sixth edition

Reading Diagnosis
for Teachers
An Instructional Approach

Rebecca Barr

National Louis University

Camille L. Z. Blachowicz

National Louis University

Ann Bates

National Louis University

Claudia Katz

National Louis University

Barbara Kaufman

National Louis University

PEARSON

Boston   Columbus   Indianapolis   New York   San Francisco   Upper Saddle River
Amsterdam   Cape Town   Dubai   London   Madrid   Milan   Munich   Paris   Montreal   Toronto
Delhi   Mexico City   Sao Paulo   Sydney   Hong Kong   Seoul   Singapore   Taipei   Tokyo

To the memory of our dear colleague, mentor, and friend,
Rebecca Barr,
and to our loving (and patient) families

Editor in Chief, Vice President: *Aurora Martínez Ramos*
Associate Sponsoring Editor: *Barbara Strickland*
Editorial Assistant: *Michelle Hochberg*
Executive Marketing Manager: *Krista Clark*
Production Editor: *Paula Carroll*
Production Manager: *Susan Hannahs*
Senior Art Director: *Jayne Conte*
Cover Art: *Microstock*
Cover Designer: *Karen Noferi*
Photo Researcher: *Annie Fuller*
Full-Service Project Management: *Sudip Sinha, Aptara®, Inc.*
Composition: *Aptara®, Inc.*
Text and Cover Printer: *R.R. Donnelley & Sons, Inc.*
Text Font: *ITC Stone Serif Std*

Photo Credits: Annie Fuller/Pearson: *pp.* 1, 247, 275, 322; Monashee Frantz/Alamy: *p.* 80; Murphy School: *p.* 341; Shutterstock: *pp.* 34, 119, 169, 209.

Credits and acknowledgments borrowed from other sources and reproduced, with permission, in this textbook appear on the appropriate page within the text.

Library of Congress Cataloging-in-Publication Data

Reading diagnosis for teachers: an instructional approach/Rebecca
   Barr [et al.].—6th ed.
      p. cm.
   Includes bibliographical references and index.
   ISBN-13: 978-0-13-269011-9
   ISBN-10:   0-13-269011-X
   1. Reading—Ability testing.   I. Barr, Rebecca.
   LB1050.46.B37 2013
   372.4076—dc23

                                                          2011029587

10 9 8 7 6 5 4 3 2 1

                                         ISBN-10:   0-13-269011-X
                                         ISBN-13:   978-0-13-269011-9

contents

- ## Our Purpose in Writing This Text

Our goal for this book is to help you, the classroom teacher or reading specialist, gain the knowledge and skills you will need to assess the reading and writing of your students and plan appropriate instruction. In planning a text to accomplish this purpose, we have been influenced by many considerations. Most important among these are our views on the nature of learning and the role of assessment in classroom instruction.

Reading and writing are active processes in which students interact with text to construct the messages of authors as well as their own messages. Research in recent years has emphasized the extent to which literacy depends on the knowledge that students have already developed. Printed symbols are signs that lead an active mind to reflect on alternatives during the process of constructing knowledge.

Children learn to read and write as they, with the support of their teachers and peers, explore alternative ways to make sense of text. Some of your students may have difficulty with this process either because of confusion they experience with printed words or because they have limited understanding of some concepts that are central to the message of an author. Still others, even with adequate knowledge of print and underlying concepts, may construe messages that depart radically from what an author intends.

Your role in this process is extremely complicated. For students who are unable to make use of the signs provided by authors because they lack adequate knowledge of print, you must find ways to develop this knowledge. Similarly, for students who lack basic concepts, this knowledge must be developed through experience, discussion, and explanation. Finally, some students with good knowledge of both print and underlying concepts profit from the experience of comparing their interpretations with those of other students and exploring their bases; others benefit from more direct help in weaving the meaning of authors from sentence to sentence and across paragraphs.

To assist you in assessing the literacy development of your students and planning appropriate instruction, the text helps you to develop your knowledge and skills in the following areas:

- Understanding the nature of literacy development—how students develop knowledge of print, vocabulary concepts, and reading comprehension strategies

- Becoming good observers of students' reading and writing and learning to make sense of what you see and hear—becoming able to understand the nature of students' problems and strengths

- Becoming familiar with alternative teaching strategies to help your students solve their problems with reading and writing

Unique Features of the Book

Just as we believe that learning is an active process for your students, we also believe that it should be an active process for you. Thus, we have planned a series of activities to promote thinking and problem solving. The text is unique in the following ways:

- We present a general model in the first chapter that will help you think about assessment and organize your observations. Each chapter provides opportunities for you to refine your observational skills; tasks of increasing complexity provide practice with previously acquired understandings.

- Your learning is grounded in more than 25 case studies that exemplify various problems that developing readers and writers may encounter. Each case provides the material from which to derive general principles and shows how the specifics of each situation shape assessment and instruction.

- We view reading and writing as reciprocal processes that are mutually supportive in their development. Throughout the text, we treat children's writing as a window into their thinking, and in a separate chapter we focus directly on the integration of writing and reading.

We encourage your active problem solving through the following features:

- **Chapter Goals for the Reader** at the beginning of each chapter to focus your learning

- **Classroom Vignettes** that tie the focus of each chapter to the classroom

- **Pause and Reflect** activities in which problems are posed for your reflection

- **Try It Out** activities at the end of each chapter through which you are encouraged to apply the understandings developed in the chapter and to build both **Student Portfolios** and **A Teaching Portfolio**

- **For Further Reading** suggestions to enable you to explore selected ideas on your own in greater depth

- ## New to This Edition:

  - **Heavily revised and updated content.** Updated **in collaboration with classroom and clinical practitioners** to reflect assessments related to Reading First and Response to Instruction and Intervention (RTI)
  - Ideas for **teaching portfolios** to meet IRA standards
  - **Increased coverage of early assessment and intervention** throughout the book to help teachers during early intervention screening and planning and monitoring instruction
  - **A revised Appendix D** that consists of a **comprehensive list of assessment tools** to help practitioners easily locate appropriate tools for the classroom
  - **An updated Appendix E** that refers the reader to sources for locating and **leveling children's early reading intervention** to help teachers with instructional planning
  - Close ties to **IRA standards** for the reading specialist in every chapter

In addition, new features include expanded treatments of early literacy development and differentiation and updated resources for teachers: (a) information on new assessment instruments including those used for RTI and (b) expanded information on fluency.

- ## How the Book Is Organized

  Unlike most texts that are topically organized, this one is developmental in design. The first chapter of the book develops a general way to think about reading assessment and instructional planning. The next six chapters develop understandings related to the assessment and instructional planning of print (Chapters 2 and 3), prior knowledge and vocabulary (Chapter 4), reading comprehension (Chapters 5 and 6), and writing (Chapter 7). The next chapter entails application and integration of previously learned concepts to informal reading inventories (Chapter 8). In the final chapter, we focus on the decision making that occurs as you organize, use, and communicate information gained through assessment.

- ## Acknowledgments

  Like all projects that involve the development of ideas over an extended period of time, this one has depended on the support and critical insight of many people. We owe a great debt to a number of students from the National College of Education of National Louis University. These students provided important insights into the diagnostic process and helped us evaluate the manuscript in its many stages. Some students provided us with case materials and helped us refine the text; we are especially indebted to Marilyn Sadow; to the clinical directors, Debra Gurvitz, Eileen Owens, Peter Fisher, and Char Cieply and their supervising assistants; to Pam Pifer Roberta Buhle and Maggie Walsh; and to Jesse and Jake Blachowicz for their examples. We also gratefully acknowledge the help of Aurora Martínez Ramos from Pearson and her assistants. Many thanks, also, to Paula Carroll and Karen Slaght for their editorial contributions and to Kristin Lems, our initial indexer. Our efforts were encouraged by our colleagues at the National College of Education of National Louis University and those from the literacy education community. In particular, Darrell Morris, Laurie Nelson, Diane Sullivan, and Renee Weisberg have contributed to our thinking about literacy assessment and instructional planning. In addition we benefited from the technical assistance of Maria Dionne Taylor, Christopher Broach and Sudip Sinha, as well as from the many comments and suggestions of the following reviewers: Lynn Saffer Domino, Florida Atlantic University; Parker C. Fawson, Utah State University; Gail Fazio, Rutgers State University; Janet Towell, Florida Atlantic University; and Carol D. Wickstrom, University of North Texas.

Rebecca Barr was Professor of Education and Director of the Doctoral Program at National College of Education of National Louis University, Chicago, Illinois. She was also editor of the *Handbooks of Reading Research*, the past president of the National Reading Conference, and Editor of *The Journal of Reading Behavior*. She was a noted educator, scholar, and researcher.

Camille Blachowicz is Professor of Education and Director of the Reading Program and The Reading Center at National College of Education of National Louis University, Chicago, Illinois. She is the author of numerous chapters, articles, and books primarily in her research area, vocabulary instruction, and speaks widely nationally and internationally. Dr. Blachowicz was named to the roster of Outstanding Teacher Educators in Reading by the International Reading Association and has been the recipient of grants and fellowships from the Institute of Educational Sciences, the Spencer and the Fulbright Foundations. Currently she is a co-principal investigator on the federally funded Multi-faceted Comprehensive Vocabulary Improvement Program Project.

Ann Bates is Assistant Professor of Education and Clinical Director of the Reading Center at National Louis University, Chicago, Illinois. She writes, researches, and speaks on clinical practice, early reading, and storytelling. Currently she is a research associate on the federally funded Multi-faceted Comprehensive Vocabulary Improvement Program Project.

Claudia Katz is Assistant Professor of Education and Director of Professional Outreach for the Reading and Language Department at National College of Education of National Louis University, Chicago, Illinois. She has been a columnist for the *Journal of Adolescent and Adult Literacy* and writes, researches, and speaks on adolescent literacy and literature.

Barbara Kaufman is Adjunct Instructor of Education at National College of Education of National Louis University, Chicago, Illinois. She is also director of The Good News Tutoring Program, one of the oldest continuous community tutoring programs in the United States. She is a coach-facilitator with Literacy Partners of The Chicago Literacy Initiative Partnership, a project in urban school reform.

Model for Reading Diagnosis and Instructional Planning

chapter goals for the reader

- To become familiar with the theoretical, historical, and research bases of reading diagnosis
- To learn to apply a model of reading diagnosis
- To understand reading diagnosis as an integral part of ongoing classroom instruction
- To become familiar with class screening purposes and procedures
- To appreciate the importance of responsive instructional planning

Tessa and Her Student, John

Tessa loves teaching fourth grade, and each year she understands her students better. This is her third year. But every year, five or six of her students pose challenges for her because of the difficulty they encounter reading some of the materials she assigns, particularly for social studies and science. Even though she has taken several courses and workshops in teaching reading and writing, she is still unable to assess her students' specific areas of strength and difficulty. Thus, Tessa has decided to take a course in reading diagnosis. She hopes to acquire sufficient skill in assessment to understand her students' reading as she meets with them daily and to learn how she can provide them with appropriate instructional support.

This year she is keeping her eye on a group of about seven students. Three of them are quite far behind; they are having difficulty reading selections from the third-grade reading series. The other four seem to do well on some days, but not on others. She is particularly curious about what John actually knows about reading and writing. She is asking the following questions: What are John's strengths on which I can build? How can I help John feel that he is a part of the classroom group and encourage him to continue to develop his reading strategies? ∎

chapter overview

The chapter is organized into four main sections. In the first, we consider the goals we had in mind as we wrote this book and describe our view of reading. We hope that our explanations and the sequence of case studies will provide the opportunities you need to develop your understanding of reading screening and diagnosis. Ultimately, we hope that you will develop your observational and interpretive skills during the course of ongoing instruction to better understand what your students need to become proficient readers.

In the second section, we consider reading diagnosis. We describe the long and distinguished history of reading diagnosis, mainly in clinical settings, and the more recent research literature. Building on this tradition, we argue that you and other classroom teachers are well positioned to diagnose the reading strengths and problems of your students. We describe a model for reading diagnosis and its major decision points. We believe this model will be particularly useful because it will help you to organize and make sense of the multitude of observations you will make about your students' reading during the rapid give-and-take of classroom activities.

In the third section, we consider some approaches to class screening that are particularly useful at the beginning of the school year. From a variety of approaches, we focus on creating a class profile from standardized reading test results, graded word lists, oral reading samples, and cloze passages. These approaches provide a basis on which to organize class instruction and identify the special needs of certain children.

In the final section of the chapter, we consider reading instruction. We discuss current trends in the field of reading and the importance of developing instruction that provides appropriate support for student growth and permits students to share their ideas about what they are reading.

chapter outline

Our Perspective on Reading and Instruction

• Goals for Reading Instruction

Reading enriches our lives. We all know the thrill of reading a good story and the satisfaction of locating needed information. As teachers we are committed to helping our students use and appreciate the experiences reading affords. Our goals are twofold: (1) to instill in our students a love for reading and (2) to support their development of reading skill. As students acquire greater proficiency in reading and read material that interests them, they will begin to appreciate the power reading gives them to enrich their own lives.

Achieving these goals is easy with some children. They learn to read easily, and the satisfaction they experience leads them to read often and with pleasure. Unfortunately, other children experience considerable difficulty in reading and view it as an unpleasant and undesirable activity. These are the children who worry us. The purpose of this book is to help you, as their teachers, develop the understanding you need to help these children. What are your views of reading and reading instruction? How do you diagnose students' reading strengths and difficulties? What do you need to know to provide them with appropriate instructional support? These questions are not easy to answer.

Our View of Reading

What do we do when we read? Some literacy experts believe that the process of reading involves translating printed symbols into speech; they assume a direct correspondence between text and meaning so that comprehension occurs easily and automatically for the reader. This view ignores the active role of the reader in constructing meaning. It also neglects the ways written language differs from spoken language. In fact, readers must actively assign one meaning to text from a variety of possible meanings, based on their prior experiences and the context of the selection.

An opposing view of reading is that knowledge is in the minds of readers, who rely on print only to test their ideas. This view fails to acknowledge print as a vehicle for information. Through print, readers are led to construct not only familiar ideas but also innovative thoughts and lines of argument.

Our view of the reading process lies between these two extremes. We see reading as an interactive activity. Foundational research suggests that proficient readers process print in a thorough and efficient manner (Adams, 1990). However, they do not automatically assign meaning to what they read. Readers construct meaning from the print they perceive using context and prior experiences to interpret what they read.

Until recently, researchers have focused on aspects of reading pertaining to thinking and knowledge (cognitive dimensions), but affective dimensions related to the interests and feeling of students may be even more important. Some children, usually those who learn to read easily, find joy in reading exciting stories and in the challenge posed by new information and arguments. Other students, usually those who encounter difficulty learning to read or those for whom reading has become a chore, experience reading negatively. When their first encounters with reading are difficult or boring, they develop an aversion toward reading, and those students who avoid reading never discover its pleasures.

Research on reading programs shows that when children's first experiences are with good children's literature, they develop more positive attitudes and interest toward reading than when instruction focuses on reading skills. Interacting with books they enjoy and find interesting leads children into a positive motivational cycle, allowing them to develop increased interest in and pleasure through reading.

For these reasons, we view reading as an interactive process. It is supported by children's knowledge of print, informed by their prior experiences and knowledge of word meanings, facilitated by their comprehension strategies, and fueled by their love for reading. Throughout this book, we encourage you to think about the implications of this perspective for reading instruction.

Research on reading diagnosis and instruction provides much information that is useful to you in meeting the needs of your students. Nevertheless, you must be able to master it in such a way that you can use it during the active give-and-take of everyday instruction. Our challenge as authors of this book is to organize and sequence the fundamentals of diagnosis and instructional planning in a form that will be most useful to you. In this book, we present principles for you to follow and descriptions of development that provide an overview of the changes children undergo. But we also use these in the context of many case studies to convey the rich details of children's lives. In the end, we hope that you develop ways for thinking and observing children's reading that enable you to design instruction that lets your students make good progress in learning to read.

Reading Diagnosis

We begin our discussion with a brief history of reading diagnosis. Much of what has been learned about the nature of children's reading difficulties has been learned in reading clinics, where clinicians work one-on-one with children. Nevertheless, classroom teachers have some important advantages in reading diagnosis; we consider these as we examine differences between the perspectives of reading clinicians and classroom teachers. Finally, we introduce a model to guide our diagnostic thinking. We show its usefulness in understanding the reading of several children, including John, the student mentioned in the introductory section of this chapter.

• History of Reading Diagnosis

Reading diagnosis as we use it in this book refers to "an astute analysis of the process by which [a student] gains meaning, significance, enjoyment, and value from printed sources" (Harris & Hodges, 1995, p. 86). We view diagnosis as an ongoing process. Assessment is similar but refers to the "process of gathering data in order to better understand some topic or area of knowledge, as through observation, testing, interviews, etc." (p. 22). Diagnosis depends, then, on careful assessment, but goes beyond it by involving judgments about the data.

Physicians were among the earliest specialists to undertake a form of reading diagnosis (e.g., Morgan, 1896). Early in the 20th century, two developments in the field of education converged to support the scientific study of reading difficulty. First, Huey (1898, 1908/1968) and others (Dearborn, 1906; Dodge, 1905, 1907) set the conceptual and empirical basis for understanding the psychology of reading. Second, advancements in psychometric theory laid the foundation for developing test instruments to measure human traits.

Before the 1920s, tests had been developed to assess school learning, and the results were used to identify the special needs of individuals (Uhl, 1916; Zirbes, 1918). The earliest diagnostic work was conducted in the school setting by teachers and other school personnel. The first professional book on reading diagnosis, *Deficiencies in Reading Ability: Their Diagnosis and Remedies,* written by Clarence T. Gray in 1922, relied in large part on what researchers had learned from school-based studies of reading difficulty.

At the same time, educators realized that more detailed study of students who were experiencing reading difficulty would provide insight into how the reading process operates. They began doing detailed case studies to develop more refined testing procedures and effective remedial instruction. Special educational laboratories and reading clinics were established in university settings for this purpose (see, for example, Fernald & Keller, 1926; Gray, Kibbe, Lucas, & Miller, 1922).

Other research in the 1920s and 1930s expanded and developed the knowledge gained through clinical case studies. Pelosi (1977) noted several developments during this period that contributed to the refinement of reading diagnosis. First, case study investigation became more elaborate and sophisticated and continued to be the dominant method of research. Second, precise diagnostic instruments and procedures were developed. Finally, there was an ever-increasing interest in the nature of reading processes and the causes of reading disability (Robinson, 1937).

During this period researchers in such related fields as medicine and psychology popularized the term *dyslexia* when referring to children with reading difficulties. Literally translated, it means a "dysfunction with words" (the Latin prefix *dys-* means "difficult" or "faulty," and the Greek root *lexia* refers to "words"). Thus, the term is simply descriptive; it does not address the underlying nature of the difficulty. Further, research by Vellutino and his associates confirms that estimates of the incidence of difficult-to-remediate disability are highly inflated (Vellutino, Scanlon, & Jaccard, 2003). We believe that such labeling is not particularly useful, especially because it often carries the connotation that the child has a central functioning impairment. Similarly, we believe that other forms of labeling such as "visual learner," "left-brain dominant," and "perceptually handicapped" are of little help to teachers in planning appropriate instruction, and they may be misleading in that they imply simplistic remedies. As we show in the following sections of this chapter, we prefer to identify the nature of the reading difficulty and strength in a way that anticipates appropriate instruction.

Developments over the ensuing decades have influenced our thinking about reading diagnosis. First is the extensive research undertaken during the 1970s and 1980s on the nature of reading processes. In contrast to the behavioristic perspectives of earlier studies, this research showed that the characteristics of readers, in particular their knowledge and expectations, influence their comprehension—that is, readers actively construct their understandings on the basis of the knowledge they bring with them and the context of what they read.

Second, following this growth in knowledge about the reading process, many reading researchers turned their attention to classroom instruction. Their work showed that some of the problems children experience result from the way they are taught. How teachers organize children for instruction, what materials they have children read, how much time they provide for reading, and what level of instructional support they give all have a direct bearing on how well children learn (Gambrell, Morrow, & Pressley, 2007).

Additional research has documented the important influence that students' writing has on their reading development. Writing enhances children's awareness of sounds in words and their skill as readers (Morris, Bloodgood, Lomax, & Perney, 2003). Writing in response to reading encourages students to reflect and deepens their understanding. Later we discuss the importance of student writing, an activity you need to consider both for assessment and in planning instruction.

Motivation is also essential in learning. Studies of literature-based and integrated curriculum classes show the important motivational consequences of having children read books they enjoy (Dahl & Freppon, 1991; Ivey & Broadus, 2001); including nonfiction (Guthrie, 2007). Helping children select high-quality books that are of interest to them not only has the immediate benefit of making instruction more enjoyable but also serves our goal of creating lifelong readers.

• Reading Diagnosis as Part of Classroom Instruction

The approach to reading diagnosis presented in this book is based not only on clinical case studies and the research literature, but also on our understanding of the goals of classroom teachers. These differ somewhat from those of teachers in the clinical setting. Classroom teachers want to help their students acquire the skill necessary to be part of the mainstream of classroom reading instruction. In contrast, clinical teachers are more concerned about whether students are reading up to their potential levels for achievement. The comparison of actual and potential reading level, used in clinical settings, may occasionally be a useful approach for teachers, but generally in the classroom, teachers prefer an approach to diagnosis that identifies students as needing special support when they are unable to read the materials used for class discussion.

This is the path we follow in this book. While it is consistent with the goals of most classroom teachers, it does have several consequences. One result is that some children with limited knowledge will be identified to receive special attention. The focus of this attention will be to develop their word knowledge and general understanding so they will be able to participate in class discussion.

Using this approach also means that some students (with a discrepancy between potential and actual reading) may receive no special support since they are able to read the class materials.

There are other differences between classrooms and clinicians. Teachers who work with groups of students do not find it easy to undertake extensive testing with individual students. But because teachers have access to a wealth of evidence about the reading, writing, and language development of students on a daily basis, extensive testing is not needed. You have the opportunity to listen to children read orally, note their answers to comprehension questions, and observe how they think, write, and talk about a variety of topics. With the time advantage that comes from working with students for many months, you can develop working hypotheses about how children learn and revise these hypotheses as you continue to observe student reading and writing. Because you can collect evidence over time, it will not be necessary for you to attempt the detailed diagnosis that clinicians undertake. Most important, you have the opportunity to modify instruction and to observe how it works. Information about students' interests and family support, along with your ongoing observations, enable you to plan instruction that is both conceptually and motivationally appropriate.

Nevertheless, the observations of teachers tend to be haphazard because of the complexity of their work. However, they may be haphazard because most teachers have not been taught useful methods for observation and interpretation. In this book we introduce these observational and interpretive strategies in a gradual manner through detailed case studies. We *do not* expect you to undertake such extensive case studies in the classroom, *nor* do we expect you to follow in a step-by-step fashion the procedures we have developed. We do hope that once you have done the detailed analyses outlined here, you will have gained the understanding necessary for more informal and ongoing observation in your classroom.

• Model for Reading Diagnosis

Our view of reading diagnosis and instructional planning assumes that students are active problem solvers. Therefore, the manner in which they develop reading skill is influenced by the instructional tasks they confront from grade to grade. For example, if students are instructed with a systematic phonics program, they learn to solve a set of problems somewhat different from the ones they encounter if they are instructed with a literature-based program that emphasizes comprehension and writing. Similarly, if students are given considerable experience reading and answering questions on expository materials, they develop comprehension skills different from those they develop if they read mainly narrative materials.

Two implications follow from this view. First, diagnostic assessment must consider how students currently approach the task of reading in relation to the reading tasks they have encountered in the past. Second, subsequent instruction must build on this foundation. Thus, diagnosis by a teacher who is familiar with the instructional history of students and who tests their response to current instructional materials provides an optimal basis for instructional planning.

What must you know in order to diagnose the nature of your students' reading difficulty? A diagnostician is much more than someone who knows how to administer tests. The diagnostician is an active explorer whose search is guided by a carefully developed conceptual scheme. This scheme identifies the major decision points in the diagnostic process and then, once a particular decision is made, identifies certain subsidiary decision points. Through this sequential decision-making procedure, you can progressively evaluate plausible explanations for reading difficulty.

Major Diagnostic Decisions

In the model of reading diagnosis shown in Figure 1.1, the central and most important process in reading is comprehension, the ability to reconstruct meaning from printed text. This means that the goal of reading is to comprehend the reading materials that are part of instruction. Certain underlying processes such as print skill and vocabulary knowledge are viewed as supporting effective comprehension. These underlying areas become important if a student is experiencing difficulty with comprehension. In this book, the main goal of reading diagnosis and reading instruction is to help all students develop effective strategies for comprehension.

Comprehending Text. The first decision you need to make is to determine whether your students comprehend the textual materials that are part of instruction; if they don't, you can conclude that they are experiencing problems in reading. We believe that a student's expected reading level—and whether he or she has a reading problem—should be established in terms of the level of materials used by the class or the student's subgroup. If a student is able to read and comprehend classroom material, we conclude that he or she has no reading problem. The student can be assigned the appropriate materials and given suitable instruction during the daily reading lesson. However, when there is evidence that a student cannot adequately understand the materials used for regular class instruction, we consider that student to have a reading problem that warrants further diagnosis.

figure 1.1 • Basic Model of Reading Diagnosis

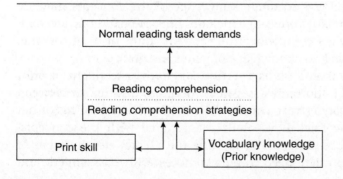

When there is evidence that a student has a reading problem, the second decision point requires you to identify the general nature of the problem. A student can have difficulties in three general areas that may interfere with comprehension: (1) inadequately developed print skill, (2) inadequate vocabulary knowledge pertaining to the ideas described in a passage, and (3) inadequately developed strategies for understanding text (see Figure 1.1).

Print skill refers to the ability of readers to translate printed symbols efficiently into spoken language or meaning. This area includes not only skill with phonics, structural analysis, and syllabication, which permit a student to identify previously unknown words, but also the acquisition of a set of words that are recognized instantaneously. It includes the proficient integration of word recognition and word identification with contextual information as a student responds to prose to develop fluency.

Most children acquire basic print skill during their early reading instruction, and this skill becomes integrated and automatic through a variety of home and school reading experiences. Note that the emphasis of early instruction can have a profound influence on the particular print concepts that students learn. Further, students who have difficulty acquiring print concepts that are taught explicitly also have difficulty inferring those that are not explicitly taught. For example, some reading programs emphasize the development of phonic concepts but do not teach the process of blending and the application of phonic knowledge in context. For students who do not spontaneously infer how to blend phonic values, a good knowledge of phonics may be of little value in identifying unknown words. Print skill is more fully described in the next two chapters.

Vocabulary knowledge refers to knowledge of the key words contained in particular reading selections as well as the encompassing concepts being conveyed and the ways word meaning is revealed by context. For example, to understand a passage about the discoveries of Copernicus and Galileo, students must be familiar with the meanings of such words as *planet* and *telescope*; beyond these, the encompassing concept of "movement" is central to an understanding of how the solar system works. Students differ in the extent to which they can comprehend a passage without adequate knowledge of the concepts they are presumed to know. Vocabulary knowledge includes both general language concepts and specific literacy concepts concerning the functions of print, writing, and communication, as well as a knowledge of genre and grammar.

For students who speak English as a second language, assessment of prior knowledge is particularly important. Assessment needs to distinguish between a student's knowledge of underlying concepts (in any language) and his or her knowledge of the specific English vocabulary associated with the concepts. The diagnostic model is useful for understanding the literacy development of bilingual students, but you may need to do a more extensive assessment and interpretation in the area of prior knowledge than will be needed for English-speaking students. Prior knowledge is more fully considered in Chapter 4.

In addition to experiencing problems in print skill and/or vocabulary knowledge, students may have problems in their **comprehension strategies.** That is, a student may have no difficulty with print translation and may be familiar with the meanings of the words and concepts that are central to understanding a passage, but may still fail to comprehend the material. This failure may indicate that the student is having difficulty integrating information across a text. Whereas a writer begins with a conception of the message to be conveyed in a passage and then confronts the problem of how to write this in words, sentences, and paragraphs, a reader must reconstruct the author's message by processing these units and recombining them into one or several arguments or descriptions. Some readers experience difficulty with this integration process as well as with the monitoring and fix-up strategies necessary to recognize and address these problems. For example, readers often encounter pronouns, nouns, or phrases that refer to a previously identified person or topic. These words or phrases are signals that more information is being provided about the same topic or person, rather than a new topic being introduced. Readers must also understand what to look for and how to reread and connect the information they missed on their first reading. Comprehension strategies are considered in Chapters 5 and 6.

Identifying the Nature of the Difficulty. As previously described, the second step in diagnosis is to determine whether a student is experiencing difficulty with print skill, vocabulary knowledge, and/or comprehension strategies. While these three areas are part of an integrated process, it is useful to consider them separately. Different sorts of information and assessment procedures are required to determine the status of each one. Print skill is typically assessed by having students read passages, words, or word parts aloud, whereas discourse processing is typically assessed by having the reader "retell" the passage content, think aloud during reading, or respond to comprehension questions based on a selection that has been read. Vocabulary knowledge assessment does not necessarily involve reading; rather, it uses questions to elicit a student's understanding of selected terms. The three areas also differ in the types of instructional procedures that enhance their development. The instruction that is useful for helping a student develop word identification strategies is quite different from what is effective in facilitating discourse comprehension.

The model for diagnosis shown in Figure 1.1 assumes not only that these three areas can be considered separately but also that two of them—print skill and vocabulary knowledge—represent conditions that facilitate the effective employment of the third: comprehension strategies. Accordingly, if a student fails to comprehend a passage, it is important to examine the student's print strategies and vocabulary knowledge for problems. Problems in either of these areas could account for the observed difficulty in comprehension. Thus, it is difficult in such cases to ascertain whether the student is experiencing problems in comprehension over and above those that stem from deficiencies in print skill or vocabulary knowledge. Comprehension strategies constitute a central category within the model: Problems are assumed to occur in this area when comprehension is weak *and* both vocabulary concepts and print skill are adequately developed.

To begin thinking in terms of the diagnostic scheme, let us consider the strengths and difficulties of four students (Cases 1.1–1.4) who have encountered problems reading classroom materials. You are encouraged to consider the evidence and determine each student's relative strength in the areas specified by the model. On this basis, you should be able to specify the area(s) in need of further diagnosis.

case 1.1

John

John is nine years and two months old and is in the fourth grade. His teacher, Tessa, has found that he has considerable difficulty understanding not only his social studies and science textbooks but also the stories in the third-grade-level reading book used by her slowest-paced group. His oral reading, however, is flawless, and he even reads the social studies and science passages with considerable fluency. Tessa first noticed that he has extremely vague concepts pertaining to biological terms and then pursued his understanding of more common terms. She found that he knows only superficially, or not at all, words from his reading book such as *revenge, comrade, foundation,* and *craftsmen.* ■

pause and reflect

Pause for a moment to consider John's case. In terms of the diagnostic scheme, which are the areas of John's difficulty? As we learned at the beginning of this chapter, Tessa is seeking a better understanding of John's reading. From this brief description of his reading, what are his areas of strength on which she could build? What are your ideas about how Tessa might provide support so that John would feel that he is a part of the classroom group and be encouraged to continue to develop his reading strategies?

Diagnosis. The oral reading evidence indicates that John has strength in the area of print skill. John's inability to answer the questions posed by Tessa therefore seems attributable to inadequate vocabulary knowledge and/or poor comprehension strategies. The possibility that he is deficient in vocabulary knowledge is suggested by his lack of knowledge about terms known by his classmates. Thus, we tentatively conclude that vocabulary knowledge is John's major problem area. It is possible that he also has comprehension difficulties, but this remains to be determined by having him read a passage for which his vocabulary knowledge is sufficient. Vocabulary knowledge, then, should be Tessa's first area of focus.

case 1.2

Mary

Mary is seven years old and in the second grade. She is currently in the middle reading group, which uses second-grade-level materials. When she reads aloud during reading instruction, she does so fluently, making few errors. However, many of her answers to postreading questions show that she has not understood major events within the story. Her answers to questions about important terms within the story reveal that she has a good command of English and is more knowledgeable than other students in the group. ■

pause and reflect

Consider the following questions: Does Mary have any problems in reading, and if so, in what area(s)? What evidence supports these conclusions?

Diagnosis. Mary's reading difficulty is not associated with inadequately developed print skill or vocabulary knowledge. Her inability to comprehend what she reads may therefore derive from sentence and paragraph comprehension inadequacies. Therefore, her teacher should consider further exploration of comprehension strategies.

case 1.3

Larry

Larry is ten years old and in fourth grade. He is in the slowest-paced group in the class, which reads from third-grade materials. Larry's teacher had almost immediately noted his difficulty in reading aloud. Although Larry had developed familiarity with some common words, he would wait for the teacher to assist him on many other words, particularly those that were multisyllabic. His comprehension of stories that he read silently was extremely low; however, he comprehended well when the others in his group read aloud. He also demonstrated good understanding of key words in the reading selections; indeed, he was one of the most knowledgeable class members when it came to science activities and social studies discussions. ■

pause and **reflect**

Consider the nature of Larry's reading. What do you consider to be his reading strengths and difficulties?

Diagnosis. Larry experiences difficulty in the area of print skill but also in comprehension of materials that he has read. He is strong in vocabulary knowledge. Therefore, we conclude that his comprehension difficulty reflects his poorly developed print skill. There is evidence to support this conclusion, namely, his good comprehension when he listens to others read. Once he acquires skill with print, he should become a proficient reader, given his well-developed vocabulary knowledge. Our task is to diagnose his print skill further in order to learn how to facilitate his development in this area.

case 1.4

Tom

Tom is seven years and nine months old and in the third grade. In second grade he was with the middle reading group, and his third-grade teacher has continued that placement. His answers to comprehension questions indicate excellent understanding of what he reads, whether silently or aloud. Further, informal questioning about key vocabulary words indicates a breadth of vocabulary knowledge and fluency of expression. However, his oral reading is characterized by frequent substitutions of words. He seems to have developed extremely careless reading procedures. ■

pause and **reflect**

Consider how we might make sense of these reading characteristics. Does Tom have a reading problem, and if so, what is its nature?

Diagnosis. It is clear that Tom's strengths are his good vocabulary knowledge and his adequate comprehension. Nevertheless, his print skill appears to be inadequately developed and should be explored further. Note that in terms of the model, Tom's pattern of reading strengths and weaknesses is one that is unlikely to occur. The model suggests that adequately developed print skill is a prerequisite for adequate comprehension, and typically this is true. Exceptions occur, however, among students with extremely well-developed vocabulary knowledge. Such students, on the basis of this knowledge and minimal information from print, are able to make sense of a story or passage. While we may conclude that Tom has no reading problem at the present time, his print skill may become inadequate to the demands of reading as the materials become more technical and precise in their informational content. Therefore, it is appropriate to treat

Tom as having a reading problem in the area of print skill and to diagnose further the nature of his difficulty.

• Diagnostic Patterns

These cases show how the diagnostic model may be used to determine whether a student has a reading problem and to identify the areas in need of further diagnostic exploration. In a more systematic fashion, Table 1.1 shows the different patterns of reading skill that are possible when comprehension, print skill, and vocabulary knowledge are considered. For example, John, the first case we considered, with poor comprehension and vocabulary knowledge but good print skill, conforms to Pattern 3. The second case, Mary, with adequate print skill and vocabulary knowledge but inadequate comprehension, conforms to Pattern 2. The third case, Larry, represents Pattern 4, with poor print skill and comprehension but good vocabulary knowledge. Finally, Tom conforms to the relatively uncommon Pattern 6, with good comprehension and vocabulary knowledge but inadequate print skill.

In Pattern 1, reading comprehension and underlying print skill and vocabulary knowledge are all sufficient for the student to cope with his or her reading tasks. Because there appears to be no reading difficulty, further diagnosis is unnecessary.

Pattern 2 consists of adequate print skill and vocabulary knowledge but inadequate reading comprehension. Clearly, the potential for adequate

table 1.1 • Diagnostic Patterns of Print Skill, Vocabulary Knowledge, and Reading Comprehension Strategies

Skill Area	Common Patterns					Uncommon Patterns		
	1	*2*	*3*	*4*	*5*	*6*	*7*	*8*
Reading comprehension	+	0	0	0	0	+	+	+
Print skill	+	+	+	0	0	0	+	0
Vocabulary knowledge	+	+	0	+	0	+	0	0
Further diagnostic exploration[a]	Discontinue diagnosis	Explore comprehension strategies	Explore vocabulary knowledge	Explore print skill				

[a]In Patterns 3, 4, and 5, comprehending strategies might also be an area of weakness. However, this area is directly explored only when vocabulary knowledge and print skill have been eliminated as major factors in reading difficulty.

comprehension is strong, but the student has not yet acquired some skills or organizing concepts for processing text. Further diagnosis in the area of comprehension is needed to determine the nature of the problem.

Pattern 3 is that of the student often identified as a "word caller"—the student who possesses adequate print skill but inadequate vocabulary knowledge and reading comprehension. Where you see this pattern, you assume that limited vocabulary and concepts interfere with reading comprehension: The student's limited experiences set a ceiling on what he or she can comprehend through print. Further exploration of the student's prior knowledge is appropriate. For example, a student may have experienced certain situations or events but failed to acquire the pertinent verbal labels. The instruction recommended for this student would be very different from that recommended for a student who also lacked the experiential base.

Pattern 4 characterizes the student who has difficulty translating print into familiar language. Here you may assume that poor print skill accounts for poor reading comprehension. The student has the strength of good language development, as indicated by strong vocabulary knowledge. Further diagnosis should focus on how he or she identifies and recognizes words.

In Pattern 5, reading comprehension and both sets of underlying skills are inadequately developed. Further exploration of the student's vocabulary knowledge and print skill is appropriate.

Because reading comprehension typically depends on the development of print skill and vocabulary knowledge, the remaining three patterns, in which comprehension is good whereas print skill and/or vocabulary knowledge are poor, occur infrequently. Pattern 6, as we have seen, occurs mainly for extremely able students with well-developed verbal skills. These students are able to compensate for rather poorly developed print skill by using a combination of contextual cues, minimal print cues, and past experience; as a result, they score at an adequate level in reading comprehension. For this pattern, further examination of print skill is recommended. Although the student will often tolerate the frustration of the reading task when working with you on an individual basis, he or she may avoid reading tasks when left to work alone. Although such students may be able to compensate for skill deficiencies at this stage, later they may be unable to comprehend more difficult reading material.

Finally, Pattern 7 rarely occurs. If it is observed, it probably reflects a kind of "production deficiency." That is, a student, although able to summarize a passage or respond to questions based on it, may have difficulty generating definitions of terms or demonstrating their use. This pattern may sometimes be seen in English language learners (ELLs). Pattern 8, in fact, occurs rarely and if observed, probably reflects invalid measurement in one of the three areas.

The purpose of diagnosis is to examine each of the three reading skill areas shown in Table 1.1 and to determine its relative status. This procedure ensures that major problem areas will not be overlooked and that areas for more intensive exploration are identified.

• Developmental Flexibility of the Model

The diagnostic model is applicable to all levels of skill, from initial reading acquisition to mature reading proficiency. That is, it is useful in helping you understand the strengths and difficulties of a beginning reader as well as that of a college student. The flexibility of this diagnostic approach derives from its conceptualization of reading as having the three component areas: reading comprehension, print skill, and vocabulary knowledge. Each area represents a different pattern of development in accordance with the different problems posed by reading materials students are expected to understand at successive levels. These changing demands of reading materials, considered here briefly, are treated more comprehensively in subsequent chapters.

The first two years of reading instruction usually emphasize the development of skill for translating print to speech or meaning. Some reading programs focus on the development of phonic concepts, others on the development of a sight vocabulary, and still others on the orchestration of strategies. Most current programs develop print concepts through direct instruction and extensive reading of contextual materials. These contextual materials are generally narrative in form, with the characters (people or animals) performing acts and speaking thoughts that are familiar to young children. Accordingly, most children already possess the relevant vocabulary knowledge and have acquired the necessary comprehension strategies through listening to stories read to them. However, when students lack this knowledge or listening experience, these aspects of reading must become areas of instructional focus for them, along with print skill.

Students refine and integrate their print skill during subsequent years in several ways. They become able to tackle longer and more complex words, some of which they have never heard before. They become so familiar with the characteristics of print that processing becomes almost automatic for "easy" materials. As a consequence, their reading rates improve dramatically.

As their print skill is refined, however, new problems arise. Beginning in the third or fourth grade, students typically encounter new forms of printed materials. They are expected to read texts other than narratives—texts that are characterized by a markedly different paragraph structure. In subject areas such as science and social studies, paragraphs are organized around a major topic, with examples of supporting information, or structured in terms of temporal, spatial, logical, or cause-and-effect relationships. Such structures differ not only from that of narrative materials but also, of course, from the oral language forms with which students are familiar. Once students encounter expository materials, they must acquire many new skills for processing information.

Along with these new genre-related processing problems, students encounter new demands on their vocabulary knowledge as they progress through the middle grades and high school. In sharp contrast to the primary materials, science, social studies, math, and more advanced literature introduce vocabulary and underlying concepts and text structures that go beyond the students' prior experiences and vocabulary knowledge. Thus, students must learn how to obtain new knowledge from text. They must become independent readers in order to accomplish homework assignments and projects.

In sum, students must become increasingly efficient in processing print, learning to evaluate information from a variety of sources, and integrating it in sophisticated reports and projects. This brief discussion indicates some of the ways in which reading demands change over time. The point to remember, however, is that despite the changing nature of reading acquisition, the diagnostic model is able to account for reading difficulties at all levels.

Class Screening

Starting the school year with a new class is challenging for all teachers, especially those just beginning their teaching careers. Whether using themed trade book materials, a reading series, literature circles, a core literature book, or other approaches, you need to know the range of your students' reading before you can choose appropriate materials. You also need to know which students might require extra support.

At the start of the school year, or when meeting a new group of students, it is helpful to take a quick "snapshot" of your class to establish starting points for more detailed diagnostic reflection. Just as a class picture on the first day of school can help you learn your students' names and faces and give you an initial point of reference, class screening procedures can help you to acquire the "sense of the class." There are many options for screening. We consider four reading tasks here in some detail: standardized reading tests, graded word lists, oral reading passages, and cloze samples.

This type of screening assessment is meant to supplement, not replace, more comprehensive indicators of your students' reading throughout the course of the school year. The following chapters describe methods for authentic assessment based on classroom materials that are collected throughout the year. Just as a snapshot doesn't capture the same full, rich "reality" as a video or home movie, so a screening measure provides only a small window on reading performance, a guide to help with later, more detailed assessment.

• Standardized Reading Test—Class Profile

One easy way to start the school year is to construct a class profile from data already on hand, typically standardized test data and the recommendations of the prior year's teachers. Teachers typically receive standardized test results as part of the portfolio of information for an incoming class. The major purpose for testing is to meet school and district needs; however, these results can also provide a starting point for you to get to know your new class.

Let's consider Tessa's fourth-grade class to understand how teachers can use the information from standardized tests to start their instructional planning at the start of the school year. Tessa's goal for the first month of school is to begin learning the reading and writing strengths of her students and the areas in which they need support. She looked over the test scores shown in Figure 1.2. This information helped her form questions about the reading

figure 1.2 • Standardized Test Results and Third-Grade Reading Group: Tessa's Fourth Graders Tested at 3.9

Student	Reading Vocabulary	Reading Comprehension	Prior Year's Third-Grade Group Placement
Ann	3.4	3.7	L
Candy	4.1	3.8	M
Carol	3.0	4.3	L
Connie	4.3	4.0	M
Cornelia	4.1	3.9	H
Daniel	4.1	3.8	H
David	4.0	4.3	M
Denise	4.5	4.0	H
Donald	4.8	3.7	H
Dorothy	4.3	5.1	M
Dottie	3.1	3.1	L
Gary	3.4	3.9	M
Gordon	3.7	3.0	M
Grace	3.5	3.0	H
Greta	4.4	3.9	H
Jean	2.9	2.0	M
Jeff	5.7	4.9	H
John	3.1	2.8	L
Kay	4.3	4.0	H
Lois	3.4	3.3	M
Lottie	2.7	1.8	L
Tia	4.5	3.9	H
Walter	1.9	2.2	L
Wanda	2.2	2.7	L

p a u s e and **r e f l e c t**

Look at the vocabulary and comprehension scores of the students listed in Figure 1.2. Which children raise questions in your mind, suggesting that you should learn more about them? What are your questions? Are the differences you see between the vocabulary and comprehension scores significant? Consider the basal group placement of the students when they were in third grade. How does this information lead you to modify some of your tentative conclusions? What further information would you want to obtain?

of certain children that can be pursued further through informal observation during reading and writing instruction.

Typically, in examining test scores, you first see that some children receive low scores and others high scores relative to their peers. Remember that these scores are only estimates and that the children's true levels of performance may be somewhat higher or lower. Tessa is particularly concerned about Lottie because of her low comprehension score. In addition, she wants to observe the reading of Dottie, Grace, Jean, John, Walter, and Wanda. She notes the relatively high scores of Dorothy and Jeff and wants to observe how independent they are when they do their classwork. Finally, she is concerned about the high discrepancy between vocabulary and comprehension scores for Carol, Donald, and Dorothy.

When she considers the third-grade group placement, she is puzzled by Carol's placement in the low group. Further, the low-group placement of Ann surprises her. On the other hand, two of the children she is concerned about, Grace and Jean, were in the high and middle groups last year, so perhaps the test scores are not valid. Obviously, Tessa cannot draw conclusions solely on the basis of this information. It does, however, raise some questions and suggest which children may need special support or more challenging work.

Let us return to Tessa's class to consider how she will organize her students for instruction. In previous years, Tessa grouped her students on the basis of their reading achievement. Typically, she forms two groups: one composed of children reading at the fourth-grade level and the other composed of children reading below grade level who need intensive instructional help to develop their reading strategies. In the past she chose to do this because the stories in the fourth-grade reading series were extremely difficult for some of the students in her class. Although she forms groups for reading instruction, every afternoon she provides 30 to 60 minutes of readers' workshop. Children read books they have selected, either alone or with a partner or interest group, and keep a reading log or journal in which they record their reactions and ideas. Tessa reads and responds to the journals, as do the children's reading partners. Finally, the entire class participates in a Friday session of readers'/writers' workshop in which books, ideas, and ongoing activities are shared.

Tessa is thinking about using this organizational arrangement again this year. If she does, she will have a large group using the fourth-grade reading series and a smaller group using the third-grade materials. Yet, she will have some

p a u s e and **r e f l e c t**

Consider the information included in Figure 1.2. How do you think Tessa will initially compose the two groups of students for reading instruction? Which students might be more independent in the large group? Which might need more guidance in the large group? Which might work best in a smaller group with lower-level materials? When you have finished, compare your judgments with those of Tessa.

activities in which she combines the two groups. For example, she may focus one of her thematic units on the special "challenges" faced by children because both levels of materials have selections appropriate for the topic.

Tessa's initial decisions about the reading needs of her students will, of course, be modified as she learns more about her class. In considering the test scores, she places more weight on the comprehension score because it involves the reading of textual passages. She decides to form a small group composed of Dottie, Grace, Jean, John, Lottie, Walter, and Wanda. These are the children she had tentatively identified as needing special instructional support in the small group setting. Tessa's goal is to have all these children reading with the rest of the class by the end of the year.

Tessa selects the remainder of the class to form the large group. Within this group, she identifies two children, Dorothy and Jeff, whom she will challenge with some independent book club activities. She is also going to find special and more demanding activities for David, who also shows strong comprehension. This initial grouping will be modified many times during the year. At different times Tessa forms focused trade book reading groups. For example, when the Holocaust is the topic of social studies, students read from a designated set of related trade books. The groups formed for this purpose are heterogeneous in composition. As needed, she provides any children from the class with special, small-group support.

Tessa's grouping each Friday for the readers'/writers' workshop includes all class members. This experience provides her the opportunity to see how well the children in the small group read more challenging materials. In the afternoon period for independent reading and writing, she observes the selections of children and the partners with whom they choose to work. She encourages children to form partnerships on the basis of their interests.

Although a profile based on standardized test results can be enlightening, many teachers prefer to collect a sample of reading performance to construct a class profile. Several different types of screening approaches will help you do this. In the following three sections, we discuss how you can develop a profile of your class using (1) a graded word list, (2) an oral reading passage, and (3) a cloze sample.

• Graded Word List—Class Profile

Word recognition, as well as automaticity of recognition, is a strong correlate of reading performance (Juel & Roper-Schneider, 1985), and the ability to recognize words on a graded word list has often been used as a quick screening measure for students. Informal Reading Inventories typically start with graded word lists as a first measure to help place students in reading materials. There are also many word reading tests available commercially such as the *Slosson Oral Reading Test*-R3 (Slosson, 2002) and the *Wide Range Achievement Test*, Fourth Edition (WRAT-4; Wilkinson, 2006). In addition, graded word lists often accompany informal reading inventories such as the *Analytic Reading Inventory* (Woods & Moe, 2007) and the *Basic Reading Inventory* (Johns, 2010). Alternatively, word lists can be constructed by sampling the graded reading materials used in your program.

We recommend lists of graded words that include at least ten words at each grade level rather than those with a few words spanning a large range (such as the WRAT). This design provides a sufficient sample to provide information for analysis as well as screening. In addition to noting word identification strategies, you can also ask children about whether they know the meanings of selected words. This will provide insight in the background experiences and vocabulary knowledge of children.

pause and reflect

Figure 1.3 shows a sample of how one student, Sam, read the first-grade word list. Examine his correct responses as well as his miscues. What reading strengths are revealed? Can he quickly recognize words? What do his miscues reveal about his skill in identifying unknown words?

To illustrate a class profile based on a graded word list, we consider the case of Eileen, a first-grade teacher whom you will meet again in Chapter 3. At Baker school, where Eileen teaches, many children come to first grade already reading. To understand their literacy development, she engages them in informal reading and writing tasks during the first weeks of school. On the first day, for example, she sees which children can recognize their own names to put on their cubbies. She notes which children actively engage in shared reading and writing activities. By the end of the first week, she has a fairly good idea which children are already reading. She has identified 10 of her 24 children that she believes are reading. To confirm her impressions, she had them read from the first few lists from the *Basic Reading Inventory* (Johns, 2010).

From the number of words Sam read correctly, we learn that he is reading quite well for a beginning first grader. He is able to recognize words that first graders are typically able to recognize in the spring of first grade. Since he recognized many of the correct words immediately, we can see that he knows these words well—automatically. There were five words that he did not know and three that he "sounded out" correctly. From this we learn that he already knows how to identify previously unknown words quite well (Figure 1.3).

After Eileen had given the ten students she thought were reading the word lists from the *Basic Reading Inventory,* she created a profile of the number of words they read correctly. To be counted as being able to recognize words

figure 1.3 • Sam's Reading of the First-Grade List from *Basic Reading Inventory* at the Beginning of the First Grade

List A 7141 (Grade 1)	Sight	Analysis	List A 7141 (Grade 1)	Sight	Analysis
1. here*	✓		12. after*	✓	
2. down*	✓		13. hill	✓	
3. then*	them	the ✓	14. men	man	✓
4. how*	✓		15. gone*	✓	
5. saw*	✓		16. ran*	run	✓
6. pocket	✓		17. gave*	✓	
7. hello	✓		18. or*	✓	
8. aunt	✓		19. way	✓	
9. never*	ner	dif	20. coat	✓	
10. puppy	✓		Number correct	15	10
11. could*	df	cold	Total		

*denotes basic sight word from Revised Dolch List

Source: From *Basic Reading Inventory, 10th Edition* by Jerry L. Johns, Copyright © 2008 by Kendall Hunt Publishing Co. Reprinted with permission.

at a certain level, students had to recognize 14, or 70 percent, of the words on the list. She used the label "Emergent Reader" for children who were not able to recognize any words on the list. Some children were reading some of the words on the Primer list, although they did not reach the criterion of 70 percent. These she called "Beginning Readers." The profile she developed is shown in Figure 1.4.

As you can see, two of the ten children, Latisha and Amy, were unable to read any words on the Preprimer list; they were, however, accomplished Emergent Readers, as indicated by Eileen's other

figure 1.4 • Profile of Ten of Eileen's First Graders Tested on the Word Lists of the *Basic Reading Inventory* at the Beginning of First Grade

Reading Level	Student
Second	Peter
First	Sam
Primer	Katie, Matthew
Preprimer	Marina
Beginning Reader	Joshua, Denise, Sasha
Emergent Reader	Latisha, Amy

informal tasks. Three children, Joshua, Denise, and Sasha, read some words and were ranked on the profile as Beginning Readers. One child, Marina, was reading at the Preprimer level, and two, Katie and Matthew, were successfully reading Primer words. However, their word recognition was often quite labored, and they showed little facility for recognizing unfamiliar words. Both Sam and Peter were reading quite independently. Their word recognition was rapid, and they were able to identify many words.

To screen the remaining 15 children in her class, Eileen assessed how well they recognized and could name the letters of the alphabet. She also administered a spelling test to assess their phoneme awareness and knowledge of letter-sound associations. Particularly at early stages of literacy development, different screening assessments may be appropriate, depending on the degree to which children have developed reading proficiency.

• Oral Reading Passage—Class Profile

Oral reading measures are also a useful means for judging the accuracy and fluency of children's reading (Strecker, Roser, & Martinez, 1998). Similar to the graded word lists, oral reading passages may come from sets of commercially constructed oral reading passages such as the *Basic Reading Inventory* (Johns, 2010), *Observation Survey*—Text Reading (Clay, 2006), the Qualitative Reading Inventory (Leslie & Caldwell, 2005), and the *Analytic Reading Inventory* (Woods & Moe, 2007). Alternatively, teachers can select one or several passages from the materials that are used as part of their instructional programs. We refer to this as "curriculum based" because you use a regular classroom text to collect a short sample of a student's oral reading.

An oral reading sample is extremely useful as a screening procedure. For an example of an oral reading record, see Figure 1.5. From it, you gain evidence on oral reading accuracy (percentage of passage words read correctly) that will let you assess the development of a child's sight word knowledge and word identification strategies. For somewhat more advanced students, you can gain information on fluency (the number of words read per minute). Fluency involves not only reading at a good rate, but also reading with a high degree of accuracy and proper intonation and phrasing (prosody or "sounding like language"). The ability to read fluently is highly correlated with many measures of reading competence (Shinn, 1989). Fluency requires that the reader possess good decoding skills, the strategies to orchestrate these skills in reading real text, and comprehension to monitor what is being read to make sure it sounds like language.

Oral reading samples are thus useful for gathering different types of information. They can help you achieve three different purposes: (1) getting a quick sense of how well your class reads in the fall, (2) identifying those students who

f i g u r e 1 . 5 • A Marked Passage of Alex's Oral Reading for a Fluency Snapshot

Directions: You are going to read part of a story about two people who meet while living in Japan. She was a Japanese schoolgirl named Aiko, and he was an American sailor named John.

Every day, my father, whose name was John, walked in the park [went]	12
with my mother, Aiko. They sat on a bench and talked. But my father [Aiko] [beach]	26
was afraid to invite my mother to dinner. [A-a-p] [in-✓]	34
If we go to a restaurant, he thought, I'll go hungry because I [res-✓] [thoughsc] [be]	47
don't know how to eat with chopsticks. And if I go hungry, I'll act like a [l]	63
bear. Then Aiko won't like me. I'd better not ask her to dinner. [Aiko]	76
My mother wondered why my father]never invited her to dinner. [w-won-p]	87
Perhaps John is afraid I don't know how to eat with a knife and fork	102
and I'll look silly, she thought. Maybe it is best if he doesn't invite me	117
to dinner.	119
So they walked and talked and never ate a bowl of rice or a	133
piece of bread together.	137
One day, the captain of my father's ship said, "John, in three	149
weeks, the ship is leaving Japan."	155
My father was sad. He wanted to marry my mother. How can I	172
ask her to marry me? he thought. I don't even know if we like the	187
same food. And if we don't, we'll go hungry. It's hard to be happy if	202
you're hungry. I'll have to find out what food she likes. And I'll have to	217
learn to eat with chopsticks.	222
So he went to a Japanese restaurant.	229
Everyone sat on cushions around low tables. My father bowed	239
to the waiter. Please teach me to eat with chopsticks.	249
Of course, said the waiter, bowing.	255

Name	Alex	Total wds. rd.	82
Date	Sept. Gr. 5	# Errors	7
		Words Read Correctly	75

Source: From Aoki, et al. *Catch a Snowflake*, "How My Parents Learned to Eat," Copyright © 1991. Used by permission of McGraw-Hill Education.

may need special support and more time when working with grade-level material, and (3) helping you to assist your students in selecting independent reading material (Blachowicz, Fisher, Massarelli, Moskal, & Obrochta, 2000). In addition, when oral reading samples are collected at the end of the school year, they are useful in charting the progress that your students made over the course of the school year.

To screen in this way, first you need to select reading material that is representative of the materials you will actually be using in class. This could, for example, be a core novel, an article from *National Geographic World,* or a short selection from a magazine or basal anthology. Try to avoid highly technical material or selections with unusual and exotic vocabulary. Choose a passage that will take the students one or two minutes to read. Make a master that you might laminate and a copy for each student being assessed.

Each student is assessed individually. Typically, students take about two minutes to read the selection. A class of 25 students can be tested in a week, if you work with about five students per day. Begin a session by sitting in a comfortable place and introducing the student to the process and the text. The directions should be something like: "I would like you to read this passage about _____. (Add any sentences to prepare the students that you think are relevant.) I'd like you to read this at a comfortable rate as accurately as you can. You may start."

You may either start timing immediately or you may let the students read the first paragraph without timing or marking. At whatever point you being timing (either the start of the first or the second paragraph) begin timing for one minute. Each time the student makes a miscue, put a tick mark in the margin or over the word, or mark the exact miscue if you are a skilled recorder. At the end of one minute, mark the last word read and let the student complete the passage.

You may add a comprehension question or retelling task. Many teachers also make anecdotal notes on each sheet to remind them of things they noticed about each child's reading, such as "Had to hold paper really close to face. Glasses?" "Had lots of trouble dropping down each line," "Very fluent . . . this is way too easy for this child," or "Raced through and couldn't tell me anything about what was read." Teachers experienced in analyzing oral reading will also note the types of miscues students make for later probing, such as "Had trouble with all the multisyllable words."

Count how many words were read in one minute and subtract the number of errors a student made. This will give you a CWPM (correct words per minute score). For example, using the oral reading sample for Alex shown in Figure 1.5, how would you interpret his reading rate? Rates will vary based on the conceptual difficulty and structure of a text. Nevertheless, some common expectations may help you think about Alex and about your class. Typically, silent reading

table 1.2 • Mean Words Correct per Minute Targets[a] for Average Students in Grades 1 through 8

Grade	Fall "Target"	Winter "Target"	Spring "Target"
1	10	20	50
2	50	70	90
3	75	90	110
4	95	110	125
5	105	125	140
6	130	140	150
7	130	140	150
8	130	140	150

[a]The targets are reported in round numbers.
Source: From *Basic Reading Inventory*, 10th Edition, by Jerry L. Johns. Copyright © 2008 by Kendall Hunt Publishing Co. Reprinted with permission.

rates become slightly faster than oral rates as children develop proficiency in reading. These are shown in Tables 1.2 and 1.3.

We illustrate this screening procedure by showing you a profile, developed by Vanessa, of her fifth-grade class. For this screening at the beginning of the school year, she had her students read a short piece about Japan from a novel she had selected for her students to read. Her class profile based on the screening is shown in Figure 1.6. From this profile, Vanessa could see that Katie, Elizabeth, RJ, Scott, Diane, and particularly Jeanne were going to have significant trouble with the novel she had chosen as the unit core book. She would need to support them in their reading and also make sure they had extra time. She planned to monitor their reading more closely during instruction and to obtain further diagnostic information. She also considered giving them an Informal Reading Inventory to obtain a more detailed picture of their reading levels, strengths, and weaknesses.

In contrast, Katie, Jamie, Sara, Jeanette, and Canessa read the sample very rapidly. Vanessa decided to check their comprehension on their next reading. If the others were as fluent as they seemed on the snapshot, and they understood what they were reading, she would need to look for some challenging material for them to read in addition to the novel. With Vera, Vanessa suspected that comprehension was sacrificed for speed. She would use comprehension strategies such as the Directed Reading-Thinking Activity (DR-TA) with her to model appropriate speed rather than rapid reading. Also, from the anecdotal comments Vanessa made, she could see that several students had trouble with multisyllable words. For these students, she would schedule a mini-lesson to do some diagnostic teaching on this topic.

table 1.3 • Oral Reading Norms for Students in Grades 1 through 8

Grade N	Percentile	Fall		Winter		Spring	
		N	WCPM	N	WCPM	N	WCPM
1 (38,239)	90	2,847	32	16,416	69	18,976	101
	75		14		40		75
	50		7		21		48
	25		2		11		26
	10		1		5		13
2 (45,446)	90	13,738	98	15,454	122	16,254	140
	75		74		98		115
	50		49		72		89
	25		23		46		64
	10		12		20		37
3 (43,717)	90	12,844	128	14,988	144	15,885	160
	75		101		117		136
	50		73		90		107
	25		48		58		78
	10		26		37		45
4 (40,072)	90	13,086	143	12,801	164	14,185	180
	75		119		139		153
	50		95		111		124
	25		70		86		99
	10		44		60		72
5 (37,238)	90	12,298	163	11,898	180	13,042	194
	75		135		154		167
	50		108		125		138
	25		85		97		108
	10		60		72		79
6 (26,547)	90	8,403	176	8,450	193	9,694	203
	75		153		165		178
	50		128		139		151
	25		98		111		123
	10		66		81		93
7 (12,597)	90	4,205	173	3,255	185	5,137	199
	75		151		159		176
	50		126		132		149
	25		102		108		122
	10		79		84		97
8 (9,728)	90	3,128	180	2,490	187	4,110	196
	75		158		163		175
	50		131		139		153
	25		102		108		125
	10		82		85		96

Source: From *Basic Reading Inventory*, 10th Edition, by Jerry L. Johns. Copyright © 2008 by Kendall Hunt Publishing Co. Reprinted with permission.

figure 1.6 • An Example of Vanessa's Class Summary of Fluency Snapshots in September of Fifth Grade

**Correct Words
Per Minute**

185	
180	
175	
170	— Vera
165	
160	
155	
150	
145	— Katie
140	— Jamie
135	— Sara
130	— Jeannette
125	— Canessa
120	— Ashley, Elizabeth K.
115	
110	— John
105	— Hmenda
100	— Jason
95	
90	— Jackie
85	— Jenny
80	
75	— Mike
70	— Alex
65	— Scott t.
60	— Shannon
55	— Sid
50	— Tony
45	— Katie P
40	— James
35	— Katie
30	— Elizabeth S.
25	— RJ
20	— Scott B. — Diane, Jeanne

Cloze Sample—Class Profile

A cloze passage is typically constructed by deleting every fifth word in a passage and replacing it with a blank. A reader, on the basis of the context, must supply the missing words. Try to make sense of the passage shown in Figure 1.7.

What terms did you insert to make a sensible passage? For the first blank, the words *experience* or *practice* would make sense. The word *cloze* would make sense in the second blank. The following represent appropriate synonyms to complete subsequent blanks: (3) *deletes/omits/leaves out,* (4) *passage/paragraph/text,* (5) *space/dash,* (6) *readers/students,* (7) *meaning/context,* and (8) *complete/create/finish/fill-in.*

A reader's ability to use the context in silent reading is highly correlated with general comprehension ability (Bormuth, 1967). To complete a cloze passage like the one in Figure 1.7, you need to use your knowledge of word meanings, sentence structure, passage meaning, and general world knowledge to predict meanings for unknown words so that what you read makes sense. Cloze passages force students to use all their cueing systems to make sense of what they are reading. Because cloze completion is a silent and untimed task, some feel it is a good measure for older readers who rely more on silent reading for their work. We talk more about using cloze procedures for instruction in Chapters 4 and 5.

After your students complete a cloze passage, you can make a class profile similar to the one in Figure 1.6. This would show the rank of your students in silent comprehension as measured by the cloze completion task. From this analysis, you can identify those students who might warrant further consideration. Because cloze passages are unusual, you need to teach students the process before using it for assessment. You might also want to include in the profile a column for qualitative comments indicating what kinds of difficulties students had with the process.

Screening is just a first look at the reading of a group of students to help identify those who *may* need further assessment. We have tried to share

figure 1.7 • A Section of a Cloze Test

More direct instruction and _____1_____ with vocabulary may be given by using the
_____2_____ procedure in its many modifications. A cloze passage _____3_____ selected
words from the _____4_____ and replaces them with a line or _____5_____ . Reading a
cloze passage requires _____6_____ to use their knowledge of _____7_____ to supply
appropriate words and concepts to _____8_____ a meaningful passage.

types of screening using standardized test results as well as several that look at
actual reading performances such as word recognition, oral reading of text, and
cloze silent reading. The process of laying out class performance on a profile is
a valuable learning experience. Early screening can help you identify students
for early information gathering; this is the first step in efficient diagnosis. Some
teachers become discouraged with the notion of reading assessment because
they feel they need to do a full-blown diagnosis on each child in the class.
Screening profiles can help you to prioritize and focus your time and effort.

Instructional Planning

In Chapters 2, 3, 4, and 5, we describe ways in which the knowledge of children
develops as they learn about print, word meanings, and comprehension strategies. In Chapter 9, we discuss ways in which assessment of these aspects of a
child's reading fit in the wider framework of school data collection and interpretation. This focus on development and learning processes may seem unusual in
a book on diagnosis. However, we have emphasized these areas because we
believe that you will not be able to plan appropriate instruction unless you have
internalized an understanding of the ways children develop knowledge as they
learn to read.

There was a time, not so long ago, when teachers typically assumed that
children entering kindergarten or first grade knew little about reading. They
were thought of as "empty vessels" or "blank slates" to be filled with sight
words, phonics skills, and other skills. Teachers typically organized their reading
instruction by following the suggestions in the manual that accompanied the
basal reading series. Learning to read was defined in terms of acquiring a variety
of skills. In other words, a behaviorist philosophy informed instruction.

In contrast to this view, studies of emergent literacy (see Chapter 2) have
shown that children enter school knowing a great deal about literacy. They
observe their parents reading, they enjoy being read to, they examine the labels
on a variety of products, and they attempt to write. They do not simply memorize information, but they make sense of their new experiences in terms of their

previous experiences. Children do not passively receive knowledge as is assumed by a behavioristic perspective; rather, they make or construct their unique interpretations of events. This activity includes events about which they read. This view of learning is identified as a constructivist perspective.

Teachers who accept this perspective on how children learn know the importance of ensuring that selections children read "make sense" and that they relate directly to the experiences of children. This attitude accounts for the increased use of children's literature in many classrooms, whether in the form of trade books or basal reading series that include children's literature. To facilitate the reading development of children you should follow three related activities:

- Identify the knowledge that children have already acquired about print, word meanings, and comprehension strategies.
- Consider this knowledge in terms of a developmental view of literacy.
- Identify the interests of students and how you can build on them.

Appropriate instructional support involves selecting reading materials that are at an appropriate level of difficulty for students and providing instruction in areas where they need support. Such instruction will enable students to progress to the next stage of development. Central to instructional planning is the view that instructional support should be geared just beyond what children are able to accomplish independently in order to help them progress to the next level of proficiency (Rogoff, 1990; Vygotsky, 1978).

In the case studies in the following chapters, we describe instruction that is responsive to students' developmental stages. We accept the position that learning develops in a social/cultural environment (Vygotsky, 1978). In other words, we believe that learning in the classroom occurs interpersonally through social interaction before individuals should be expected to use strategies on their own. Accordingly, we recommend that new concepts and ideas be introduced and discussed with your support. Concepts and strategies developed in this manner will later be applied independently by individuals. We also recommend that you select instructional materials with students to reflect their areas of interest.

summary

Reading diagnosis entails analyzing the process by which students gain meaning from text. Building on the insights and methods that have developed historically, we describe a model to guide the observations and judgments you will make about your students' reading in the classroom.

The model draws your attention to three major decisions. The first decision concerns whether a student comprehends the materials being read in your classroom. If not, your diagnosis continues to the second decision point, where you consider whether difficulties in (1) print skill, (2) vocabulary knowledge, and/or (3) reading comprehension strategies are interfering with comprehension. The pattern of strengths and difficulties that students show in these three areas will influence your third decision concerning instruction. Your understanding gained through diagnosis and your observations concerning the interests and feelings of your students will help you to identify instructional materials that are appropriate for them in difficulty and interest and will assist you in providing them with needed instructional support.

try it out

1. **Reflection on Reading Patterns:** Look at Table 1.1 (p. 15), and think about children you know and have observed reading. Can you see reading patterns that describe their reading? Think about the data you used—what you observed—in drawing your conclusion. Given your tentative conclusions about their reading and your knowledge of their interests, what sort of instructional materials and support would be appropriate?

2. **Student Portfolio Ideas:** Ask students from your class to collect materials that reflect the three areas of the model in Figure 1.1. That is, have them reflect on their skill with print, their knowledge of word meanings, and their comprehension strategies. What from their work reflects their skill in each of these areas? As a class, discuss, compare, and evaluate what they choose to represent each area.

3. **For Your Teaching Portfolio:** Consider the assessment you already carry out in your classroom. Do you collect data reflecting all the relevant areas of Figure 1.1? Do you collect data on the interests and feelings of your students? Are there areas that you would like to make more explicit in the model by adding subheadings or new headings? File this as your model of diagnosis. Revisit it as you complete the book.

4. **Do a Class Screening:** Select ten students from the same classroom and develop a reading profile. Administer a graded word list, a grade-appropriate passage, or a cloze task. After scoring the screening results, chart the students on a graph ranked by performance, examine the variability among students in the class, and discuss the implications of this for instruction.

for further reading

Klenk, L., & Kibby, M. W. (2000). Remediating reading difficulties: Appraising the past, reconciling the present, constructing the future. In M. Kamil, P. Mosenthal, P. D. Pearson, & R. Barr (Eds.), *Handbook of reading research* (Vol. 3, pp. 667–690). Mahwah, NJ: Erlbaum. For a reconsideration of remediation as currently practiced in schools and in the future.

Morris, D. (1999). The role of clinical training in the teaching of reading. In D. E. Evensen & P. B. Mosenthal (Eds.), *Advances in reading/ language research* (Vol. 6, pp. 69–100). For a thoughtful analysis of the implications of clinical teaching.

Wixson, K. K., & Lipson, M. Y. (1991). Perspectives on reading disability research. In R. Barr, M. Kamil, P. Mosenthal, & P. D. Pearson (Eds.), *Handbook of reading research* (Vol. 2, pp. 539–570). White Plains, NY: Longman. For a comprehensive summary of perspectives on reading disability that have been used to guide research.

2 Knowledge of Print: Its Development, Assessment, and Instructional Support

chapter goals for the reader

- To understand how children become aware of reading and writing and the purposes of both
- To understand how children learn about print
- To understand how children consolidate their strategies to become fluent readers
- To develop skill in assessing and interpreting the reading and writing of emergent and beginning readers
- To develop skill in planning instruction for emergent and beginning readers

Rachel and Her Students, Keshawn and Jesse

Rachel is a dynamic first-grade teacher with several years' experience. She fully appreciates the fact that most of her fledgling first graders will not be reading when she receives them in the fall. She is equally prepared for the fact that they will arrive with a wide range of print-related knowledge prerequisite to reading, including such knowledge as alphabet letter recognition, letter-sound awareness, and concept of word (the understanding of how language matches print). Rachel knows that some of her new first graders will be readers already. She has the daunting task of assessing the level of print knowledge *each* young new reader brings to the task of reading and writing so that she can help every child progress.

In this chapter, we consider two of Rachel's students, Keshawn and Jesse. Keshawn is an active, bright child, but he has expressed little interest in attempting to learn to read. As you read the section on emergent literacy, think about how this description may be useful in helping Rachel to understand Keshawn's literacy development. Jesse is an active, enthusiastic student who admits proudly that she has always liked to read and write. The section on the development of print-related concepts examines the growing orthographic awareness seen in early readers like Jesse. The chapter will describe some assessments Rachel relies on to gain continuing insights into the children's understandings of how print works, as well as some instructional plans she hopes can support each child's continuing development. ■

chapter overview

This chapter explores the stages that children pass through as they learn about print and the relationship of print to speech and meaning. We consider some of the following questions:

How do very young children make sense of printed language?

What are the different sorts of problems they solve as they learn to read?

How does their knowledge become consolidated so that they read fluently?

The chapter takes a look at some literacy "snapshots" Rachel uses to examine the knowledge that the children have about print and how she uses that information to plan differentiated and appropriate instruction for both Keshawn and Jesse and children like them in her classroom.

Rachel uses assessments that are helpful in the rapid give and take of daily instruction. As you read this chapter and the chapters that follow, it is important to keep in mind the distinction between assessment and diagnosis. We define assessment here as a process of *gathering data* for the purpose of guiding instructional decisions. Diagnosis involves interpretation or judgment of gathered data toward the development of a working hypothesis.

chapter outline

How Children Develop Knowledge of Print: Stages of Understanding Print

The child's world is full of print, and sooner or later the child will notice it. . . . Everything that children eat, wear, play with or pass in the streets has a sign or symbol. (Margaret Meek, p. 41)

Learning to read is a complex process in which children solve many different problems. Both this chapter and the next focus on the problems that children must solve and the stages they pass through in learning how print relates to speech and meaning. Did you know that literacy development begins early in life and progresses in stages? Long before children receive formal instruction, they are learning about the *functions* of literacy in their homes and in their community. Later they come to learn about the *forms* of literacy through both their continued active engagement in literacy events in their environment and through the direct instruction they receive in school.

We believe that teachers need to understand changes that occur in the awareness and knowledge that children possess about printed text. Accordingly,

figure 2.1 • Stagelike Development of Print Knowledge Necessary for Learning to Read

Print Awareness	Print Knowledge	Integration and Fluency
Understands that print is meaningful	Has alphabet knowledge	Has growing orthographic knowledge
Orients to text	Has sound/symbol knowledge	Has decoding strategies
Has concept of story	Has some concept of word	Uses contextual strategies
Uses "story talk" when "reading" books	Has some sight vocabulary	Uses "cross-checking" of cues
Has ability to rhyme	Has limited decoding	Has increasing sight vocabulary
Has auditory discrimination of beginning/ending sounds		Increases reading rates and prosody
Engages in environmental reading		

as shown in Figure 2.1, we have delineated three major or broad stages through which children progress as they learn about the nature and functions of print. We refer to the first stage as the development of *print awareness*. During this stage, children begin to notice the print that is all around them and to speculate about its meaning. Some children may begin to figure out that print is related to speech and meaning in complicated ways still beyond their understanding.

During the second stage, the development of *knowledge of print,* children acquire systematic knowledge about the nature of words and letters. At first, word learning for children with limited alphabet knowledge is based on the use of partial and often arbitrary visual cues. Word recognition might rely on a beginning letter, word length, an unusual letter, or even a smudge on the card bearing the printed word. Children may be using letters to visually discriminate words but are not using letter-sound relationships. As the children gain more experience with reading and writing, they learn more about the nature of words. Children begin to attend to words in a more systematic fashion, such as noting initial and final consonants, letter-sound cues, medial letters, and a greater number of features in combination. During this stage, children are also solving the problem of how their oral language, in particular, and meaning, in general, relate to print. It is a period of growing phonics knowledge and developing sight words.

It is in the next stage that children struggle to integrate the reading cues that come from the letters that make up the words and the cues that come from the sentence context. *Integration* refers to putting together information from a variety of sources including a child's prior knowledge about a topic, story and sentence context, as well as print cues to identify words in running text. The third stage is the development of integration and *reading fluency,* in which children consolidate knowledge of print and recognize words rapidly and automatically, permitting them to give their undivided attention toward comprehending the meaning. Reading fluency depends on well-developed knowledge about print as well as the integration of this print knowledge with syntactic and semantic information derived from context ("What sounds right? What makes sense?").

In this chapter, we discuss these three stages to help you build an understanding of how the knowledge children develop about print evolves over time. We consider Keshawn and Jesse, two first graders at different stages of print knowledge, and describe some assessment tools that can be used by the classroom teacher to look at both emergent and early reading. Last, because we believe that assessment is meaningless unless it leads to appropriate instruction, we describe lesson plans informed by our assessment results.

• Development of Print Awareness

The skills, knowledge, and attitudes that are developmental precursors to authentic reading and writing begin early in life. Even the development of oral language is significant to early literacy learning. *Emergent literacy* is a useful term coined by Marie Clay and used by others (Clay, 1975, 1979; Teale & Sulzby, 1986) to describe children's growing print awareness, which begins in the context of the home and in the community. This emergent literacy develops best in an environment that fosters the active exploration of spoken and written language.

Emerging Concepts of Print. Printed words are a common part of our culture. Walking down the street, we notice street signs, advertisements, T-shirt slogans, and printed directions. Inside our homes we see magazines, letters, labels, and trademarks. Even when we watch television, we frequently see printed words. Because of the number of printed messages in our environment, almost all children encounter printed words and see people reading and writing. Some become aware of print at a very early age (Orellana & Hernandez, 1999; Taylor, 1983). In this sense, learning to "read" print begins long before children engage in formal reading instruction.

Many children come to understand why people read and write by actually participating in acts of reading and writing. If they are read stories, they see that reading provides entertainment. If they participate in reading recipes, they see that reading provides information. If they help in writing lists, they see the value of writing as an aid to memory. Actively participating in and observing literacy activities is important because once children view these activities as pleasurable, useful, and informative, these experiences form the basis for their wanting to learn to read and write.

It is not outwardly apparent what goes on in the minds of adults and older children when they look at print as they read or write. Children must guess about what is read or written and how the process works. Studies of young children inform us about some of the ideas children have about reading and writing and how these change over time (Harste, Woodward, & Burke, 1984). From being familiar with stories, children learn about the conventions for writing English and other languages. Learning about the arrangement of text involves knowing where a book begins, where to begin reading on a page, in what direction to move, what to do at the end of a line, and what to do at the end of a page. Further, it involves learning that printed words—not just pictures—are reliable cues to speech and meaning.

Studies reveal that children differ considerably in their knowledge about print (Clay, 1975, 1979). For many children, learning about books and print begins long before school instruction. At home and in preschool, they have been read to from books, and they examine books themselves. They ask questions about reading, try to mimic reading, and sometimes ask a reader to demonstrate reading by pointing to words as the story progresses. Knowledge about the arrangement of print develops through a variety of experiences extended over time. Some children, however, come to school without the advantage of these experiences and, accordingly, lack much of the knowledge about print that their more fortunate peers have acquired. They may have only vague notions of why and how people read and write.

Children also vary in their understanding of the nature of stories and what it means to read. Sulzby (1985), for example, had preschool and kindergarten children read their favorite stories to her. She found that they could be divided into two main groups: those who depended mainly on the pictures or memory of a story as the basis for their story telling and those who had begun to cue into the print as the basis for reading. Further, she found that children in the first group differed in the extent to which their stories were well formed and reflected oral versus written language patterns. Some children mainly labeled or commented on the pictures, whereas others retold the actions in the story. Some told stories in a fashion similar to the way they talked, and others sounded as if they were reading (although their story showed little conformity to the story as printed in the book).

Sulzby also found differences among children who were aware that print in storybooks serves as the basis for reading. Such awareness was demonstrated by some children in their refusal to read because of not knowing the "words"; others focused on a limited number of known letters or words; and still others demonstrated varying degrees of reading proficiency. Studies such as this show that children vary in their understanding of the nature of stories and what it means to read.

One of the earliest problems to be solved by children concerns the nature of print. Children must come to realize that print is more than a series of marks. For a while, print is seen as being no different from any other mark or design on a page. Hiebert (1981) reported that many three-year-olds and some older preschoolers pointed to pictures when they were asked what readers should look at in books. Later, when children distinguished pictures from print, some continued to identify numbers as letters. Even when children have learned that letters are different from other marks on the page, they fail to appreciate the representational nature of writing. This is characteristic of children in the early print awareness stage (Ferreiro & Teberosky, 1982). For example, Ferreiro (1984) reported that when asked, "What could be read here?" (pointing to the text), a three-year-old responded "Letters." When asked further, "What does it say in the letters?" he responded "Letters." This and other evidence suggested that the child was not yet aware that letters were more than letters; he had not discerned the symbolic function of writing. Print was seen as being no different from other marks or designs. Gradually, children form a concept of what people do when they read and write. Thus a major development toward literacy is achieved when children understand that writing represents meaning.

As part of this process, children must determine where writing goes in relation to pictures. On the basis of responses of preschoolers, Ferreiro (1984) speculated that children believe that writing must be inserted into drawings or abutted next to them to have meaning. Only later do they learn that the position of writing on a page can change in relation to the picture without changing the meaning of the text.

Somewhat later, children experiment with the number of letters that should be used to represent words. For example, Ferreiro (1984) reported that Fernando, at 4 years 11 months, represented "one corncob" with a single letter and "three corncobs" with three. Four months later he represented both "one child" and "five children" with three letters. He had progressed from believing that each letter corresponded to each object to the concept of words as composed of a fixed number of letters. Ferreiro also found that some children at a later stage represented longer spoken words with more letters than shorter words, one for each syllable. Her research also showed that different children approach the problem in different ways and develop somewhat different hypotheses.

During this period of early print awareness, children also learn to "read" words in context. That is, they can recognize labels and other signs that regularly occur in the same contexts, such as "stop" on an octagonal red sign at the street corner or "PEPSI" within a red-white-and-blue design. Careful studies show, however, that when the words were taken out of context, young children do not always recognize them; further, when the writing itself is altered ("XEPSI" instead of "PEPSI"), they don't always detect the change (Masonheimer, Drum, & Ehri, 1984; see also Mason, 1980). This means that children identifying words in this manner have not yet entered the stage of word learning when they depend solely on the letters to recognize printed words.

Increased Language Awareness. Each of these studies helps us to gain insight into the problems that young children must solve as they grow in their understanding of printed messages. To gain even greater appreciation of the complexity of the task, consider the ways in which children's knowledge about their language must be related to the printed words they see. When they first become aware of print, they already possess a well-formed language system. Nevertheless, they have not learned to think about their language in an objective fashion. For linguists, language is a complex, hierarchical system in which smaller units of language are nested within larger ones. For example, large units of discourse can be divided into sentences, and sentences into words, or morphemes. Words are themselves composed of smaller units—syllables—which in turn are composed of sounds—phonemes. Although students do not need to acquire the sophisticated perspective of a linguist to learn to read, they must become more aware of the nature of their language to understand the various ways spoken language corresponds to writing.

The correspondence between speech and writing is complicated because relationships occur on a number of levels and are not always obvious. At the most general level, the message of written exposition relates to a spoken counterpart. At a lower level, a printed sentence will also correspond to a spoken sentence. But whereas a capital letter and a period indicate the boundaries of the printed sentence, inflectional characteristics may indicate the boundaries of the spoken sentence. Spoken words also relate to printed words; but whereas printed words are marked by spaces, spoken words are not delineated from each other. There are no spaces in the oral speech stream. Indeed, children may begin reading with little awareness of how speech becomes partitioned into word units. As children begin to read, they must, however, learn how their oral language matches specifically to the printed word. This ability to map oral speech forms to print is called *concept of word* and is a key development that enables children to focus on individual words and to explore the nature of words. Until children can read a sentence, pointing to each word systematically, they will not progress far in either learning sight words or in exploring letter relationships within words (Clay, 1979).

Below the level of meaningful words, spoken phonemes and syllables correspond to letters (graphemes) and series of letters. Establishing the relations between sounds and letters is complicated for several reasons. First, just as children are not aware of word units in their spoken language, so they are not aware of the sounds that compose spoken words. In fact, some researchers have argued that it is experience with letters that sensitizes children to the phonemes of words (Ehri, 1983, 1991). Second, while English has a relatively principled orthography (writing system), children must develop a growing awareness of these principles. They must, for example, learn to understand that a letter, particularly certain letters (vowels), may stand for several different phonemes. Eventually, they must learn that more than one letter is sometimes needed to represent a single phoneme (*oa* represents the sound of the letter name *o*).

Recent research supports the importance of children being able to develop their ability to hear and objectify subunits of language. In particular, phonemic awareness has been identified as critical in the development of reading skill, and it has been associated with differences in end-of-first-grade reading achievement (Bradley & Bryant, 1983; Ehri, 1998; Goswami & Bryant, 1990). For very young children and those in the emergent stage of literacy development, phonemic awareness can be encouraged and nurtured through informal word games played at home and through instructional tasks that help children hear sound units in words (Lundberg, Frost, & Peterson, 1988; Yopp, 1992). However, this ability is most naturally developed in classrooms in the context of reading and writing tasks where children are seeing how words are written.

It is important for teachers to understand how to identify each student's evolving word and phonemic awareness. For example, children give evidence of word awareness, or concept of word, when their storybook reading closely conforms to the text. Children's spelling approximations usually referred to as invented spellings are further evidence of their stage of orthographic sophistication; their efforts to map the sounds they hear to letters can be a "window" to their phonemic awareness. In this chapter, you will see how our first-grade teacher, Rachel, examines the word and phonemic awareness of Keshawn and Jesse.

In sum, children unconsciously begin to understand language in an objective fashion. At the level of stories and other textual messages, they learn to relate sentences and messages to each other within the larger context in which they occur. This form of metacognitive strategy is discussed in Chapter 5 with regard to comprehension. At the level of sentences, they develop a sense of how the words in sentences relate to each other. For example, children reading a sentence use both syntactic and semantic cues to anticipate a word by asking themselves what sounds right or what makes sense. At the level of words, they develop the understanding of how language is segmented into printed word units (concept of word). Finally, at the level of word elements, children develop phonemic awareness, or the ability to hear and manipulate subunits of words.

pause and reflect

Imagine for a moment that you are Rachel and that Keshawn is one of your students. What would you want to learn about Keshawn's growing awareness of literacy? What are three things that you would do with Keshawn in order to learn more about his knowledge of reading and writing?

• Development of Print Knowledge

Instructional Influences. Teachers in preschools and some in kindergartens view their role as supporting the emergence of print awareness through informal activities such as story reading, language experience stories, and simple writing tasks. Traditionally, more direct reading instruction occurs in first grade, though in many schools across the country, direct reading instruction is initiated in kindergarten classes. In thinking about the development of print knowledge, it is important for you to consider the instruction that children have received because their learning, and to some extent their confusions, may reflect the nature of their past reading instructional program.

Many children learn to read from basal programs that include opportunities to read stories and informational selections, to write, and to develop skills and strategies (Chall & Squire, 1991). Typically, the skill instruction in word elements (compound words, word endings, letter-sound associations, and so on) proceeds in an orderly fashion, with a new concept introduced in each lesson. The stories and other selections children read are sequenced to increase in difficulty. For example, stories they read at the beginning of first grade may be composed of sentences that are predictable in pattern. Stories they read later in first grade are typically more complex in sentence pattern and in the number of different printed words included. The materials are sequenced in terms of difficulty so that children will not become frustrated by having to deal with too many new concepts (sentence patterns or words). Words such as *in, the, but,* and *are* tend to recur in stories, and this repetition helps children develop a set of quickly recognized words. Some teachers refer to these words as "sight words" because readers recognize them instantly without resorting to letter-sound identification.

Over a decade ago, many American children read from basal programs in which the difficulty of reading selections was controlled in an artificial fashion. The number of new words, letters, or spelling patterns introduced and repeated in successive stories was carefully measured. This systematic introduction and repetition of words or letters was done to simplify the complexities of early reading and to help children learn printed words and letter-sound associations. At the same time, many of the sentences that resulted were stilted and unlike those children were accustomed to hearing, either in conversation or in stories read aloud to them. Consequently, children had difficulty using their understanding of story and sentence context to help them with word recognition. Research has shown that children who had been taught with beginning reading materials controlled in these ways made distinctive reading errors. Learning from materials in which letters were controlled, children frequently produced either nonwords or words that violated the sense of a passage. Those reading from word-controlled materials tended to make the error of using real words that made sense in terms of sentence context, but that were not the words printed on the page (Barr, 1974; Cohen, 1974–1975; Juel & Roper-Schneider, 1985).

Generally, in education, there has been a shift away from behaviorist views to those that emphasize the constructive nature of learning. While earlier behaviorist theory was centered more on item learning (words, letters), the focus has shifted now toward integrated strategies that children use to make sense of text. *Integrated strategies* entail the coordination of information from prior knowledge, story and sentence context, and print. This shift in the way we view learning led to a modification of basal programs as well as literacy instruction in which children learn to read from real text (both narrative and informational texts written by children's authors) in addition to or instead of basal stories and are encouraged to write. To make the books accessible, teachers ensure that the stories are familiar to children, either by previewing the book or, initially, reading aloud. As children read from trade books, by themselves or with a friend, they are encouraged to construct meaning from a variety of sources: their memories of the story, clues that the pictures provide, story and sentence context, and associations from print.

Regardless of the materials used in beginning reading instruction, teachers need to be mindful that the texts children experience in learning to read impact, often profoundly, what children learn. Hiebert (1999) examined the genres of texts used to teach beginning readers: texts based on high-frequency words, phonetically controlled texts, trade books, and texts written using predictable sentence or text pattern, commonly with strong picture cues. Her research suggests that each of these "single-criterion" beginning reading material provides unique opportunities for beginning readers to gain proficiency over an aspect of the learning-to-read process, but sometimes, at the expense of other important learning. She likens the beginning reader's consistent exposure to particular types of text to a diet where children eat particular food groups but not others. To carry through the analogy, children on a steady diet of one particular instructional text may be acquiring some "nutrients" (skills) but not others. Specifically, Hiebert's analysis points out that texts based on high-frequency words encourage the learning of an important automatic sight vocabulary. However, these texts contain a high percentage of irregularly spelled words, thus impeding the learning of consistent letter-sound relationships. The flip side is also true. Phonetically regular texts teach phonic patterns but may shortchange opportunities to develop frequently occurring sight word vocabularies. Trade books, literature anthologies, and predictable "little books," increasingly popular in classrooms, pose different challenges, particularly for the "at-risk" readers. While these texts foster contextual reading strategies, they are demanding for novice readers because of the sheer number of different high-frequency and phonetically irregular words.

Given that most reading materials for emergent and early readers are "single criterion," teachers may find themselves confused about how to provide the optimal learning experience. Hiebert makes a plea for teachers to find multiple criteria texts that provide children with the chance to examine and apply information about different aspects of written English. *Matching Books to Readers: Using Leveled Books in Guided Reading, K–3* (Fountas & Pinnel, 1999) is a treasure trove for books that meet multiple criteria description for emergent and beginning readers. Poetry can also serve this purpose. Teachers use a variety of single-criterion texts in their literacy programs, including poems that focus on specific phonics elements or leveled little books where there is repetition of sight words and new vocabulary supported by patterned sentences. The central point of this discussion remains the importance of a seldom acknowledged fact: beginning reading materials can influence what children learn about print.

Word Awareness and Learning Words by Sight. The discussion on emergent literacy shows how children develop a growing understanding of print and its relation to speech and meaning through their participation in reading and writing activities. Through story reading, they learn how stories are arranged in books and come to understand that printed words are meaningful. When children write, they explore the nature of writing and how it relates to spoken words. At some point in their development, they realize that printed words are individual nameable objects. It is when children become aware of this concept that they are able to learn words and to explore the complex relationships within words and between letters and sounds.

Interestingly, some knowledge of letter-name/sound relationships seems to help children develop a stable concept of word (Ehri, 1980; Morris, 1988). As Ehri (1980) argues, knowledge of letter-sound associations constitutes the "glue" that holds word images in memory. The development would seem to be reciprocal in that some knowledge of letter-sounds makes new words more familiar. At the same time, the awareness of specific words in speech and a sense of their *printed* word boundaries allow children to make increasingly more sophisticated inferences about letter-sound correspondences within discrete word units. Thus, children begin to learn words and to begin to discriminate one word from another.

Ehri (1980) describes the complex process of word learning. She explains that children form fragmentary mental images of printed words that become stored in their memories along with the spoken identity of the words and their meanings. Children's early spelling attempts, or invented spellings, are excellent evidence of these incomplete word images (like–*lc;* ride–*rd;* play–*pa*). As children repeatedly read the words and increase their ability to segment words phonemically, they build a more complete image, often reflected in increasingly more standard-like spelling. Ehri says:

> Since beginners already know how words are pronounced, their task is to assimilate the word's printed form to its phonological (speech sound) structure. They do this by matching at least some of the letters to phonetic or phonemic segments detected in the word. These segments serve as "slots" in lexical memory which are filled by images of letters seen in the word's spelling. (1980, p. 313)

It is clear that within this developmental view, the ability to learn words is closely interwoven with the ability to learn the sound components of words. Research suggests that the development of phoneme awareness is a critical achievement in the process of learning to read (Bradley & Bryant, 1983; Goswami & Bryant, 1990; Lundberg, Frost, & Petersen, 1988; Tunmer, Herriman, & Nesdale, 1988).

One of a child's most important achievements in reading is learning to recognize printed words instantaneously. In word learning, beginning readers must confront two problems. The first is learning to segment oral language into parts that correspond to printed words. The second is learning to discriminate among the printed words. In the following sections we consider the nature of word awareness and learning first, and then the development of phoneme awareness and word identification strategies. We treat these two aspects of learning to read separately, but remember that the two develop concurrently and are interconnected.

Word Awareness. Literate adults have difficulty imagining that young children may listen to sentences without being aware of the specific words that compose them, yet evidence from research indicates that this is true. Perhaps the study that has most influenced our thinking about the development of word awareness was conducted by Karpova (1955, as described in Slobin, 1966). Karpova found that the word consciousness of children develops in three stages. In the first, at three to four years of age, children understand sentences as semantic (meaningful) units, without distinguishing individual words. For example, they report that a sentence such as *Galyla and Vova went walking* contains two words: *Galyla-went-walking* and *Vova-went-walking*. During the next stage, prereaders become able to separate sentences into subject and predicate. Finally, during the third stage, children learn to identify the words that compose sentences, although they may experience difficulty with compound and multisyllabic words and fail to distinguish some function words as separate units.

Failure to develop word awareness during the initial stages of reading is manifested in oral reading that bears little or no correspondence to the printed words being read. The development of such awareness is evident in Clay's (1967) description of the stages through which beginning readers progressed while being instructed in a sentence method:

> As [the children] developed skill in matching behavior, fingers were used to point to those parts of the text that were supposed to correspond to the vocal responses. Fluency gave way to word by word reading. At this point the child's reading became staccato as he over-emphasized the breaks between words. He could be thought of as "reading the spaces" or "voice pointing" at the words. (p. 16)

Thus, pointing to words during the initial stages of reading indicates the development of awareness of words and of the correspondence between spoken and written language. Voice pointing and, subsequently, natural phrasing reflects increasing familiarity with and control over print. Both finger and voice pointing should be interpreted as signs of progress, and as Clay noted, they are not behaviors to be "hurriedly trained out." Timed reading is not recommended for emergent readers for this reason.

Most children do not encounter difficulty in becoming aware of words and establishing an automatic sight vocabulary. However, some children, like Keshawn, require explicit instruction before they make the connection between their own oral language and the print and before they can attend carefully to the structure of printed words. Instructional methods described later in this chapter show how teachers can help children develop a concept of word and the word awareness that underlies it.

Sight Word Learning. The development of sight words is an important component in the learning-to-read process. The acquisition of an automatic sight word repertoire plays a critical role in fluent reading. Sight word learning involves comparing new words with previously learned words to identify features that are useful for distinguishing among them (Goswami & Bryant, 1990; Goswami & Mead, 1992). For example, in learning the words *red, blue, yellow, green,* and *orange,* children need only attend to the initial letter of each word to discriminate among them and give a correct response. If, however, the word *brown* is added to the set, the children will need to consider more than the initial consonant to discriminate correctly, since *blue* and *brown* begin with the same letter.

Thus, a problem with the discrimination learning of printed words is that as the set of words learned becomes larger, features that were initially useful in discriminating among words are no longer sufficient, and students must attend to other features. Primary teachers observe this problem most often in the failure of students to distinguish among words with similar beginning and ending letters but different medial vowels (e.g., *but, bat,* and *bit*). Most children eventually learn to attend to enough word features that they rarely confuse words. In addition, they learn to use other sources of information, such as phonics and contextual cues, to facilitate rapid word recognition. Discrimination among printed words is also reinforced when children write sentences based on what they have read. By writing words, children become increasingly conscious of all letters in a word. Many teachers use "word walls," which contain words children read and use often in their independent writing. Generally, words are introduced, a few each week, and organized alphabetically in a prominent place in the classroom. Teachers refer to this growing core group of words frequently to reinforce their quick identification.

Beyond word discrimination, the ease with which children learn words is associated with the meaning the words carry. Abstract words, such as *in, the,* and *very* are more difficult for children to remember and identify quickly than more concrete and meaningful words such as *baby, ball,* and *dinosaur.* Repeated exposure to words makes it more likely that children will remember and identify them quickly. Basal program authors who control the repetition of words are attempting to help children learn words through concentrated practice. When children read from books with limited amounts of print and predictably patterned sentences, they are more likely, in the initial stages of learning words, to remember the set of words being stressed.

Many children receive reading instruction in books where the vocabulary is not controlled. While these books support emergent and beginning readers by the repetition of pattern, use of rhyme, and strong picture cues, sight word learning is achieved through multiple readings. Often, teachers "spot check" sight words that occur in context in order to highlight their visual forms for the children. These words might be used in individual or group word banks where children practice associating the printed forms with their spoken identity in isolation, but only after the words have been successfully recognized in context. It is, however, through contextual reading that children begin to relate the printed form with its meaning as well as its pronunciation.

Practice with isolated words is quite different from practice in context. Isolated word drill may help children associate the printed forms of words with their spoken counterparts, but without context, children do not have to specify the meaning of words in terms of story content and prior experience. As a result, the concepts of words stored in memory are less semantically rich and less easily recalled.

Initial word learning can be achieved with limited phonics concepts. However, children cannot be skilled readers by relying exclusively on memorizing sight words. All printed words are built using a pool of 26 symbols to represent 44 speech sounds. Because these few symbols are used over and over, visual forms begin to look very much alike. To be a successful reader, a child must develop insights about the connections between visual letter forms and the sounds they represent in order to access the myriad vocabulary a child encounters as she becomes a fluent reader. In the next section, we consider how students learn word elements.

Knowledge of Word Elements. Knowledge about words and their elements develops over time as words are learned. Knowledge of *word elements* means the knowledge that children have of English spelling (orthography) that enables them to identify words they have not seen before. Knowledge of word elements pertains to letter-sound associations and the structural components of words, such as root words and affixes (e.g., *-ing, -ed, re-, un-*), as well as procedural knowledge about word elements. The latter includes knowing how to blend word elements to form a word as well as how to analogize from a known to an unknown word, as in using the ending of *sat* to help in identifying *mat* (Goswami & Bryant, 1990; Goswami & Mead, 1992). Underlying the development of knowledge of word elements is phoneme awareness.

Phoneme Awareness. Phoneme awareness refers to a child's sensitivity to the sound components of oral speech and, in particular, the processing of sound units across words. Awareness of discrete sound units continues to be refined as children ultimately learn to match phonological structures to their orthographic correlates. When children are first learning to speak, they discern differences at the phonemic level within words; that is, they are able to distinguish between words that differ in only one sound (e.g., *cat* and *bat*). At the same time, they have little conscious awareness over phonemes as distinctive units; they are unable to treat them in an objective fashion. Various research strategies suggest that children become aware of phonemes only gradually. For example, children below the age of seven experience considerable difficulty reporting the word that remains when a phoneme is deleted (e.g., when /h/ is deleted from *hill* or /d/ from *card*); Bruce (1964), Rosner and Simon (1971), and Liberman, Shankweiler, Fischer, and Carter (1974) reported that none of a preschool group and only 17 percent of a kindergarten group were able to segment words into their phonemic components, whereas 70 percent of a first-grade group were successful at this task. The problem of distinguishing phonemes within words is complicated by the fact that each phoneme may have several sound variants, and these are treated as equivalent in the writing system. This situation makes it difficult to explain and illustrate the concept of phonemes.

Research has established a convincing correlation between the development of phoneme awareness and reading, but there is debate over whether phonemic awareness is a prerequisite or a facilitator of reading development, whether it develops concurrently with reading, or whether reading leads to phoneme awareness (Ehri, 1979). Although we know that instruction to develop phoneme awareness enhances later reading achievement (Bradley & Bryant, 1983; Lundberg, Frost, & Petersen, 1988), we also have seen that reading influences the way children perceive phonemes (Ehri, 1983). As a teacher you need to be conscious that many children profit from instruction that encourages them to hear phonemes in words. Rather than providing intensive instruction in phoneme awareness followed by instruction in letter-sound associations, we believe that the two should occur together as part of reading and writing activities.

How do children learn to hear phonemes in words? One natural approach is through hearing and seeing rhyming words. Playing with word families helps children become aware of how the beginning consonants or consonant blends (onsets) change, while the word endings (rimes) stay the same (Treiman, 1985; Adams, 1990). Another way to get children to attend to phonemes is to encourage children to invent spellings. Before the 1980s, most children were not encouraged to explore writing until they had learned to read. We now know that if children have even a little knowledge of sound-letter correspondences, they can approximate writing real words as they compose. By learning to say words in a slightly elongated fashion, stretching the words out to exaggerate

figure 2.2 • Developmental Spelling Stages Showing Increasing Orthographic Awareness

Ardon	Marni	David	Hans	Jane
Stage 1	*Stage 2*	*Stage 3*	*Stage 4*	*Correct*
BE3Q	BCA	BAK	BACKE	BACK
ED	MLA	MAL	MAEL	MAIL
LIz	SPA	SAP	STAP	STEP
C	JLK	JAP	JUNGK	JUNK
CB	PTA	PET	PEEKT	PEEKED
N	HA	CEH	CHIN	CHIN

the distinct phonemic units, children are able to hear the sounds, initially in a limited way. They may first be able to distinguish and represent only the beginning sound, then later perhaps a beginning and end sound. A middle sound is represented particularly if it is a long vowel that says its alphabet letter name or salient consonant (Clay, 1979; Elkonin, 1963). If we use the metaphor of a dimmer switch on a light, we can think of children moving developmentally over time into increasingly fuller light (or more standard spelling). Since children's inventions tend to advance in predictable stages representing continued experience and exposure to appropriate reading and directed word study, their writing can inform our instruction to support continued progress. Developmental spelling can be indentified in stages (Henderson, 1981, 1985; Invernizzi & Hayes, 2004; Morris, 1999; Read, 1971).

In the first stage, as shown in Figure 2.2, children represent words by letters and, sometimes, numbers, and the spellings bear no resemblance to the target word. Thus, this spelling stage is labeled the *prephonemic stage.* As we have come to understand phonemic awareness, the label may be misleading. In fact, children in this stage are able to process distinct sound units to some extent. However, they lack the alphabet knowledge to link sound with an appropriate symbol representation.

In the second stage—early phonemic spelling—children begin to use alphabetic writing, representing some sounds of words in a systematic way, particularly those at the beginning of words. This stage can be divided into two substages: the first, or "initial consonant" stage, in which only initial consonants are represented, and second, or "consonant frame," in which both initial and final consonants are represented. In the third stage, often called the "letter name" or phonemic stage, sounds across words are represented more fully. Most sounds across words are matched with a corresponding *letter name.* The *dr* in *dragon,* for example, is represented by a *j* or a *g* because that is actually the letter name articulated when pronouncing *dr.* Long vowels are generally represented correctly because their sound is clearly also their letter name. On the other hand, short vowels that have no corresponding letter name are often represented by the vowel letter name closest in place of articulation. For example, the *e* in *bed* has no letter name equivalent but is closest to the letter name *a* in the vocal tract. Children write *b-a-d* for the word *bed* (Read, 1971). In the fourth stage, often called the transition stage, children represent within-word patterns; they no longer use a one-sound/one-letter strategy to spell. In particular, children begin to spell using correct vowels and silent letters that mark the pronunciation of vowels (the final *e* pattern, for example). This new knowledge is assimilated from exposure to pattern words in the children's contextual reading and the children's increasingly sophisticated phonics (they begin to notice that the letters *t-a-p* do not spell *tape*). Nevertheless, as is shown in Figure 2.2, the spellings still depart in systematic ways from standard spelling for some words (Henderson & Beers, 1980).

This development in spelling reflects growth in the underlying knowledge that children have about words and a growing sophistication in representing the sound elements processed. To think of this development in terms described earlier by Ehri (1980), the images of words that children store in memory become more complete. Her research shows that children spell words not simply on the basis of letter-sound knowledge but also on the basis of their stored images of words because silent as well as voiced letters are represented in their spelling.

Beyond the relationship of phonemic awareness and developmental spelling, there are more advanced stages where children are negotiating syllables and affixes and connections between word meanings and spelling. The developmental stages described in Figure 2.2 can be extended upward through the grades showing the increasing orthographic knowledge that underlies all that children do related to literacy (reading, vocabulary acquisition, writing). As in the early stages, children's spelling errors can be seen as a conservative measure of what children know about our English orthography and what they can or cannot apply as they write. A full discussion is beyond the scope of this chapter. Teachers who want to understand the range of development in spelling and the synchrony of literacy development, as well as ways to assess spelling and provide appropriate instruction, can refer to the work of Donald Bear (Bear, Invernizzi, Templeton, & Johnston, 2008).

Word Identification. The phonemes (sounds) of English correspond, more or less well, to graphemes (letters), and these correspondences are referred to as *phonic* concepts. Almost all beginning reading programs now in common use introduce phonic concepts. Where programs with a heavy emphasis on phonics are used, students' reading progress is heavily dependent on their mastery of phonic concepts. However, in some phonic programs, phonemes are introduced in isolated form, and students miss the important learning that words can be segmented into phonemes. Accordingly, students learn phonic correspondences on an item-by-item basis and fail to acquire a general procedure by which to relate word forms and phonemes.

Many children learn to read from programs that include instruction in phonics and other word elements. Others learn word elements inductively: They discover spelling patterns through writing. There is evidence that those children who learn to read easily also develop knowledge about word elements easily, beyond what has been taught to them through direct instruction. The knowledge of average and less-proficient learners, by contrast, tends to reflect the concepts they have been taught directly through their writing and reading programs (Barr & Dreeben, 1983). Further, while some children may demonstrate knowledge of word elements, unless they can organize this knowledge systematically to support word identification (and spelling), it is of little functional value. Therefore, a teacher needs to be able to assess children's knowledge of word elements and their ability to use their phonics knowledge to learn new words. If children are not making progress, they may need supportive and direct instruction to help them to hear sounds in words and learn spelling-sound relationships (Stahl, Duffy-Hester, & Stahl, 1998).

pause and reflect

Examine the message in Figure 2.3 that Jesse wrote. Is there evidence that she understands that sounds are represented by letters? What do you conclude about her knowledge of word elements? What sounds does she represent in her spelling, and how does she represent those sounds? How would you characterize Jesse's spellings in terms of the spelling stages? Last, what evidence is there that Jesse is beginning to develop a sight vocabulary? Can we conclude that Jesse is, at least, a beginning reader?

Children progress through spelling stages that reveal increasing orthographic awareness, as shown in Figure 2.2. Children progress through similar stages in their ability to identify unknown words. Reading aloud, children reveal their knowledge of sight words and also their skill in identifying unknown words. By analyzing the match between the printed words and a child's miscues, you can develop some hypotheses about the nature of his or her knowledge of word elements. These procedures are demonstrated in Chapter 3 when we consider children's oral reading.

• Development of Integration and Fluency

In this section we focus on the integration of reading strategies and reading fluency. *Integration* is the ability to use prior knowledge, contextual information, and print cues simultaneously in a coordinated fashion. *Fluency* is reading unfamiliar as well as familiar selections with appropriate intonation, phrasing, and rate. It is possible for children to demonstrate fluent reading with familiar stories they have read many times, but unless this same fluency is demonstrated with unfamiliar selections, we cannot conclude that they are fluent readers. The

f i g u r e 2 . 3 • Message Written by Jesse

Dear Aunt Diane, How are you? Have you gotten the mouse
you got me when I lost Marshall. I hope so. Jacob's
birthday was or will be soon, on February 27th, Wednesday.

Source: Printed with permission from Jesse Blachowicz. We thank her for this contribution.

capability to read fluently depends on two conditions: (1) instantaneous recognition of an extensive set of printed words, and (2) considerable practice reading contextual selections. Some skillful young readers achieve fluency in their first year of reading. Many, however, require several years of reading experience before they acquire sufficient word knowledge and contextual practice to read unfamiliar material fluently. The focus of this section is on determining whether children have achieved fluency when reading unfamiliar selections and delineating the reading experiences they need to further their development of fluency.

Integration and Reading Strategies. Biemiller (1970) described three stages of development in beginning reading skill. In the first stage, beginning readers, when reading contextual selections, attend mainly to contextual information; that is, when they come to words they do not know, the words they substitute are words they have guessed on the basis of context. For example, the sentence *The red wagon rolled down the hill* might be read as "The red wagon *sped* down the hill." The substitution of *sped* for *rolled* suggests that the child, failing to recognize the word *rolled,* used the contextual meaning of the sentence to determine an appropriate substitute.

In the second stage, children appear to focus much more on the print: When they encounter an unknown word, their substitutions tend to match some part of the unknown word. For example, a child at this stage reading the sentence *The red wagon rolled down the hill* might substitute the nonsense word *railed* for *rolled* if he or she did not know the word *rolled.* Children at this stage are beginning to attend much more closely to the features of printed words, sometimes at the expense of meaning.

In the final stage, children integrate information from print and context when identifying unknown words. Biemiller found that errors they made tended to be appropriate both to the context of the sentence and the graphic features of the word. For example, in reading the same sentence the student might substitute the word *raced* for *rolled.* The substitution makes sense in terms of the meaning of the sentence, and it matches some of the features of the printed word. During this stage readers learn to integrate information from context and print to aid them in identifying unknown words.

All readers in the process of becoming proficient readers learn to incorporate information from a variety of sources while reading. This integration of information can be seen most clearly in beginning readers. In the early stages, they seem able to consider only one source of information (context or print) at a time. Later when they confront unknown words, their substitutions indicate use of information from several sources (Biemiller, 1970; Weber, 1968).

Fluent Reading. An issue of considerable importance is whether the ability to integrate information from a variety of sources underlies fluent reading, or whether fluent reading comes about in some other way. In essence, the debate focuses on whether fluent reading is achieved through coordination of print and contextual information, with decreased attention to print in favor of meaning, or whether knowledge of words and word identification proficiency are solely or mainly responsible for fluent reading (Stanovich, 1986).

On one side, many reading experts argue that fluent reading arises from the complex coordination of information sources (Bussis, Chittenden, Amarel, & Klausner, 1985; Clay, 1979). Goodman (1976) asserted, "Skill in reading involves not greater precision, but more accurate first guesses based on better sampling techniques, greater control over language structure, broadened experiences and increased conceptual development" (p. 504). Some adherents to this position even argue that heavy dependence on print causes poor reading. Smith (1971) claimed that "the more difficulty a reader has with reading, the more he relies on visual information; this statement applies to both the fluent reader and the beginner" (p. 221).

Others have articulated an opposing position. Among the first to focus on the development of fluency or automaticity, LaBerge and Samuels (1974) proposed that instantaneous processing of print evolves as component skills of word identification become automatic through practice. They suggest that practice facilitates two different developments. First, it helps the reader consolidate separate processes. At a basic level, for example, he or she consolidates phonic associations and blending within word identification. That is, children learn to blend letter-sound associations to identify previously unknown words. At a more advanced level, visual recognition leads immediately to awareness of meaning with or without consciousness of the sound of the letter or word. Readers are no longer aware of the visual forms or sound of words they read—only their meaning. This consolidation is revealed when children no longer hesitate in recognizing words. Second, practice permits the reader to grasp larger units, allowing him or her to go from reading word by word to reading word groups or phrases. This reorganization is sometimes manifested in an increase in reading rate.

In the initial version of the formulation of theories about fluency, it was seen as developing through automaticity of word knowledge; the role of context was not considered (see Samuels, 1979, for later versions that consider the role of contextual facilitation in the development of fluency). Later researchers have attempted to clarify the role of context in fluent reading. Perfetti (1985) has shown that there is a linear relation between isolated word recognition time and contextual facilitation: The more difficult a word is to recognize (because a reader lacks word knowledge or because a word is printed unclearly), the more important context becomes in contributing information.

Stanovich (1980, 1986) developed this position further by distinguishing between two forms of contextual support: an automatic contextual facilitation that occurs outside conscious control and a consciously controlled process. The automatic process is viewed as operating in memory without reader awareness; the topic under consideration triggers or activates related concepts, thereby making them easier for a reader to retrieve. The conscious process is directed by the purpose of the reader, with his or her full attention. Stanovich argued that this conscious use of context occurs when readers encounter problems recognizing words; one negative consequence, however, is that the resulting focus of attention on word recognition detracts from comprehension. Good readers who have developed automaticity in word knowledge encounter few problems with word identification when they read and therefore can direct all their attention toward meaning. Poor readers who encounter many problems with print are forced to use context to help them identify words, and this division of attention between print and meaning leads not only to poorer comprehension but also to less adequate contextual information to support word identification.

In this book we suggest that the goal of reading is comprehension, and that adequate comprehension depends on the integration of knowledge from different sources, including the reader's background knowledge on a topic, his or her developing understanding of an author's message, knowledge of language structures, and knowledge of print. At the same time, we believe that fluent processing of print depends on automaticity of word knowledge, when the reader quickly recognizes words without having to devote effort to their analysis. We agree with Stanovich that when readers encounter few problems in word identification, they are able to focus more completely on reconstructing the messages of authors. Remember, however, that there is a stage before fluent reading when most readers profit from learning to integrate information from print and context to aid their word identification.

Assessing Children's Emergent Literacy and Beginning Reading Knowledge

During their early years, children become aware of the nature of print and its relation to speech and meaning in many ways. Children differ greatly in the understanding they have achieved at the time they enter school. Some, despite extensive story reading and exposure to print, fail to make connections about the nature of storybook reading and writing. Others experience a less rich print environment and are read stories infrequently. Often these children have not had the opportunities or encouragement to begin exploring the nature of print. Teachers must be able to assess their student's awareness of print and language if they are to plan appropriate instructional activities for them. Assessment tasks should be easy for the classroom teacher to administer and score and should provide a clear picture of each child's literacy knowledge. The assessments should also provide important baseline information from which teachers can

f i g u r e   2 . 4 • Reading Dimensions Tapped in Assessing Emergent and Beginning Readers

Phoneme Awareness—A child's awareness that spoken words are made up of distinct sounds seems to be crucial in learning to read because in our language, individual letters or letter combinations map to a phonemic (sound) equivalent.

The Sound of Written Language—This refers to a child's awareness of differences between spoken and story language. Children who have had experiences with books tacitly learn the rhythm of written language that is different from conversation.

Concept of Story—Children who have the experiences of being read to know that stories have a beginning, middle, and end.

Alphabet Knowledge—Children must be able to name and produce letters before they can make much progress in reading and writing.

Letter-Sound Knowledge—Children must learn that letters are symbols for sounds and be able to associate sound for each letter symbol.

Word Awareness—Reading requires the matching of the spoken word to its written equivalent. Children must understand how written words are separated by white spaces across a line of text.

Sight Vocabulary—Sight words are those words that a child can recognize automatically without conscience analysis.

Decoding Ability—Children must eventually apply letter-sound knowledge to "sound out" unknown words.

Spelling Ability—This refers to a child's ability to match the sounds heard to alphabet letter names (a first grader spells *step* s-a-p because he or she processes the *s* at the beginning and the *p* at the end and the sound relationship between the short *e* sound and the letter name *a*).

Contextual Reading—Teachers of beginning readers must have a sense of the child's oral reading in order to place the child in materials of an appropriate level of challenge.

compare future growth. When assessing emergent and beginning readers like Keshawn and Jesse, Figure 2.4 shows some of the reading dimensions that should be examined.

This is not an exhaustive list but might help a classroom teacher begin to organize a meaningful assessment battery. As Rachel considers Keshawn and Jesse, she is focusing on both an emergent reader with little print knowledge and a beginning reader who has some strong early literacy skills. It is Rachel's job to assess their differing abilities to process print. As you read the following case studies and the assessments Rachel has selected, think about what kinds of information about print each task taps and how Rachel can use that information when planning instruction for Keshawn and Jesse.

• Assessing Emergent Literacy

case 2.1

Keshawn

Short and stocky with a head of curls and steely black eyes, Keshawn is a lively, sociable six-year-old only child. Keshawn's parents both work and have been forced to move several times over the last few years. As a consequence, Keshawn has had little consistency in preschool and kindergarten. However, there are books in his home, and bedtime stories are an important ritual. Doing well in school is valued by Keshawn's parents. They have told him that school is *his* job. Keshawn has lots to say, and Rachel has noted his strong verbal skills. However, Keshawn starts first grade "at risk" because he lacks knowledge of print-related concepts needed for reading to progress. Rachel knows that Keshawn may not have had the kindergarten experiences where many children engage in reading-like tasks and where the foundations for certain print skills are established. Because Keshawn is not reading at all, Rachel wants to know as precisely as possible what Keshawn does know about written language. Over the course of several days, she will administer some key "snapshots" (including the *Illinois Snapshot of Early Literacy,* described by Barr et al., 2002) that can inform her and guide her subsequent instruction. ■

Storybook Reading Procedure. One of the easiest ways a teacher can gain insight into the knowledge a child has about print is to listen to that child read aloud. The storybook reading procedure, in which a child reads a "favorite" storybook, was developed by Sulzby (1985). It is one effective way to explore a student's understandings of reading and writing, even in cases where a child's print knowledge may be very limited. Thus the procedure is useful in looking at preschoolers, kindergartners, and high-risk first graders. To begin this informal diagnostic process, ask the child to select a favorite book from the classroom library, then take the child to a quiet corner of the room and place the book sideways cover down on the table. Say, "Read me your book." If the child hesitates or refuses, provide encouragement by saying, "Well, just pretend that you can read it. Pretend-read it to me."

While the child reads or pretends to read the story, you need to draw conclusions about how well the conventions of writing are understood and whether the reading is based on pictures in the book or on the text. The form shown in Figure 2.5 can be used to summarize your observations during the assessment of a child's storybook reading. With respect to the conventions of reading, you should note whether the child:

figure 2.5 • Form for Summarizing Results from Storybook Reading

SUMMARY FORM—STORYBOOK READING CHECKLIST

Date

Conventions of Writing

Little knowledge _____

Some knowledge _____

Complete knowledge _____

Picture-Based Reading

Labeling and commenting _____

Well-formed story in the form of oral language _____

Well-formed story in the form of written language _____

Text-Based Reading

Refusal—doesn't know the words _____

Identifies a limited number of words/letters _____

Reads known words with substitutions for unknown words _____

Reads word by word _____

Reads fluently _____

Comments:

- Knows how to hold the book right side up
- Begins at the beginning of the story
- Begins reading at the top of the left-hand page
- Reads across the page left to right

    While the child "reads," you need to judge whether the reading is based on pictures or text. If what is read does not match the text, you need to determine whether the "story" is a series of comments or a well-formed narrative. If the story is well formed, listen to the intonation: Is it similar to the way the child speaks, or is it in the form of written language?

    If the reading corresponds to the text, you need to determine whether the child watches the print or is "reading" from memory. When a child responds to the print, you can then determine the extent of that knowledge: Can he or she identify some letters or words, read some words substituting responses for unknown words, read word by word, or read fluently? Sometimes there will be a mixture of reading and storytelling. Other times the child may refuse to read because of not knowing the words. This refusal shows that the child knows that what is read must be text based.

2.1 When Rachel begins the storybook procedure with Keshawn, he curls up close to her, delighted to have her undivided attention. He has picked out his favorite book, *Gregory, the Terrible Eater* (M. Weinman Sharmat). Rachel asks him to read it to her, but he reminds her that he can't *really* read the words. After being reassured that he can pretend read, Keshawn proceeds to read the story using the pictures to prompt him. Keshawn does not attend to the words on each page but he uses a distinct written language intonation. His telling of the story is rich in detail. He knows how to handle the book and "reads" from front to back. He can point to an example of a word and can point to an example of a letter. Some other tasks will give Rachel further important insights into Keshawn's print knowledge. ■

Alphabet Knowledge. The alphabet is the centerpiece of our written language, so letter knowledge is central to learning to read and write. At the beginning of kindergarten, alphabet knowledge is the best predictor of end of first-grade reading achievement (Morris, Bloodgood, Lomax, & Perney, 2003). Many letter names carry the sound represented by the letter; knowing the names is helpful in a child's initial attempts to read and write.

2.1 Rachel calls Keshawn to her desk while the other children are at activity centers. She presents him with a random list of first uppercase then lowercase letters. Rachel asks Keshawn to name the letters as she points to each one. On a separate score sheet (Figure 2.6), Rachel marks Keshawn's responses. Keshawn recognizes 14 uppercase letters and 10 lowercase letters. Rachel notices that Keshawn correctly identifies the letters in his own name, except for the lowercase *n*. The alphabet assessment confirms that Keshawn's alphabet knowledge is below the expectation for beginning first grade, which is a score of 53 upper- and lowercase letters (*Illinois Snapshot of Early Literacy* norms, Barr et al., 2002). Rachel will use this alphabet information for instructional planning. ■

figure 2.6 • Alphabet Recognition—Upper- and Lowercase: Keshawn

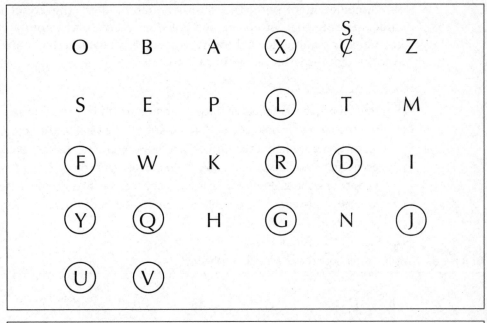

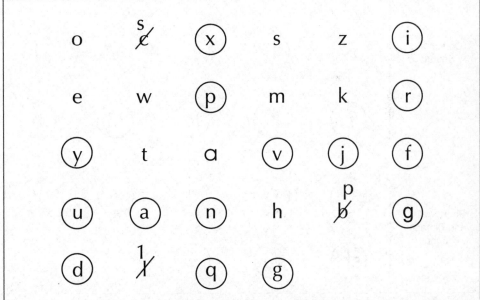

Score 1 point for each correct letter. Self-corrections are correct. Reversals are <u>not</u> correct.

Alphabet Recognition	Uppercase 14/26	24/54
	Lowercase 10/28	

Source: Illinois Snapshot of Early Literacy (2002). By permission of the authors.

Alphabet knowledge includes recognizing the letter symbols, but it also includes identifying the sound represented by the visual letter forms. Understanding that letters are symbols for sound is an important benchmark in emergent reading. Rachel wants to assess Keshawn's letter-sound knowledge, even though his letter recognition is weak.

2.1   Rachel presents Keshawn with a random list of letters. She says, "You told me the name of the letters. Now I want you to tell me the sound you make when you see each letter." Rachel models what she wants Keshawn to do by pointing to the letter *M* saying, "When I see this letter, I say /M/." On a separate score sheet (Figure 2.7), Rachel scores the letter-sounds Keshawn can identify. This information will help direct Rachel's instructional planning. ■

f i g u r e   2 . 7 • Letter-Sound Knowledge: Keshawn

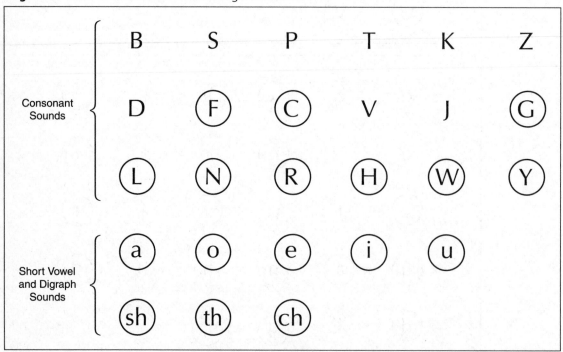

Score 1 point for every correct sound. Count self-corrections as correct.

| | **Letter Sounds**   9/26 |

Source: Illinois Snapshot of Early Literacy (2002). By permission of the authors.

Spelling Knowledge. For reading to progress, children need to learn to segment words into phonemes (distinct sound units). For example, the word *man* has three phonemes. Looking at children's spelling is an excellent and efficient way to evaluate a child's phoneme awareness. Further, spelling performance at the beginning of first grade is a strong predictor of end-of-year reading achievement (Morris & Perney, 1984). Keshawn's journal entries are drawings, so they give Rachel no insight into how he can apply his letter-sound knowledge to writing words. Despite Keshawn's limited alphabet knowledge, Rachel makes the decision to administer a short spelling assessment. The six-word spelling list (shown in Figure 2.8) contains characteristic spelling features for which first graders will be held accountable.

2.1

Rachel makes sure that Keshawn understands the spelling task by modeling two example words with him. She prompts Keshawn, first, through the word *mat* by asking what sound he hears first. When Keshawn correctly replies /m/, Rachel asks what letter makes that sound. Keshawn responds correctly. Rachel prompts for the next sound, but when Keshawn cannot answer, Rachel quickly supplies the correct sound and letter *a*. Rachel asks what Keshawn hears at the end of the word. Keshawn cannot identify the final sound /t/, so Rachel proceeds to model the correct response. Rachel prompts Keshawn through another word, *lip,* where Keshawn can only match the final sound /p/ with the letter *p.* Finally, Rachel begins the spelling task by saying, "Now you are going to spell some words on your own. When I say a word, think about the sounds you hear and write the letters that go with the sounds. If you can only write the letter that goes with the beginning sound, that is fine. Put down all the sounds you hear."

Rachel is mindful that alphabet production (the ability to write the letters) may impact Keshawn's performance. Keshawn's spelling is shown in Figure 2.8. You will note that Rachel scores Keshawn's spelling by assigning points based on his representation of phonemes with the correct letters or developmentally appropriate letter substitutions. Keshawn must be able to represent at least the initial consonant sound to receive points. Rachel also evaluates his spelling qualitatively. She notes that his spelling attempts reveal some representation of initial consonant sounds (*b* in *back; m* in *mail; c* in *step*—an appropriate substitution; and *p* in *peeked*). For the word *step,* Keshawn correctly hears the /t/. He correctly represents the final sound in *junk.* Rachel feels that Keshawn is using what he knows effectively and describes Keshawn's spelling efforts according to stages of spelling development described earlier in this chapter (page 50). Keshawn is an early phonetic

figure 2.8 • Developmental Spelling: Keshawn

	Student's Spelling	Correct & Acceptable Letters				Letter Points	Bonus Point (Correctly Spelled)	Total Points
1. back	b	(b) p	a	ck c k g		1 [3]	[1]	1 [4]
2. mail	M	(m)	ai a ay	l le o		1 [3]	Award Bonus Point for MAIL or MALE [1]	1 [4]
3. step	ct	s (c)	(t) d	e a	p b	2 [4]	[1]	2 [5]
4. junk	k	j g	u o	n	(k) c ck g	[4]	[1]	0 [5]
5. peeked	p	(p) b	ee ea e	k c g	ed t d	1 [4]	Award Bonus Point for PEEKED or PEAKED [1]	1 [5]
6. chin	–	ch h sh t c j g	i e	n		[3]	[1]	0 [4]

1. Circle first consonant. Discontinue scoring a word if first consonant *IS NOT* represented by a letter listed for that word under CORRECT & ACCEPTABLE LETTERS. If first consonant is not represented, there is no score for that word.
2. If first consonant *IS* represented by a correct or acceptable letter, circle it and all subsequent letters *if they occur in the same order from left to right* as listed in columns under CORRECT & ACCEPTABLE LETTERS. Ignore inserted letters.
3. For each word, count the number of columns that contain a circled letter. Only one point can be given per column (i.e., a column with two circled letters earns only one point). Enter number under LETTER POINTS.
4. Award one additional point under BONUS POINT for any word that is *correctly* spelled.
5. Add number of LETTER POINTS plus BONUS POINT (if earned) for each word and enter under TOTAL POINTS for that word. Add final column for a total score. Enter below.

Developmental Spelling   5/27

Source: Illinois Snapshot of Early Literacy (2002). By permission of the authors.

speller. An instructional priority for Keshawn will be to consolidate his alphabet recognition and his ability to match letters to their corresponding sound and for Rachel to provide frequent opportunities for him to write. This would include labeling his pictures, journal writing, and story writing. ■

Word Awareness. When children first begin to learn to read, they are not aware of how their own spoken language matches the print. Ultimately, they do need to learn how to read a sentence and point to the individual words. This understanding, often called *concept of word,* is closely tied to the child's ability to learn sight words and to attend to letters within words (Clay, 1979; Morris, 1980). During the first few weeks of school, Rachel relies heavily on class-dictated experience stories, initially written on large chart paper. An elaborated discussion of this instructional procedure follows later in this chapter. Once the children have ample time to essentially memorize the short three- to four-sentence "story," they are given their own copy on which they are encouraged to make an illustration and practice reading. It is during this time that teachers can monitor each child reading the text.

For Keshawn, Rachel models a finger-point reading of each sentence and asks him to finger-point read the same sentence in order to observe Keshawn's understanding of how his speech matches the printed words. Keshawn has lots of difficulty with this finger-point reading task. While he remembers each sentence, he cannot coordinate his oral language to the printed word. He cannot use letter cues to "locate" words along a line of memorized text. This has been an easy-to-administer task because it is part of a class activity, but it gives Rachel important information about Keshawn. While Rachel uses a classroom chart story to examine Keshawn's word awareness, many other short reading selections would be just as appropriate. These include a familiar short poem, a selection from any of the predictable texts currently available, or the concept of word tasks described in the *Illinois Snapshot of Early Literacy* (Barr et al., 2002).

Using four simple-to-administer tasks over the course of several days Rachel corroborates what she has observed in the classroom. Figure 2.9 lists the tasks described earlier and also lists some useful phonological assessments and activities that Rachel might have included. Rachel understands that Keshawn will require instruction in alphabet recognition and opportunities to read easily memorized short text where he can practice finger-point matching. Developing a small core sight vocabulary will be a priority as well. Later in this chapter, we describe Rachel's instructional plans for Keshawn and other children like him in her class.

figure 2.9 • Tasks Useful in Examining the Print and the
Phonemic Awareness of Emergent Readers

storybook reading procedures
alphabet recognition and production
letter-sound knowledge
finger point reading
developmental spelling test
phonological awareness assessments and activities:
    Phonological Awareness Literacy Screening (PALS)
    Yopp-Singer Test of Phoneme Segmentation
    Dynamic Indicators and Basic Literacy Skills (DIBELS)
    Illinois Snapshot of Early Literacy (ISEL)

Rachel learns early in the school year that there is a wide range of reading and writing skills in her class. It is her wish to identify as quickly as possible the disparate needs of the children that comprise her classroom. While Keshawn represents a place on one end of the print knowledge spectrum, Jesse occupies a spot at the other. ■

• Assessing Beginning Reading Knowledge

case 2.2

Jesse

Dark haired and tall for her age, Jesse is an engaging, friendly child. She has great oral language skills and an ebullient personality. She announces to Rachel that she is really ready for first grade and is matter-of-fact about her ability to read and write, as though there was never a time that she couldn't. Both of her parents are professors who encouraged Jesse's interest in reading. Books were seen early and often in Jesse's home life as both a source of enjoyment and information. While Jesse's kindergarten experience did not include formal reading instruction, there was an abundance of literacy activities, including listening to books, story telling, and writing opportunities. She began to figure out the mysteries of reading easily and by the beginning of first grade is already a capable and confident reader and writer. Many of the children in the class, including Keshawn, look up to her for her academic self-assuredness.

No less than Keshawn, Jesse deserves a literacy curriculum that will support her reading and writing efforts and ensure her further growth. Rachel sets up some assessment tasks that will help her place Jesse in the right kinds of reading and word study.

Word Awareness

In the first month of school, Rachel finds opportunities to hear each of her children read using, as one of her tools, the classroom chart stories referred to earlier in this chapter. Rachel initially models a finger-point reading, one sentence at a time, for Jesse. However, she quickly finds that Jesse can accurately and confidently finger-point read a familiar text without the modeling. Rachel wants a bit more information regarding Jesse's sight vocabulary. When she isolates a few high-frequency sight words in context, Jesse identifies them quickly. Unlike some other children, she does not need to track from the beginning of the sentence to read the target words. Rachel may take simple running records (see Chapter 3 for a full explanation) as Jesse reads short sections from graded materials and little leveled books to establish an instructional reading level.

Spelling

While Rachel administers a short developmental spelling task to Jesse as she did with Keshawn, she finds that Jesse's journal writing contains a wealth of information on her knowledge of words and word elements. Refer back to Figure 2.3, the message written by Jesse to her aunt. Rachel notes that Jesse accurately represents consonant sounds in her writing. Even for longer words, such as *birthday* and *Marshall* she writes all the sounds that she is able to hear. *Wednesday* is a particularly telling example because the only consonant Jesse does not write is the *d*, which is not pronounced. Two consonants occurring together in a word may still pose problems for Jesse; for example, the *n* in *aunt* and the *t* in *went* were omitted.

Vowels are also represented in most of the words she wrote. She is able to write most short vowel sounds, particularly when they occur in short words. She seems to be working on the problem of how to represent digraphs (*how, mouse, soon, dear*). Rachel notes that Jesse does not use long vowel markers (*hope*), but she also notes that Jesse manages to maneuver her way through multisyllablic words, representing sounds in unconventional but strategic ways. Jesse is able to write a handful of words correctly suggesting a beginning sight vocabulary (*are, you, the, me, I, so, was, or, be, on*). According to developmental stage theory, Jesse is a strong letter-name speller.

Word Recognition

2.2

A word recognition test would be frustrating for a fledgling reader like Keshawn. However, Jesse and a handful of others in Rachel's class begin first grade with a sight vocabulary. Considering a child's automatic isolated word recognition can help determine a reasonable instructional reading level. As part of Jesse's initial assessment, Rachel asks her to read a list of 22 words that increase in difficulty, to the beginning of grade two (Figure 2.10), as well as a set of strictly decodable words (Figure 2.11).

Both tests are quick to administer. Further, the decodable list of words gives Rachel some nice information on Jesse's ability to apply her phonics skills where the words have a uniform consonant–short vowel–consonant

figure 2.10 • Word Recognition: Jesse

1. cat _____ + _____	9. and _____ + _____	17. into _____ + _____
2. go _____ + _____	10. look _____ + _____	18. tree _____ + _____
3 is _____ + _____	11. play _____ + _____	19. friend _____ + _____
4. red _____ + _____	12. this _____ + _____	20. made _____ + _____
5. you _____ + _____	13. there _three_ s.c.	21. ready _rē_ .....
6. can _____ + _____	14. men _____ + _____	22. because _____ + _____
7. me _____ + _____	15. road _____ + _____	
8. big _____ + _____	16. never _____ + _____	

➤ Score 1 point for each correctly identified word.
➤ Count self-corrections as correct.
➤ Words <u>laboriously</u> <u>decoded</u> are not counted as correct.

Word Recognition	21/22

Source: Illinois Snapshot of Early Literacy (2002). By permission of the authors.

figure 2.11 • Word Recognition Task
(Decodable Words)

1. cat	**5.** fat	**9.** job
2. net	**6.** mop	**10.** mud
3. win	**7.** led	
4. bug	**8.** dig	

Source: Early Reading Screening Instrument (Morris, 1992).

figure 2.12 • Tasks Useful in Examining the
Print Knowledge of the Beginning Reader

> writing sample
>
> developmental spelling test
>
> isolated word recognition tests (high-frequency
>   sight words and decodable words)
>
> graded reading passages

pattern. Rachel simply lets Jesse read the words off the lists and records
her miscues. Rachel may examine any mistakes for the quality of the error.
In other words, how close was the response to the target word (*big* for *dig*,
for example)?

Figure 2.12 reviews tasks useful for assessing the print knowledge of
beginning readers like Jesse. Jesse is a part of a small group of readers in
Rachel's class. She has a core sight vocabulary and strong phonetic knowledge. Rachel knows that it will be important to continue to challenge Jesse
with appropriate reading and writing opportunities and a word study program that will further strengthen her understanding of word elements. ■

Planning Appropriate Instruction

Assessment is of little value unless it helps identify the activities and instructional support that will help children further develop their reading and writing
skills. Although assessment necessarily focuses on the needs of children one at a
time, teachers typically organize instruction for groups of children. Thus it is
necessary for you to consider the special needs of *all* children in a group and to
provide instruction that will meet their needs. For example, Keshawn is a member of a small group of children with similar reading skills in first grade. When
planning instruction, Rachel must consider not only Keshawn's special needs
but also those of the other children in the group.

Instructional planning consists of three main steps: (1) identifying the needs
and appropriate instruction for individual children; (2) considering the range of
needs and instructional possibilities for a group of children; and (3) selecting those
instructional approaches that will further the development of all children. Rachel
must make some initial grouping decisions. She knows that she can reasonably
organize four reading groups within her two-hour literacy block. Rachel looks
carefully at the individual performances in four literacy assessments that correlate
with reading achievement in making her grouping decisions (see Figure 2.13).

f i g u r e   2 . 1 3 • Rachel's First-Grade Class: Summary of Fall Literacy Snapshots
(Highest Score Possible Is in Parentheses)

	Alphabet Recognition (54)	Letter-sound (26)	Spelling (27)	Word Recognition (22)
Laura			21	21
Jesse			21	21
Daniel			19	22
Alvin			19	18
Enrique			19	11
Jason	48	22	16	12
Zakyra	48	22	14	4
Marvin	49	22	15	0
Ashley	53	21	16	6
Shelly	52	21	16	6
Reggie	54	21	17	0
Justin	54	21	14	6
Juan	54	20	15	0
Wayne	53	20	15	0
Danya	50	19	14	2
Jasmine	47	17	14	0
Shawnee	43	17	10	
Edgar	43	13	7	
Keshawn	24	9	5	
Ebony	33	6	8	
Rebecca	13	3	0	

Note that Rachel has not given *all* the children in her class *all* four assessments. For example, Keshawn did not see the word recognition task because Rachel knew he did not have the requisite print knowledge for that assessment to provide her any insights. Jesse did not need to have her alphabet knowledge assessed. Rachel uses the alphabet recognition task and the letter-sound task to group Keshawn, Rebecca, Ebony, Edgar, and Shawnee. She feels that this group has similar needs in building alphabet knowledge. While Jasmine has similar deficits, she seems to have a stronger ability to apply what she knows about letter–sound relationship as evidenced by her spelling score. Rachel considers the spelling and word recognition performances in grouping Jesse, Laura, Daniel, Alvin, Enrique, and Jason.

Though Jason and Enrique lack the sight vocabulary strength of the others in the group, they have, nevertheless, begun to build a sight vocabulary and will hopefully continue to make progress with the high group. These groupings are starting points for Rachel and are fluid, allowing Rachel the chance to adjust as children progress (or fail to progress) in their reading and writing skills.

Next, instructional plans that Rachel has developed for both Keshawn and Jesse and the children who will be part of each of their reading groups are broadly described. Rachel will be constantly monitoring the children's progress and making changes in group assignments as the year goes on.

Instruction to Support Emergent Reading

• An Instructional Plan for Keshawn

Rachel wants to make sure that all her first graders receive a careful balance of contextual reading and writing opportunities as well as directed word study where words are examined out of context. Rachel prefers to use an instructional framework that helps structure the limited time she has with her reading groups daily. The lesson framework includes these components: supported contextual reading with opportunities for rereading, word study, and writing for the purpose of exploring sound–letter relationships. In order for Rachel to feel she is engaged in ongoing assessment and monitoring of every child in her class, she has a daily "focus" child in each of her reading groups. Rachel pays particular attention to her focus child of the day, recording strengths and weaknesses, providing timely reinforcement and corrective feedback as that child performs more of the tasks than the others (Morrow et al., 1986). You will learn how to do a running record in Chapter 3.

Rachel wants to organize her instructional plans around those areas of reading and writing where Keshawn needs practice and consolidation: alphabet recognition and production, concept of word in text, use of beginning consonants as a word identification cue in reading, increased ability to represent sounds across words, and the acquisition of a functional sight vocabulary.

Book Reading. Rachel introduces new reading each time she meets with her small group. Emergent readers like Keshawn need to engage in meaningful reading where they can practice finger-point matching and begin to build a core of easily identified sight words. In addition to the chart stories elaborated on later, Rachel uses an assortment of little books that she has carefully sequenced according to difficulty. Many of these books are not controlled phonetically or in terms of vocabulary, but they have a structure that supports early readers, which includes a limited number of words on a page, strong picture–text matches, rhyme, and repetition. Rachel always carefully introduces each new book to her group. She points out words or phrases that might be "tricky." She makes sure that the children know the names of the characters or can identify animals, for example. She knows that her rich orientation to the story will support the children's initial attempts to read the new material successfully (Clay, 1991). Rachel echo reads with Keshawn and his group, finger-point modeling. The story is choral read several times and the children may break into pairs for partner reading. The new book will become the basis for rereading over several days. It is during the rereading that Rachel will teach and reinforce word identification strategies. For Keshawn and his group, this will involve using initial consonant cues and sentence context to identify words not remembered.

Sometimes Rachel alternates the use of the more conventional little predictable books with **Big Books**. Just as the name implies, Big Books are big. Intended to be used for both small-group instruction or for whole-class instruction, many Big Books share titles with their little book counterparts. Put up on an easel, Big Books are visually compelling. Rachel likes to use Big Books to model the reading process. She invites the children to participate by reading along with her or echo reading as she finger-point reads the large print. She may engage the children in various "word finds" or "letter finds." Often the most at-risk children find focusing on the Big Book on the easel and engaging in reading activities set by the teacher less of an effort than following along in their own little books.

With both Big Books and little books, Rachel will build sight word banks. After Keshawn and his group have read a story several times, Rachel selects high-frequency words encountered in the reading for Keshawn to identify in context. If Keshawn can recognize the words embedded in a sentence, then the word is written on a card to be subsequently recognized in isolation. Words are kept in a small bag or file and are reviewed often. These learned high-frequency words will greatly facilitate Keshawn's reading. Furthermore, his ability to retain and build sight vocabulary is an important indicator of reading progress.

Word Study. Rachel is concerned that Keshawn may not acquire the phonetic awareness (awareness of sounds within spoken words) and orthographic awareness (letter-sound knowledge) without direct assistance from the teacher. She uses an instructional approach called word sorting where children categorize words according to certain orthographic features. The words are carefully sequenced and paced to a group's level of word knowledge. To facilitate Keshawn's alphabet knowledge, Rachel has him sorting pictures into columns based on their initial consonant sounds (Figure 2.14). Keshawn must place each picture card in one of three rows, saying each picture as he does. Subsequently, he must match a proper alphabet letter representing the initial consonant sound heard to each column. Once Keshawn has mastered most consonant sounds, he and his small group of emergent readers will categorize word families, or rhyming families (-*at*, -*ap*, -*an*, for example). For a fuller discussion on word sorting, see Morris (1982) and Johnston (1999).

figure 2.14 • Picture Sorting for Developing Sound-Letter Recognition

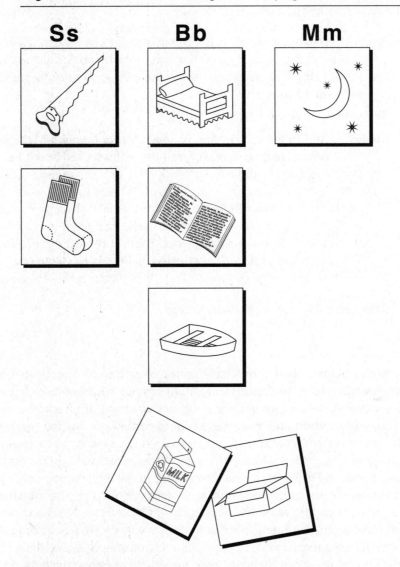

Sentence Writing. Rachel knows guided writing opportunities are also excel-lent ways to improve Keshawn's phonemic awareness and to continue prog-ress in developing letter-sound knowledge. Rachel requires Keshawn and his small group to compose a daily "story," actually a single sentence. The focus child is generally responsible for the story, and while the other children do their best to work through the sounds on their own, the focus child is care-fully guided through the process of representing sounds across each word. Rachel's standard of expectation depends on each child's level of orthographic sophistication. A typical writing lesson with Keshawn and his group in the fall might go like this:

> *Rachel:*   What are you all going to write today? Keshawn, it's your turn to make a story. Today you read about a snail who thinks he can't do a lot of things. Then he remembers he can do something special. What can you do that is special?
>
> *Keshawn:*   I can ride my two wheeler.
>
> *Rachel:*   That's a great story! Are we all ready to try to write? Let's say the sentence one more time so we have all the words locked in our heads. Then, you can go ahead and write on your own, or you can listen to me work with Keshawn and work along with us. What is the first word in your sentence, Keshawn? That's an easy word because there is only one letter in the word. Can you write it? What is the next word in your sentence? What sound do you hear at the beginning of the word *can*? What letter makes that sound /k/? What else do you hear in the word *can*? What do you hear at the end of the word? . . . What letter makes the /n/ sound?

Keshawn's sentence eventually yields:

I kn rid mi t ylr.

Rachel helps Keshawn stretch the sounds in each word. She tries to get Keshawn to represent, at least, beginning and ending sounds with her help. She will model letter formation where needed. She holds Keshawn accountable for spaces between each word invention and encourages him to control the writing process by going back to the beginning and tracking up to each target word as he begins to think about how it is spelled. During the early weeks, Keshawn's group may represent only a few sound elements for each word. But Rachel will require richer inventions as the children increase their word knowledge through their contextual reading, growing sight vocabularies, and word sorting. Notice that Rachel accepts letter substitutions that make sense (*k* for *c* in *can*; *y* for *w* in *wheeler*). Following the writing attempt, Rachel may choose to work on a few of these spelling elements to teach Keshawn and the other children some important phonics concepts. For example, Rachel might ask Keshawn if he knows another letter that makes the same sound as *k*. She may point out that the /w/ sound he hears in *wheeler* is a *w,* not *y.* Rachel will try to reinforce these concepts in the group's contextual reading, asking the group to note words that begin with *c* or *y* as they are encountered in the little books.

Rachel's instructional priorities will change as her group of emergent readers begins to develop increasing independence. She will pace the reading so that the children have opportunities to practice newly acquired reading skills in books that slowly increase in difficulty.

Instruction for Children Developing Knowledge of Print

• An Instructional Plan for Jesse

Rachel uses essentially the same instructional framework for Jesse and her group. Jesse's group uses an assortment of reading materials, including little books, stories pulled from the basal, and stories from a basal anthology. These books have considerably more print than the books Rachel uses with Keshawn and more ambiguous picture cues. Rachel works with Jesse on the use of both contextual information and print cues to identify unknown words. Rachel is looking for the integration of print and context cues in Jesse's rereadings and her ability to identify increasingly more words automatically.

When Rachel introduces a new reading to Jesse and her group, she does not echo the text first. Even though the stories are harder than the ones Keshawn is reading, Rachel provides less support because Jesse and her group have sight vocabularies and decoding ability that allow them more independence to "struggle" with the text. Rachel, does, however, continue to provide a rich orientation before the children try a first reading.

Even though Jesse seems to be quickly building word knowledge through her reading and writing, Rachel provides some directed word study. As with Keshawn, Rachel uses categorization activities to highlight important orthographic elements (Figure 2.15). Based on Jesse's spelling samples, Rachel decides that Jesse will benefit from examining single-syllable words across different short vowel sounds (*cat, plan, back/frog, pot, clock/spin, hit, pig,* for example).

Because Jesse and her group members are all eager and confident writers, Rachel concentrates her group lesson on consolidating word identification strategies and building fluency. Individual conferencing around writing journals is adequate to address spelling issues, where accountability is closely tied to word sorting activities.

Rachel is sensitive to the differing needs of Keshawn and Jesse. She uses regular small-group time to address their respective skill levels. During this group time, Rachel is careful to select reading that allows the children to practice new reading strategies and learn new words. Rachel knows that reading material that is too difficult or, conversely, too easy will not support optimal growth. With this in mind and with a commitment to differentiated reading instruction, Rachel has teamed with other first- and second-grade teachers in her

figure 2.15 • Cross-Vowel Sorting

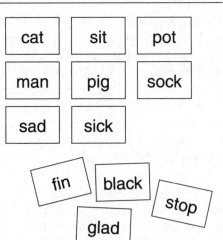

building to level the reading materials in the classroom including stories in the basals, anthologies where the stories can differ widely in terms of difficulty, trade books, and little books. The small increments separating the levels mean that children, particularly those at risk, can practice reading multiple stories at a particular level of difficulty before moving to more challenging material. Teachers can match reading to children's evolving reading competencies. Books are leveled by teams of expert teachers who consider

the amount of text on a page

the print size and spacing between words

the picture support

the placement of the text on the page

the amount of repetition and rhyme and new vocabulary

the complexity of the story line

In addition to teacher-derived leveling systems, teachers can take advantage of existing leveling systems that have been developed such as one of the most frequently used by Fountas and Pinnell (1999). Appendix E lists Internet sites where teachers can access book titles and their levels, as well as books and resources.

The Language Experience Approach

While Rachel believes in the value of small homogeneous guided reading groups in her class, she also likes to engage the children in whole-class reading activities. She reads them good literature and takes time to discuss the stories. She engages them in group reading of Big Books. She also involves them in writing and reading a shared experience. Rachel knows that one effective way to develop print awareness is to provide her new first graders with the chance to see print as it is being written and read in order to understand how print is arranged and related to speech. An excellent procedure used in kindergarten and as a bridge into first grade is the **Language Experience Approach** (LEA; Stauffer, 1981). The LEA encourages children, with the support of the teacher, to write a story about a shared experience. The story must be written large enough on a big sheet of paper or blackboard that all the children can see it as it is being composed and reread. These instructional procedures have been incorporated into a three-day cycle of activities (Morris, 1986) as follows:

Day 1: The teacher leads the children in a discussion of a shared experience: for example, making popcorn, making valentine cards, watching snowflakes fall, visiting the school library or cafeteria, planting a seed, retelling the story of Columbus's voyage, and so on. Following the oral discussion, the children dictate two or three sentences describing the experience, and the teacher records these few sentences in manuscript print on a large sheet of chart paper.

Making Popcorn

We made popcorn.
We made it in a popcorn popper.
We put butter and salt on the popcorn.

Next, the teacher models a reading of the completed experience story, pointing to each word as she reads. Finally, the children join in choral-reading the story several times, with the teacher continuing to point to the words on the chart paper as the group reads.

Day 2: The Day 1 story is brought out and choral-read several times, with the teacher again modeling finger-point reading. Next, some informal questions can be asked and games played with the now familiar story. For example:

- Who can come up to the chart and show me where we start reading? Where we end? Where do we go when we reach the end of a line?
- These little dots in our story are called "periods." What do they tell us?
- Who knows this word (teacher points to *popcorn*)? Good! Can someone else find the same word at another place in the story?
- What is the first letter in this word (teacher points to the *p* in *put*)? Can you find another word in our story that begins with *p*?

Day 3: On Day 3 the teacher works at a table with groups of seven to eight children at a time. The "popcorn" story has been transferred from the large chart paper to the bottom of an 8½ × 11 piece of paper, and each child at the table has a copy. The teacher reads the story several times and the children attempt to follow along on their own copy. Next, the teacher instructs the children to illustrate the popcorn story on the top half of the paper. As the children begin drawing, the teacher moves around to each child and asks him or her to finger-point read the three-line story. (Note: Early in the year the teacher may have to use an echo-reading strategy. That is, the teacher reads one or two lines and then the child attempts to echo-read these lines while pointing to the words on the page.) If the child is successful in finger-point reading the story—that is, matching spoken words to written words in an appropriate manner—the teacher can later point randomly to individual words in the text and see if the child can identify them, immediately or by using context.[1]

Beginning first graders—and certainly kindergarten children—will differ considerably in their ability to finger-point read a short, familiar text like

---

[1]From *Teaching reading in kindergarten: A language-experience approach* (Occasional Paper No. 12, pp. 4–6) by D. Morris (1986). Evanston, IL: The Reading Center, National College of Education. Reprinted by permission.

"Making Popcorn." Therefore, the Day 3 procedure described here, aside from its instructional value, is important diagnostically. It allows the teacher to observe carefully the reading development of individual children at a low cost in time, one to two minutes spent with each child (Morris, 1986, pp. 5–6). Teachers can develop a simple observational sheet or monitoring form on which they can note important print-related behaviors for each child. In order of descending competencies, behaviors to observe would include strong finger-point matching across the LEA text, automatic sight word recognition, use of tracking for word identification (child tracks across sentence to target word), some echo support needed to "read" LEA, no memory for text, and no language-print matching.

With strong teacher-supported reading, developmentally appropriate word study, and lots of opportunities to write and receive feedback, Rachel ensures that both Keshawn and Jesse will continue to develop as readers and writers.

summary

In this chapter we considered the complex knowledge involved in learning about print and becoming fluent readers. We identified three phases of learning. Young children become aware of the nature of reading by being read to, by observing print at home and in the neighborhood, by "pretend-reading" storybooks, and by observing others read. Similarly, they become aware of writing by seeing their parents and others write and by writing themselves. Through these experiences and more formal instruction, they gradually develop knowledge of print. They begin to understand how words are composed of sounds and how these sounds relate to letters. Through practice reading stories and informational text, they develop as fluent readers.

We looked at two typical first graders, Keshawn and Jesse, who arrive in Rachel's class in the fall with very different levels of print knowledge and who require very different levels of instructional support in order to progress as readers. We described simple informal assessment procedures that Rachel used to develop a clear picture of each child's instructional needs. We learned how "rereading" situations allowed Rachel to observe Keshawn's and Jesse's ability to read printed words in context, the degree to which each child had a concept of word, the ability to use print cues to remember words, and the ability to recognize words automatically. We also noted how Rachel used the children's writing to further infer their knowledge of sound–letter associations. Last, we discussed some appropriate instructional procedures underscoring the idea that there should always be instructional implications following any kind of meaningful assessment.

Some children come to school with a well-developed awareness of print; many, however, need supportive instruction with stories and writing to help them develop greater familiarity and security with printed messages. These experiences prepare children to learn printed words and the relationships between letters and sounds within words.

try it out

1. The next time you have the chance to work with emergent readers, try a short LEA. Evaluate their concept of word. Think what print knowledge will help them learn to "read the spaces."

2. **Student Portfolio Ideas:** Extensive reading constitutes one of the best ways for children to expand their sight vocabularies, apply their developing word identification strategies, and become fluent readers. Thus, having students keep a record of the books they are reading each week represents an essential component of their portfolios. Beyond this, depending on the stage of your students, you might like to have them keep track of the new words they are learning or keep a list of the new strategies they have learned for word identification.

3. **For Your Teaching Portfolio:** Use what you have learned from this chapter to add to your teaching portfolio. You might include
   - Your response to the assessment tools Rachel used to make some hunches about Keshawn and Jesse.
   - In response to the "Try It Out" suggested in number 1, develop a monitoring form in order to track individual growth of the children in your class. See page 77 for ideas on what behaviors to include.
   - A sample instructional lesson on reading one of the little books or beginning writing that you tried and evaluated.
   - Your reflections on one of the "For Further Reading" selections for this chapter.

for further reading

Caldwell, J. S., & Ford, M. P. (2002). *Where have all the bluebirds gone? How to soar with flexible grouping.* Portsmouth, NH: Heinemann. A detailed explanation of alternative groupings and minilessons.

Clay, M. M. (1991). Introducing a new storybook to young readers. *The Reading Teacher, 45*(4), 264–273. Excellent strategies for introducing storybooks to children learning to read.

Dorn, L., French, C., & Jones, T. (1998). *Apprenticeship in literacy: Transitions across reading and writing.* York, ME: Stenhouse. Strategies for providing rich literacy experiences for emergent and beginning readers, including shared and interactive reading and writing activities.

Morris, Darrel. (2008). *Diagnosis and correction of reading problems.* New York: Guilford. In-depth case studies model systematic approaches to assessment and instruction and address the interrelationship of reading, writing and word study.

 **3**

Knowledge of Print: Oral Reading Analysis and Instructional Support

chapter goals for the reader

- To understand how students' oral reading can be used to learn about their knowledge of print
- To develop skill in taking running records and interpreting the oral reading of children
- To develop skill in recording and interpreting the oral reading of more advanced students
- To develop skill in using informal techniques to explore students' print knowledge
- To understand how to plan appropriate instructional support for students based on your analysis of their oral reading

classroom vignette

Two Students and Their Teachers

In this chapter, we consider how two teachers observe and make sense of the oral reading of their students. Eileen, a first-grade teacher, was contacted by one of her student's parents in the spring of the year. They were concerned about their son Ken's slow progress learning to read and requested a meeting with her. They asked if she thought he would need to be tutored during the summer following first grade. Eileen wondered if they were worried about his being retained in first grade.

Before the conference, Eileen listened to him read orally to assess his word learning, knowledge of word elements, and reading fluency. This assessment raised certain questions in her mind about his sight vocabulary and knowledge of word elements; she pursued these more informally. Finally, based on this information, along with her experience with him during the year, she considered several ways to support the further development of his reading strategies.

The second teacher, Martha, has been teaching fifth grade at Hyde School, an inner-city school, for the past four years. Early in the school year, she became concerned about the failure of one of her students, Eva, to complete her homework assignments. Martha had Eva read aloud a story from her core anthology so that Martha could learn more about her strategies with print. From the oral reading analysis and interpretation, Martha assessed Eva's strengths and identified the problems she has yet to solve.

We include these case studies later in the chapter so that you can learn how two teachers used oral reading analysis to better understand the reading of their students and to plan appropriate instruction. As you read the cases, consider what you might do if you were the teachers. ■

chapter overview

This chapter has three main parts. In a brief first section, we describe how you can explore your students' knowledge of print by having them read aloud. In the second section, we provide an overview of the procedures you will follow while recording the oral reading of students. In the case study sections, we first consider the case of Ken and describe the procedures Eileen followed in making and interpreting a *running record* for him. A running record, developed in New Zealand, is a way to conduct an oral reading analysis with a beginning reader

(Clay, 1985). All a teacher needs to make this record is a blank piece of paper. In the second case study, we consider an oral reading analysis procedure that is more useful with readers who have advanced beyond the beginning stages. These records are made on a copy of the text. To demonstrate these procedures, we consider the case of Eva and describe the procedures Martha followed in recording and interpreting Eva's oral reading. In the final section, we describe procedures you can use to help children develop their sight word vocabularies, their understanding of word elements, and their reading integration and fluency.

chapter outline

Oral Reading Analysis: Areas of Reading Assessed

By listening to students read contextual selections, you can identify problems that exist in three areas: (1) knowledge of print, (2) integration of knowledge sources, and (3) reading fluency. In Chapter 1, we described the fluency snapshot, an oral reading assessment that can be used to quickly screen a classroom of students. In this section, we describe the areas of reading that are assessed in greater depth through oral reading of contextual selections. Following this we describe the specific procedures that you may follow to learn how to assess oral reading competently.

• Knowledge of Print: Sight Word Vocabulary

As children become familiar with print, they are able to identify an increasing number of words instantaneously without analysis. We refer to these words as the child's **sight word vocabulary.** Included in the child's sight word vocabulary are **high-frequency words**, those words that account for about 70 percent of running text. These high-frequency words include some common nouns, verbs, and adjectives; in addition, many words that form the structure of sentences, such as *the, his, here,* and *but*, are considered high-frequency words. Edward Dolch (1936) was among the first to describe the set of commonly occurring words that children tend to learn first as sight words (see Dolch list, Appendix A). Each child will develop a sight word vocabulary that uniquely reflects the stories and other selections he or she has been reading.

Some children learning to read have a difficult time learning and remembering the high-frequency words. Thus, it is useful for you, as their teacher, to note whether they are quickly identifying this specific set of words. When you assess students' oral reading, it is important to note how quickly and accurately they recognize the high-frequency words. It is also instructive to observe how their oral responses differ from the printed words. Proficient readers develop large sight word vocabularies; their word identification skills enable them to recognize words instantaneously.

• Knowledge of Print: Word Identification

Children learning to read develop strategies for identifying words they do not yet know. These strategies may take a variety of forms: letter-by-letter synthesis of the sounds associated with letters, analogizing the pronunciation of unknown words from known words, guessing on the basis of context. Content words that children mispronounce during contextual reading provide a window into their word identification strategies. While you listen to children read aloud, note whether they read portions of words correctly and whether they can deal with multisyllabic words. It is also useful to consider how their oral responses differ from the printed words.

Methods for examining sight word knowledge and word identification based on oral reading are described in the second section of the chapter. There we observe Eileen and Martha as they learn about the sight word knowledge and word identification of their students, Ken and Eva.

• Integration of Reading Strategies

Listening to students' oral reading of contextual selections allows you to assess their knowledge of print and also to examine how well they can combine this knowledge with information from other sources to identify unknown words. In addition to knowledge of letter-sound associations and words parts, picture cues, story themes, prior sentence context, knowledge of syntax, and experience with a topic are all useful sources of information that may aid a student in identifying unknown words. Students who have not developed balanced strategies for word identification need to be shown how to use information from a variety of sources to identify words more efficiently and effectively.

Students' oral reading responses can be analyzed in terms of *how* as well as *whether* they match responses that are expected on the basis of the text (Goodman, 1965, 1967, 1969). Some incorrect responses, or *miscues,* as Goodman prefers to call them, may reflect use of information about print; others may be influenced by prior sentence context. That is, they may make sense in terms of contextual meaning derived from the story topic, pictures, or the previously read portion of the sentence. Some responses may reflect both these factors, whereas others may show the influence of neither. Some children in the beginning stages of reading rely on context or picture cues to the neglect of print cues; others produce non-words that are cued by print but show no influence of contextual meaning. Analyzing how oral reading responses match expected responses permits you to learn about the strategies students use when they encounter unfamiliar words.

The number and types of miscues that readers attempt to correct also give you information on their ability to integrate contextual and print information and to monitor their reading. Researchers have identified several categories of correction behavior in oral reading (Page & Barr, 1975). When a reader corrects a response, he or she is showing dissatisfaction with the original response. Conversely, when a reader fails to attempt a correction, that indicates a lack of dissatisfaction or insufficient knowledge on which to base a correction. Consider an oral reading response that is semantically and syntactically acceptable but differs in letter–sound correspondence from the expected response, as in *Tim ran down the* **road** for *Tim ran down the lane.* If the reader does not attempt to correct the miscue, you can assume that semantic and grammatical cues from the context permitted him or her to verify the response and to feel satisfied with it. We can also assume that, to some degree, the phonic discrepancy did not cause a feeling of dissatisfaction.

If no pauses or other miscues immediately precede or follow the response, your assumption concerning a lack of influence from letter–sound or visual cues is strengthened. If the reader uses *road* and *lane* interchangeably in a semantically acceptable way throughout the passage, your assumption is further strengthened. If, on the other hand, the reader attempts to correct the substitution of *road* for *lane,* you may assume that the phonics or visual cues are operating at this point because the original response caused some dissatisfaction. This attempt to correct may be successful or unsuccessful. If it is successful, you may assume that phonics cues are influencing the reader's processing.

The production of a semantically and grammatically unacceptable response, such as *Tim ran down the* **lone**, would lead to a similar interpretation in terms of corrections. If the reader did not attempt a correction, you could assume that he or she was not processing adequately the available semantic, grammatical, and phonics information. If a correction is made with a vowel change such as *lean* for *lane,* the phonics cues are probably generating the correction attempt. On the other hand, if the reader inserts *line* for *lane,* he or she may be using all sources of information. In any event, if you look carefully at why the reader makes the correction changes that he or she does and what miscues are not corrected, you can learn a great deal about the student's reading process.

It is also important to ask students how they were able to identify unfamiliar words. Often students are able to describe their methods in ways that may provide you with ideas for further instruction.

• Reading Fluency

Fluency or lack of fluency is evident when you listen to the oral reading of students (Strecker, Roser, & Martinez, 1998). For children who have not yet mastered the component skills of print processing, their reading shows substitution errors, long pauses, frequent repetitions, and inappropriate phrasing. For these children, disfluency is an indicator of their problems with print skills. Thus, this problem should not be addressed as a fluency issue.

For other children, oral reading analysis sometimes reveals no major problems with decoding—few substitutions, pauses, or repetitions—but will reveal phrasing that is inappropriate to the syntax and meaning of the selection. These children read word by word or in clusters of words with brief pauses between them. You can distinguish this, a primary fluency problem, from one that is secondary to other reading problems by having the student read text that is extremely easy for him or her. If the characteristics of nonfluent reading—poor intonation, inappropriate phrasing, long pauses, and word-by-word reading—persist even when the child experiences few problems with print, then you can conclude that the problem is primarily one of fluency.

Finally, some readers become extremely anxious when asked to read aloud, and their oral reading is disrupted, not necessarily because they lack fluency but because of their anxiety. In such cases, it is not possible to assess reading fluency accurately by having the students read aloud. However, you can gain some understanding of their fluency by noting their rate of silent reading.

From about third-grade level and beyond, a reading rate in the average range can be used to determine adequate fluency. When this information is combined with oral reading evidence, you can draw useful conclusions about the development of print knowledge and reading fluency. Once students no longer have problems with word identification, you may appropriately help them develop their reading rate.

As is illustrated in Table 3.1, students' reading rates on unfamiliar selections improve dramatically from first to second grade and thereafter show steady but more moderate increases. Although a comparison of the average reading rates of students on a number of reading tests shows wide variation (Harris & Sipay, 1980, p. 556), this variability in part reflects differences in the difficulty of the test material. Some tests consist of extremely easy passages while others include

table 3.1 • Mean Words Correct per Minute Targets[a] for Average Students in Grades One through Eight

Grade	Fall Target	Winter Target	Spring Target
1	10	20	50
2	50	70	90
3	75	90	110
4	95	110	125
5	105	125	140
6	130	140	150
7	130	140	150
8	130	140	150

[a]The targets are reported in round numbers.

Source: From *Basic Reading Inventory, 10th edition* by Jerry L. Johns. Copyright © 2008 by Kendall Hunt Publishing Co. Reprinted with permission.

more technical material. The rates shown in Table 3.1 are based on passages that are appropriate in difficulty to the grade of the students tested. Silent reading rates are somewhat higher than the ranges shown for oral reading, particularly for the intermediate grades and beyond (Carver, 1983; Morris, 1999; Taylor, 1965). Table 3.1 shows target oral reading fluency rates for average students at three points in the school year (Johns, 2005).

To conclude, listening to students read a selection orally enables you to judge their fluency in terms of phrasing, intonation, and reading rate. Your conclusions about their fluency and word knowledge will help you plan appropriate instruction. The goal of the diagnosis is to determine the fluency of the student's reading as well as the level of material where he or she encounters few problems with print. If the reading is not fluent, it is important for you to provide instruction that will help the student build knowledge about print and to encourage him or her to reread materials in order to develop reading fluency.

Procedures for Recording Oral Reading

To learn how to listen to students as they read aloud, it is important for you to practice oral reading assessment following systematic procedures. Many complex decisions are involved in selecting an appropriate story or expository passage, learning to record oral reading responses, analyzing the responses, gaining further needed information, and finally, interpreting the results. It is necessary for you to practice oral reading assessment with children individually before you become sufficiently proficient to undertake such assessment informally during the rapid give-and-take of classroom instruction.

The procedures for oral reading response analysis are described here in considerable detail. If oral reading analysis is new to you, you should follow each recommended step. As always in learning a new skill, your first attempts to use these procedures will be difficult and time consuming. However, with practice, the appropriate skills and knowledge will become automatic—so that you can accomplish oral reading response analysis easily. Indeed, after you have developed listening and interpretive skills, you can perform a useful diagnosis by simply listening to students' oral reading. The procedures involve four main steps. First, some *preparation* is necessary before you listen to a student read. Following this preparation, you *administer* the passage and record the student's oral reading. Then you *analyze* the response patterns.

Once this phase of the assessment is completed, you may formulate additional questions that you wish to pursue. The final step is to *develop an appropriate plan* for instructional support, based on all the information you have about the student's reading. Next we consider the preparation you must make before you have a student read aloud.

• Preparation

Normally you will select a passage from instructional materials being used in the classroom. You should make a judgment about the level at which the student is able to read. A trial run with several short selections may be necessary. Oral reading may be from any appropriate book, including the student's core anthology. The portion used for analysis should be 50 to 100 words in length for beginning readers and 100 to 200 words or more for more advanced readers. The total length should approximate the amount students typically read at any one time in the classroom.

The oral reading responses of any student can be recorded and analyzed to determine how he or she translates print into spoken language. In this chapter, we describe two methods of recording oral reading. The first, running records (Clay, 1993b), is particularly useful when you are working with children in the beginning stages of learning to read. The second is one traditionally used to record oral reading responses.

Running Records. All you need to make a record of a child's oral reading is a pencil and a blank sheet of paper—and, of course, a child willing to read aloud for you. For each word the child reads correctly, you make a checkmark (✓). When he or she substitutes a different word for a printed word, you write the printed word, draw a line above it, and then write the word spoken by the child. When he or she omits a word, you write the printed word with a line above it and then a period (.) to indicate the omission. When he or she repeats a word or phrase, draw a line with an arrow over the repeated portion, with an "R" to

figure 3.1 • Running Record of Child's Oral Reading

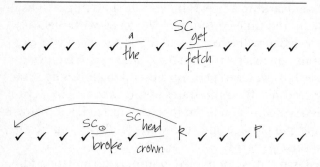

indicate a repetition. When the child self-corrects a miscalled word, write "SC." When he pauses, write "P."

The record for a child reading the nursery rhyme "Jack and Jill" might be recorded as shown in Figure 3.1. From the record, we know the child read correctly all the words recorded as a "." In the first sentence, he substituted the word *a* for *the*. The word *get* was substituted for *fetch* but then he self-corrected (SC) the substitution. He repeated the first phrase of the second sentence and corrected the omission of *broke* and the substitution of *head* for *crown*. Finally, the child paused in the final phrase, likely to examine the word *tumbling* more carefully.

In the Case Study section, you will see Eileen's record of Ken's oral reading and her interpretation of its meaning. For a more detailed description of running record procedures, see Clay (1985).

Traditional Method of Recording Oral Reading. The symbols used for recording oral reading responses using traditional procedures are similar. Figure 3.2 shows one method of recording the ways a student's oral reading departs from the responses expected on the basis of the text. However, if you have already

figure 3.2 • Symbols for Recording Oral Reading Responses

Omissions. Circle the word, group of words, or part of a word omitted.

Insertions. Write in the word or word part inserted. Indicate its position with a caret.

Substitutions or mispronunciations. Identify the mispronounced word(s) by drawing a line over it (them). Write in the substituted word(s).

Repetitions. Underline or overline repeated words using a line and arrow.

Corrections. Indicate corrected responses by "SC" or "C" for self-correct.

Pauses. Indicate pauses by a "P."

Punctuation. Indicate failure to pause for a comma or period by circling.

Danny ran up to the door.

on
He rode his bicycle.

pic   black
He bicycled around the block.

                             black
He rode around the block.
                             black SC
He rode around the block.

He got a glass of milk.
The milk tasted funny, Danny thought it might be too warm.

learned a somewhat different system, you should continue to use that system. As shown in Figure 3.2, substituted words are recorded by crossing out the mispronounced word and writing the student's pronunciation over the miscued word. Similarly, pauses (breaks in phrasing) are recorded with a "P." You should be familiar with this or some similar scheme. We recommend that the student's oral reading be tape-recorded as well, so that you can check the accuracy of your recording. The reason for the assessment should be discussed with the student (e.g., it may be to find ways to help the student read better or to understand how he or she approaches reading tasks).

Administration

Make sure your student is comfortable and sufficiently relaxed. If the oral reading is to be tape-recorded, you should obtain the student's permission. It is important for you to make a brief statement to help orient the student to the content and theme of the selection (see Beck, Omanson, & McKeown, 1982, for procedural suggestions). It is also important to explain to the student what he or she should do. For example, you may say the following:

> This is a story in which … [theme-related preparatory statement]. Please read this story aloud for me. If you come to a word you don't know, try to figure it out, guess at it, or skip it. I will not be able to help you, so do the best you can.

You should record the student's responses on a photocopy or typed version of the story. You should record responses even if the oral reading is tape-recorded. The time that the student begins and finishes reading the passage should also be noted.

If the student becomes frustrated at some point, you should provide reassurance that it is all right to guess at a word or skip it. If the reading passage proves generally too frustrating, or if the student becomes upset, discontinue the assessment and try it at a later time with an easier passage.

Analysis

Examine the oral reading record to determine whether the passage is of appropriate difficulty and is adequate to assess the student's sight word recognition, word identification strategies, and reading integration and fluency.

Passage Difficulty. This analysis pertains to the level of material that would be appropriate for various purposes such as for reading instruction, as opposed to independent reading, and is based on the student's overall accuracy and fluency of word recognition. The criteria for judging whether a passage is appropriate, summarized in Table 3.2, was derived from those originally recommended by Betts (1954). Betts suggests that more than one error for every ten words read

table 3.2 • Criteria for Determining Reading Levels

Level	Oral Reading Accuracy (%)
Independent	98–100
Instructional	95–970
Borderline	90–940
Frustration	Below 90

indicates that the material is too difficult for the student. That is, when the student reads less than 90 percent of a passage correctly, the material is at the student's frustration level. Betts claims that students should make no more than one error per twenty words on materials they read as part of instruction. That is, when instructional support is provided, students should be able to read passages with 95 percent accuracy or greater. There is, thus, a borderline range of 90 to 94 percent accuracy. What should you do when students perform in this region? Typically, students are asked to read diagnostic passages with little or no instructional support. Therefore, when students perform in the borderline range, you should study the kinds of problems they encounter to determine whether instructional support might be developed to bring their oral reading accuracy into the acceptable instructional range (95 percent accuracy or greater).

Betts states that materials intended for independent reading should pose very few problems for students. Specifically, he recommends that there be no more than one problem per 100 words read. However, this standard is based on testing wherein students read a passage silently before they read it aloud. Thus, we recommend a slightly lower standard for oral reading on sight: no more than two errors per 100 words. Perhaps more important than the number of errors is evidence of the student's fluency. The material that a student reads independently should be sufficiently easy that he or she reads with good intonation and phrasing.

Powell's research (Powell, 1970; Powell & Dunkeld, 1971) suggests more lenient oral reading standards for primary grade readers than those noted by Betts. However, subsequent research (Ekwall, 1976; Pikulski, 1974) shows some inconsistency with Powell's findings. Given this inconsistency and our own clinical experience, we suggest standards that are generally in line with those originally suggested by Betts. We caution you, however, that these standards should not be used mindlessly. In addition to counting the number of errors, it is also extremely important to consider the quality of the errors (Biemiller, 1979; Kibby, 1979; Whaley & Kibby, 1981). Some, for example, may indicate serious problems with print, while others may suggest carelessness.

These criteria pertain to oral reading accuracy. Obviously, in judging the appropriateness of materials, you must consider comprehension as well. In Chapters 5 and 6, criteria for evaluating comprehension are discussed.

figure 3.3 • Formula for Calculating an Accuracy Score for Oral Reading

Formula	Sample
Total Words (*TW*) − Errors (*E*) = Correct Words (*CW*)	140 (*TW*) − 7(*E*) = 133 *CW*
CW/TW × 100 = Accuracy %	133/140 × 100 = 95% Accuracy
(percent of words read correctly)	

In determining whether a passage is of appropriate difficulty, you should study the entire passage for dialect influence and for repeated errors (i.e., where a character name or word is mispronounced more than twice). Note whether the student ever solves the identification of the word, especially when it is a key word. All dialect-influenced responses should be disregarded in further analysis.

Repeated mispronunciations of proper names are only counted once.

You will need to determine the percentage of the passage that was error-free. This is the accuracy score: (1) Calculate the total number of errors (omission, substitution, insertions, mispronunciation, and self-corrections). (2) Subtract this error number (*E*) from the total number of words the child read (*TW*). This is the number of words read correctly (*CW*). (3) Divide the number of words read correctly from the total number of words in the passage; multiply that number by 100 to get an accuracy percentage. You will find a calculator useful here. Figure 3.3 demonstrates the formula with sample numbers for a passage where the child read 140 words and made 7 errors. The criterion scores shown in Table 3.2 should be used for judging oral reading performance. The results from this assessment of passage difficulty should be recorded on the oral reading summary form shown in Figure 3.4 in the space provided under "A."

High-Frequency Word Recognition. You should separate the high-frequency word errors from the miscues made in response to unfamiliar content words. For miscues in response to high-frequency words, the following questions should be considered:

1. What is the proportion of high-frequency word errors in relation to the total number of words in the passage?
2. Is the reading fluent, and do these miscues distort the author's meaning?
3. Are these miscues corrected by the reader?

On the basis of this evidence, you should determine whether high-frequency word errors pose a problem and decide whether word recognition should be checked further. High-frequency word errors should be recorded under "B," on

figure 3.4 • Oral Reading Response Analysis Form

ORAL READING ANALYSIS

Name _____ Grade _____ Date _____

Book/Page _____ Level _____

A. Difficulty

_____ /_____   _____% Correct

Level: Independent Instructional
       Borderline   Frustration

B. Word Learning: High-Frequency Word Errors

Printed Word	Oral Response	Further Exploration	Evaluation
_____	_____	_____	_____
_____	_____	_____	_____
_____	_____	_____	_____
_____	_____	_____	_____
_____	_____	_____	_____
_____	_____	_____	_____
_____	_____	_____	_____
_____	_____	_____	_____
_____	_____	_____	_____

C. Word Identification: Content Word Errors

Printed Word	Oral Response	Further Exploration	Evaluation
_____	_____	_____	_____
_____	_____	_____	_____
_____	_____	_____	_____
_____	_____	_____	_____
_____	_____	_____	_____
_____	_____	_____	_____
_____	_____	_____	_____
_____	_____	_____	_____
_____	_____	_____	_____
_____	_____	_____	_____
_____	_____	_____	_____
_____	_____	_____	_____
_____	_____	_____	_____
_____	_____	_____	_____

D. Integration–Fluency

Integration: _____

_____

Fluency: Rate _____ /_____ = _____ wpm Evaluation _____

         Phrasing _____

the left side of the analysis form (Figure 3.4). If further exploration is necessary, the "Evaluation" section on the right side of the form should not be completed until this is accomplished.

Word Identification. To study the student's word identification strategies, you should record unfamiliar word miscues in section "C" of the form in the following way. Single-syllable words should be separated from multiple-syllable words. Classifying miscues in this fashion makes it easier to identify patterns in a student's approach to word identification and hence facilitates further exploration of word identification skills.

After the printed words and miscues are recorded, you should examine them to identify patterns. The following questions should be considered:

1. To what extent do the errors resemble the expected response graphically? Is the reader in command of the following phonics associations: consonants, consonant blends and digraphs, vowels, and vowel digraphs? Is the function of markers understood?

2. Are miscues corrected by the reader and, if so, on what basis?

3. What does the evidence reveal about the reader's ability to identify affixes and syllables?

On the basis of this evidence, you should decide whether the student has difficulty in any area of word identification and whether skill in selected areas should be explored further. When additional exploration is indicated, the "Evaluation" section should not be completed until this has been done.

Integration and Fluency. You should determine whether the student's miscues show use of contextual information. For example, are more than half the errors contextually appropriate and does the student have and use contextually based correction strategies? You should also describe the student's reading fluency and calculate his or her reading rate. To calculate the rate, divide the number of seconds that the student took to read the passage by 60 to get the number of minutes involved; then divide the number of words in the passage by the number of minutes to get a words-per-minute rate. This information should be recorded in section "D" of the oral reading summary form.

Summary. In summarizing the results, the following questions should be addressed:

1. Does the passage represent an appropriate level of difficulty in terms of the reader's print skill?

2. Is the reader developing a sight vocabulary, or are there problems in this area?

3. Has the reader evolved a successful strategy for identifying unknown words, or is further development needed?

4. Has the reader evolved a strategy that is based on the integrated processing of graphic and contextual information? Is the reader's rate of reading in accord with that of his or her classmates, or are there problems of reading fluency that need correction?

Sometimes, it will be unnecessary for you to analyze results systematically in the ways described in this section. This will be especially true once you have gained skill in more systematic analysis. If you are developing your skill in oral reading analysis, however, we recommend that you follow these more systematic procedures.

In the case described next, Eileen uses systematic procedures in analyzing the running record of Ken's reading; but she does not use the form shown in Figure 3.4 to organize her results. Typically, the form is more useful as an organizational device when you are studying the oral reading patterns of more proficient readers. Martha, in trying to understand Eva's oral reading, does use the form to organize and extend her observations. In any analysis, whether you use the form or not, you should address the questions summarized earlier. To answer these questions, you may need to gather evidence beyond that gained through the oral reading analysis. In the two cases described next, we present such exploratory procedures.

case 3.1

Ken—Use of Running Records

Ken had transferred into the school in the fall of the year, and compared with other children in the class, his prior experiences with reading and writing had been limited. Ken's teacher, Eileen, was developing a program for her class where a variety of reading materials, both fiction and informational, would be used. She believed that language experience stories and reading from predictable, patterned books were appropriate experiences for all her children, including those who were having some difficulty learning to read.

Prior to the spring conference she had arranged with Ken's parents, she obtained one more sample of his oral reading. In addition, she had one sample from December and one from February, as well as many samples of his writing. She had Ken read aloud a book that he had not read before: *The Carrot Seed* by Ruth Krauss—one that she judged to be of appropriate difficulty for him. During reading instruction with her class, she always introduced stories by "talking" with the children as they paged through the story prior to their reading it.

Since her goal was to replicate the instructional setting, she followed the same procedure with Ken. She paged through the story, first providing an overview of the story ("In this story, the author tells us about a little boy who planted a carrot seed"), a sense of the characters ("His mother and father and big brother are afraid the seed won't grow"), and the work the little boy undertook ("What's he doing here? Yes, he's pulling the weeds and sprinkling the ground with water"). She then asked Ken, "Do you think the seed will come up?" After his response, she turned to the end of the book and asked, "What happened?" She then turned back to the beginning of the story saying, "Now I'd like you to read the story about the little boy and his carrot seed to me." ■

Administration of the Running Record

While he read, Eileen observed his reading and made notes using a running record format described on page 96. Eileen's running record is shown on the right half of the page in Figure 3.5, and we've included the text Ken read on the left, although this would not ordinarily be part of the record. In other words, as described previously, the running record consists of checkmarks (3) for correctly read words, mispronounced words written above printed words, "SC" for self-corrections, "P" for pauses, and "R" plus a line and arrow for reread portions of the story. Eileen also made a tape recording so she would be able to share and discuss Ken's reading with his parents.

Eileen noted that Ken pointed to each word as he read. Only twice, once while reading the fifth sentence and then again in the final sentence, did he lose the match between his spoken word and the printed word to which he was pointing. She also noted that this reading seemed to be a valid one. That is, Ken seemed to "be having a good day," and his reading was typical of his daily reading.

Analysis of the Running Record

Once an oral reading sample has been obtained, only through analysis and reflection will we gain insight into the ways Ken's understanding of print is developing. It is important to reflect on how the prereading preparation may have influenced his reading. The book overview seemed to prepare him for some new words that would have been unfamiliar to him such as *planted*, *carrot*, *seed*, and *afraid*, and it seemed

pause and reflect

Think about Ken's responses. One useful way to gain insight into his reading is for you to read aloud the story in the way he read it. That is, using the running record, reconstruct his reading. What are three things that you notice about his reading?

figure 3.5 • Text From *The Carrot Seed* and the Running Record of Ken's Oral Reading

Sentence (Text)	(Running Record)
1 A little boy planted a carrot seed.	
2 His mother said, "I'm afraid it won't come up."	
3 His father said, "I'm afraid it won't come up."	
4 And his big brother said, "It won't come up."	
5a Every day the little boy pulled up the weeds around	
5b the seed and sprinkled the ground with water.	
6 But nothing came up.	
7 And nothing came up.	
8 Everyone kept saying it wouldn't come up.	
9a But he still pulled up the weeds around it every day	
9b and sprinkled the ground with water.	
10 And then one day, a carrot came up.	
11 Just as the little boy had known it would.	

Source: Text only from *The Carrot Seed* by Ruth Krauss, illustrated by Crockett Johnson. Text copyright © 1945 by Ruth Krauss. Illustrations © 1945 by Crockett Johnson. Used by permission of HarperCollins Publishers.

to provide him with a sense of the story. In general, Ken's oral reading indicates that he has learned a lot about print.

There is no simple, linear way to undertake an analysis, although the questions discussed in the prior section offer guidance. The scoring of self-corrections is one area of analysis that teachers need to consider carefully. It is our view that self-corrections should be counted as errors when analyzing primary children's oral reading in order to determine the most accurate instructional level. In the analysis of a child's self-monitoring capability, self-correcting can be viewed as a strength. This does not, however, alter the fact that an error occurred at the print level, where many early readers are experiencing difficulty.

figure 3.6 • List of Ken's Omitted and Miscued Words

Omitted Words	Miscued Words	
	Printed Word	Oral Response
around (SC)	said	did (SC)
Kept	His	The
still	And	said (SC)
had	big	brother (SC)
	Every	each
	wouldn't	won't
	known	knew

For running records, you may not choose to use the systematic form shown in Figure 3.6. Instead, you may prefer to follow the more informal procedures used by Eileen. Because of the brevity of most running records, the formal approach may be unnecessary. Even so, you will address the same basic questions.

One question that you need to consider is whether the story is too difficult. Ken was able to read many of the words in the story correctly (90 of 101 words for 90 percent accuracy). What sense do we make of this? Is this story too hard for him? As we learned earlier, an accuracy level between 90 percent and 94 percent is usually considered to be in the borderline range for children. But we believe, in the early stages of reading, that such standards may be too stringent. It may be more useful to consider the sense-making strategies that a child is using and his or her growing knowledge of sight words and word elements. From this perspective, we would consider this story to be appropriate for Ken, particularly with instructional support and rereading.

In understanding a child's reading strategies, it is particularly useful to examine pauses and repetitions. We learn that Ken pauses while he is thinking of some unfamiliar words. For example, he paused before correctly identifying *planted* and *sprinkled*. He also paused before the high-frequency word *And,* which he first misidentified as *Said,* and then correctly identified as *And.* He also uses repetitions (rereading a portion of a sentence) sometimes to reinforce the meaning of a sentence (sentences 1, 5b, and 7), sometimes to fill in omitted words (*around* of sentence 5a), and perhaps to aid subsequent word identification (*sprinkled* in sentence 5b). These strategies indicate that he is actively making sense of text. His omissions (sentences 9a and 11) are not corrected when they make sense, but are when they do not make sense (sentence 5a). If you read sentences 9 and 11 aloud as they were read by Ken, you will see that they make sense.

At the same time we are pleased with Ken's awareness that reading should make sense, we need to be concerned about the development of his sight vocabulary. Sometimes it is useful to examine the words omitted and miscued by listing them. In the lists shown in Figure 3.6, we include words that were self-corrected (SC) as well as those that were not.

This form of listing makes it easier to see the types of words that Ken is choosing to omit. All are basic high-frequency words, and most are words that Eileen thought were in his sight vocabulary. Thus, she will explore whether he actually knows these words in isolated form; he may have had difficulty with them in context because of the other problems he was trying to solve.

Ken's reading miscues indicate several areas of strength. First, he was able to correct three of the seven substitutions. This suggests that the words may well be known by him. Second, his difficulties, as indicated by substitutions as well as omissions, tend to occur at the beginnings of sentences, where there is less available context. This type of error again suggests his reliance on meaning as part of his reading strategy.

The nature of his substitutions suggests his awareness of graphic cues. Six of the seven substitutions show a match at the beginning of the word in initial letter (4), at the end (3), or both (1). Only the substitution of *The* for *His* shows little correspondence in terms of print; but the miscue does make sense in terms of sentence context. Thus, we see that Ken is aware of letter cues and makes use of this knowledge. Most of his miscues not only match the print in some way, but also make sense in context. Eileen has questions about the nature of his knowledge of print: Is he making use of a visual match, or has he learned letter–sound associations, using these as a cuing system?

Further Exploration of Ken's Reading

• High-Frequency Words

Eileen explored Ken's knowledge of sight words in two ways. First, she wanted to see whether he knew the words he miscued when he read *The Carrot Seed*. She wrote the words on a paper and had him read them aloud. As she had thought, he had no difficulty recognizing each of the words to which she pointed.

In order to check his sight word development more systematically, she had him respond to a subset of the list of "basic" high-frequency words developed by Dolch (1936). If she had been using a basal reading program with Ken, she might have tested him on the set of words that tended to recur in those materials. She wanted to see how he might respond to the reading selections he would encounter in second grade; thus, she decided that the Dolch list would provide some evidence of his knowledge in this area. The high-frequency word list (shown in Appendix A) and other similar lists (Harris & Jacobson, 1982) include words that frequently occur in early reading materials. Because they account for about 70 percent of running text, they are an important set of words for children to learn. These words should be written on cards or in list form and presented one at a time.

Eileen had written the Dolch words on cards. When she presented them to Ken, she observed whether he was able to recognize them immediately or after a delay. She found that he was able to recognize about half of the words immediately. This is appropriate for children nearing the end of first grade. He did not, however, seem to have any strategies for identifying those he did not know by sight. In interpreting the results, she considered whether Ken had had the opportunity to learn the words he did not know. There were a few that he had encountered earlier in the year that he no longer knew, but generally he was able to recognize most words that he had previously read and reread in stories.

• Word Elements

Eileen wanted to know more about Ken's knowledge of word elements. She knew from the running record that his substitutions tended to match in the beginning and final consonants. She had learned from the sight word task that he was not able to identify unknown words when they were printed in isolation. Thus, she further explored his knowledge in two ways. The first involved additional exploration of the sight words he did not know. The exploration of unknown words takes the form of assisting students in their attempts to pronounce the words correctly. When children have difficulty, the task is simplified by having them respond to only part of the word, first the initial consonant or consonant blend and then the word ending.

Eileen listed four words for Ken to identify and wrote them (*his, kept, still,* and *had*) on a piece of paper. She then had him look at *his* and asked him if he knew it. He said no. She then covered all but the initial consonant (*h*). He was able to give the sound corresponding to *h*. She then covered the initial consonant and asked him to pronounce the portion remaining. He did this successfully. She then asked him if he knew the word. He said he couldn't get it. She next said the consonant sound followed by the word ending. On the other three words, he identified *k* and *h* and the word ending *ill,* but had difficulty with the word elements that included consonant blends. She tentatively concluded that Ken might profit from instructional support in writing and recognizing consonant blends and from instruction in blending word parts.

The second approach Eileen used to gain information about Ken's knowledge of word elements involved a spelling task in which she had him write ten words. His

pause and reflect

Think over what you have learned about Ken. What special instructional support do you believe a tutor should offer? List two things you would want a tutor to do.

performance on this task is described in Chapter 7. The knowledge he displayed was consistent with that revealed when Eileen asked him to respond to word parts. She confirmed that Ken has good command of consonants in the beginnings and endings of words but that he is not yet able to blend consonants and vowels.

Providing Instructional Support

The results from these analyses show that Ken is developing his sight vocabulary, but that he sometimes does not recognize words he knows when they appear in context. He has fairly good knowledge of initial and final consonants, but is not yet able to undertake more systematic forms of decoding. The nature of his corrections and repetitions shows that he views reading as a meaning-making process.

Eileen believes that he would benefit from the rereading of familiar stories to consolidate his sight vocabulary. She also believes he would profit from instruction that focuses on the representation of consonant blends in his writing and the blending of word parts. In general, she believes that his classroom program is appropriate, but she will provide more specialized support in writing and blending word elements, either individually or as part of class instruction.

Because Ken entered first grade with less reading and writing background than most of the other children in the class, special tutorial support during the summer may be appropriate. After sharing samples of Ken's work with his parents, Eileen will discuss this possibility with them.

The running record procedure Eileen used with Ken is particularly valuable for children during their first year of reading. Thereafter, we prefer to make a record of the oral reading on a duplicate copy of the text being read: Older readers typically read longer segments, and it is easier to compare their responses with the text when the record is marked directly on the text. In the following section where we consider the case of Eva, the procedures for oral reading analysis are described in detail.

case 3.2

Eva—Oral Reading Analysis

As we discussed earlier, Martha was concerned about Eva's lack of interest in classwork and homework. She suspected that Eva might be having difficulty with reading and wanted to know how she could help her. Martha decided to analyze Eva's oral reading. Eva was 10 years, 5 months old at the time and in the second month of fifth grade. She had changed schools four times in the previous four years, and there was little in her record to help Martha understand her achievement problems.

It should be noted that although Eva is fluent in English, Spanish is sometimes spoken in her home. Because of this, it is important for Martha to listen carefully to Eva's pronunciation of English. During oral reading, if she pronounces words or sentences as she speaks them, these deviations from Standard English should not be counted as errors. In an oral rendering of a text, it is not unusual for children to translate the print into their spoken language. Our purpose here is to determine how well Eva reads rather than how well she speaks Standard English. ∎

Administration of the Oral Reading Task

Martha selected a story from the third-grade reading materials that were being read by her group of students who were experiencing some difficulty with reading and writing. Eva met regularly with this group. The story selected was "The Picnic Mystery." Although Eva read the entire story, only a representative portion is analyzed here. Martha told Eva that the story was about a boy and his uncle who happened upon a picnic and asked her to read the story to see whether she was able to figure out what happened to the people. The record of Eva's oral reading, which was also tape-recorded, is shown in Figure 3.7.

f i g u r e   3 . 7 • Record of Oral Reading: Eva

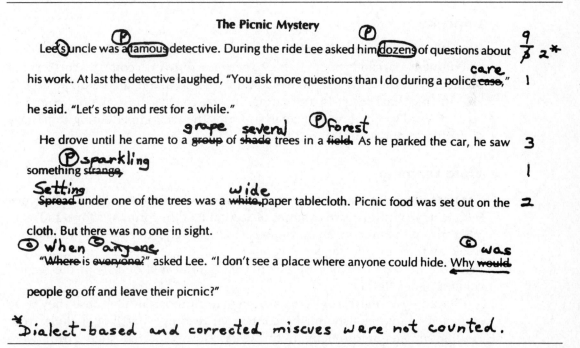

Source: The Abandoned Picnic. From *The Second Baffle Book* by Lassiter Wren and Randle McKay, copyright © 1929 by Doubleday & Company. Used by permission of Doubleday, a division of Random House, Inc.

Analysis of Oral Reading

Immediately following the oral reading, Martha considered whether she could trust its results. Was Eva comfortable? Was she involved? Was the reading typical for her?

Martha felt that Eva had been comfortable during the reading and that this oral reading sample was representative of her reading. Some of her substitutions, however, should not be counted as substitutions since they reflect her dialect. She tends to drop the final *s* during conversation, and here has mispronounced *Lee's* as *Lee*. This was therefore not counted as a miscue.

pause and **reflect**

Think about Eva's oral reading. What strategies does she have for making sense of text? On what evidence are you basing your ideas? How would you characterize her knowledge of print? Does she possess a well-developed sight vocabulary? What does she know about word elements? Would you characterize her reading as fluent?

The numbers at the right of each line in Figure 3.7 indicate the number of miscues per line. Note that miscues subsequently corrected are not counted as errors, even though they may be indications of difficulty. That they were subsequently corrected is noted by a © on the oral reading analysis sheet, and these corrections are considered a sign of strength.

• Difficulty

If we divide 106 (correct words) by 115 (total words) and multiply by 100, we determine her accuracy score to be 92 percent. When we compare this level of accuracy with the criteria levels in Table 3.2 we find that it falls below an acceptable instructional level, in the borderline range. Martha can now complete Section A of Eva's oral reading analysis form (the section pertaining to passage difficulty), as shown in Figure 3.8.

• Word Learning

The next step is for Martha to record the miscues in response to high-frequency sight words in the first two columns of Section B of the form. As shown in Figure 3.8, three of the miscues are in response to high-frequency words. Eva had corrected all three miscues, apparently on the basis of subsequent contextual information. The fact that they were corrected is indicated by a © in the second column under "B."

Because the sight word errors are few in number and because they were corrected spontaneously during contextual reading, Martha concludes that Eva has no major problem in this area. However, that such errors were made at all suggests that Eva has not consolidated her high-frequency sight vocabulary.

figure 3.8 • Analysis of Oral Reading Responses: Eva

ORAL READING ANALYSIS

Name _Eva. W._ Grade _5_ Date _April_

Book/Page _Discovering Treasure_ Level _gr. 3_

Level: Independent Instructional
(Borderline) Frustration

A. Difficulty

_9_ / _115_   _92_ % Correct

B. Word Learning: High-Frequency Word Errors

Printed Word	Oral Response	Further Exploration
where	when ©️	✓
everyone	anyone ©️	✓
would	was ©️	✓

Evaluation

High-frequency word errors are few in number and were corrected during contextual reading. Thus, no major problem exists. However, Eva needs to consolidate her sight word knowledge.

C. Word Identification: Content Word Errors

Printed Word	Oral Response	Further Exploration
shade	several	should
field	forest	fill
strange	sparkling	NR*
case	care	care
group	grape	grape
spread	setting	NR
white	wide	wide
famous	[omitted]	NR
dozens	[omitted]	NR

Evaluation

On one syllable words, she uses initial consonants— but word middles and endings do not always correspond. Her knowledge of initial consonants is limited. On a probe of word elements, she produced a word rather than a sound in response to initial consonants. She seems to recognize words on the basis of visual cues and context. She does not attempt unknown multisyllabic words.

* NR = no response

D. Integration—Fluency

Integration: Overreliance on prior context; most miscues violate author meaning. Effective use of repetitions and pauses to correct errors.

Fluency: Rate 115 / 1.8 = _64_ wpm Evaluation Slow even for a second grader,

Phrasing Rapid reading interspersed with long pauses for word recognition.

• Word Identification

The next step is for Martha to record in Section C of the oral reading summary miscues Eva made in response to unfamiliar content words. She first begins with miscues in response to single-syllable, then to multisyllabic printed words. Errors of omission are listed following the substitution errors, as shown in Figure 3.8. In contrast to high-frequency sight word recognition, Eva makes no successful corrections of unfamiliar content words.

Three of the seven miscues deviate from the printed word in more than one element and involve substitution of multisyllabic for single-syllable words. The next two miscues, which show a close correspondence, are also in response to single-syllable words. Finally, Eva omits rather than attempts two words that are two syllables in length. This pattern of response suggests that Eva has serious difficulty in word identification.

Although almost all of Eva's miscues show an initial consonant match, she erred on four of five initial consonant blends and digraphs. Vowels in miscued words are mispronounced more often than not, and she seems to have no knowledge of vowel digraphs and markers. Affixed words were, however, an area of strength; Eva correctly pronounced *laughed, during, asked,* and *parked.* Overall, the evidence suggests that Eva has little skill in word identification. This possibility will be explored further.

• Integration and Fluency

Eva does not integrate well, relying heavily on context in identifying unknown words. With few exceptions, her substitutions in response to content words are plausible with respect to prior sentence context, but they show low correspondence with print. Although Eva uses repetition effectively to correct sight word errors, she is unable to correct her content word miscues.

Her reading is not fluent, as it is characterized by many pauses before unfamiliar words. She read this portion of the story in 108 seconds. By dividing the number of seconds by 60, Martha gets a time of 1.8 minutes, as shown in Figure 3.8. Then by dividing the number of words in the passage 115 ÷ 1.8, Martha determines Eva's reading rate: 64 words per minute. This rate is extremely slow; it is below even the average range for second graders shown in Table 3.1. Martha expects, however, that Eva's rate would be faster on easier materials that posed fewer word identification problems for her. Because word identification difficulties are seriously interfering with her reading fluency, Martha will not make further exploration of this aspect of Eva's reading at this time. Rather, further exploration will focus on the consolidation of her sight vocabulary and development of her word identification skills.

Further Exploration of Oral Reading

• High-Frequency Sight Words

Eva's response to the three high-frequency sight words that she missed during contextual reading was rapid. Further, she pronounced all of them correctly (indicated by a check in the third column of "B" in Figure 3.8). The results from the exploration suggest that Eva knows these words, even if she at times confuses certain similar words. These results support the hypothesis that her main problem in word learning is in being able to recognize them quickly when under the pressure of difficult contextual reading. Eva needs to consolidate her existing set of high-frequency sight words through contextual reading of easy materials as summarized under Evaluation in Section B.

• Word Identification

Further exploration focused on Eva's ability to deal with unfamiliar content words. As shown in Figure 3.8, when words that were miscued during contextual reading were presented in isolation, Eva was still unable to recognize them. During the further exploration, Martha first asked Eva to respond to initial consonants, in order to confirm their apparent effectiveness as a cue system. Surprisingly, Eva experienced extreme difficulty producing the sounds that correspond to the initial consonant letters identified. This finding suggests that she uses initial consonants as effective visual cues to search for known words in her memory but not as elements that cue an appropriate initial sound. Because of Eva's extreme difficulty with initial consonants, she assessed her ability to segment words into phonemic components. With support, Eva was able to segment off the initial phoneme of a known word. This is probably the point from which instruction should begin.

Assessment of Eva's knowledge of the structural characteristics of words revealed that she is familiar with most common word endings (e.g., -ing, -ed, -er, -est). She does not know how to segment multisyllabic words into pronounceable units. However, when some of the words were divided for her, she was able to pronounce a few syllables correctly because they resembled known words. This facility suggests that Eva may be able to use her relatively well-developed sight vocabulary to help her identify syllables through an analogizing procedure.

pause and reflect

Think over what you have learned about Eva. What special instructional support do you believe Martha should offer? List two things you would want her to do.

Providing Instructional Support

The instruction you develop must follow from the understanding you gain through ongoing diagnosis. In Eva's case, Martha must determine whether she can profit from the instruction appropriate for Martha's low group members and/or whether Eva should receive individualized instruction. Because Eva lacks knowledge in the area of word identification, instruction must be designed to develop her underlying knowledge of word elements. Martha's initial plan (to be modified with new evidence) was as follows:

• Reading Materials

Eva should be reading from materials at two levels of difficulty. First, in order for her to consolidate her sight vocabulary, material should be at a level that poses few word identification problems for her. Whether second-grade-level materials would be appropriate for this purpose needs to be established. Second, Martha should experiment with instructional support prior to and during the reading of the current third-grade materials to determine if these can be used for Eva's instruction. It is important to keep Eva involved in ongoing class activities if at all possible. However, if the third-grade basal materials are still too difficult with instructional support, Martha will need to establish an individual reading program for Eva with somewhat easier materials.

• High-Frequency Sight Words

Eva's high-frequency sight vocabulary is quite well developed, as indicated by the large number of these words she recognized during contextual reading and her ability to pronounce them correctly when they were presented in isolation. However, the fact that she miscued on high-frequency sight words during contextual reading means that she has not yet learned them to the level of immediate and automatic recognition. Eva should be encouraged to read and reread easy, highly interesting materials. Martha should keep charts to let Eva see her reading progress.

• Word Identification

Martha would like to help Eva develop strategies for independent word identification. Building on Eva's strengths, she will help her to become more aware of her implicit knowledge of sounds at the beginnings of words (initial consonant associations). She will do this through writing and spelling activities. As Eva writes words, Martha will help her to pronounce each word slowly and to think how the initial sound might be represented.

Next, she will introduce a method for identifying multisyllabic words. Again building on Eva's strength with sight words, Martha will help her chunk words into syllabic units and to analogize from known words to identify the syllables of unknown words.

Teaching syllabication and syllable pronunciation can easily be incorporated into small-group reading instruction. After introducing a new story but before reading it, Martha should present any unfamiliar content words. Using some of these words, Martha can conduct the following two-part exercise. She writes the words on the board, one at a time. After a word is written, students should speculate how it might be divided into "chunks" that can be pronounced. A line should be drawn after each chunk, and Martha should proceed to the right until the word has been completely divided. Even when the final product does not conform exactly to what is specified by rules for syllabication, Martha should proceed with the lesson. If students wish to revise their prior decisions, they should be allowed to do so.

In the second part of this exercise, students learn analogizing. After examining the first chunk, students are asked if it looks like any word they know. Martha should then write the word the students suggest above the syllable to see if they can use it to identify the syllable. If they are unable to think of a word, Martha should supply one or provide the phonogram with which the syllable ends as an alternative. The students should then use a consonant substitution (word family) approach to identify the syllable. Correct and incorrect attempts should be presented to the group for their evaluation.

Martha can use this procedure for three or four of the multisyllabic words appearing in the story, as long as the attention of the group is sustained. She should simply pronounce other unfamiliar words as part of a discussion of the meaning of all unfamiliar words and how they pertain to the theme of the story.

• Integration

Eva's overreliance on contextual information indicates that integration is a problem for her. Her difficulty reflects the lack of a proper balance between the use of contextual information and attention to graphic information. Therefore, her integration should be reexamined after she develops greater proficiency with word identification. Her learning more about print should lead automatically to a more balanced use of cues from print and context.

• Fluency

As part of her program, it is important for Eva to experience "problem-free" reading, that is, reading selections that pose few word identification problems for her. This easy reading and rereading will help to consolidate her sight vocabulary and give her the opportunity to focus on meaning free from word identification distractions. It is on material at this level that Martha may wish to incorporate some of the instructional approaches designed to promote integration and fluency that are described in the following section.

Instruction to Enhance Facility with Print

Some children develop knowledge of print and reading fluency simply by reading many stories and informational selections. Others need more direct forms of instruction to help them solve problems related to print. In this section of the chapter, we review several approaches that you may use to help children learn sight words. We also describe instructional support designed to help students develop their knowledge of word elements. The heart of your instruction will focus, however, on helping students to develop an integrated set of reading strategies and fluency through contextual reading. Thus, we also describe instruction that you may use to promote integration and fluency.

• Instruction to Develop a Sight Word Vocabulary

It is not our intention in this section to describe procedures that are introduced in most reading methods courses. We will, however, describe supplementary procedures that you can use with your reading groups to reinforce learning. You should draw new sight words to be taught to the students from contextual materials. Instruction should never involve only words in isolation. Contextual reading should be a part of every instructional session so that it reinforces the development of sight word vocabulary. The number of new sight words you introduce each day should depend on the students' mastery. For example, if you introduce five new words but students master only two, reduce the number to two or three at the next session. You can adjust the degree of instructional reinforcement to what students need for retention. Word-sort activities, writing, and spelling can all be used to reinforce students' initial learning of sight words.

Word Banks.   The use of word banks is an outgrowth of the language experience approach in which various reinforcement activities help students learn and remember words (Stauffer, 1980). The **word bank** consists of words a student is learning through contextual reading (basal materials or language experience materials) and other words of interest. When a new word is encountered or identified, it is printed on a 3 × 5-inch card for each student. Since some beginning readers have limited ability to write evenly and accurately, it is sometimes better for you to print the words in a form similar to print in books. The student can use the back of the card to draw a picture or write a sentence that will cue him or her to the identity of the word. As students learn new words, the cards accumulate. Give students a box and rubber bands to help them keep and organize their word cards.

The cards may be used for a variety of reinforcement activities. Children may review them working individually or in pairs. They may use them to form sentences as a small-group or individual activity. One of the most productive activities involves sorting the words into various classes on the basis of specified features (see Gillet, Temple, Crawford, Cooney, & Crawford, 2003, for a more detailed description of procedures to be followed during word sorts). During small-group instruction you may ask children to go through their cards to find words that have a certain characteristic. For example, ask them to select words that begin or end like the word *balloon,* that name an animal, or that are three syllables in length. Alternatively, invite students to identify words that conform to a criterion of their choosing. Once they have identified and displayed a group of four to six words to their classmates, they can see whether the other students can determine the characteristic the selected words share.

Writing and Spelling. Beginning readers who have difficulty learning words are often helped to remember them by being encouraged to spell and write names (Bloodgood, 1999) and words you introduce in their reading materials. These activities prompt children to scrutinize words carefully, particularly the medial portions, and to become more aware of the words' phonemic correlates. Further, once they have learned to write basic sight words, students often draw on these high-frequency words during their other writing activities. Thus, writing is made easier, and basic sight words are reinforced. Classroom word walls provide a resource for both reading and writing.

Contextual Reading Practice. One of the best ways to consolidate sight vocabulary is through extensive contextual reading. Many basal programs are designed to provide practice on words that have been introduced by including them in subsequent stories. However, such practice may be insufficient for students who have great difficulty remembering words. Thus, it is important for you to devise ways to give students more practice on the words they are learning. Easy-to-read books such as the *Frog and Toad* series by Arnold Lobel are appropriate. Also, some basal series provide supplementary materials for this purpose. Alternatively, students may reread stories they have previously read. For example, once a book is completed, you may ask students to identify their favorite stories from the book and then let them take turns reading the stories. You may pose a new question about a previously read story and have children read the story silently to find the answer. Sometimes a prior edition of a basal series provides a different set of stories that include many of the words introduced in the newer edition. These texts may be useful as supplementary reading for students having difficulty learning words.

One reason teachers fail to provide supplementary reading is that students in the slowest-paced group do not read very fast at best. To take time for more contextual practice would seem to place an additional burden on these already slow readers. However, they cannot increase their reading skill without practice. Thus, in order to provide additional practice, you may have to plan extra small-group instructional time. For example, you may want to meet with children progressing most slowly twice daily (morning and afternoon) rather than once a day.

• Instruction to Develop Knowledge of Word Elements

In considering instruction in the area of word identification, it is helpful to distinguish between students who have difficulty identifying single-syllable words and those who have difficulty mainly with words of two or more syllables. The first group of students needs to become aware of letter–sound associations and/ or how to apply such knowledge when identifying single-syllable words. The second group needs to learn how to divide words into pronounceable "chunks" to be able to identify these units with the knowledge they possess.

Some students lack basic knowledge of word elements and must be taught them (Stahl, 1992; Stahl, Duffy-Hester, & Stahl, 1998). Learning to hear the phonemes (sounds) in a word is the first step in learning phonics associations (Griffith & Olson, 1992; Yopp, 1992). Some students may need to develop phoneme awareness by listening to words of two or three phonemes to identify the number of different sounds they hear. During this process, children should be encouraged to say the words in elongated fashion, as they do when attempting to spell the word. Sometimes drawing a series of connected boxes corresponding to the number of phonemes in a word helps children to hear the sounds (Elkonin, 1963; Joseph, 1998/1999). You can write the letters corresponding to phonemes as the children say them and then supply any unknown elements.

Each phonics association to be taught should be introduced through a series of words in which the phoneme occurs in initial position (Moustafa & Maldonado-Colon, 1999). If students have difficulty remembering the phoneme, you can introduce a key word (which contains the phoneme at the beginning) in printed form. Word sorts are useful activities for helping children to hear words beginning with the same sounds. Whenever students encounter words beginning with the newly learned phonics association, they should be encouraged to pronounce that portion of the word. This activity teaches them that phonics associations provide valuable cues for word identification. Finally, students should be encouraged to use phonics knowledge in conjunction with contextual information during contextual reading.

In teaching phonics associations, it may be useful to introduce the concept of *markers* (see Venezky, 1970, for discussion of this concept). In certain contexts, vowel letters generally and some consonant letters as well "mark" the pronunciation of another letter in that context (e.g., the *e* or *i* following a *c* marks the pronunciation of *c* as /s/). However, the concept of markers should not be taught as a rule but rather by presenting examples from which students can infer the generalization. You should begin with the final *e* concept (*can–cane, mat–mate, tap–tape*) and then move to vowel combinations (*pad–paid, ran–rain, bat–bait, man–main*). Though most students pick up this concept rather easily, they sometimes have problems applying it during contextual reading.

Some students experience extreme difficulty learning phonics associations. An alternative for them that depends on a sight vocabulary is to analogize from known to unknown words (Johnston, 1999). Students are encouraged to think of a word that ends in the same way as the unknown word and then to use a consonant-substitution method to identify the word. For example, in identifying the word *tar,* students are encouraged to think of a word that ends the same as *tar,* such as *car.* If the students have difficulty thinking of an appropriate word, you should supply one. Finally, the cue word is written on top of the unknown word and students are encouraged to identify the unknown word by substituting initial consonants. Once the procedure is mastered, words without obvious analogies should be attempted under your guidance.

For students who have considerable difficulty thinking of appropriate cue words, the systematic training procedure described by Cunningham (1978; see also 1975–1976, 1979) may be effective. In this approach, students are made aware that they are familiar with a large number of sight words that can be used to identify unknown words. In the first step, ask students to write the words *he, went, her, can,* and *car* on index cards. Then ask them to select two of the cards that match parts of such unknown words as *banter, ferment, meter, barber, percent,* and *garment.* Add additional sight words during the second and third steps and provide further matching practice. In the fourth step, encourage students to use "the whole store of words in their heads as words to match to unfamiliar [two-syllable] words." In the fifth and final step, apply the procedures to words of three or more syllables.

Some students have acquired extensive knowledge of word elements (consonants, consonant blends, vowels, vowel markers, word endings) but fail to apply this knowledge when identifying unknown words, particularly during contextual reading. For some students, this is because they have developed a habit of hastily guessing at words, particularly those in context, on the basis of partial information. They need to be taught a new procedure for dealing with unknown words. This procedure consists of five steps:

1. Pause (instead of guess).
2. Look at the initial part of the word and pronounce it.
3. Look at the remainder of the word and pronounce it.
4. Blend the word parts together into a word.
5. Check to see if the word makes sense in context.

After applying this procedure slowly and systematically, students will become able to scan words more rapidly and pronounce them accurately using their print knowledge.

Some students, however, have difficulty with the fourth step of the procedure: blending word elements together. To teach blending skill, you can use the following procedures, either with individual students or with groups. Instruction should begin with the blending of syllables (*but-ter, wag-on, ti-ger*). If this is difficult for the students, compound words such as *football, doghouse,* and *cowboy* should be presented along with pictures corresponding to the component words. The students should identify the picture that corresponds to the "word-syllable" being pronounced. When students can blend compound words, they can attempt other two-syllable words. Next, phoneme blending should be developed. First, a vowel unit should be blended into a final consonant (*ca-t, bo-x, de-sk*), then a consonant into an ending (*f-oot, h-and, p-en*), and finally, three units should be blended (*r-a-t, f-a-ce, p-a-ge*). Many students are helped by seeing the sequence of letters while they hear you pronounce the sounds and by imitating the way you separate and blend sounds within words. Blending should be practiced for short periods every day for several weeks.

Students who experience difficulty mainly with longer words and relatively little difficulty with single-syllable words need to be taught how to "chunk" or divide multisyllable words into pronounceable units. To learn the concept of syllables, students should listen to you pronounce two-, three-, and even four-syllable words and tap the number of syllables they hear. Next, they should examine the syllables of two-syllable words that are regular in pattern (*butter, rabbit, window, pencil, apron, table, open,* and *paper*) to see whether they can figure out what constitutes a syllable (that it contains at least one vowel) and determine typical syllable patterns.

You can advise students to pronounce vowels in multisyllabic words as they would in one-syllable words and then to blend the syllables into a word that makes sense. The concept of an "open" syllable (e.g., *be*) suggesting a long vowel pronunciation and a "closed" syllable (e.g., *bet*) indicating a short vowel pronunciation is difficult for some students to learn. The most effective procedure for developing the concept involves word comparisons or word sorts (for further discussion, see Henderson, 1985). To begin, select two-syllable words familiar to the students. The first set should include words such as *hopped* and *hoped, dinner* and *diner.* The students should focus on the first syllable, and you can guide them to see that the nature of the syllable (open or closed) influences vowel pronunciation. Then words within the same initial vowel can be compared: *hopped, potter, hoped, hotel, cotton.* Students should be able to give a reason for sorting certain words together. Finally, the words compared or sorted can include several different vowels: *butter, paper, rabbit, window, favor.*

Some students have difficulty with syllable pronunciation because syllables are *nonsense*. One way to help students deal with this problem is to use a word family approach: Students should identify several known words first, then related syllables (*bat, cat-lat, tat*), next a real word followed by a syllable (*bed-med, rod-fod, cab-pab*), and finally a list of nonsense syllables.

Once students understand how to divide longer words into syllables and to identify the syllables, it is important that you provide them with regular practice doing this as part of their reading instruction. When you assign stories or expository selections, you should identify approximately three to five multisyllabic words that may pose a problem for the students and write these words on the blackboard. You should ask the students how the first word can be divided into syllables. Sometimes there will be disagreement among group members. Students should then be encouraged to pronounce the syllables, identify the word, and draw a conclusion about the best way to divide the word. Once the words are identified, you should check to see that the meanings are familiar to all students in the group. The concepts underlying any unfamiliar words should be discussed using procedures described in Chapter 4.

Instruction to Promote Integration

Students frequently encounter words that they do not know. Those who have not developed balanced strategies for word identification need to be shown how using information from a variety of sources leads to more efficient and effective word identification.

Cloze Tasks. If few of a student's oral reading miscues are contextually appropriate, you should explore further, through tasks such as the cloze test, to determine whether the student is able to use context to anticipate words (see, e.g., Blachowicz, 1977; Bortnick & Lopardo, 1973). In a modified cloze approach, words that students were unable to pronounce during contextual oral reading are identified, and students are instructed to read the sentences in which the words occurred, saying "blank" for the unknown words. After they have read the sentence with the "blank," they are encouraged to think of words that might make sense in the blank. If they are able to produce words that are semantically acceptable within the sentence, we conclude that they are able to make use of context for word identification. It should be noted, however, that some sentence contexts provide little relevant information to aid word identification. Such sentences should not be used for this activity.

Application. If students are able to complete a cloze blank correctly but show little use of contextual information during oral reading, we can conclude that the problem is one of application. The students know how to use contextual information but have developed a reading strategy that usually does not draw on context as a source of information for anticipating responses and for correction. This type of strategy development is not unusual for some students who have been instructed with a synthetic phonics approach. Students who are able to complete cloze blanks, once alerted to context as a source of information and encouraged to use it, usually learn quite easily to use contextual information during passage reading.

Finally, during activities when students read aloud, it is appropriate for you to ask students who pronounce difficult words correctly how they identified the words. It is also appropriate after cloze procedures have been introduced to ask students whether a response "makes sense." Once students have received instruction focusing on the division of words into syllables and syllable identification, you may ask them to identify the first syllable of an unknown word and then attempt to identify the word on the basis of context and the first syllable.

• Instruction to Develop Fluency

Reading Practice. Contextual reading practice is the most effective means for developing fluency (Morrow & Weinstein, 1986; Richards, 2000). Many slowly progressing readers fail to achieve fluency because they are continually asked to read materials that are too difficult. They have little opportunity to experience the pleasure of problem-free reading and to develop reading fluency (Allington, 1983). Thus, if they are to improve fluency through practice, they *must* have material that is easy for them to read. It should pose few word identification problems and no comprehension problems. Methods for monitoring independent reading selections can be implemented in both the primary (Maro, 2001) and upper grades (Katz, Polkoff, & Gurvitz, 2005).

Having students reread selections can often eliminate many problems posed by a selection. After a first reading, the student is familiar with the context and can recognize most difficult words. Thus, he or she is more able to focus directly on meaning and to read at a faster rate. The method of repeated readings can also be used more formally (Blachowicz, Fisher, Massarelli, Moskal, & Obrochta, 2000; Dowhower, 1994; Nelson & Morris, 1988). First you identify a segment to be read orally and have the student read it aloud, noting the errors and the reading speed. The student then rereads the same selection, and you compare the number of errors and reading speed for the second reading with those of the first. The procedure can be continued one or two more times.

Some teachers schedule a daily independent reading time in their classrooms in order to provide the practice necessary to improve fluency. One model for this that we have found successful is Read and Relax (Maro, 2001), whereby students are instructed to select "easy books" that will allow them to experience error-free reading and full comprehension.

Typically, reluctant readers need tangible forms of reinforcement to encourage them to practice reading. Charts showing the number of pages read per day or week within a certain period of time (e.g., 15 to 30 minutes) provide a tangible record allowing students to see the amount they have read and any increase in the number of pages read within the time period (reading rate). Similarly, records of repeated reading can be used to show student improvement in reading accuracy and speed over a period of weeks.

Modeling Fluent Reading. It is sometimes useful for either you or an older student who is a proficient reader to read to a student to demonstrate the nature of fluent reading. One method effective for disfluent readers is to *model phrase reading* (Walker, 2003). First you tape-record the student reading a short selection that is of appropriate difficulty (instructional level). Then you read a sentence with brief pauses between phrases of the sentence. The student reads the same sentence with similar phrasing. Once the student demonstrates adequate phrasing, you read more than one sentence, with the student repeating what you have read. Finally, the student reads the remainder of the selection independently or along with you. You then record the student reading the entire selection and compare the phrasing and general fluency on the final reading with that of the first reading.

An alternative method consists of having a student read with a fluent reader or slightly after the proficient reader. The model reads slightly ahead and somewhat louder than the student, finger pointing to the line of print as it is read. Once the student reads fluently, the model can relinquish control to the student by reading more softly and somewhat behind the student. In general, the purpose of providing a model of fluent reading is to show clearly the nature of fluent reading and to get the student to compare his or her earlier reading with reading that is fluent. A third alternative is to engage in a meaningful activity such as reader's theatre, where students hear each other read (Martinez, Roser, & Strecker, 1998/1999).

Reading Rate Improvement. Teachers are well aware of differences in reading speeds among their students. It is appropriate to encourage them to improve their rates once they have developed a sight vocabulary, word identification strategies, and reading fluency. To read material at a faster rate, they must be able to maintain accuracy without word-by-word reading, and focus instead on silent reading of phrases.

Two types of reading selections should be used: easy, independent-level materials that the student is interested in reading (for example, a novel, biography, or science fiction) and expository selections followed by comprehension questions (it is also useful if a word count is included). The student first reads the easy materials for a specified time period (approximately 15 minutes) and counts the number of pages read or, alternatively, reads a specified number of pages and records the time taken. He or she then reads the expository selection and responds to the comprehension questions. Finally, the student determines his or her reading speed on the easy material (the average number of words per page times the number of pages read divided by the number of minutes), the reading speed on the expository selection, and the percentage of comprehension questions correctly answered.

This information is recorded on a chart and compared with that from the prior reading session. The student should be encouraged to increase reading speed on the easy material while maintaining adequate comprehension on the expository material. As reading rate on the easy material increases, a corresponding speed increase on the study-type materials is typically observed. If no check is made of the comprehension of study-type materials, the student may develop skimming procedures that sacrifice comprehension.

summary

Oral reading analysis provides a window into the knowledge that your students have about sight words and word identification. Even more important, it reveals how students integrate and make sense of information from various sources—context, sight words, phonic cues, pictures—as they read. It permits you to hear the reading rate, pauses, and intonational patterns of children in order to draw conclusions about their fluency.

In order to learn to use diagnostic strategies, such as oral reading analysis, you must study them and then use them with children on an individual basis. Later, once you are familiar with the procedures, you can use them more informally in the classroom while children work on reading and writing activities independently or during small-group instruction. Your knowledge about what particular children know about words and word elements will become more precise over time. Eileen's running record of Ken's oral reading and Martha's analysis of Eva's oral reading show the steps that are useful in recording oral reading and the types of information being used by children.

Such analyses are useful only when they lead to instruction to help students further develop their reading strategies. We described word banks, word sorts, writing and spelling activities, and extensive easy reading as ways to help children who have difficulty remembering sight words. We reviewed instruction strategies for developing knowledge of word elements and for enhancing integration. Finally, we encouraged reading practice, modeling fluent reading, and reading rate improvement activities as ways to support the development of reading fluency.

try it out

1. Working with first graders and other children in the beginning stages of reading demands expertise both in appropriately structuring the oral reading task for them and in analyzing the results. Repeated practice is essential. Find a child who is in the beginning stages of learning to read. Select a storybook with predictable text. Introduce the story and use the running record format to record the child's reading. Examine the record to see what it reveals about the child's reading strategies and his or her knowledge of print.

2. Find an older student for whom reading is challenging, and ask about the selections he or she is currently reading and those he or she prefers. Explain that you are learning how to record oral reading, and ask if the student would be willing to read aloud for you. Make a photocopy of the text you have selected. Preview the selection with the student. If possible, audio-record as you mark the oral reading on the photocopy of the text. Later, replay the oral reading and check the accuracy of your record. Then examine the record to see what it reveals about the student's reading strategies and knowledge of print.

3. **Student Portfolio Ideas:** For any of your students who are developing either their knowledge of print or their fluency, set up a recording booth so they can record their oral reading several times during the year. Have them select a section of their oral reading from the beginning of the school year to compare with more recent recordings. Ask them to identify the changes they notice.

4. **For Your Teaching Portfolio:** Use what you have learned from this chapter to add to your teaching portfolio. You might include
   - Your responses to "Pause and Reflect" on Ken and Eva
   - Your response to the "Try It Out" suggested in number 1 or number 2
   - A sample instructional lesson related to the development of sight words, knowledge of word elements, or fluency that you tried and evaluated
   - Your reflections on one of the "For Further Reading" selections for this chapter

for further reading

Clay, M. M. (1991). *Becoming literate. The construction of inner control.* Portsmouth, NH: Heinemann. Detailed description of the methods for making running records, interpreting results, and planning Reading Recovery instructional support.

Duffy-Hester, A. M. (1999). Teaching struggling readers in elementary school classrooms: A review of classroom reading programs and principles for instruction. *The Reading Teacher, 52,* 480–495. An examination of programs designed to support the progress of students who encounter difficulty.

Morrow, L. M., Tracey, D. H., Woo, D. G., & Pressley, M. (1999). Characteristics of exemplary first-grade literacy instruction. *The Reading Teacher, 52*, 462–476. A detailed study of exemplary teachers, coupled with an analysis of their approaches to teaching reading.

Maro, N. (2001). Reading to improve fluency. *The Illinois Reading Council Journal, 29,* 10–19. A guide to implementing a classroom

independent reading time that support fluency development.

Moskal, M. K., & Blachowicz, C. (2006). *Partnering for fluency.* New York: Guilford. An examination of the components of fluency, the related research, and methods for making fluency instruction part of a classroom reading program.

Pilkulski, J. J., & Chard, D. J. (2005). Fluency: Bridge between decoding and reading comprehension. *The Reading Teacher, 58,* 510–519.

4 Prior Knowledge and Vocabulary: Development, Assessment, and Instructional Support

<u>**chapter goals** for the reader</u>

- To understand the connection between knowledge, words, and meaning and how these develop in children
- To develop skill in assessing and interpreting background and vocabulary knowledge through the reading of an extended passage
- To understand the essential components of comprehensive vocabulary instruction
- To build a portfolio of ideas for vocabulary instruction

classroom vignette

Two Students

Raymond and Tanya are two seventh-grade classmates who may be like students you've encountered. Raymond is a lively student who usually does well in class activities when getting the general idea of a selection is required. However, he sometimes has difficulty when important ideas depend on specific vocabulary. Tanya is a student for whom English is a second language (an ESL student), and sometimes her intelligence doesn't show through in discussions following reading. She often appears lost or is silent. In both cases, their teacher, Paul, wants to take a deeper look at these students' vocabulary knowledge and find ways to help them in their classwork and participation.

This chapter presents an overview that can help you understand how vocabularies grow and how instruction can affect that process. Then detailed cases for Raymond and Tanya are presented to give you examples of how vocabulary knowledge can be investigated and developed. ∎

chapter overview

This chapter has three parts. The first section introduces some of the background issues essential to understanding the development of prior knowledge and vocabulary. Here are some questions to consider:

How are the terms *word, meaning,* and *concepts* related? How are they different?

How do students learn words?

How can instruction influence word learning?

The second section focuses on assessment and the cases of Raymond and Tanya. Although these students both have problems with new vocabulary, they have different profiles. The third section focuses on instructional techniques including learning from context; relating new words to what students already know; and extending, elaborating, and recalling word meaning.

chapter outline

Understanding Vocabulary Knowledge and Development
- Words and Meanings

- Words, Meanings, and Concepts
- How Words Are Learned

Understanding Vocabulary Knowledge and Development

Unifying the three parts of this chapter is the assumption that words are basic units of meaning in language. When we examine the relationship between vocabulary knowledge and reading comprehension, we typically find a very high correlation (Davis, 1968; Thorndike, 1973). Yet attempts to demonstrate a simple causal relation between knowledge of specific words and the comprehension of texts containing those words have not been uniformly successful. Markedly increasing the number of difficult words in a text leads to poorer comprehension, just as decreasing the number of difficult words leads to better comprehension (Wittrock, Marks, & Doctorow, 1975), but teaching students the difficult words before reading does not necessarily result in comprehension gains (Memory, 1990).

One explanation of this latter result is that knowing words well enough to select appropriate synonyms on a multiple-choice vocabulary test is not necessarily sufficient for comprehension. The reader must also be somewhat familiar with the **domain of knowledge** and cultural context in which the words occur. A high school student may know that a geologist studies the history of the earth through its rock formations, but this student will have difficulty comprehending the function of a geologist on a deep-sea expedition unless he or she is also aware of recent technological advances that make it possible to study the earth beneath the ocean floor. Thus, we need to recognize a distinction between word knowledge as traditionally conceived (and measured) and the cultural or general knowledge that may be necessary for understanding a given text. This distinction is somewhat analogous to the difference between a dictionary and an encyclopedia or between a definition and a full-fledged concept. Nevertheless, it is through words that readers gain access to their relevant stores of knowledge—their mental encyclopedias as well as their mental dictionaries—and through them that we assess that knowledge in diagnosing comprehension difficulties.

121

When a student fails to show good comprehension, and print skill is not the primary source of difficulty, the problem can often be traced to lack of familiarity with a particular word or words or the concepts that underlie them. In this chapter we discuss and illustrate some procedures for investigating this possibility. To understand how to assess a student's vocabulary knowledge, some background is needed. The first part of this chapter will take you through the murky fields of words, meaning, concepts, and strategies. Figure 4.1 presents an organizer that fleshes out the Vocabulary Knowledge "box," the diagnostic model presented in Chapter 1.

The words of a language make up its lexicon. Different languages have different lexicons in the sense that they use different sequences of *sounds* (phonemes) to express the same *meanings*. But languages also differ in the meanings or concepts, the aspects of experience, and have words that reflect the different

figure 4.1 • Vocabulary Knowledge: What's in the Box?

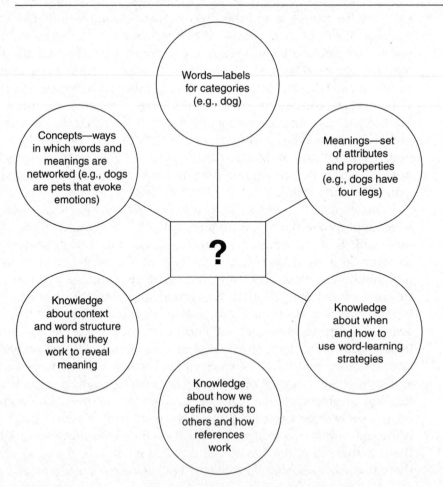

concerns and interests of the communities that speak them. For this reason, the lexicon of a language is never static. Words are constantly being added to express new thoughts and conditions, and some words fall into disuse while others undergo changes in primary meaning or intent. In a very real sense, the lexicon is an inventory of the concepts available to a language community, a map of the categories into which reality has been segmented and organized. Although words are the names we give to objects and actions, events and experiences, and so on, this naming activity involves, in the first place, the construction of concepts that determine the way in which the environment is subdivided into parts and the parts grouped into categories. For example, in English we divide the color spectrum in such a way that the colors blue and green are placed into separate categories designated by the words *blue* and *green*. Some languages, however, do not have different words for the colors blue and green but use a single word to designate this portion of the color spectrum. To take another example, some languages have words for individual kinds of trees but lack a general term for the entire class analogous to the English term *tree*. These differences are not just linguistic curiosities. They reflect differences in the categorization of experience and illustrate the important principle that the categories of objects, actions, and properties labeled by words are not "given" by the nature of things but rather reflect our desire to organize our experiences.

• Words and Meanings

What does it mean to know a word in the lexicon? It means, first of all, knowing how the word sounds when it is spoken and, in the case of literate speakers, how it looks in printed or written form. Proficient readers occasionally have print knowledge but not spoken knowledge. We have all had the experience of discovering, on hearing a word for the first time after years of encountering it in print, that it is pronounced quite differently from what we had thought. This is most evident when we first encounter "loan words," which come into English from another language. If someone pronounces *détente* to rhyme with *repent-y*, it is a fair inference that the speaker learned the word from print, not from hearing it used in everyday speech. Both the spoken and printed forms of a word can provide direct access to the listener's/reader's stored knowledge of its meaning; that is, either can provide a virtually instantaneous pairing of word with meaning.

But "knowing" a word goes well beyond decoding it. We can all decode *dolorist* but won't find that much help if it is not a word in our oral vocabulary. Knowing a word means knowing the aspect of reality to which it refers—which entities in the universe of entities it labels. In the case of a noun, this means knowing the objects or ideas, persons, and places to which it refers. In the case of a verb, it means knowing the actions it denotes. And in the case of adjectives and adverbs, it means knowing the qualities of objects and actions these words designate. When you tell students that a *snare* is a trap or that a *squabble* is a quarrel, you are identifying the real-world referents of these words, the known objects or ideas they name (on the assumption that traps and quarrels are familiar as real-world entities).

Yet, it should be clear that words are not simply verbal labels for particular experiences or individual segments of reality. They are labels for *categories* of things. The child who believes that the word *dog* refers only to the family pet does not know the meaning of the word, for that entails understanding that the word applies to all other animals of a similar kind.

To be sure, we use words to refer to specific things—the *car* we drive, the *meal* we ate, the *anger* we feel. But the meaning of a word is not so much embodied in its referents as in the attributes of its referents that are criteria in distinguishing them from the referents of other words. That is, it consists of the properties that determine whether something is or is not an instance of a category. The meaning of the word *story,* for example, does not begin and end with any particular story, or type of story, or even all the stories in the world. It consists, rather, of what a thing must be like to be considered a story, as distinguished, for example, from a poem or essay.

The meaning of a word may be seen as closely akin to what dictionaries attempt to record. The typical dictionary definition gives the essential properties of a category of objects, actions, or qualities, which may be used to identify word referents or instances of that category. And it does this in a most economical way, by naming the extensive, or superordinate, category to which the word referents belong and then setting forth the special characteristics that distinguish them within this more extensive category. This system eliminates the need for specifying for each word the properties of the extensive category to which it belongs.

That word meanings and (dictionary-type) definitions are more or less equivalent, at least in common parlance, is nowhere more evident than in the responses people make to questions about meaning. When adults are asked "What does ____ mean?" or "What is (a) ____?" they most commonly use the dictionary format—that is, they name the superordinate and the differentiating features, or give a word with similar meaning (a synonym). Students aged nine or ten also use this definitional form more often than any other (and this tendency increases with age). Younger children, on the other hand, are most likely to define words in terms of function or salient physical characteristics. Thus, an adult will say that *straw* is "dried grass," *gown* is a "long dress," and *orange* is "a fruit," whereas a young child will say of *straw,* "It's yellow"; of a *gown,* "You wear it, what you sleep in"; and of an *orange,* "You eat it." Similarly, a young child will say that *puddle* is "what you step in," while an older child will say that it is a "small pool of water" or "water that gathers after a rain." An explanation type of response (e.g., *skill* is "being able to do something"; *priceless* means "worth a lot of money") is infrequent among younger children but occurs at age 11 or 12 as the second-most-frequent response, though still considerably less frequent than the superordinate or synonym response (Feifel & Lorge, 1950).

Researchers have long believed that these age-related differences in definitional form reflect the developmental changes in conceptual processes. Accordingly, "functional" definitions, which seem to be more personal and less generalized than explanations, superordinates, and synonyms, are considered less mature. However, Anglin (1977) points out that adults and older children often include use, or function, in their definitions, "the difference being that children mention only use whereas adults mention a superordinate category as well" (p. 21). Nelson (1974) has also argued that function is an important aspect of word meaning for adults as well as children. Moreover, all types of definitions are found at all ages, and the shift from predominantly functional to categorical meaning is gradual (Wolman & Barker, 1965). If the form in which children defined words were primarily a manifestation of their stage of cognitive development, each stage being qualitatively different from the preceding one, we would expect the transition from one form to another to be more sudden. It may be that children's definitions gradually become more like those of adults mainly as reflections of their gradually increasing knowledge about the nature, origin, and categorization of things.

In other words, as children gain in knowledge of where things come from and how they are made, used, and classified, their definitions are likely to include such information. After all, one must know that straw *is* dried grass in order to define it that way. Another knowledge-related explanation suggests that children sometimes may not use superordinate terms because they are not familiar with them. When asked to define a word such as *robin,* a majority of children may give a "mature" definition because they almost all know the superordinate term, *bird.* In contrast, when defining a word with a low-frequency superordinate (e.g., *pencil*), students may use a "semantically empty" superordinate, such as *something* (e.g., "A pencil is something to write with."). This suggests they know that a superordinate is required, but don't have the correct term available (Blachowicz & Fisher, 1989).

So we can see that knowing a word is related to our experiences and that these experiences differ culturally and developmentally. A word is a category of experience that has specific attributes for membership in that category. When we talk about what a word "means," we are often talking about those attributes that are important for membership in that category, though we often represent this meaning in a classical definition that places the word in a superordinate category and then specifies attributes. But, as we have seen, the properties that define a category are only part of what an individual knows about that category, only part of his or her word knowledge. Underlying each word in an individual's lexicon is a concept. Let's consider concepts and their relations to words and meanings.

• Words, Meanings, and Concepts

It is common to talk about concepts as those things that underlie the word that labels them. We tend to think of concepts as precisely formulated ideas concerning the essential attributes of classes of things. This tendency stems in part from the close association between concepts and scientific thought and also from a long tradition in psychological research. In this tradition, concepts are generally considered to involve a limited set of stable features (e.g., red geometric figures that have four sides and are surrounded by dots). However, it is mainly scientific concepts that are so well defined. Most "natural" concepts—the ones we use in everyday thought and action—do not have clear-cut boundaries. Is a wooden shoe "clothing"? Is coffee "food"?

A further complication is that the various members of a category are not necessarily considered equivalent: Some members seem to be much more central or dominant than others. For instance, people are much more likely to name a sparrow or a robin as an example of a bird than they are to name a penguin or a duck. Almost 100 percent of college students in an experiment gave *chemistry*, *football*, and *carrot* the highest rating as examples of a science, a sport, and a vegetable, respectively, whereas *history*, *weight lifting*, and *pickle*, respectively, were given low ratings in these same three categories by a majority of subjects (Rosch, 1973).

It appears that children develop knowledge of categories from the central to the peripheral. When 9- to 11-year-old children were asked to verify category membership by answering yes or no to statements like "A chicken is a bird," they made no errors on the items that were rated as "central" by adults, whereas 25 percent of their responses were incorrect on the items rated peripheral (Rosch, 1973). In a similar study, Anglin (1977) found that even preschoolers tended to include the "good examples" as members of a category and exclude the less exemplary ones. What is particularly interesting about Anglin's results is that the good examples did not have to be familiar to the children in order to be classified correctly: pictures of a wombat, an aardvark, and an anteater were identified as animals just as frequently as pictures of a cow, a horse, and a cat. Anglin interprets this as evidence of the "inferential or generative nature of the child's concepts, for they will consistently include in concepts various kinds of instances which they have never seen before, provided they are central instances" (p. 156). On the other hand, familiar items were sometimes misclassified (though not by the majority of children) if they were peripheral. For example, an ant, a butterfly, and a starfish were not considered animals by a few children. This tendency seemed to be related to the fact that the children had another name for familiar objects such as these—they would say, "That's a tree, not a plant"; "That's a butterfly, not an animal."

What these studies suggest is that concepts are much more than definitions. Concepts include (at least when reasonably well developed) not only the attributes necessary for category membership (i.e., the criteria for determining what is or is not a category member), but also what is *characteristic* of most members—information about the people and places, objects and actions with which they are commonly associated as and functions of category members. Thus, an adult's concept of flowers is not limited to the idea that they are the part of a plant in which seeds are formed. Rather, it includes the knowledge that flowers wilt, are considered pretty, are likely to be seen at funerals as well as weddings and parties, and much more. It is conceptual or vocabulary knowledge, and not definitional knowledge alone, that is important for comprehension.

So we do not use words merely to refer to things or identify their category of membership. We use words in sentences to describe situations—that is, the relations between objects and actions and the qualities of objects and actions. Even a simple sentence such as *John pulled Mary's hair* involves a series of relationships, between *John* and *pull,* between *hair* and *pull,* and between *Mary* and *hair.* More important, sentences are used in discourse, so that the situations they describe become part of a larger complex. We cannot understand the following vignette unless our concept of hair includes the knowledge that having it pulled is painful:

> John pulled Mary's hair. She ran home crying, and he was sent to the principal's office.

To conclude, words are the names we give to categories of objects, actions, and the qualities of objects and actions, and their meanings lie in the properties that distinguish one category from another. A statement of these properties constitutes a definition, and the things to which a word applies by virtue of having these properties are its word referents. Thus, words are terms of reference for specific objects as well as units of the language with intrinsic meaning. But, as we have seen, the properties that define a category are only part of what an individual knows about that category, only part of that person's word knowledge. Underlying each word in an individual's lexicon is a concept, and this may be thought of as comprising all the significant knowledge an individual possesses in association with that word (including its definition). *Vocabulary knowledge, then, involves the meaning of words in the strict sense and in the broader sense of the concepts underlying words.* It is the sum total of knowledge associated with words. We can also refer to this as "verbal knowledge."

What further complicates this picture is the fact that we often use the same word to refer to categories of experience in different domains. Some are unrelated (multiple meanings), whereas others are closely related (figurative language).

Multiple Meanings. Many words in the English language have more than one meaning. In fact, there are relatively few words that do not. This situation normally causes little difficulty in communication, however, because the reader or listener can usually tell which meaning is intended from the immediate context or the topic of discourse. For example, the word *cell* is almost sure to refer to the cells of the human body in a biology text and to a small room or apartment in a treatise on monasteries. In a book on reading, the word *passage* will generally refer to a portion of printed text rather than to a hallway. However, words with several meanings pose no special problem *only* if we know the intended meaning and it is readily accessible in memory. If we have never before encountered the word *passage* in reference to written material, we might interpret a "reading passage" as a "hallway in which to read." A word with several meanings is especially likely to confuse. If the reader knows one of its meanings, but not the intended one, he or she will be more bewildered than if completely unfamiliar with the word. When a reader knows one meaning, not realizing that there are others, he or she will be drawn into an erroneous interpretation. On the other hand, the reader who does not know the word at all will approach it simply as an unknown.

Figurative Language. The several meanings of a word sometimes have little in common. *Bat* is an example. It seems to be purely coincidental that two entirely different entities—a small flying mammal and an item of equipment used in baseball—have the same verbal label. The word *fair* in the sense of "just" and *fair* in the sense of "light-colored, blonde" is another example.

On the other hand, the several meanings of a word can often be closely related. Think of the word *sharp*. In *sharp mind,* it means "quick, intelligent"; in *sharp picture,* it means "not blurry"; a *sharp outfit* is "stylish"; and a *sharp knife* is one that "cuts well." Yet all these senses seem to share a common core of meaning. These types of usages are often referred to as figurative language.

Such extensions of meaning are extremely frequent in English. They are closely related to metaphor as they involve attribution of a quality commonly associated with one kind of thing to another, completely different kind of thing. That is, comparisons are drawn across different realms of experience. If it is common to speak of *pure* water, *pure* food, *pure* air, and so forth, then we can also, by extension, speak of a *pure* heart or mind. And we can have *strong* evidence as well as *strong* muscles. The difference is that in extension the quality we wish to impute is specified, whereas in true metaphor we merely liken one thing to another, and the reader must infer which property (or properties) of the one is shared by the other. When Romeo says Juliet is "the sun," we must understand that he is referring to the sun's warmth, brilliance, and life-sustaining qualities (and not to its shape or color).

Research on how we comprehend metaphors is not extensive, but a few interesting observations have been made. For example, many adjectives describing physical sensations are also used to describe psychological characteristics (e.g., *sweet, warm, cold, rough, hard,* and *loud*). In one study, children ranging in age from 3 to 12 years were first asked about the literal meanings of several such dual-function words (to verify mastery at this level), and then they were asked about the words' figurative meanings (e.g., "Are people cold? What do they say or do when they are cold?"). Not until children were 7 or 8 years did they show some understanding of the psychological meaning of these terms. Even then they were unaware of the connection between psychological and physical meanings, believing the meanings to be entirely unrelated. By 9 and 10, children were more sensitive to this connection, and 11- and 12-year-olds were often actually able to explain the connection (e.g., "hard things and hard people are both unmanageable"; Asch & Nerlove, 1960, cited in Gardner, Winner, Bechhofer, & Wolf, 1978, p. 8). To summarize, children in preschool generally understand the physical or concrete meanings of dual-function adjectives; during the early years of schooling they master the psychological meanings; and during preadolescence, they begin to recognize the metaphoric connection (Gardner et al., 1978).

This pattern of development holds true for metaphoric comprehension in general. Children of 8 or 9 years can understand the meaning conveyed by a metaphor, but only on an intuitive basis: They can match a picture to the statement "He has a very heavy heart" but cannot easily paraphrase the statement. This limitation may reflect the avoidance of figurative usage in their own speech by children of this age; perhaps because of their concern with dictionary definitions, they tend to prefer ordinary, established meanings and comparisons, occasionally protesting that figurative expressions are "silly": "A tie can't be loud"; "A person can't be a rock." This may be a necessary stage of development; children must understand what words usually (and literally) mean before they can appreciate the departures and extensions of metaphoric comparisons (Gardner et al., 1978).

This point was demonstrated, to some extent, in a study of instruction in the comprehension of metaphors and similes (Readence, Baldwin, & Rickelman, 1983). The investigators hypothesized that the key to comprehension of these expressions is vocabulary knowledge. More specifically, they pointed out that a person must be sufficiently familiar with the "vehicle" term to know which of its features is being attributed to the "topic," the thing being described. For example, in "His hands were sandpaper," *hands* is the topic and *sandpaper* the vehicle; that is, *sandpaper* is the means for conveying the idea that his hands were rough. To understand this metaphor, you must be familiar enough with sandpaper to know that roughness is its most significant characteristic. To cite another example, "The smoke from the forest was pea soup" can be understood only if you know that pea soup is thick; knowing that it is green or edible provides no help. The investigators found that when fifth- and sixth-grade students misinterpreted metaphors and similes, usually they did not associate the necessary attribute with the vehicle term. For example, they might not think of pea soup as thick. However, when these students were given lists of attributes (including the one being ascribed to the topic) for the vehicle terms of the metaphorical statements they had misinterpreted, they were able to correct 77 percent of their misinterpretations (Baldwin, Luce, & Readence, 1982).

These studies suggest that students' failure to understand metaphorical language is not primarily due to their lack of the necessary reasoning powers or inability to recognize the type of comparison involved. Consequently, "drill exercises in discriminating between literal and metaphorical statements or matching interpretations with metaphors and similes may have little effect" (Readence et al., 1983, p. 111). Rather, direct instruction in the critical attributes of word referents seems more appropriate.

Nevertheless, the difficulty of understanding figurative language must not be underestimated. Familiarity with the terms used is certainly essential, but it is not sufficient. In order to determine which of the possible attributes of a metaphoric vehicle is the intended one, the reader must understand the situational context. We understand what Romeo means when he says Juliet is "the sun" because we know from what has gone before how he feels about her.

By the time students reach the age of 10 or 11, they can paraphrase as well as understand metaphors. Evidently, their conceptual and lexical knowledge is sufficiently consolidated that they do not resist or protest against comparisons between animate and inanimate objects, physical and psychological properties, and so on. However, it is not until adolescence that students are likely to fully appreciate the nature of metaphor; to recognize the links between sensory, physical, and psychological realms; and to perceive the significance of comparisons drawn across them (Gardner et al., 1978). Having a clear distinction (and seeing the relationships) between the terms *word, meaning,* and *concepts* can help us understand some aspects of comprehension difficulty related to vocabulary knowledge. But we must also understand how words are learned.

How Words Are Learned

An eminent psycholinguist, George Miller (1977), observed that young children seem to learn the words that name colors before they learn to match those words to specific color stimuli. That is, they will answer "red," "blue," "green" (or some other color word) in response to the question, "What color is this?" even though the color they name is not the correct one. And when asked to point to all the blue things in any array of objects, they may point to all the tan ones, showing that they can distinguish between colors without knowing which color-name to apply. The same phenomenon has been observed with respect to time words: Children will give time units in response to questions about time, but the numbers they give are often quite bizarre in relation to the questions (e.g., in answer to the question, "When was your daddy little?" a three-year-old will respond, "Last week").

These observations led Miller to reflect on his own vocabulary knowledge, and he recognized that he, too, knew many words whose specific referents he could not identify or did not understand. For example, he knew that the words *camellia, nasturtium,* and *marigold* were the names of flowers but he did not know what these flowers looked like. Many adults are probably in a similar position with regard to tree names like *sassafras* and *cottonwood* or animal names like *wombat* and *aardvark*.

These observations suggest that both children and adults often learn the general domain of knowledge or experience to which a word belongs before they understand its precise meaning. We should not be surprised, therefore, when students can give only the most general information about certain words—that *anxiety* means "feeling"; *soliloquy* is "a statement"; *penance* means "punishment" (Drum, 1983). This probably represents a first stage in the process of learning words. With further experiences in a variety of contexts, they will be able to differentiate word meanings more precisely.

The phenomenon of overgeneralization of word meaning is well documented among very young children (Clark, 1973). They commonly use the term *dog* as a label for other animals (horses, cows, sheep), *baby* for young children, *tick-tock* for instruments with round dials (gas meter, bathroom scale), *ball* for spherical objects (marbles, balloons), *Christmas tree* for all evergreens, and so on. One child used *open* for both untying of shoes and the peeling of fruit! We can understand these overextensions as stemming from the perceptual similarity of "correct" and "incorrect" word referents. And, to some extent, the child may be aware of the difference between babies and children, a clock and other dialed instruments, and so on, but may not yet have acquired the appropriate verbal labels. This would also explain the child's use of the terms *big* and *little* to cover all dimensions of size—long and short, wide and narrow, thick and thin, high and low. In other words, some overgeneralizations undoubtedly emerge because children must use the terms that are available to them to refer to new objects and ideas.

More difficult to explain is the common confusion between antonym pairs such as *more* and *less, before* and *after, same* and *different*. One theory (the **Semantic Feature Hypothesis**) is that the meanings of words can be broken down into smaller units or elementary components of meaning (semantic features), and words that share many features are likely to be confused. More specifically, the meaning of one word in an antonym pair is likely, at first, to be extended to cover the meaning of the other as well because the contrastive feature of the second word has not yet entered the child's "mental dictionary." In other words, the child may not have differentiated the meanings of *less, after,* or *different* from the meanings of *more, before,* or *same;* the lexical entry for these words is incomplete (Clark, 1973). Perhaps this same notion of incomplete entry accounts for the confusion, found even among adults, between *affect* and *effect, imply* and *infer.*

The Semantic Feature Hypothesis represents just one attempt to understand the development of word meaning, and much can be said about its limitations (cf., Anglin, 1977; Nelson, 1974). From our point of view, one serious limitation is that it is based on observations of preschool children. Nevertheless, it is sometimes useful to think of words as "bundles" of semantic features and to understand students' partial or vague knowledge of words in these terms.

Possibly more frequent than overgeneralizations of word meanings are undergeneralizations. These tend to go unnoticed in spontaneous speech (on which much of the research on child language is based) because they do not result in erroneous verbal labels—the child merely applies a word to a more restricted range of objects than is necessary. Consequently, undergeneralizations have been relatively neglected in the study of word meaning. They are, however, much in evidence when observations are based on comprehension tasks (Anglin, 1977). Whether a word is overgeneralized or undergeneralized appears to depend somewhat on its level of generality. The reason for this is that perceptual similarity plays an important role in children's categorizing behavior. General terms tend to refer to an assortment of dissimilar items and therefore to be undergeneralized. Thus, Anglin found that with the general terms *food, plant,* and *animal,* atypical instances such as ketchup, trees, and insects, respectively, were excluded. Rarely were these terms overgeneralized. Specific terms, on the other hand, were often overgeneralized to perceptually similar items—*apple* to tomato, *flower* to other plants (cacti, philodendron). In general, then, children's acquisition of word labels cannot be said to progress either from specific to general or from general to specific. Rather, "vocabulary development is characterized by the complementary trends of differentiation and of hierarchic integration" (Anglin, 1977, p. 237).

In conclusion, we believe that underlying the meaning a student attaches to a word is a concept. This includes, even for young children, knowledge of what instances of the concept look like, smell like, taste like, and so on, where they are found, the uses to which they can be put, and what they can do. With development, a child expands a concept to include knowledge of the relations of instances to other things, their internal constituents, and their origins (Anglin, 1977). But it should be clear that there can be concepts without words, just as there can be words without conceptual underpinnings. The distinction between words and concepts is an important one for vocabulary instruction; it implies that teaching definitions is not the same as teaching concepts. The teaching of definitions (or synonyms) makes sense when words pertain to well-developed concepts. Even then, new words must be practiced in a variety of verbal contexts if they are to be useful in comprehending discourse. But when the concepts underlying words are somewhat unfamiliar, definitions will be inadequate; instruction must also provide the verbal and nonverbal experiences necessary for concept development.

• How Instruction Influences Vocabulary Learning

We noted earlier that the high correlation between vocabulary and comprehension is not well understood. There is persistent controversy over whether word knowledge is directly "instrumental" in a person's understanding text or is itself a reflection of deeper and broader knowledge of the culture. On the one hand, students who score high on a vocabulary test may simply "know more of the words in most texts they encounter"; on the other hand, it may be that "possessing a certain word meaning is only a sign that the individual may possess the knowledge needed to understand a text." The second position assumes that students who select the right responses on a multiple-choice test know more about words than their definitions (though that is all that is demonstrated on the test). This position is consistent with the view of verbal knowledge we have proposed.

Unfortunately, as Anderson and Freebody (1981) point out, there is little besides logic and intuition to support the view that vocabulary scores reflect primarily conceptual or background knowledge. The sheer number of words learned by school-aged children year by year suggests that a great deal of vocabulary is learned through encountering words in context (Cunninghan & Stanovich, 1998), with meanings growing and developing as learners add new featural information to their internal word and conceptual maps. The tendency among reading researchers has been to study background knowledge as separate and distinct from vocabulary. However, there is a kind of support for the vocabulary-as-background-knowledge view, by default, in the finding that simply teaching definitions does *not* tend to improve comprehension. Out of eight studies reviewed by Mezynski (1983), four resulted in comprehension gains due to vocabulary instruction and four did not. In each of the four that proved unsuccessful, students were taught simple definitions or synonyms, accompanied in some cases by illustrative sentences. By contrast, in each of the successful studies, instruction went beyond this narrow type of drill, a conclusion supported by other meta-analyses of research (Stahl & Fairbanks, 1986).

In one of the successful studies, the additional instruction amounted to little more than answering two questions about each word. For example, in addition to learning that *altercations* are "fights," students answered these questions: "Do you have altercations with your teacher? Do you have altercations with a tree?" (Kameenui, Carnine, & Freschi, 1982). One wonders why this should make the difference between success and failure. Perhaps the questions helped students associate the new word with an underlying concept—meaningful experiences or knowledge—rather than with a rote definition. Some researchers have suggested that the conceptually rich discussion generated by the questions is the real source of word learning (Stahl & Vancil, 1986).

Whereas Kameenui et al. (1982) taught a small number of words (six) and used a short experimental passage incorporating these words to assess the effect of instruction on comprehension, the other successful studies involved large numbers of words taught over a period of many months and assessed the effects of instruction through standardized comprehension tests. Thus, there is evidence in favor of instruction that is geared toward improving students' *general* vocabulary as well as support for direct instruction in difficult passage words. More significantly, in the general vocabulary studies, words not only were taught (i.e., defined, illustrated, explained, and discussed), but also were presented in rich contexts. The Draper and Moeller (1971) study constituted a veritable "barrage" of new words—1,800 in all—presented in the context of fables, folktales, and Greek and Roman myths. The Lieberman study (cited in Mezynski, 1983) used social studies and English curriculum materials as the context for new words. A slightly different approach was taken by Beck, Perfetti, and McKeown (1982) and in their later instructional work, which suggested that robust vocabulary instruction could have a significant effect on comprehension (research amplified in later instructional studies; Beck, McKeow, & Kucan, 2002; Beck & McKeown, 2007). Instead of providing narrative or expository contexts for newly learned words, they designed activities in which students explored and refined the meanings of words. For example, students completed sentences or answered multiple-choice questions about the situations, behaviors, or events in which word referents might be involved. To illustrate, for the word *accomplice,* students were asked, "Would an accomplice be more likely to (a) squeal to the police in return for not having to go to jail? (b) rob a bank by himself? (c) enjoy baby-sitting?" (p. 510). Also, the words taught in the Beck, Perfetti, and McKeown study were grouped into semantically related sets, eight to nine words per set, and some questions were designed to probe the overlap among words in a set. For example, *accomplice, novice,* and *hermit* were in the "people" set of words, and the students were asked: "Could an accomplice be a novice? Would a hermit likely be an accomplice?" (p. 510).

This body of research suggests that instruction in definitions alone does not adequately prepare students for the task of comprehending discourse. Also, contextual learning is a powerful force in the vocabulary development of the school-age child (Nagy & Herman, 1987; Sternberg, 1987). Though the exact size and growth rate of children's vocabularies are arguable, it is clear that instruction cannot account for a major part of our word learning. In their meta-analysis of vocabulary research, Stahl and Fairbanks (1986) concluded that a combination of definitional and contextual learning is more effective than either alternative alone. A broad, rich range of experiences seems to be necessary before newly learned words can be understood in novel contexts. Such experiences can evidently be provided through exploratory questions as well as through contextual exercises that engage the learner in discussing, using, analyzing, and playing with new words. These experiences make definitions "come alive": They enable students to connect words with real-world events, situations, and behaviors—with existing conceptual knowledge.

Many suggested guidelines have been given for vocabulary programs in the classroom (Blachowicz & Fisher, 2006; Carr & Wixson, 1986), and some can also be drawn from research and meta-analyses of instructional programs (Blachowicz & Fisher, 2000). The process of word learning should be an active one for learners with the goal of connecting the new words to what they already know.

The goal should be to augment both the breadth and depth of existing word knowledge and to build independent word learning habits. For maximum effect, this development takes place within the context of content learning or, at a minimum, in concert with textual reading instruction and should incorporate the following, though not necessarily in this order:

1. *Assessing what students already know.* Briefly worded explanations, synonyms, associations, or hypotheses about the word's meaning should be elicited from the student, if possible, and elaborated on by the teacher. When the word is connected to a well-established concept, the dictionary can be consulted (Parker, 1984). For variation, you might present sentences from which target words have been omitted but that contain clear clues to the words' meanings. Students can then supply synonyms to match a new word's meaning (Blachowicz, 1977). If defining is the first instructional step, whatever defining characteristics are proposed should be viewed as tentative and reevaluated after students gain more experience with the word.

2. *Providing rich and active language opportunities that include discussion, writing, and charting.* The concepts underlying words should be developed through discussion of illustrative situations; meanings should be expanded and clarified through associations with familiar people, places, objects, and actions. Students' own experiences are, of course, elicited wherever possible. However, when students' experiences are limited, you should invent appropriate scenarios and provide information (Beck & McKeown, 2007).

3. *Application.* Students should reinforce and refine concepts through further interaction with illustrative contexts. This activity can take the form of exploratory questions similar to those used by Kameenui et al. (1982) and by Beck et al. (2002), or it can involve instructional materials regularly used in reading or content area instruction. In addition, when time permits, you may give students writing assignments in which they generate sentences and paragraphs around the newly learned words.

4. *Use and practice.* Wide reading in context is essential for vocabulary development (Nagy & Herman, 1987; Cunningham & Stanovich, 1998) as is hearing the new words used in oral language, storytelling, and story reading (Eller, Pappas, & Brown, 1988). Also, using it in writing is an excellent—and traditional—way to cement a new meaning. Word games and word play provide both practice and motivation for word learning, which is so essential for growth.

5. *Teaching independent strategies.* Our goal is to have students move away from the support of their teachers and become independent. At this point, they need the independent strategies to learn new words on their own. Studies of strategic behaviors in readers emphasize not only the need for declarative knowledge (knowledge about something) but also the need to

know when to use that knowledge (conditional knowledge) and how to go about using it (procedural knowledge). For students to be independent word learners, they need to know about context and how it works, both the external context of the text (the context around the word) and the internal context of the word morphology). Then they need to know when to use that knowledge and how to go about gathering information for meaning and what to do when these are not sufficient (read on, ask someone, use a reference tool).

Balanced, Comprehensive Vocabulary Instruction

Knowing about teaching vocabulary is not the same as structuring a sensible classroom approach. It essential that teachers and researchers begin to document what a balanced approach to vocabulary actually looks like in the classroom (Blachowicz, Watts-Taffe, & Fisher, 2006).

Studies of long-term vocabulary programs are just beginning to emerge. Lubliner and Smetana (2005) examined the effects of a multi-dimensional vocabulary instructional program on low-achieving fifth-grade students' word learning and comprehension. Following 12 weeks of metacognitive instruction on vocabulary from a social studies unit, students demonstrated pretest/posttest growth on experimenter-constructed vocabulary and comprehension tests. The students in the program also demonstrated that they closed the gap on vocabulary and comprehension compared to students in a higher-achieving school who did not experience the program. Although these results are encouraging, the relative brevity of the program and lack of an equivalent comparison group make it difficult to make generalizations to students participating in longer-term programs.

A paper by Block and Mangieri (2006a) reported an evaluation study of a commercial vocabulary program they authored (Block & Mangieri, 2006b). The workbook-based program provided lessons in using context, learning about affixes and roots, learning subject-matter-specific vocabulary, and learning words from other languages and words reflecting linguistic devices such as idioms and onomatopoeia. Following 22 weeks of brief daily lessons, Block and Mangieri reported that experimentals in Grades 3 to 6 statistically outperformed controls at the same grade levels on several standardized and experimenter-constructed measures of vocabulary and comprehension.

Baumann, Ware, and Edwards (2007) conducted a year-long formative experiment using Graves's four-part program (2000, 2006). The classroom teacher and two university researchers worked together implementing the vocabulary program in reading/language arts and social studies classes. Students demonstrated growth beyond that expected for maturation alone on some vocabulary measures, and rich, descriptive data indicated that students grew in interest and motivation with respect to vocabulary learning. All these studies, however, have limited generalizability due to various research issues. However, they have provided stimulus for other studies looking into the ways in which teachers can structure a comprehensive approach to classroom vocabulary instruction.

One final issue should be mentioned before we conclude this discussion of instructional research. It concerns the special importance of vocabulary instruction for less able readers who generally exhibit poor performance on vocabulary assessment measures. Though research continues to emphasize contextual reading as essential for growth in word knowledge, it may not be sufficient for these readers who begin school knowing fewer school-type words than their more proficient counterparts (Becker, Dixon, & Inman-Anderson, 1980). These are the readers who are frequently unmotivated or unable to do the amount of contextual reading that would close the gap with their age mates, and they often have second language issues as well (Carlo et al., 2004; Snow & Kim, 2007). Further, McKeown (1985) found that poor readers lagged behind more capable readers in the use of strategies that allow readers to gain new word meaning from context, knowing that one needs to use context, generating possible meanings for an unknown word, and using the prior and subsequent context to choose among generated alternatives.

Roser and Juel (1982) looked at readers' performance on word learning tasks in regular reading classrooms. They selected children in first through fifth grades who were either average or poor readers (i.e., who were reading either at or one year below grade level). Each group read stories from their classroom reader, one with vocabulary instruction and one without. The words taught were those identified in the teacher's manual as "new words," and the instructional method emphasized the relationship of each new word to the children's lives. Specifically, new words were presented along with sentences in which blanks were substituted for the new words; the teacher guided the group in selecting the appropriate word for each sentence, centering the discussion on students' knowledge and previous experiences. The results showed a marked increase in passage comprehension after vocabulary instruction only for the poorer readers in third, fourth, and fifth grades. The average readers in all grades performed just about as well without instruction as with it. In first and second grades, not only did instruction have no effect, but also the poorer readers performed as well as the average readers. These results are not unexpected, given the fact that beginning reading materials make fewer demands on students' vocabulary knowledge. A noteworthy feature of this experiment was the use of instructional-level materials in regular reading lessons conducted by the classroom teacher. Therefore, an appropriate instructional program for disabled readers with poor vocabularies would include motivation and time for wide reading but would also provide instruction on key concept vocabulary and strategy development for effective context use.

Assessing Prior Knowledge and Vocabulary Difficulty

We have learned from the review of experimental research discussed earlier that knowing the definitions of words in a passage does not always lead to increased comprehension for students. By the same token, *not* knowing word meanings does not necessarily interfere with their comprehension. Why should this be so? Clearly, much depends on how many unknown words there are and on how important they are to the central content (Freebody & Anderson, 1983a). The influence of these factors on comprehension will depend, in turn, on students' familiarity with the content (cf., Freebody & Anderson, 1983b). A large number of unknown words may present no obstacle to their comprehension in a highly predictable context. For example, a simple 100-word fairy-tale-style story was readily understood by a group of average readers in fifth grade, even though ten of the words were taken from an eighth-grade list and, moreover, an average of seven of those words were marked incorrectly by the experimental group on a multiple-choice test given after instruction (Stahl, 1983). On the other hand, even a few unknown words can severely disrupt comprehension if they represent key concepts in an expository passage on an unfamiliar topic.

In the usual case, however, unknown words usually cause losses or misinterpretations of information that are more limited in scope. By way of illustration, a child who did not know the meaning of *snare* and *clipped* read a story that began as follows: "A miller laid a snare, and a baby eagle flew into it. The miller tied him to a pole and clipped his wings" (Hughes, Bernier, & Gurren, 1979, p. 19). The unknown words prevented that child from answering questions about the *causes* of the bird's predicament; but the *facts* of its predicament—captivity and inability to fly—were clearly understood from ensuing events. In general, students appear to tolerate unknown words as long as other, compensatory sources of information are available to them, either from the passage itself, in the form of redundant information, or from their own store of knowledge.

• Ways to Assess Vocabulary

In the following section we present two case studies illustrating how word knowledge and topic familiarity influence comprehension. The first case represents the moderate loss in comprehension likely to be observed when passages are not overly demanding relative to the reader's conceptual knowledge. The second shows a more severe loss, as it makes greater demands on the reader. The presentation of these cases, in addition, demonstrates the diagnostic procedures useful in assessing word knowledge and evaluating its effect on comprehension. These cases represent the gathering of vocabulary knowledge data in rich contextual situations. We believe this is the most reliable diagnostic method, using the reading of a text that is rich enough and long enough to provide insights into vocabulary learning. Such analysis depends on the judicious use of probe questions to attempt to pinpoint some issues about vocabulary. For example, after reading you might ask:

Question	*Purpose*
1. Were there any words in here that gave you trouble and that you think are really important?	1. To see if student can monitor own word knowledge.
2. Do you know what _____ means? (Have the student read the word for you or pronounce it for the student if he or she cannot read it.)	2. To see if the word is in the student's oral vocabulary.
3. Can you use it in a sentence?	3. To see if the student has any functional knowledge of a word that he or she may not be able to define.
4. Is there anything you know about the word or associate with it?	4. To determine if a student has any featural information or associations with the word. Can the student place it in a domain?
5. If I told you the word had a connection with _____ (introduce a concept) does that make you think of anything?	5. To see if providing the domain activates any knowledge.
6. Let's look back at the text. Does this give you any help?	6. To see if students can reexamine context for meaning. (Use only when such clues exist and are relevant.)
7. Let's break this word into parts. Does this give you any help?	7. To see if word structure information (internal context) can help. (Use only when such clues exist and are relevant.)
8. Here's the dictionary definition of this word. Does this help you with any meaning in this context?	8. To see if students can use a dictionary and connect with context.

Besides an individual assessment, classroom information can provide and flesh out our pictures of a student's vocabulary knowledge. Some productive ways to gather data include the following:

- *Classroom observation.* Classroom behavior is often most revealing of difficulties with vocabulary. Using these observations for assessment require that teachers have some way of keeping anecdotal records for analysis. Keep a tally of words that cause difficulty on running records, guided reading, classroom content activities, or informal reading inventories, and probe using some of the preceding questions.

- *Analyze retellings.* Responses to questions and writing show when words are misused or when specific vocabulary is characteristically not used. Responses to questions can often reveal misconceptions about words as in the cases that follow.

- *Teacher assessment.* Note which students have particular difficulty on teacher tests of vocabulary. Spelling series often have meaning-focused activities that highlight students with divergent vocabulary knowledge.

- *Self-assessment.* Have older students keep *difficult word* lists. Note which students routinely include more- or less-difficult words on their lists.

- *Standardized tests of vocabulary.* Though most general reading survey tests contain some measure of vocabulary, they are not typically designed for use in individual diagnoses. However, teachers should be aware of issues related to standardized vocabulary assessment and the choice of tools to use for broad scale assessment. Formats for assessment vary, including words presented in isolation or in context with response formats ranging from matching synonyms to choice of phrases using the words. In a review of these options, Farr and Carey (1986) suggested that teachers choose tests presenting words in context with a word content reflecting their instructional program.

  Several standardized tests assess vocabulary in context using a modified cloze format. You may wish to investigate the following: Degrees of Reading Power (DRP); Diagnostic Reading Scales; Woodcock Reading Mastery Tests. Other standardized assessments may offer insights into analysis (Stanford Diagnostic Reading Test; Metropolitan Reading Diagnostic Tests); receptive vocabulary (Peabody Picture Vocabulary Test); content area vocabulary (Tests of Reading Comprehension); or analogical reasoning with vocabulary (Woodcock Reading Mastery Tests).

- *Modified administration of standardized tests.* In using any vocabulary test, you must be clear about whether vocabulary knowledge or decoding is being assessed. An effective practice for making this determination is first to administer a test to the student in writing and then to assess further by administering the same test orally to factor out decoding as a problem. When students have incorrect answers, probe the answers. Tests may also be administered in an untimed format to have a measure of "power" rather than of speed.

- *Word list scans.* Use vocabulary lists from a prior or current year's textbook or reading series. Choose every tenth word from the list and ask the students for a meaning. If possible, locate the word in context so that students can go back to the context if the word is not known initially or if context is needed to unravel multiple meanings or figurative usage.

- *Cloze testing.* Cloze passages from a text about to be used for instruction can tell you if the vocabulary level will be difficult for your students. We have shared examples of cloze assessment in Chapter 6.

Using postreading probes, a pattern of vocabulary difficulty may emerge. Students who are lacking both concepts and labels need rich conceptual instruction to develop both simultaneously. Students who have some conceptual knowledge but overgeneralize or undergeneralize terms can benefit from work elaborating categories and attributes of words. Students who have difficulty with multiple meanings may need direct instruction with terms used in particular domains. And last, students who have difficulty using the context to pick up attribute and category cues for words may need experience and instruction with using context to tease out word meanings.

Steps in Individual Vocabulary Assessment

If you have a hunch that a student is having difficulty with vocabulary, you may wish to prepare a vocabulary probe to use in conjunction with an extended passage reading. The passage must be long and complicated enough to provide sufficiently rich context for this kind of analysis. After preparing an extended passage (see Chapter 8), follow these steps for preparing a vocabulary probe:

Step 1: Preparation: Selection of Words. Select three to eight words (depending on passage length) for an initial appraisal of vocabulary knowledge. The words should be important to the passage that is chosen from instructional material—that is, they should convey information pertaining to the main ideas and essential details. Figurative expressions and phrases of a technical nature should also be selected because they too represent possible obstacles to comprehension. Basic to this step, then, is a careful reading of the passage to identify its central content. You must also be alert to the occurrence of common words used in uncommon or metaphorical senses. In selecting words for presentation, try to distinguish between those explained by the context of the passage and those without such illuminating contexts. The former can be used to probe for context use strategies, whereas the latter words are more appropriate for estimating the difficulty of a particular material for student use.

Step 2: Administration: Presentation of Words. Following the comprehension questions, present each word from your selected list to the student separately after asking the comprehension questions. Ask "What does _____ mean?" or "What is a _____?"or any other probe questions. For words with multiple meanings, you may also provide the context in which the word occurred. If the student cannot formulate a definition, or leaves some doubt as to the accuracy or fullness of his or her vocabulary knowledge, seek additional information, asking for an exemplary object or situation to which the word would apply or requesting that the student use the word in a sentence. Examples as well as sentences often have to be explored still further. For example, Raymond (see Case 4.1) suggested that the word *sophisticated* could be applied to a truck. Although this usage is potentially correct, further questioning indicated that he thought it was motion (rather than modern design or engineering) that made a truck sophisticated.

Step 3: Preliminary Analysis of Results. In this step note the degree of success the student achieves in defining the words presented in Step 2. If the student does not know as many as half the words presented, you should consider vocabulary knowledge an area of general weakness. The diagnosis does not end there, however. You must also determine the extent to which the unknown words impede comprehension. To do this you must examine the student's incorrect responses to comprehension questions. In particular, you must determine, for each question that was answered incorrectly, whether the information needed to answer it was unavailable to the student because of an unknown word. If this is true for a majority of incorrect responses, then the student's reading difficulty can be attributed to inadequate vocabulary knowledge.

Obviously, you cannot always anticipate the words and ideas that will cause confusion and misunderstanding for a student during your initial selection of words; often the student's responses to questions reveal difficulties that were entirely unexpected. In Raymond's case, for example, Paul, his teacher, did not recognize the word *crude* as a possible source of difficulty in his first analysis of the passage; therefore, he did not include it in the initial set of words presented. In such situations, you should select additional words for presentation to the student during the next step.

You should examine the student's performance on the comprehension questions at this point for evidence that he or she lacked the conceptual knowledge or specific information necessary for general comprehension of the passage. If you find such evidence, formulate questions to explore this possibility and present them during Step 4. This procedure is particularly important when a student's overall comprehension is poor—say 50 percent or less—and specific words do not seem to be directly implicated.

Step 4: Further Assessment. The additional words identified in Step 3 as potential obstacles to comprehension are presented to the student as in Step 2. The results will enable you to complete the determination, begun in Step 3, of whether the student answered particular questions incorrectly because he or she did not know the meanings of certain words. The questions devised to explore conceptual knowledge and information are also administered in this step. Further, discussing the words explained by context and letting the student refer to the text can provide a window from which you can evaluate the student's context use strategy. These results can give you further insight into the source of his or her comprehension difficulty.

Steps 5 and 6: Interpretation and Instructional Plan. The results of Steps 3 and 4 combined serve as the basis for your final evaluation of the role of vocabulary knowledge in the student's reading difficulties. If the student cannot answer questions about the passage because he or she lacks vocabulary knowledge, then vocabulary knowledge represents an area of weakness in reading for the student and warrants instructional emphasis. For instructional purposes, the passage may be too difficult for this student because of a vocabulary knowledge deficit. You can determine this by assessing the severity of the student's comprehension loss. If the loss is limited in scope, as in Raymond's case, then passages of equivalent difficulty will probably be suitable for instruction as long as the student learns important words before reading. On the other hand, if the loss in comprehension is widespread, extending to information not specifically related to unknown words (as will be seen when we look at Tanya, Case 4.2), then the student should be assigned an easier level of materials.

Let's look now at our first case. As we progress through the analysis, stop at the "Pause and Reflect" points to develop your own assessment ideas for Raymond. If you are working with a group, develop your own interpretation, then share and compare.

case 4.1

Raymond

Raymond is a seventh grader whose work in school is generally above average. However, he is ambitious and expresses some concern about his reading ability. His teacher did an assessment to identify areas of his performance that might be strengthened through specific instruction.

Preparation

An expository passage from his seventh-grade text, entitled "Kinds of Housing" (275 words in length), was selected for Raymond to read. It is shown in Figure 4.2 along with the comprehension questions, which include vocabulary questions.

figure 4.2 • Diagnostic Reading Passage: Raymond

Kinds of Housing

With a few exceptions, environment determines the kinds of shelter people choose. So, houses are usually built from materials that are most readily available in the surrounding areas.

The temporary dwelling, as its name suggests, is not built to last. Nomads, people who are always on the move, build temporary dwellings. For example, Native Americans of the plains developed the tepee made of buffalo hides. When buffalo were plentiful, they were an important food source. To avoid waste, Native Americans found a practical use for the hides of the animals. When the tribe moved on, the tepees were left behind.

The grass lean-to is favored by the Bush people of the Kalahari Desert. It is made from grasses and sticks found in the area in which they live.

There are two kinds of permanent housing: crude and sophisticated. Igloos, log cabins, and adobe huts are crude permanent housing. They are built to last. The surfaces, however, are rough and unfinished.

The igloo is a dome made of blocks of hard-packed snow. The snow acts as an insulator. It makes the igloo surprisingly warm.

Log cabins were common during America's westward expansion. As settlers headed west, the thick forests provided timber for housing.

Adobe is sun-dried mud. Adobe huts are found in warm, dry areas, such as parts of Mexico and the American Southwest.

Sophisticated permanent housing can be made from many materials. Homes with concrete foundations are built to last from owner to owner. Very often, these houses have a framework of wood, iron, or steel. The location of steel mills and ironworks often determines the areas where this housing is found.

Source: "Kinds of Housing" from *Taking Flight* copyright © 1983 Margaret Earley, Donald Gallo, and Gwendolyn Kerr reprinted by permission of Houghton Mifflin Harcourt Publishing Company.

4.1   Raymond's teacher, Paul, selected six words based on a conceptual analysis of the passage. The first, *environment,* is important for understanding the thesis of the passage. The second word, *determines,* is central in understanding the main idea of the passage, that environmental conditions influence the nature of housing. The third, *available,* is a general vocabulary word that is important for understanding why kinds of housing vary according to the locale. The fourth, fifth, and sixth words—*temporary, permanent,* and *sophisticated*—represent major concepts that distinguish major types of housing. Paul did not include the word *insulator* both because the insulating property of snow was deemed incidental to the main point of the passage and because the meaning of *insulator* was explained in the sentence following the one in which it was introduced. This is an example of the type of word that can be used to explore contextual strategies.

pause and **reflect**
Which words would you choose as central content words for Raymond's assessment?

Paul also identified *adobe, igloo,* and *nomads,* also well explained by the context of the selection. Paul can ask Raymond to locate clues to the word's meaning in the passage during the comprehension probe if vocabulary knowledge appears to be a problem.

The preparation stage involved selection of key vocabulary items as well as development of comprehension questions (to be discussed in the next two chapters). These are shown, together with the vocabulary items, in Figure 4.3; the expected answers are in parentheses. The first nine questions can be answered from information either stated or implied in the text; the remaining three require interpretation or application of text information.

Administration

Raymond read the passage aloud while Paul recorded his errors and noted the amount of time he took to read it. The comprehension and vocabulary knowledge questions were administered immediately thereafter. Raymond's responses are shown in Figures 4.4 and 4.5. You should study his answers to make a tentative judgment about the adequacy of his comprehension and vocabulary knowledge.

Preliminary Analysis

Print Skill. Raymond had difficulty decoding only three words, or fewer than 1 percent of the words in the passage. Two miscues involved inserted and omitted sight words that did not alter the meaning of the passage. The third was potentially more serious; it involved the mispronunciation of the word *determines,* with the third syllable pronounced like the word *mines.* Raymond read the passage in 2 minutes and 12 seconds, at a rate of 125 words per minute. This is within the average range for seventh graders. On the basis of this evidence, Raymond's print-processing strategies seem to represent an area of strength.

pause and **reflect**
Look at Raymond's responses to the comprehension questions in Figure 4.4 and to the vocabulary knowledge questions in Figure 4.5. How would you evaluate his overall comprehension? Is lack of vocabulary knowledge affecting his comprehension?

Comprehension. Of the nine questions that pertained to text information, Raymond answered five

figure 4.3 • Comprehension and Vocabulary Knowledge Questions: Raymond

1. **a.** What determines the kind of shelter people choose? (environment; available materials)
   b. Where do we usually get the materials we build houses from? (environment; surrounding area)
2. What is a temporary dwelling? (one that is not built to last)
3. What are the people called who build temporary dwellings? (nomads)
4. Why do some people build temporary dwellings? (they are always on the move)
5. What are the two types of permanent housing? (crude and sophisticated)
6. What is the difference between crude and sophisticated permanent housing? (crude are rough and unfinished; sophisticated are made from modern materials)
7. Name some types of crude permanent housing. (igloo, adobe, log cabin)
8. What are some materials sophisticated permanent housing is made of? (wood, iron, steel)
9. What determines where sophisticated permanent houses are built? (location of materials)
*10. If you had the choice between living in an igloo, a log cabin, or an adobe hut, which would you choose and why? (discuss climate and comfort)
*11. Of all the types of housing mentioned in the passage—temporary and permanent, crude permanent, and sophisticated permanent—which type do you live in? (permanent sophisticated)
*12. Do climate and environment still govern what materials we use to build houses today? (discuss role of climate and environment and today's construction)
    *Beyond-text question

Vocabulary Knowledge
Key Concept Words
1. environment
2. determines
3. available
4. temporary
5. permanent
6. sophisticated

Contextually Explained
7. insulator
8. adobe
9. igloo
10. nomads

correctly and two incorrectly (items 6 and 8). His answers were only partially correct on the remaining two questions (items 1 and 9). The partially correct answers involved use of examples rather than the more general formulations called for by the questions. Thus, Raymond's comprehension score (6 out of 9) was below 75 percent. Is there a possibility that his incorrect

figure 4.4 • Responses to Comprehension Questions: Raymond

$\frac{1}{2}$ **1. a.** $\frac{1}{2}$ What determines the kind of shelter people choose? (environment; available materials)
RESPONSE: It can be the grounds, maybe grass or sand; and like if it's cold or sunny.

    b. $\frac{1}{2}$ Where do we usually get the materials we build houses from? (environment; surrounding area)
RESPONSE: Sometimes we can make it. Like the log cabins, you could get it from the trees around you. The igloos, you could pack the snow yourself.

✓ **2.** What is a temporary dwelling? (one that is not built to last)
RESPONSE: It's not built to stay long.

✓ **3.** What are the people called who build temporary dwellings? (nomads)
RESPONSE: Nomads.

✓ **4.** Why do some people build temporary dwellings? (they are always on the move)
RESPONSE: They are always moving around.

✓ **5.** What are the two types of permanent housing? (crude and sophisticated)
RESPONSE: Crude and sophisticated.

✗ **6.** What is the difference between crude and sophisticated permanent housing? (crude are rough and unfinished; sophisticated are made from modern materials)
RESPONSE: Not sure—crude are built to stay longer and sophisticated is not that long.

✓ **7.** Name some types of crude permanent housing. (igloo, adobe, log cabin)
RESPONSE: Log cabin, adobe hut, igloo.

✗ **8.** What are some materials sophisticated permanent housing is made of? (wood, iron, steel)
RESPONSE: I think one of the houses are igloos made out of snow—or I think wood. [Anything else?] Steel.

$\frac{1}{2}$ **9.** What determines where sophisticated permanent houses are built? (location of materials)
RESPONSE: Well, if they were wood, they would be by a forest.

$\frac{1}{2}$ ***10.** If you had the choice between living in an igloo, a log cabin, or an adobe hut, which would you choose and why? (discuss climate and comfort)
RESPONSE: Igloo, or log cabin.... Well, I would choose an igloo because it keeps you warm. Maybe a log cabin; it was built like a house—and that's what we mostly live in, like in cabins in the woods. [So, which would you choose?] Log cabin 'cause it's built like a house.

✓ ***11.** Of all the types of housing mentioned in the passage—temporary and permanent, crude permanent and sophisticated permanent—which type do you live in? (permanent sophisticated)
RESPONSE: I think sophisticated. [Is it permanent or temporary?] Permanent.

✗ ***12.** Do climate and environment still govern what materials we use to build houses today? (discuss climate, environment, today's construction)
RESPONSE: Not sure. [Do you think people can build any kind of house no matter what the climate is?] Well, not exactly—don't know how to explain it.

*Beyond-text question

f i g u r e 4 . 5 • Responses to Vocabulary Knowledge Questions: Raymond

✓ **1.** *environment*
  RESPONSE: The things around you.

✗ **2.** *determines*
  RESPONSE: They…say it, they predict.
  TEACHER: Can you use the word *determines* in a sentence?
  RESPONSE: He determined that the number was gonna be five.

✓ **3.** *available*
  RESPONSE: That is…. I can't explain it.
  TEACHER: Then use it in a sentence.
  RESPONSE: This pen is available for anybody that wants to use it.

✓ **4.** *temporary*
  RESPONSE: It's not built to stay long.

✓ **5.** *permanent*
  RESPONSE: That it stays there…the house stays up longer.

✗ **6.** *sophisticated*
  RESPONSE: I don't know the meaning of that word from the other thing, but I think
              I know another meaning.
  TEACHER: O.K. Tell me the meaning you know.
  RESPONSE: Well, I don't know how to explain it.
  TEACHER: Could you put it in a sentence?
  RESPONSE: This is a sophisticated truck.
  TEACHER: What does that mean about the truck?
  RESPONSE: That it's in a kind of motion or something. A kind of way.

(or incomplete) answers were due to unknown words? We believe it will
be useful for you to consider this issue before reading on; in particular, it is
important to examine the way in which information pertinent to the questions Raymond missed was presented in the passage.

Raymond's incorrect responses to the comprehension questions suggest that he might be confused over the terms *crude* and *sophisticated*.
In response to the question of the difference between these two types of
housing (item 6), he replied that "crude is built to stay longer and sophisticated is not that long." In addition, he could not remember the kinds of
materials used in sophisticated housing (item 8), a plausible consequence
of unfamiliarity with this term. Again, to gain experience with the diagnostic process, examine Raymond's responses on the vocabulary knowledge
assessment at this point. Is there corroborating evidence that vocabulary
knowledge interfered with his comprehension?

Vocabulary Knowledge. Of the six words selected for assessment, there
were only two that Raymond could not define: *sophisticated* and *determines*.

For *sophisticated,* he thought that he knew "another meaning" for it—other than the one intended in the passage—but the meaning he gave ("a kind of motion") was incorrect. Note that the passage characterizes *crude* permanent housing (as in igloos, log cabins, and adobe huts) as "rough and unfinished" and later states that *sophisticated* houses have concrete foundations and frameworks made of wood, iron, or steel. Thus, the meaning of *sophisticated* in the sense of smooth, finished, and involving advanced technology is not given; this must be inferred from the contrast with *crude.* Raymond was evidently unable to make this inference; possibly he did not know what *crude* meant.

Because Raymond's difficulties on the comprehension questions seemed to be caused by his limited understanding of such words as *determines, crude,* and *sophisticated,* Paul decided to focus the further assessment on his vocabulary knowledge. In addition to assessing Raymond's understanding of *crude* and further specifying his knowledge of *determines,* Paul planned to explore his understanding of the words *plentiful, readily,* and *insulator.*

pause and reflect

How would you use the same passage to further assess Raymond's vocabulary knowledge? Can you think of any way to explore his ability to use context? Compare your choices with those of Paul.

Further Assessment

The next day, after having Raymond reread the passage, Paul asked what *crude* meant. Raymond replied that *crude* "was a kind of housing" (as stated in the text), and he recalled the three examples that were given in the passage. Further questioning revealed that he had never before heard the word used nor could he use it in a sentence himself. It now seemed reasonable to consider Raymond's difficulty with item 6 on the comprehension test as stemming primarily from the unfamiliarity of *crude* and *sophisticated.* Without prior knowledge of these two words, Raymond could only assume that the difference in the materials used in these two types of housing made for a difference in degree of permanence. Although the terms *rough* and *unfinished* were used in the passage to describe crude housing, he evidently failed to relate these words to the meaning of *crude.* Consequently, he could not, in turn, grasp the idea that *sophisticated* was the opposite of rough and unfinished.

In the case of *determines,* Raymond seemed to know what it would mean in the context of people making decisions or predicting outcomes, but he seemed unable to grasp the idea that existing conditions could (so to speak) do the same:

> **Paul:** The passage states the environment determines the kinds of housing people choose. What does *determines* mean?
>
> **Raymond:** If they lived in a cold place, that would show that they lived in an igloo. If it was hot, that would say that they would live in a hut maybe.
>
> **P:** Okay. Then what would *determine* the kind of shelter people choose?
>
> **R:** Well, like the people who run the city, they can choose if they wanted brick or wood.
>
> **P:** Yes. But what does *determine* mean?
>
> **R:** They . . . say it, they predict.
>
> **P:** Can you use the word *determines* in a sentence?
>
> **R:** He determined that the house was gonna be wood.

Thus, it was not so much the meaning of the word itself that gave Raymond difficulty; it was rather the underlying concept, that environmental conditions could set limits on people's choices, that escaped him. His failure to grasp this concept could explain his inability to give generalized answers to the questions, "What determines the kind of shelter people choose?" and "Where do we usually get the materials we build houses from?"

To explore further the possibility that vocabulary knowledge was a limiting factor in Raymond's comprehension, Paul asked him to define several other words. Raymond knew that *plentiful* meant "there is a lot." However, for *readily,* he said, "that it's done, finished, used . . . I'm not sure." And for *insulator,* he understood that it was related to keeping warm but thought it was "a type of machine, a heater." Further, he could not pick out any clue sentences in the selection (such as, "The snow acts as an insulator") to suggest whether his idea of a machine made sense. Paul continued to probe context use. Raymond knew the word *igloo* but couldn't define *nomad* or *adobe.* When he reinspected the passage, he was able to locate their meanings, which were explicitly cued by the context. Although his unfamiliarity with these words did not interfere directly with his overall passage comprehension, the words provided additional evidence that his vocabulary knowledge was somewhat inadequate. With respect to context use strategies, when Raymond was allowed to look back, he could

pause and **reflect**

How would you pull together your information on Raymond to explain your analysis to Paul? What instructional suggestions would you give?

locate and use contextual information that was quite explicit, but he had a harder time picking up contextual clues that were given less explicitly and located across the selection.

Interpretation

Raymond's responses to the vocabulary knowledge and comprehension questions are summarized in Figure 4.6. The summary indicates that Raymond's comprehension (67 percent) is somewhat below the instructional range (75–89 percent comprehension), but not at his frustration level (less than 50 percent; see Table 8.1). When comprehension falls within the borderline range between instructional and frustration levels, it is appropriate to consider whether additional instructional support, directly in the major area of reading difficulty, may enable Raymond to read passages similar to this one with adequate comprehension.

Raymond's performance on the initial administration of the questions and during further assessment indicates that he has difficulty in the area of vocabulary knowledge. Generally, he is able to process text with good understanding. However, when the text and/or the questions used to assess comprehension involve terms that are unfamiliar to him, his comprehension is not entirely adequate. For example, he misconstrued the salient features of and difference between "crude" and "sophisticated" housing. Similarly, although he understood the use of available materials in the specific instances cited in the passage, he did not grasp the general principle these instances exemplified. In both these failures of comprehension, unknown words were directly implicated. Raymond was also unable to employ the context scanning strategies necessary to monitor or supplement his understanding of words.

Instructional Plan for Raymond

Because of his relative strength with print, the passage represents an appropriate level of difficulty for instructional purposes as long as important word meanings are discussed before the material is read. Paul's instruction for Raymond should focus on two major areas: First, the development of word meanings should be emphasized during prereading and postreading by analyzing features to extend word meanings. Second, systematic instruction should be developed in the area of using text information to infer word meanings by analyzing the words in context (Blachowicz & Zabroske, 1990). Examples of the kinds of instruction Paul used with Raymond are included later in this chapter. ■

COMPREHENSION–VOCABULARY KNOWLEDGE SUMMARY

Name Raymond Grade 7 Date Feb.

Book/Page Exploring Paths 82-83 Level 13

COMPREHENSION

6 / 9 67 % Correct

Level: Independent Instructional (Borderline) Frustration

A. Retelling: Complete Main Idea Partial (Inadequate)

Comments: Missed main idea

B. Text-Related Comprehension

Item #	Response	Further Assessment (Comments)	Item #	Response	Further Assessment (Comments)
1	½	Examples rather than main idea	6	X	
2	✓		7	✓	
3	✓		8	X	
4	✓		9	½	
5	✓				

C. Beyond-Text Generalization

Item #	Response	Further Assessment (Comments)	Item #	Response	Further Assessment (Comments)
10	½		12	X	
11	✓				

VOCABULARY KNOWLEDGE

5 / 10 50 % Correct

Item Tested	Response	Comments	Item Tested	Response	Comments
environment	✓		crude (P)*	X	never heard word before
determines	X		plentiful (P)	✓	"a lot"
available	✓		readily (P)	X	defined "ready"
temporary	✓		insulator (P)	X	knew relation to warmth
permanent	✓		adobe (P)	✓	} could use context to find
sophisticated	X		nomads (P)	✓	

* Prefers to probe items

EVALUATION

A. Comprehension: Remembered examples and details but did not grasp the main idea of the passage; problems are directly related to unknown words.

B. Vocabulary Knowledge: Deficiencies in word knowledge currently interfere with comprehension; prereading activities focused on vocabulary development should improve comprehension.

case 4.2

Tanya

Tanya is a seventh grader who has been in the United States for four years and whose home language is not English. Though Tanya is friendly and talkative before and after class, in class, where seventh-grade materials are used, her performance is erratic. Sometimes she is an active participant; at other times she is silent and withdrawn. Paul decides to use a seventh-grade text to determine whether the level of the material is appropriate for Tanya as well as to explore the nature of her difficulty.

Preparation

Paul selected a passage entitled "And Then There Were None" from the *Bookmark Reading Program,* which was being used for class instruction. The passage, 342 words in length, is shown in Figure 4.7. Paul prepared both word meaning and comprehension questions to be administered after Tanya read the passage. Before proceeding, compare the words you selected with those Paul chose: *specimens, slaughtered, surviving, refuge, prospective, immense,* and *extinct.*

> **pause and reflect**
>
> Which words would you choose for assessment from Figure 4.7? Would they have been different from the ones Paul chose? Why?

Administration

Tanya read the passage in three minutes, a rate of 98 words per minute. The record of her oral reading is given in Figure 4.8. Examine the evidence to decide whether print translation represents an area of reading difficulty for her.

Her comprehension and word knowledge responses are shown in Figure 4.9. Examine this evidence to formulate tentative answers to the following three questions. First, is Tanya experiencing difficulty with reading comprehension? Second, is her knowledge of word meanings limited? Third, if she is experiencing difficulty with both comprehension and word knowledge, is there evidence that her inadequate knowledge of word meanings accounts for her comprehension difficulty?

> **pause and reflect**
>
> Look at Tanya's responses in Figures 4.9–4.11. How would you analyze her print skill, comprehension, and vocabulary knowledge? What would you assess further?

figure 4.7 • Diagnostic Reading Passage: Tanya

And Then There Were None

In 1534, a French sea captain reported that his men had killed more than a thousand "northern penguins" in a single day. But the bird to which the captain referred was not a penguin at all. It was the great auk, which at one time nested safely by the millions from Newfoundland to Scandinavia. Today the only specimens are in museums.

Like the penguin, the great auk could not fly but was a powerful swimmer. Each season, a female laid only one enormous egg, measuring about five inches long. Fully grown, a great auk stood three feet tall.

Originally, the great auk's largest nesting ground was an island off the eastern coast of Newfoundland. But by the early 1800's, fishermen had completely destroyed them. They used the birds' bodies for food or rendered them into cooking oil.

While the Napoleonic wars were raging across Europe, ships were sailing from Reykjavik, Iceland, to nearby Penguin Island, the second largest great-auk nesting colony, to kill the birds for food. There, using only large sticks, sailors slaughtered the proud birds by the thousands. Then, in the spring of 1830, another terrible blow struck the few great auks still at Penguin Island. The island just disappeared beneath the frigid ocean waters. Most of the surviving great auks took refuge on the small island of Eldey. This island was not far from where their home had been.

But Eldey was not to remain their home for long. The birds had become famous in Europe. Collectors paid immense sums for great auk skins throughout the 1830's. In 1884, Carl Siemson of Reykjavik, an agent for prospective buyers, offered a large cash reward in hopes of getting just a few more skins of the almost extinct bird. A daring Icelandic fisherman answered the challenge and went to Eldey with a small crew. There, he looked for and finally discovered two great auks. He promptly killed them both. Soon after, he returned to Reykjavik to collect his reward; 100 crowns ($60) for the last two great auks on earth.

Source: From *Exploring Paths: Skills Reader,* HBJ Bookmark Reading Program, by Margaret Early, Donald Gallo, and Gwendolyn Kerr, copyright © 1979. Passage by Mark Wexler, copyright © 1974 by the National Wildlife Federation. Reprinted by permission of Houghton Mifflin Harcourt School Publishers.

Preliminary Analysis

Print Skill. The results from Tanya's oral reading are summarized in Figure 4.10, which shows a total of 18 oral reading errors. Of these, five were sight word errors, mainly insertions and omissions. A few of the sight word errors seemed to result when she was attempting to pronounce a difficult name; the others are typical of mature readers and do little harm to meaning. The majority of miscues were in response to content words, and almost half of these were responses to somewhat unusual names. The others involved important content words (e.g., *extinct, rendered, refuge, prospective*). These errors may indicate some difficulty with the pronunciation of multisyllabic words. On the other hand, she pronounced many difficult content words accurately (e.g.,

figure 4.8 • Record of Oral Reading: Tanya

And Then There Were None   18

In 1534, a French sea captain reported that his men had killed more than a thousand

"northern penguins" in a single day. But the bird to which the captain referred was not a

penguin at all. It was the great auk, which at one time nested safely by the millions from   1

Newfoundland to Scandinavia. Today the only specimens are in museums.

   Like the penguin, the great auk could not fly but was a powerful swimmer. Each season, a

female laid only one enormous egg, measuring about five inches long. Fully grown, a great

auk stood three feet tall.   · 1

   Originally, the great auk's largest nesting ground was an island off the eastern coast of

Newfoundland. But by the early 1800's, fishermen had completely destroyed them. They

used the birds' bodies for food or ~~rendered~~ them into cooking oil.   1

While ~~the Napoleonic~~ wars were raging across Europe, ships were sailing from ~~Reykjavik~~,   4

Iceland, to nearby Penguin Island, the second largest great-auk nesting colony, to kill the

birds for food. There, using only large sticks, sailors slaughtered the proud birds by the

thousands. Then, in the spring of 1830, another terrible blow struck the few great auks still at

Penguin Island. The island just disappeared beneath the frigid ocean waters. Most of the

surviving great auks took ~~refuge~~ on the small island ~~of Eldey~~. This island was not far from   3

where their home had been.

But ~~Eldey~~ was not to remain their home for long. The birds had become famous in Europe.   1

Collectors paid immense sums for great auk skins through out the 1830's. In 1884, Carl   1

~~Siemson~~ of ~~Reykjavik~~, an agent for prospective buyers, offered a large cash reward in hopes   3

of getting just a few more skins of the almost ~~extinct~~ bird. A daring Icelandic fisherman   1

answered the challenge and went to Eldey with a small crew. There, he looked for and ~~finally~~   1

discovered two great auks. He promptly killed them both. Soon after, he returned to   1

~~Reykjavik~~ to collect his reward; 100 crowns ($60) for the last two great auks on earth.   ✗ 0 *

* Miscues occurring more than twice were not counted.

Source: From *Exploring Paths: Skills Reader,* HBJ Bookmark Reading Program, by Margaret Early, Donald Gallo, and Gwendolyn Kerr, copyright © 1979. Passage by Mark Wexler, copyright © 1974 by the National Wildlife Federation. Reprinted by permission of Houghton Mifflin Harcourt School Publishers.

Comprehension

½ **1.** What is this passage about? (the great auk; its extinction)
RESPONSE: About two auks.

X **2.** In what part of the world did the great auks live? (Newfoundland, Scandinavia, Iceland, etc.)
RESPONSE: On an island. [Do you know where it was?] No.

X **3.** When did the events in the story take place? (1500–1800)
RESPONSE: Don't know.

½ **4,**X**a.** What did the great auks look like? (penguins)
RESPONSE: Like hawks; big birds.

b. How big were they? (3 feet)
RESPONSE: Three feet.

½ **5.** What problem did these birds have? (hunted and killed)
RESPONSE: They couldn't stay in one place. The place where they were at would disappear under the ocean.

½ **6.** Why were the birds hunted and killed? (for food, cooking oil, skins)
RESPONSE: For the money. If they caught two hawks, they get $50 worth, get 50 coins each. So they got 100 coins, they got $60.

½ **7.** What happened to Penguin Island in 1830 and what did the birds do? (it sank into the ocean; the birds swam to another island)
RESPONSE: It disappeared under the ocean. [What did the auks do when this happened?] They flew away.

½ **8.** Why did Carl Siemson offer a large sum of money for the birds? (he was an agent for prospective buyers of skins)
RESPONSE: He wanted to get some money for himself for the birds. So if he got'em, then he would kill them. Then he would get some money for them and they both would have been even about the money.

✓ **9.** How much were the hunters paid for the last two great auks? ($60)
RESPONSE: (not asked; answered in response to item 6)

X **10.** What happens when animals are hunted and killed with no protection from the law? (extinction)
RESPONSE: They'd be kind of scared. They'd be dead. Men would go to jail.

Vocabulary Knowledge

X **1.** specimens
RESPONSE: Leaves. [Tell me more about it]. I not sure.

✓ **2.** slaughtered
RESPONSE: Kill someone.

✓ **3.** surviving
RESPONSE: They lived on.

X **4.** refuge
RESPONSE: Don't know.

X **5.** prospective
RESPONSE: You're looking at it…thinking about it.
Teacher: Can you use it in a sentence?
RESPONSE: The prospective was easy.

X **6.** immense
RESPONSE: Clever.

X **7.** extinct
RESPONSE: Don't know.

figure 4.10 • Analysis of Oral Reading Responses: Tanya

ORAL READING ANALYSIS

Name Tanya   Grade 7   Date Oct.

Book/Page Exploring Paths   Level 13

A. Difficulty

18 / 342   95 % Correct

Level: Independent   (Instructional)
        Borderline   Frustration

B. Word Learning: Sight Word Errors

Printed Word	Oral Response	Further Exploration	Evaluation
of	at		No problem
finally	foond		
the	[omitted]		
were	[omitted]		
at	[inserted]		

C. Word Identification: Content Word Errors

Printed Word	Oral Response	Further Exploration	Evaluation
great	greatest	✓	generally little difficulty
throughout	through	✓	with word identification
prospective	prospect	✓	when meanings and
			pronunciations of words
refuge	rē-uge	re-fuge	are known.
rendered	reneered	✓	
Napoleonic	Nupolentlc	Nā-pol-e-nic	
② Reykjavik	Reja	Rē-ka-vik	
② Eldey	Italy	✓	
Siemson	Simmons	Simson	
extinct	estic	✓	
discovered	[omitted]	✓	

D. Integration–Fluency

Integration: Most sight word and affixed word errors are contextually appropriate. No use of correction strategies.

Fluency: Rate 342 / 3.5 = 98 wpm   Evaluation Slower than average.

Phrasing Fluent except when she encountered unknown words.

COMPREHENSION–VOCABULARY KNOWLEDGE SUMMARY

Name _Tanya_ Grade _7_ Date _Oct._

Book/Page _Exploring Paths_ Level _13_
_334-335_

COMPREHENSION

_4_ / _9_ _44_ % Correct

Level: Independent   Instructional
      Borderline   (Frustration)

A. Retelling: Complete   Main Idea   Partial   (Inadequate)

Comments: _Remembered only minor details_

B. Text-Related Comprehension

Item #	Response	Further Assessment (Comments)	Item #	Response	Further Assessment (Comments)
1	½		6	½	
2	X		7	½	
3	X		8	½	
4	½		9	√	
5	½				

C. Beyond-Text Generalization

Item #	Response	Further Assessment (Comments)	Item #	Response	Further Assessment (Comments)
10	X				

VOCABULARY KNOWLEDGE

_2_ / _8_ _25_ % Correct

Item Tested	Response	Comments	Item Tested	Response	Comments
specimens	X		extinct	X	unknown concept
slaughtered	X		penguins (P)*	X	"tiny creatures" unfamiliar
surviving	√				
refuge	X		sums (P)	X	could not
prospective	X		reward (P)	√	use context
immense	X		agent (P)	X	to find clues

* P indicates a probe item

EVALUATION

A. COMPREHENSION: _Not probed because basic concepts were unfamiliar_

B. Vocabulary Knowledge _Lacks much background knowledge presumed by this material (e.g., didn't know what penguins looked like; could not locate Newfoundland, Scandinavia, or Iceland on globe; completely unfamiliar with concept of animal extinction)_

Scandinavia, specimens, slaughtered, frigid). Thus, her apparent print translation difficulty may actually reflect unfamiliarity with these words.

Comprehension. The results from Tanya's comprehension questions are summarized in Figure 4.11. Of the nine text-related comprehension questions she was asked, she answered only one (item 9) correctly and six only partially correctly, yielding a comprehension score of 44 percent. Tanya showed some understanding of the destruction of the last two great auks, but seemed unaware that this was the culmination of a series of destructive events. Her grasp of the details of time and place and the auks' resemblance to penguins was also quite limited.

It is not always possible to identify specific words that might be implicated in failures of comprehension. And so it was in Tanya's case. An examination of the passage in relation to the questions she answered incorrectly provided a few good leads regarding specific words that might be sources of difficulty for her. There were, however, two words central to the general topic or theme of the passage that could have interfered with her overall comprehension. The word *specimens* in the first paragraph provided an important clue that the birds were not extinct; unfamiliarity with this word would certainly make the rest of the passage more difficult to understand. Similarly, the word *extinct* in the last paragraph, if unknown, would represent a significant loss of information about the topic at large. In addition a number of place names mentioned in the passage could have been unfamiliar to Tanya, and the auks' resemblance to penguins would have little meaning if she had no knowledge of penguins. Paul planned to explore these items during further assessment. In the meantime, he examined the results of the vocabulary assessment.

Vocabulary Knowledge

As summarized in Figure 4.11, Tanya was able to define or use in a sentence only two of the seven words she was asked about. On this basis, her vocabulary knowledge was definitely an area of weakness. However, the unknown words alone could not fully account for her low comprehension score because they were not directly related to incorrectly answered questions. Additional questioning was undertaken, therefore, during the further assessment that followed, to determine whether Tanya's general information and conceptual knowledge were adequate for this passage.

Further Assessment

This stage focused on Tanya's knowledge of a few key words (e.g., *penguins* and *extinct*) and on her knowledge of the places mentioned in the passage. When asked if she knew anything about penguins, Tanya replied they were tiny creatures but she did not know what they looked like. When shown a picture book of types of birds, she could name the dove and pigeon in English and did recognize the penguin and label it in Spanish. With regard to the problem of extinction, Tanya did not know of any other animals that had been hunted and killed until none were left on earth, and she was unaware that anything was currently being done to protect wildlife from extinction. For example, she assumed that hunting and fishing licenses were primarily for the purpose of raising money and that wildlife preserves were designed to make it easy for people to see the animals. Further, she did not know where Newfoundland, Scandinavia, or Iceland could be found on the globe. Finally, she could not use context to suggest clues to the meanings of *sums* or *agent*.

Interpretation and Instruction for Tanya

Tanya's comprehension of the diagnostic passage was extremely limited, as was her knowledge of important words in it. One of her problems in vocabulary knowledge was lack of the appropriate terms in English for concepts she knew. However, she also lacked some of the basic concepts necessary for understanding the significance of the events described. Paul decided that passages at this level of difficulty were inappropriate for Tanya and began to look for simpler books on the topics under study to use with her. When he followed up with penguin books written at a fourth-grade level of difficulty, her decoding and comprehension were improved.

Bilingual students who do well in informal conversation, as Tanya did, often lack the academic and conceptual vocabulary for academic reading (Huckin & Bloch, 1993; Krashen, 1989). Paul planned to focus on important concepts, background knowledge, and comparison of English–Spanish vocabulary to help Tanya build a conceptual network that would allow her to understand the unit under study. ■

Instruction to Support Vocabulary Development

Within the framework of effective instruction outlined earlier, a wide variety of techniques and activities are possible. In most instructional situations, you would negotiate among various objectives and constraints and make a number of instructional choices based on elements such as the student's initial knowledge level, the importance of the word to the study at hand, and the time available for instruction. All those factors make up what have been called the cost and benefits of instruction (Graves & Prenn, 1986). Both the nature of the vocabulary words chosen for instruction and your purpose—as well as the student's prior knowledge about the words and their base concepts—can influence your decision to choose one technique over another.

Your purpose in working with vocabulary is twofold. A first goal is the development of independent word-learning strategies, such as use of context, references, and word structure. Your students need to build habits of self-reflection and monitoring of vocabulary and concept knowledge. "Do I know anything about this?" and "Is my definition adequate for this context?" become important questions for students to ask themselves.

A second consideration is enlarging the student's conceptual base and recognition vocabulary so that impediments to effective comprehension are removed. If this is a major objective, prereading instruction on key concepts may be called for, especially for those terms that are not well developed by the context, such as the words chosen as assessment words in the case studies of Raymond and Tanya. This goal suggests an alternative instructional decision. Words can be highlighted before readings, and predictive activities generating tentative meanings can be emphasized, so that the reader has a focus for contextual learning. Postreading monitoring, evaluation, refinement, and verification of meaning then become essential elements in the instructional cycle. The words that have well-developed contextual references in a reading selection lend themselves to this focus.

Your task then is to help the students "contextualize" the word in a relevant way. The context created should be drawn from or related to that provided by the text and should draw on what the student already knows to mediate the new learning. For example, when discussing equipment for the unfamiliar game of pelota that is the subject of a reading selection, you may wish to contextualize the words by using the student's knowledge of racquetball or other racquet sports. In a situation where a concept is completely unfamiliar, you may choose to build knowledge first before teaching by analogy. In creating these contexts, students can "hypothesize" the meanings of unknown words from sentence or paragraph contexts before reading the selection or consulting a reference. Alternatively, the concept underlying each unknown word can be discussed before the word itself is introduced. For example, to introduce *assassination,* discussion would begin with the idea of "kill" or "murder" and lead toward the murder of a political figure (Vaughan, Castle, Gilbert, & Love, 1982). Described next are a number of additional strategies for introducing, hypothesizing about, and helping students manipulate words and relate them to real-world contexts. They are designed primarily for showing the interrelationships among word meanings and include opportunities for self-questioning and monitoring.

• Learning Word Meanings from Context

Many of the words we know—perhaps most—have probably been learned spontaneously in the course of general reading and listening experience (Nagy & Herman, 1987). Yet research suggests that vocabulary building is a slow and gradual process (Eller et al., 1988; Gray & Holmes, 1938). This is not really surprising. When we encounter unfamiliar words in a text we are not, in general, inclined to develop and commit to memory precise meanings for them. Because we are attending to passage meaning rather than to individual words, we are more likely to infer vague meanings consistent with the text, or else read around unknown words as long as the passage remains comprehensible. In unusual circumstances we may consult a dictionary or a friend.

McKeown (1985) has documented the basic steps involved in learning from context: noting that an important word is unknown; generating hypotheses about meaning; and cross-checking by reading on, going back, or consulting a friend or reference. Variations of the cloze procedure (Blachowicz, 1977) may be employed or direct instruction with natural contexts or teacher-prepared sentences may be used (Blachowicz, 1993; Buikema & Graves, 1993). In all cases, the process should involve students in predicting and monitoring meanings with a process involving the following:

- Look—before, at, and after the word
- Reason—to connect what students know with the clues from the author
- Predict—a possible meaning
- Resolve/Redo—use what you know, the clues from the author, a reference, to confirm your prediction or start the cycle again (Blachowicz & Zabroske, 1990, p. 506)

Reference use can also be an important tool in learning from context. If reference materials are used *after* a word is encountered in context, students have identified a specific domain ("This word is some kind of animal") or questions to answer ("Could this be a type of deer?") that will help them use the dictionary effectively.

Schwartz and Raphael (1985) have suggested that employing a "concept-of-definition" template can provide a framework for approaching and evaluating contextual learning. Their instructional methodology focuses on having students develop expectations for adequate definitions through the process of filling out a concept-of-definition frame (see Figure 4.12) and models a step-by-step approach to achieving and utilizing such frameworks. A related process, the PAVE (*P*redict, *A*ssociate, *V*erify, *E*laborate) procedure, can assist teachers in strategically connecting contextual and reference learning. With PAVE, students make predictions about a word's meaning, which they verify from context and references (Bannon, Fisher, Pozzi, & Wessel, 1990). Such processes appear productive for the development of context-sensitive independent learning strategies.

• Read-Alouds

For young children, read-alouds are productive for vocabulary development. There has been substantial research on the nature and effects of storybook

figure 4.12 • Word Map

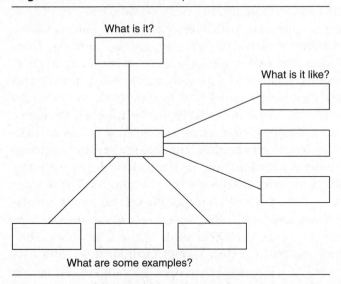

What is it?

What is it like?

What are some examples?

Source: R. Schwartz and T. Raphael, "Concept of Definition: A Key to Improving Students' Vocabulary." *The Reading Teacher, 39,* 1985. Reprinted by permission of the International Reading Association.

reading in both home and school settings (Neuman & Dickinson, 2001). Some of the findings include the following:

- Children can learn the meaning of unknown words through incidental exposure during storybook reading.

- Children learn more words when books are read in small groups.

- Children learn more words when books are read multiple times.

- Children do not benefit from being *talked at* or *read to,* but from being *talked with* and *read with.*

This last research finding suggests a more dynamic view of read-alouds in the classroom. Most researchers agree on several principles related to teaching vocabulary with read-aloud storybook reading in schools. First, there should be some direct teaching of vocabulary during storybook reading in school settings. Second, adult–child discussion should be interactive, and discussion should focus on cognitively challenging ways to interact with the text rather than literal, one-word, or yes/no questions. The students need to be able to contribute to the discussion in a substantial way, and smaller groups of five or six allow for this type of interaction. Third, the rereading of texts in which vocabulary is repeated can maximize learning. Last, the nature of the learning that occurs is different with familiar and unfamiliar books. In an initial reading the children may focus on the plot or storyline. In subsequent readings, the reasons for characters' actions and especially unfamiliar vocabulary may become the focus of their interest.

• Vocabulary Visits

Related to issues of genre, much new research on young students and their learning suggests that the primary curriculum is ripe for content learning and that there now exist many more resources for content reading for young children (Duke, Bennett-Armistead, & Roberts, 2003). One strategy of using content area trade books to build vocabulary is "Vocabulary Visits" (Blachowicz & Obrochta,

2005). "Vocabulary Visits" are virtual field trips in which vivid visuals and books are used to develop concepts and vocabulary for primary-grade students.

Teachers assemble thematic text sets, which, because of their nature, have a repeated conceptually related vocabulary (e.g., *weather—storms, hurricane, thunder, lightning, damp*). They locate or create an engaging visual, blown up to chart size, to stimulate discussion of what can be seen, heard, smelled, tasted, and felt—the senses that students use on an actual field trip; for example: What do you see? (lightning, flash, storm); What do you hear? (crash, boom, thunder); What can you feel? (wet, rain, damp, soggy). These can be constructed as dual-language charts to scaffold the learning of English language learners in the group.

The process involves students in brainstorming to activate what they already know and then engages them in active listening to content books. The teacher works with students to make a chart where conceptually related words are displayed. These labeled charts are used for "active listening" where students are called on to signal "thumbs up" when they hear some of the new words. They also add to the chart as they are read the other books in the text set. Students also take part in semantic sorting and writing activities. "Vocabulary Visits" are motivating, help develop concepts and both oral and written vocabulary for young students, and help them take advantage of contextual information.

Building Conceptual Networks

Along with becoming effective independent users of context, readers must be encouraged to learn and retain new words by connecting them to concepts and words they already know. Methods to help them activate what they already know, establish connections, organize their knowledge, and manipulate it are suggested next. Many of these can also be incorporated into a metacognitive approach to instruction, one that asks students to evaluate what they know before reading, make tentative connections to new words, establish predictions about words they know something about, and construct questions about those that are unfamiliar. Then, after reading, students can go back and evaluate their earlier predictions about word meaning and establish or refine meanings for words they have questions about. Note that all these examples are intended to be applied within the context of a selection being read or a content area being studied. This connection to the topic of their reading provides the contextualization necessary for true vocabulary development.

1. *Brainstorming and Classification.* In activities of this type, students create what might be called a **concept map**, a representation of what they already know in relation to a given word. Working in small groups, students are given a limited amount of time to list as many related words as they can. You then combine the students' contributions into a master list, and the students group the words on the list into categories. You may provide the categories, or the students may derive their own. This technique is often

recommended as an interesting way of introducing a major concept related to a unit of study. Concepts associated with terms such as *propaganda, pollution, nutrition,* and *revolution* lend themselves to this technique because students are likely to have a degree of knowledge in these areas.

Many other options such as exclusion brainstorming, knowledge rating (Blachowicz, 1986), and concept ladders (Gillet & Temple, 1986) are useful as formats for prereading of new vocabulary. You can design all these with a cognitive monitoring component by focusing on some works for prereading prediction and some for postreading evaluation and refinement.

2. *Using Graphic Organizers.* Structured overviews (Barron, 1969), semantic maps and webs (Johnson & Pearson, 1984), and vocab-o-grams (Blachowicz, 1986) all utilize a graphic model to present new words and make explicit the connections among new and already known concepts and structures. You identify the words to be taught and in a diagram show how they are related to each other. You do not present a finished diagram to the students, however. Rather, you build the diagram *with* the students as you explain and discuss each new word. Students participate by recalling prior knowledge, relevant experiences, examples, and so on. The diagram then remains on display as a reference point and an aid to memory while instruction proceeds. Thus the structured overview is actually an "advance organizer" for the key concepts, as represented by the technical vocabulary, to be taught in a content area lesson or unit. As such, it may contain familiar as well as unfamiliar words, relating what is to be taught to what is already known about a particular topic.

3. *Creating Personal Contexts.* Along with techniques stressing semantic and categorical relatedness noted earlier, the creation of personal contexts for words is another way to explore and develop meanings. Developing importance ratings for words (Dole, Sloan, & Trathen, 1995); creating and enacting dramatic contexts (Duffelmeyer, 1980); creating analogies (Bean, Singer, & Cowan, 1985); and self-selection and explanation (Fisher, Blachowicz, & Smith, 1991; Blachowicz, Fisher, Costa, & Pozzi, 1993) are also useful ways to relate new words to what students already know. In these instances, as in the ones listed earlier, you must provide scaffolding and feedback to the learner in the form of information or questions that help monitor and refine meaning.

• Extending and Elaborating Word Meaning

Once words have been introduced and discussed, students need opportunities to experiment with them in meaningful ways and to add new features to their mental word maps. This helps them to refine, extend, and elaborate their meanings and to become comfortable with nuances of usage. Use in oral language and writing are the best ways for students to explore with words. Also useful is going back to refine graphic organizers, concept maps, or other structures used before or during reading. Some simple postreading activities can also help students extend and elaborate meaning. As in all good vocabulary activities, discussion, explanation, and use are critical to real learning.

1. *Insult or Compliment?* (Lake, 1971). This activity works well with adjectives because it deals with the favorable or unfavorable connotations of words. You prepare a list of words and give it to the students. The words may be unfamiliar, in which case students will use a dictionary, or they may be words that have already been defined and discussed, in which case the activity may be considered an application of word meanings. The students' task is to decide whether the use of these words to describe them personally would be a compliment or an insult. You follow these with a discussion.

2. *Choose and Use.* Have students think about the features of words to answer questions that make them think, For example:

    Would a *street urchin* be well dressed?

    Should you trust someone who *bamboozled* you?

    Discussion and explanation should follow along with further use of the words (Hafner, 1977; Beck, McKeown, & Kucan, 2002).

3. *Word Sorts.* In this activity students organize words into categories. You can provide the categories, or the students may be required to search for the relationships among word concepts in order to derive their own.

4. *Post-Structured Overviews.* This activity is somewhat similar to a word sort, but it allows greater freedom in portraying relationships. Students must be familiar with structured overviews or various diagram formats, however, before they can exploit this freedom. Small groups are each given a list of words and a set of 3 × 5-inch cards; each word on the list is written on a card. The students then "work together to decide upon a spatial arrangement among the cards which depicts the major relationships among the words" (Vacca, 1981, p. 251). Discussion of each group's solution follows. You should recognize that more than one solution is possible.

5. *Create Keywords.* Students can generate a "keyword," which will serve as a mnemonic for the definition of the word to be learned (Pressley, Levin, & Miller, 1981). The keyword is a familiar word that is in some way similar in sound to the target word. It may, for example, rhyme with it or begin with the same syllable. The keyword is then used to construct an image (or verbal cue) that represents the meaning of the target word. For example, to remember the definition of *carlin* (an old woman), one might select *car* as the keyword and visualize an old woman riding in (or atop) a car. Then, the word *carlin* would bring to mind *car,* and this in turn would bring to mind the image of the old

woman and, hence, the meaning of *carlin*. Keywords and images are some-times difficult to create, especially for abstract words. However, the activity is likely to be interesting as well as useful to students, at least for some words or in some learning situations. The procedure should be introduced to students accordingly—as one possible strategy for remembering definitions.

summary

We have described procedures for investigating the influence of unknown words on reading comprehension. We have also illustrated the application of those procedures in two case studies. The studies demonstrate how the assess-ment of word knowledge is related to the diagnostic process as a whole; they also highlight the way in which unknown words may underlie incorrect responses to comprehension questions. The first case study showed that spe-cific words may lead directly to incorrect answers. In the second case study, however, the relationship was less direct, and unknown words took their toll in fragmentation of overall comprehension. This latter phenomenon reflects the important principles discussed in the first part of the chapter regarding the nature of word knowledge. It reflects the fact that we ordinarily know much more about word referents than just their definitional attributes and that it is this sum total of knowledge that "drives" the comprehension pro-cess. If this knowledge is inadequate with respect to the major theme of a pas-sage, overall comprehension is likely to be disrupted. (In other words, had Tanya been aware of the *problem* of extinction, even though she did not know the word itself, she might have been able to recognize the events described in the passage as instances of that problem.) This view of word knowledge has clear implications—supported by recent research—for the design of instruc-tion. In general, instruction in word meanings must go beyond definitions and include experiences in which the learner constructs relationships between new words and what he or she knows. The process must be one of active learning, in which self-monitoring of word knowledge and relating this knowledge to real-world situations and events are important components.

try it out

1. Select a student from your class who might have a problem with vocabu-lary knowledge. Choose a diagnostic passage from a reading selection your students will be using next week, such as the ones chosen for Raymond and Tanya. Select key vocabulary and assess. What is your conclusion?

2. Find one of the standardized tests with a vocabulary subtest noted in Appendix D or any one you use in your school. Look over the vocabulary subsection and answer some of the items. Are the words chosen reflective of your curriculum? Is vocabulary presented in context? Are the students asked to respond in a clear and sensible way? Also, find the most recent review for this test in the *Mental Measurements Yearbook* (Buros, 1938–1985) or online at www.unl.edu/buros to give you other views on strengths and weaknesses. What is your overall evaluation of this measure? What insights do you have for its use and interpretation as a vocabulary measure?

3. **Student Portfolio Ideas:** You might ask students to create semantic maps or webs relating some of the central vocabulary in a selection or chapter to keep in their portfolios. This is particularly useful for content area chapters. Another portfolio addition might be an "importance list," a short list of words they choose as key vocabulary from a selection they are currently reading. Along with the list, have students give a short explanation of *why* each word is central to their reading. This helps students develop the habit of self-selection for study and can give you insight into their interpretation of their reading.

4. **For Your Teaching Portfolio:** Add to your teaching portfolio from this chapter. You might include the following:
   - Your responses to "Pause and Reflect" on Raymond and Tanya
   - "Try It Out" number 1 and number 2
   - A sample vocabulary instructional number lesson that you tried and evaluated
   - A response to one of the "For Further Reading" selections from this chapter

for further reading

Beck, I. L., McKeown, M. G., & Kucan, L. (2002) *Bringing words to life: Robust vocabulary instruction*. New York: Guilford. Excellent overall look at vocabulary.

Baumann, J. F., Ware, D., & Edwards, E. C. (2007). "Bumping into spicy, tasty words that catch your tongue": A formative experiment on vocabulary instruction. *The Reading Teacher, 62*, 108–122. Excellent example of what a comprehensive approach to vocabulary instruction looks like in action.

Blachowicz, C., & Fisher, P. (2010). *Teaching vocabulary in all classrooms* (4th ed.). Columbus, OH: Prentice Hall. Describes a framework for vocabulary selection and many ideas for instruction in all classrooms.

Graves, M. F. (2006). *The vocabulary book*. New York: Teachers College Press. Framework for comprehensive instruction with examples.

Johnson, D. (2001). *Vocabulary in the elementary and middle school*. Boston: Allyn & Bacon. Strong chapters on structural analysis and affixes.

Nagy, W. E. (1988). *Teaching vocabulary to improve reading comprehension*. Urbana, IL: National Council of Teachers of English. Excellent ideas for content reading.

5 Reading Comprehension: Its Nature and Development

chapter goals for the reader

- To understand the strategic, constructive nature of reading
- To understand the interaction between reader and author that underlies comprehension
- To appreciate how readers' prior knowledge, language, and understanding of text organization influence their comprehension
- To develop a framework for questioning and develop skill in analyzing text and composing questions

One Classroom

Case 5.0: Omar and Leticia

"You read that perfectly, Omar," Sandra said, gazing fondly at one of her favorite bilingual students. "Now, tell me what you just read."

"I don't know," the little boy stammered. "We don't have those little words in my language."

Sandra was bewildered. She knew that the eager readers in her fourth-grade class had a wide range of abilities, but two of these children really confounded her. Omar could read the text accurately, but he had real trouble understanding passages that were well below the reading level of most of the fourth graders. As he struggled to tell her what a sentence was about, he would look up at her helplessly with liquid brown eyes that broke her heart.

Sandra related to Leticia's problems differently. She had little patience for the smug way Leticia focused on the factual part of a passage. No matter how Sandra probed, she couldn't get Leticia to infer new information from her own knowledge or experience. "It's about Disney World," Leticia insisted.

"But you've been there," Sandra urged. "Can't you think of anything else to say?"

"No," Leticia muttered, chewing on the ends of her curly blond braids. "It's about Disney World. That's what the words say."

Where could she go to solve these puzzles? She knew in her heart that Omar and Leticia were only the tip of the iceberg. All her students struggled with content area text. If there were no clear transitions, they were unable to organize the information they encountered. In previous years, scores on the Science and Social Studies portions of the state tests reflected this difficulty. She found herself abandoning the text and giving lectures on the material. Deep in her heart she knew she had taken over the job of reading and interpreting the text from her students. How could she engage them in reading the text? Perhaps she wasn't asking the right questions.

Sandra decided to focus on four specific questions about reading comprehension:

What could she do to help students who are unfamiliar with the topic of their reading?

How could she help students tackle diverse language that is unlike their native language?

How could her students organize the information they were reading into meaningful patterns?

What strategies do skilled readers use for understanding the text they encounter?

Sandra might feel better if she knew she was not alone. Most teachers encounter these problems in their classrooms. Strategies, knowledge, language, and organization—these are key words for understanding comprehension that are examined in this chapter. ■

chapter overview

This chapter has three parts. The first section presents an overview of the constructive nature of comprehension by focusing on the characteristics of students who comprehend well. This approach reinforces not only the general importance of the reader's prior knowledge, but also focuses on strategic and constructive processes for using that knowledge. The second section explores different factors that influence instruction: the knowledge and language of both the reader and the author, the need to make inferences and elaborations during reading, and the importance of informational organization to comprehension. The third section stresses the importance of questioning and retelling to assessment of comprehension. An awareness of all these issues is critical to the reflective assessment of comprehension, which is discussed in Chapter 6.

chapter outline

We observe comprehension by listening to what students say in discussion, reading what they write in response to reading, probing with questions, and interpreting what they tell us about their own introspection and understanding. If students have comprehension difficulties that do not seem to depend on print or word knowledge, we begin to examine the process of comprehension itself, the process of integrating and organizing information across a text and connecting it with what is already known. Assessing comprehension plays a central role in the diagnostic process. It enables you, the teacher, to estimate the level of materials that are appropriate for instruction and also serves as a backdrop against which word-level skills and knowledge may be evaluated.

The purpose of this chapter is to examine those aspects of comprehension that most directly affect the assessment process: the nature of comprehension as a strategic and constructive activity and as revealed in the behaviors of good readers, factors with the reader and within the text that affect comprehension, and a framework for questions and retellings that reflect what we know about texts and their structures.

Comprehension: A Strategic and Constructive Process

There are many ways to view comprehension. It is "thought-getting and thought manipulating" (Huey, 1908/1968); it is "reasoning" (Thorndike, 1917); it is the constructing and progressive refinement of hypotheses to comprehend, interpret, or evaluate text information. These are all apt descriptions of reading comprehension, and they share the characteristic of being process oriented. The redefinition of reading as an active, constructive process has stimulated a major strand of reading research over the last three decades. Central to this redefinition has been the emphasis on reading as a process by which the reader interacts, or "transacts" (Rosenblatt, 1985), with the text being read.

From this perspective, the process of making meaning is a constructive one (Blachowicz & Ogle, 2008) in which the reader connects what he or she already knows to information and clues supplied by the author in a text. Significant for comprehension, then, is what the reader already knows (commonly referred to as prior knowledge), what the author supplies, and the strategies the reader employs to construct something meaningful through interaction or transaction with the text (see Figure 5.1). Making meaning involves interactions with others; therefore, comprehension is also viewed as a process of social construction (Bakhtin, 1981; Bloome & Egan-Robertson, 1993; Kucan & Beck, 1997; Smith & Wilhelm, 2002). We construct meanings based on our own community backgrounds, goals, and values. Because of this, teachers must put themselves inside the cultures of the children they teach to understand their comprehension difficulties.

figure 5.1 • What Influences Comprehension

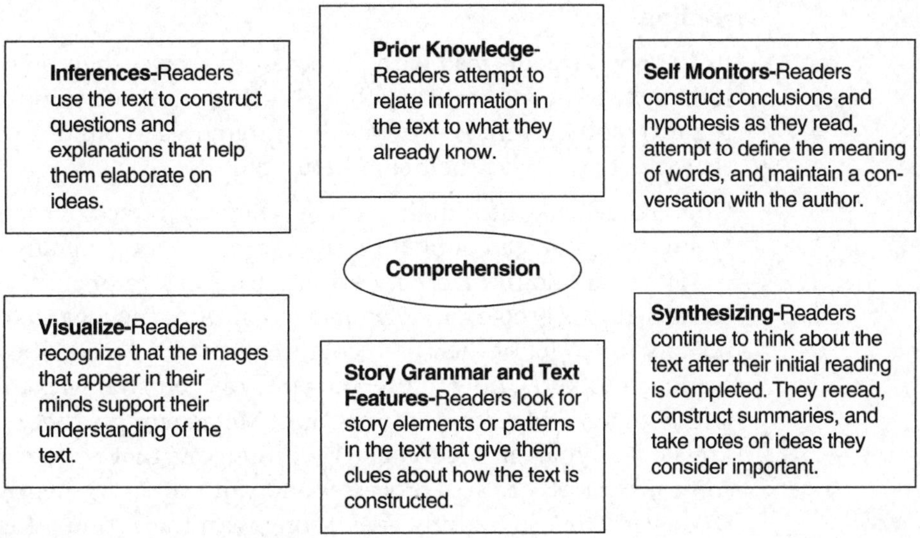

Inferences-Readers use the text to construct questions and explanations that help them elaborate on ideas.

Prior Knowledge- Readers attempt to relate information in the text to what they already know.

Self Monitors-Readers construct conclusions and hypothesis as they read, attempt to define the meaning of words, and maintain a conversation with the author.

Comprehension

Visualize-Readers recognize that the images that appear in their minds support their understanding of the text.

Story Grammar and Text Features-Readers look for story elements or patterns in the text that give them clues about how the text is constructed.

Synthesizing-Readers continue to think about the text after their initial reading is completed. They reread, construct summaries, and take notes on ideas they consider important.

(Adapted from Pressley, 1997)

The strategic aspect of reading is central to understanding comprehension, as it is to all the issues considered in this book. One way to get a "feel" for the strategic nature of reading is to focus on what good readers do. Good and poor readers have been observed and compared in many reading situations: in classroom and experimental reading tasks (Afflerbach, Pearson, & Paris, 2008; Lapp, Fisher, & Grant, 2008; Spiro, 1980; Villaume & Brabham, 2002); while thinking aloud during reading (Kucan & Beck, 1997; McKeown & Gentilucci, 2007; Meyers & Lytle, 1986; Pantaleo, 2007); and when faced with reading difficulty that they must repair (Fisher & Ivy, 2006; Garner, 1987; McClanahan, 2009; Reis, Eckert, McCoach, Jacobs, & Coyne, 2008). Although terminology and research methods differ, there is an emerging consensus about strategic processes that seem characteristic of good readers.

1. Good readers use what they know. They realize that reading is more than remembering exact wording from the text; it also involves reasoning. Adding personal knowledge is a critical component of the comprehension process.

2. Good readers self-question to establish what they *don't* know and what they want and need to know. For many things they read, their knowledge

is limited. Asking good questions helps them make hypotheses, draw analogies from experience, and set some purposes and guidelines for reading.

3. Just as good readers read with purpose—to answer their questions, to fill in knowledge, or to confirm a hunch—they integrate information across the text, add information by making inferences to build cohesion, and use structure to organize their comprehension.

4. Good readers monitor their reading. They keep track of their hunches, change them, reread, look for more evidence, but generally keep a sense of "How am I doing? Do I understand this?" as an ongoing evaluative standard. This process is called metacognition, the idea that good readers are aware of their own cognitive behavior while they are reading and know how to use and control their strategies to read, learn, and remember ideas and information. Metacognitive theory (Paris, 1984; Pressley & Wharton-Mcdonald, 1997) suggests that good readers have some awareness of these processes and can call on a repertoire of strategies when something goes wrong with their comprehension (see Figures 5.2 and 5.3). How explicit or tacit this awareness may be, however, is still a subject of debate.

5. Good readers respond thoughtfully to what they have read. Newly emerging research suggests that readers who respond personally to what they read exhibit high degrees of critical and analytical thinking (Bass & Woo, 2008; Berne & Clark, 2008; Galda, 1990; McGee, 1992; Mendelson, 2007/2008; Paul & Elder, 2004; Van Tassel-Baska, Bracken, Feng, & Brown, 2009). Teachers who are curious about their students' use of strategic reading approaches might try either the metacognitive survey (Figure 5.2) or the metacognitive self-rating sheet (Figure 5.3) with their students as a class or with a student individually.

figure 5.2 • Metacognitive Survey

Reading Strategies

1. What do you do before reading to help you understand?

2. While you read, what do you do if you don't understand something?

3. What do you do when you come to a word you don't know?

4. After you read, what can you do to help you understand better?

figure 5.3 • Metacognitive Self-Rating Sheet

Reading Strategies

Name _____   Date _____

Reading selection:_____

Before reading:

- I use pictures, titles, and headings to help me think about what I'm going to read. Fiction? Nonfiction? What type?
- I think about what I already know about this type of reading selection.
- I set my purpose and/or make predictions before reading. During reading:
- I think about what might come next.
- I revise my predictions and/or make new ones.
- I imagine pictures of what I'm reading.
- I look for author clues to what will happen/be coming.
- I pick out important ideas; keep track of the "drift."
- I skip hard words/parts and try to go on.
- I notice when something doesn't make sense.
- I go back and reread.
- I ask myself questions. After reading:
- I ask myself what I understood.
- I compare what I read with what I predicted.
- I discuss with others or write for myself.

case 5.1

Isaac

Even with a class full of less-skilled readers, Sandra decided to look at a skilled reader first to understand the nature of skilled reading. Isaac's parents were very proud of his reading ability, but they were also concerned about the kind of instruction he was receiving. They did not want him to fall back while Sandra devoted her time to the less-skilled readers. Sandra often let Isaac progress on his own. This made Isaac a good choice for a Think-Aloud (Tierney, Readence, & Dishner, 1995) assessment. In this way, Sandra could confirm her belief that Isaac would prosper with less instruction and more reading experience. The session with Isaac took about ten minutes. Sandra was able to do it during recess time. Sandra asked Isaac to read the story, "The Restless Kangaroo," which appears on pages 201–202 of this text. She asked Isaac to read the story silently and tell her his thoughts as he was reading. It did not take much prompting to get Isaac to talk about his reading. Sandra decided to tape-record Isaac's remarks and transcribe his comments so that she could reflect on them later. The transcription and notes took about ten minutes. Isaac's bright eyes sparkled as he picked up the pages and began reading. Figure 5.4 is a transcript of Isaac's Think-Aloud and Sandra's notes.

figure 5.4 • Isaac's Transcripts and Comments

Oh, I see this is a story about a Kangaroo. I love those animals. They live in Australia don't they?	Accessing prior knowledge, uses the title
Oh, I see, this story takes place in a zoo.	Self questioning, What does he know? What does he want to know?
(He reads silently for a while.)	
Is the mother kangaroo taking the baby out of her pouch? Why would she do that? The story says she's a good mother. Why would a good mother do that?	
Who is Joey?	
(Isaac reads silently for a short time.)	He knows the story is not over…uses the structure of the story to aid understanding.
Umm…Pete is in trouble with the zoo director. I wonder if he will lose his job?	
He's really dedicated to stay up all night after a day's work. He must love the animals. I once tried to stay up all night. It was really hard to do.	A personal response
(He reads some more.)	
The "scritch-scratch" I wonder…is someone coming into the cage? No, it's the baby.… So that's what a joey is…a baby one…I didn't know that before.	More self-questioning…confirms a guess…adding information….
Is the joey getting out of the pouch?	
Yes, he must crawl out and get back in.… I'm going to read back a little… The joey only puts his paw out and takes the rocks in.…	Self-questioning…proposes a possible consequence…rereads to confirm…adjusts his belief…he is aware of the rereading strategy…METACOGNITION!
What are they going to do about that?	
(More reading.)	
Oh, a blanket.… That's a good idea. I think I'd like a joey as a pet. Do you have any more stories like this?	Another personal response…he wants to know more… Oh, a blanket… Note: I must ask Isaac to journal as he reads.

pause and **reflect**

Observe your own reading as you continue this chapter. Which of the five characteristics of good readers do you exhibit? Keep track of the ones you don't understand to see how the chapter clarifies them.

With an investment of ten minutes, Sandra was able to give herself a better sense of what a skilled reader could do. This helped her set her goals for her less-skilled readers. There were some other benefits as well. When Isaac's parents came in for conferences late in the fall, Sandra was able to describe his reading skills to them in detail. She gave Isaac free rein in his reading, and she encouraged him to work independently. After Sandra's description of Isaac's skilled approach to reading, his parents understood why intensive, wide-range reading with more and more challenging text was the best instructional plan for Isaac. The information she shared during the conference also supported their concept of Sandra as an astute professional. ■

What Influences Comprehension?

But what happens when students struggle with comprehension?

From the previous chapters describing the emergence of literacy and the development of print skills, vocabulary, and concept knowledge, we have seen that the influences on the comprehension process can come from many sources—from the reader's knowledge and experience with the world, books, and literacy; from the way the author writes and structures the texts; and from the context or social situation within which the reading is done. When there is a mismatch between the language of the reader and that of the author, when the reader does not integrate information across the text, when the text is badly organized or the reader does not use the organization, or when the reader is not engaged and responsive, comprehension may suffer. Let's look at each of these in turn.

• The Knowledge and Language of the Reader and the Author

The Reader. We noted earlier in this text the importance of experience for the development of the conceptual knowledge on which all comprehension is based. In Chapter 2 the significance of early literacy experiences, such as dramatic play and storytelling, being read to, and early experimentation with writing and reading, are observed. In Chapter 4, the development of the reader's conceptual and vocabulary knowledge is emphasized. All these help readers develop an awareness of the transactional nature of reading and writing and give them pleasure that motivates them to become independent readers and capable users of language. The intertwining of all language functions is a major developmental influence on reading performance.

Certainly reading is intimately related to language. Words that look alike tend to sound alike, and words and sentences have the same meaning when they are written as when they are spoken. Indeed, reading is commonly characterized as "a language process." But what is language? Is it the words we use when we speak? Or the sounds that make up the words? Or is it the organization of words in sentences? The very fact that we can ask these different questions suggests something about the answer: Language involves all these—sounds, words, and sentences along with the meaning they create. (See Figure 5.5.)

Words, of course, have both sound (i.e., phonemes) and meaning. Thus, we can say that language is a system of sounds that conveys meaning. To know a language is to know that system, its phonology.

But the sequence of sounds that make up a word conveys meaning only to those who already know what thing, or action, or quality of things or actions the word stands for. Knowing a language, then, involves some knowledge of its lexicon as well as its phonological workings.

Finally, the sequence of words that make up a phrase or sentence is meaningful only if one knows the third component of language, its syntax. Language, then, is not speaking or listening; these are language behaviors. It is, rather, a three-part system of knowledge that we use when we speak or listen (and when we write or read as well). It is this knowledge that enables us to express our thoughts and feelings (in speech or writing) and to understand others (in listening and reading). In other words, we use our knowledge of language in reading and writing just as we do in speaking and listening. And it is in this sense that we can say, "Reading is a language process."

Imagine taking a book out of the library and finding that the page is covered with jelly. Scratching with your finger, you find a four letter word that starts with *h*.

$$h\_\ \_\ \_$$

You could imagine that the word might be *help, hard, hear, here, home, held,* and so forth. Probably you could generate quite a few words, but you are not likely to predict *hzpq*. In English *h* would never be followed by *z*, *p* would not precede *q*, and *q* would not appear at the end of a word. As a speaker of English, you know that words have both sound and meaning, so you look for a pattern

f i g u r e   5.5 • Components of the Language Process

PHONOLOGY	*LEXICON*	*SYNTAX*
A system of **sounds** that conveys meaning.	What thing, action, or quality of action the **words** stand for.	The meaningful **sequence** of words that make up a sentence.

of sounds that convey meaning. This sound system is phonology, sometimes referred to as the phonological cueing system or the graphophonic system when we talk about sounds and the letters that represent them (Juel & Minden-Cupp, 1999). When you decide a word is a real word in a particular language, you consider it part of the lexicon, the word units in that language.

If you scratch off more jelly and see "the h _ _ _," you can deduce that the word is either a noun, like *home,* or an adjective like *hard* (the hard candy). You can do this because the marker *the* cues your knowledge of syntax, the sequence of words, and types of words that make a sentence meaningful. Revealing more of the sentence, you find "She put the glove on the h_ _ _ of her small child." This causes most of us to think *hand,* because that word would make the whole sentence make sense. We use semantics, or meaning, to help in this decision.

Besides sentence and text context, other types of signals help us when we read. If we were out walking and saw a flashing neon sign with several letters flashing

B _ N _ O

we could make some predictions from the world context. If the sign were flashing over a church hall on a Wednesday night and scores of people were entering the hall carrying heavy purses filled with coins, we might conclude that the word was *BINGO*! If the sign were over the Old Town School of Folk Music when the Bluegrass Boys were playing, *BANJO* might come more readily to mind. This is world context used to help reading comprehension.

Where the author chooses words not in the reader's lexicon or sentence structures unfamiliar to the reader, comprehension can be difficult. If the text context and world context is unfamiliar, comprehension may also suffer.

Because reading and language are so closely related, we sometimes think that reading comprehension—the comprehension of written language—is the comprehension of spoken language. We assume that a student should have no difficulty understanding a written passage as long as the words and sentence structures in it are familiar and express ideas that are within the student's cognitive grasp. But this is only partly true. Reading differs from listening in a number of important ways, and accommodating these differences is part of the process of learning to read. Except in the special case of oral reading in the classroom, reading is a solitary activity whereas spoken language generally involves the presence of another human being. This may be one reason many children find it difficult to concentrate during independent (silent) reading. In addition, written language provides less information: The stress, pause, and intonation of spoken language are absent in reading, as are the relevant social and physical contexts, which supply important nonlinguistic clues (Knoblauch & Johnston, 1990; Johnston, 1997). Reading places the burden of comprehension more squarely on language alone. Children must become aware that written language is processed in much the same way as spoken language—that it relates to real-world situations and can be understood by reference to prior knowledge and experience. Instruction in meaningful and focus conversation can help children link written and spoken language (Berne & Clark, 2008; Evers, Lang, & Smith, 2009; Goldenberg, 1992/1993; Ketch, 2005; Kong & Fitch, 2002/2003; Villaume & Brabham, 2002; Zembat & Sulfikar, 2006).

For the child in the primary grades, the transition from spoken to written language entails a major adjustment over and above the adjustment to the print translation task (Zembat & Sulfikar, 2006). This adjustment is facilitated by the traditional practice of simulating in beginning reading materials the language of ordinary conversation (Evers et al., 2009). In the intermediate grades and beyond, students must adjust to written language that is more precise and tightly organized, more closely reasoned, and more complex in style and content than the language they are likely to hear in ordinary discourse (Berne & Clark, 2008). At all stages of learning to read, students need language and literacy experiences that will help them make the necessary adjustments and develop skill in reading comprehension (Goldenberg, 1992/1993; Ketch, 2005; Kong & Fitch, 2002/2003).

The Author. The author's lexical, linguistic, and structural decisions affect the processes a reader must call into play to understand a selection. That what we read should make sense is self-evident. What is not so evident, perhaps, is that coherence is constructed through the cooperative effort of the reader and the writer; readers need to employ specific strategies to connect the language of the author with their own knowledge and language (Beck, McKeown, Hamilton, & Kucan, 1997; Beers, 2003; Buehl, 2007). Critical to all these strategies is the need to integrate information and to make inferences (Wood, Pressley, & Winne, 1990). The term integration is used here in a somewhat broader sense than in Chapter 2. It refers to the process of combining information across sentences.

pause and **reflect**

What types of games could children play to enhance their understanding of these aspects of reading comprehension?

case 5.2

Sandra

Sandra decided to try a cloze procedure (Blachowicz, 1977; Cain & Oakhill, 2006; Hagtvet, 2003; Mokhtari & Thompson, 2006; Scott, 2009; Senechal, Pagan, Lever, & Ouellette, 2008; Valenzuela & Hilferty, 2007) with her entire class. She took two short stories from the basal reading text. She retyped them, dropping every fifth word in the stories, and presented them to the students. The students were encouraged to work on the first story in small groups. They had fun trying to determine what words would fit in the blanks. Students were invited to work on the second story by themselves. Everyone enjoyed this exercise, and Sandra added the results of the second attempt to each student's reading folder. It became another diagnostic tool to help her understand how much students understood this feature of the reading process. ■

• Integrating Information and Making Inferences

Not only is the language match between reader and author important to comprehension, but so are the processes the reader uses to make a text coherent. Readers need to merge information across the text to make inferences. Terminology relating to these processes differ; for the purposes of this text, we will call making connections when the information is all given "integration." "Inference" will describe the situation when the reader must add information the author doesn't supply. Some authors call both of these instances inferences, the first a text-based inference and the second a text and world knowledge inference (Pressley & Wharton-Mcdonald, 1997; Raphael & Pearson, 1985).

c a s e   5 . 3

Omar and Leticia

Sandra wanted to make aspects of comprehension visible to her students. She decided to introduce a strategy she called "Visible Thinking" to her guided reading group. Omar and Leticia were in this group. Sandra was hoping that both students would expand their understanding of comprehension by experiencing this strategy. Sandra placed the following text in a column on a large piece of chart paper. She covered up the sentences so that only the first was showing :

> Father said, "Happy birthday!"
> as he handed Jimmy a box.
> Jimmy opened up the box.
> There he saw a small brown puppy.

"As I read the sentence, look into your mind and tell me what you are thinking." Sandra read the first sentence. Hands flew up.

"There's going to be a party," Leticia said. "I just had a birthday party with cake and ice cream. It was great!"

Sandra wrote, "Leticia's birthday party" next to the first line. She wrote "Connections" at the top of the chart. "Leticia, you are doing what good readers do. Good readers make connections between the text and their own experiences. You connected your experience to the text." Sandra uncovered the next line.

Omar looked concerned. "In this sentence, who is "he"?

"That's a good question, Omar. The 'he' is a pronoun that refers to 'father' in the previous line. You just did what good readers do. You found something that didn't make sense. We call that an "anomaly." Sandra wrote "Anomalies" at the top of the chart. Next to the second line, she wrote, " 'He' refers to 'Father.' " She drew a line between the two words.

"Is 'the box' a present?" Leticia asked. "At my party, I got presents in boxes."

"Leticia, you also asked a question about 'the box.' Good readers ask questions as they read." Sandra wrote "Questions" at the top of the chart. Next to the second line, she wrote, "Is the box a present?"

Omar's eyes were dancing, "Is it Jimmy's birthday? Is that why Father gave him the box? Father said, "Happy birthday" to him."

Sandra was thrilled. She realized that Omar had just made a powerful inference. He was able to "integrate" the information from one part of the sentence to another. "Omar," she bubbled, "you just made an inference. You took information from one part of the sentence and put it with another. Good readers make inferences." Sandra wrote "Inferences" at the top of the chart. She drew a line from "happy birthday" to "the box." Then she added, "It was Jimmy's birthday." to the chart and uncovered the next line.

"I think this story takes place at their home," Leticia added. "I had my party at home. I think Jimmy is wondering what is in that box. I would want to know what my present was."

"I have the smartest students!" Sandra explained. "Leticia, you are trying to determine the 'story grammar' in this story. You are looking for the setting and the problem in the story. Good readers try to determine what the 'story grammar' is. You are doing what good readers do." Sandra wrote Story Grammar at the top of the poster. Next to the third line, she wrote "Setting: home; Problem: What is in the box?" She uncovered the fourth line and read it aloud.

Now it was Omar's turn, "When you read that line, I can see a cute brown puppy in my mind. It has floppy ears, and it is wagging a long tail!"

Sandra wrote Visualizing at the top of the chart. "Omar, you are visualizing. Good readers make pictures in their minds as they read." She wrote "cute brown puppy" next to the line she had just uncovered.

"Visible Thinking" had taken less than eight minutes, but it had covered almost all the aspects of comprehension. Sandra asked her students to open the little books they had been reading. As they read, they discussed the aspects of comprehension that had been made evident to them (Pressley, 2000). ■

p a u s e and **r e f l e c t**
Stop and think. What kind of instruction would
help Omar? What types of instruction might be
useful for Leticia?

Stop and think. What additional instruction would help Omar?
What other types of instruction
might be useful for Leticia?

Besides integrating information based on author cues such as
referents, readers must also make
inferences by using their own knowledge to provide what the author leaves
unsaid. In the previous sample, Leticia was able to infer that the box is Jimmy's
birthday present, something not explicitly stated by the author but an inference
that would make sense from what the author tells us.

In general, the integrative process enables the reader to store information
more efficiently (in condensed form), and the inferential process determines the
particular way in which information is interrelated (and thus the form in which
it can be condensed). In the example, inferences involved linguistic elements,
spatial relations, and cultural knowledge. But inferences may also involve temporal and causal relations, not to mention many others.

As the example shows, integrative and inferential processes are by no means
unique to written language. Linguistic linkages and spatial, temporal, and causal
relations all appear among statements in ordinary conversation as well as in
connected text. And these relations are inferred on much the same basis in both
cases—on the basis of general knowledge and previous experiences with the
contextual situation. Perhaps it is because these processes are so much a part of
the ordinary flow of everyday language that they have so long been taken for
granted and have become the object of serious study. In any event, like other
aspects of spoken language that are important to reading progress (e.g., vocabulary knowledge and knowledge of sentence structure), it is largely through reading that these processes develop, and it is through their development that a
student is able to understand more and more "difficult" prose.

• Linguistic Devices

The processes of integration and inference are highly dependent on the reader's
store of general knowledge and personal experience. There are, however, certain
linguistic devices used by authors, most notably those related to text structure
and coherence that appear to facilitate the integration of information. A few of
these devices are described next. Comprehension is most likely to break down at
those points in a text where these devices have not been used effectively by the
reader (or writer). (See Figure 5.6.)

1. *Topic Sentence.* A topic sentence at the beginning of a paragraph assists the
   reader in integrating information and points the reader's attention to the

figure 5.6 • Six Linguistic Devices

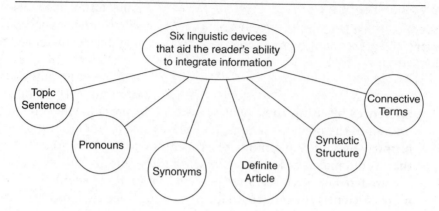

topic of the paragraph and certain concepts in his or her knowledge store. These concepts thus activated serve as sources of information for making inferences about how subsequent sentences are related to the first one and to each other. For example, consider an opening sentence that reads as follows: "Tom slammed the door as he came out of the house wearing old clothes and carrying a bucket of paint." This points the reader to the idea that someone was or will be painting something (as suggested by the old clothes and, of course, the bucket of paint) and that he may be angry, possibly about having to paint. With these ideas in mind, the reader can understand the next sentence—"The barn was a long way off"—as probably telling what was to be painted. If the paragraph is well structured, subsequent sentences will relate back to the slamming of the door as well as expand on the significance of the location of the barn. Thus, the opening sentence establishes a situational or conceptual context within which each sentence may be related to what has gone before.

2. *Pronouns.* Another linguistic device that signals how a sentence is related to earlier material is the pronoun. Typically, an author will make repeated references to the same object, event, or idea. The use of a pronoun in such instances alerts the reader to the commonality of reference and thus facilitates (at least for adults) the integration of incoming information with prior information. The pronoun signals that something is related to "old" information and directs the reader to search his or her memory (or the text) for the previous mention of its referent to integrate the new information with the old. For example, in the following paragraph, the pronoun *some* facilitates integration of the information in the final sentence with the "old" information about "medals."

A photo of Houdini at seventeen shows him proudly adorned with track medals. Although some were real, others were fake. (Krull, 2005, p. 6)

3. *Synonyms and Synonymous Expressions.* Repeated reference to a topic that has already been introduced may also be made through synonyms. This device is a more difficult one for the reader than the pronoun. Although the antecedent of a pronoun may be ambiguous at times, the pronoun itself always clearly signals that the referent has been mentioned before. A synonym, on the other hand, is not marked as another word or expression for something previously mentioned and hence does not instruct the reader to search for its previous mention. If the reader does not recognize, from the referential context, that a word or expression refers to an item mentioned earlier, the integrative process will be disrupted, and there will be some loss in comprehension. For example, notice the word *fear* in the second sentence here:

Houdini decided that his worst enemy was not physical danger but panic. So he practiced hardest at conquering fear—of the dark, the pain, lack of air, the cold. (Krull, 2005, p. 13)

The reader must infer that the word *panic* refers to "fear—of the dark, the pain, lack of air, the cold." This understanding requires an awareness that panic comes from fear, so that panic in individuals can be the cause of fear. Thus, familiarity with the important facets of a referential situation is often required for the reader to recognize coreferents.

4. *Definite Article.* The use of the definite article *the* in a text also marks a distinction between old and new information and thus facilitates comprehension. " 'The' implies that the item now mentioned has a unique and specific referent that has previously been established, and therefore cues the listener/reader to match this item with one already in memory" (Arciuli & Monaghan, 2009, pp. 73–93; Ehri, Cairns, & Zipke, 2009, p. 302; Gourley, 1978, p. 177).
    The following pairs of sentences illustrate how dependent we are on this device:
    a. Yesterday Beth sold her old Ford to a dealer. Jack bought *the* car [the one Beth sold] today.
    b. Yesterday Beth sold her old Ford to a dealer. Jack bought a car [not the one Beth sold] today.

5. *Syntactic Structure.* The structure of a sentence is itself a device by which information may be tagged as new. In general, the information at the end of a sentence is assumed to be the new information. In the simple active sentence, "John loves Mary," the fact that John loves someone is interpreted as old information and the identity of that someone is interpreted as new (Carpenter & Just, 1977, p. 232). Similarly, in the passive counterpart of that sentence (i.e., Mary is loved by John), Mary's being loved by someone is

marked as old information, and the identity of that someone, John, which appears in the last part of the sentence, is the new information being conveyed. When new information is given at the beginning of a sentence, it is often marked as such in the syntactic structure, for example, through "it clefts": It was Mary whom John loved. It was John who loved Mary.

6. *Connective Terms.* The vast majority of words in a language—the nouns, verbs, adjectives, and adverbs, or so-called content words—are referential in nature. That is, they refer directly to particular objects, actions, attributes, and qualities. Every language includes, as well, a small set of words that are relational, sometimes called "function words." Unlike the linguistic devices described earlier, which simply signal the advent of new information related to what has gone before, *relational* words specify the way in which new information is related to the old:

Causal relations are marked by causal conjunctions, "since," "because," "due to." The description of a process include temporal inter-unit links, "first," "next," and "then." Contrastive elaborations may be marked by adversative conjunctions, "however," "on the other hand." List-like elaborations are marked by additive conjunctions, "in addition," "likewise," and "furthermore." Conclusions are preceded by temporal conjunctions, "in conclusion" or "to sum up." Examples are signaled by the additive conjunctions, "for example" and "for instance." (Geva, 1983, p. 385)

While nouns, verbs, adjectives, and adverbs represent the propositional content of a passage, the relational words express its structure and the connections between propositions.

case 5.4

Sandra

Sandra knew that understanding these types of linguistic devices would help her students make greater meaning of their texts. And she knew that Omar and Leticia were especially confused about these kinds of relationships. Sandra decided to approach this aspect of written language with the whole class. She believed that helping the entire class become aware of how language works would be useful for everyone. She copied the opening paragraphs of the current basal selection and worked with the entire class to find the topic sentence. They noted that the topic sentence appears early in the selection. As the class read the selection together, they looked for ideas that related to the topic sentence and made note of them as well. When the students finished reading, they checked to see if their predictions about the topic sentence were correct.

Sandra was pleased with this lesson. It supported students as they struggled with the difficulty of linguistic devices, and it provided students with an invitation into the text. She felt that students were more engaged in reading this way. She decided to replicate the lesson with the next text selection. This time students not only looked for the topic sentence, but Sandra also used colored marking pens to indicate a particular noun and its pronoun referents. Once again she found that students were more engaged with their reading. Sandra continued this lesson format until she had discussed all six linguistic devices with her students. ■

• The Need to Make Inferences

The linguistic devices described help the reader relate incoming information to information previously given. Inferential processes play an important role in this aspect of comprehension. Certain types of inferences required for text coherence are not directly motivated by linguistic cues. These might be considered "high-level" inferences. High-level inferences require the reader to add information to a text—to make certain connections are implicit not so much in the language as in the ideation. They are necessary when a text does not contain all the information needed for a reader to understand it fully. Writers—like speakers—must make assumptions about the range of knowledge and social sophistication their readers—or listeners—already possess so they are not burdened with unnecessary detail. Thus, matters of common knowledge or shared cultural values and experiences tend not to be made explicit. This means that there is almost always an implicit as well as an explicit text; understanding the implicit text is what is sometimes referred to as "reading between the lines."

The implicit text, however, does not consist of all inferences that can be made; it consists of those that must or should be made for purposes of coherence. For example, if we read that "Mike's brother took Mike to a quiet street to teach him to ride his new bike," we may infer that Mike's brother is kind and helpful and that a quiet street in this context is one with little traffic. But these inferences may not be required for text coherence; they may be only incidental, in the same way that certain details found in the explicit text—the color of the bike, perhaps—may be incidental to the story. Only if inferences are connected in some way to what has gone before or what is to come after can they be considered part of the implicit text and necessary for text coherence. (See Figure 5.7.)

1. *Making Connective Inferences.* The temporal, causal, or other connections between sentences are frequently left implicit in discourse text. In these cases, the reader must make connective inferences. Such connectives can usually be made explicit by familiar terms such as *and, but, or, since/*

figure 5.7 • Two Types of Inferential Text

Connective:
Shows the relationship between one proposition and another.
Key Terms:
and, but, or, since/because, so/therefore/that is why, for example, this means, namely

Propositional:
Information is itself a proposition linking two other propositions in the text.

---

because, so/therefore/that is why, for example, this means, and *namely.* Note how this type of inference (shown in brackets above the line of actual text) clarifies the information in the following paragraph.

Most people believe that earthworms are of little use except for fish
[for example]
bait. But scientists have found that they are very important. /Earth-
[In this way]/
worms eat soil. They make the soil better by grinding it up as it passes
[For another example]/
through their bodies. The holes that earthworms make as they burrow
in the earth make it easier for the roots of plants to enter the soil.
[For still another example]
/Earthworms use leaves to line their underground homes. These leaves
[Thus]
make the soil richer. /Scientists have found that earthworms are the
[because]
earth's plowmen. /They keep stirring up the soil which helps to raise better crops.

2. *Making Propositional Inferences.* These are "additions of new propositions to the text base" (Crothers, 1978, p. 63; Ehri, Cairns, & Zipke, 2009, p. 302). They add the information and ideas that are plausible as "reasons, causes, effects, and the like" (p. 63). The preceding paragraph on earthworms states that the leaves the earthworms use to line their underground homes "make the soil richer." Because this information represents an example of how earthworms make the soil better, the propositional inference may be drawn that "richer soil is better soil."

pause and reflect

Choose a chapter or selection that your class is working on this week. Scan through it and note places where integration and inference are required. Do you see examples of the types of structures noted above?

In any event, integration and inferencing are two critical strategic behaviors for connecting the language and knowledge of the author with the language and knowledge of the reader.

The Organization of Information

Beyond the processes of integration and inference, reading also involves the organization of information. This organization is made possible by internal text frames (Jones, Palinscar, Ogle, & Carr, 1987) or schemata. The schemata are built on familiarity with text frames attained by the individual over relatively long periods of time as a result of acquired knowledge, experience, and understanding. But they are more than a simple store of information and ideas. They represent the high-level order an individual imposes on experiences (including school experiences), and they represent the order an individual can bring to new experiences. New experiences are "assimilated" into existing schemata, and schemata are always changing as a result of new experiences. Acquiring certain kinds of new knowledge takes a long time because the development of whole systems or networks of knowledge is required.

Text frames (Buehl & Stumpf, 2007) are hypothetical constructs that help us understand why people remember certain things and forget others. Because people tend to remember the information in a text that is important or relevant to the central theme, we assume that they have available some internal mechanisms for sorting and organizing incoming information. These mechanisms can be thought of as generalized ideas about the high-level organization of information. Thus, we probably have a text frame that guides our reading of news stories in the daily newspapers, a different text frame for reading editorials, and still different ones for mystery stories, romantic fiction, or science fiction.

Educational experiences are surely an important factor in the development of an individual's schemata—in the way an individual comes to organize and understand social and natural phenomena. The high-level organization of knowledge in a text should be reflected in the questions we ask.

Narrative Structure—Story Grammar

Readers seem to remember best the parts of a story that "make up" the "structurally important units." They represent the kinds of information commonly found in most stories, and this is probably the reason they tend to be remembered so well. What we call a story is normally made up of certain basic elements—setting, characters, and actions or problems. When readers are asked to recall a story, they usually remember something about each of these elements. Through the experience of reading 8 many stories, readers develop a set of expectations. These expectations are like "slots," which people fill as they read. A story that conforms to these expectations permits the reader to find the information.

The idea that stories are made up of certain common elements is part of the more general theory of comprehension discussed in the preceding section—the theory that organized systems of knowledge, called schemata or text frames, play a central role in comprehension by serving as "advance organizers" for incoming information. A story schema represents the reader's generalized knowledge of the elements common to most stories.

A number of investigators in the field of cognitive psychology have attempted to describe the basic elements of a well-formed story (Boulineau, Fore, & Hagan-Burke, 2004; Fitzgerald, 1989; Murfett, Powell, & Snow, 2008; Yan, Wiles, & Yu-Ying, 2008). Such descriptions are called story grammars. These grammars categorize story events in much the same way that traditional grammar categorizes words (into nouns, verbs, adjectives, etc.). The grammars that have been developed thus far apply to only very simple stories and are often highly complex, so a detailed study of them would not be useful for our purposes. However, we describe a simplified version of a story grammar in the belief that it may prove useful to teachers in charting the main line of a story and writing questions that pertain to it.

A story consists of a setting and one or more episodes. The setting includes the time and place in which the events occur, the introduction of the main characters, and any additional information that might be necessary to make the ensuing events understandable. An episode consists of (1) an initiating event, (2) the reaction of the main character to that event, (3) an action on the part of the main character that is motivated by his reaction, and (4) a consequence that is a direct outcome of the action. The initiating event is what sets the story in motion. It may be a sudden change in the external environment (e.g., "Mary heard a strange noise in the kitchen"; "Bob came to Jill with the news that the ice was too thin for skating") or it may be some internal event (e.g., "Joe remembered that today was Lisa's birthday"; "Bill remembered he hadn't seen Joe in a long time"). In either case, the initiating event sets up a situation to which the main character responds. The character's internal reaction involves some feeling, thought, desire, or goal ("Joe knew she wanted a gold necklace") and this in turn motivates the character to take some external action. The action itself may be simple and direct ("He told his secretary to pick out a gift at Tiffany's"), or it may involve some subsidiary goals, plans, and attempts to carry them out (for example, canceling a luncheon engagement or borrowing money from a friend). The action is likely to be the most elaborated part of the story. Finally, the action is responsible for some consequence, and that ends the episode. The consequence may then serve as the initiating event of another episode.

The order in which story information is given may deviate from that described earlier. Setting information may be postponed and introduced in an episode at the point at which it is relevant, or a consequence may be described before its antecedent action: "They couldn't find the ball anywhere. Judy had hit it as hard as she could."

What story grammars do is describe in general terms the basic outline of a simple, well-formed story in Western societies. They suggest that the reader not only expects a story to be about some action or series of actions taken by a main character, but the reader also expects those actions to be purposeful. In other words, an action is expected to have both an antecedent (in the form of some initiating event and/or internal reaction) and a consequence. We believe that this view of stories can serve as a guide to you in the process of writing questions. If the basic outline of a story typically involves five broad categories of information, we can think of a story as providing the answers to five categorical or generic questions, somewhat like the following:

[Setting]
1. Where and when did the story take place? Who were the main characters in the story?

[Initiating event]
2. How did it all begin? [What was the predicament of the main character(s)?]

[Action]
3. What did the main character(s) do?

[Internal reaction]
4. Why did he (she, they) do it?

[Consequence]
5. What happened as a result?

These generic questions reflect the idea of a story as a progression of related events—one thing leads to another, which leads to still another, and so on. With these questions in mind, following the initial reading of the story, the teacher should be able to derive a set of questions that reflects the main story line. There may be more than one question in any category, and some categories may be too vague or nonspecific to be questioned. This type of generic questions should make us sensitive to any ambiguities, missing information, or other weaknesses of the story structure.

• Informational Structures—Text Frames

Although the structures of stories are familiar to most school-age readers, the structures of expository text, such as social studies and science textbooks, are much less predictable. Not only is there greater variation in expository structures, but many different structures can be used within a single article or chapter.

As is true with narrative structure, familiarity with expository structures enhances comprehension (Buehl & Stumpf, 2007; Jones et al., 1987; McGee & Richgels, 1985) and can also form the basis for three basic questions:

1. What is the topic?

2. How does the author organize the information about the topic?

3. How could I summarize the author's message?

An informal outline or map of selection content can help isolate the topic and the organizational pattern. The most common patterns of overall expository organization, sometimes called macrostructures, are the following:

1. Chronological order—shows a sequential pattern of ideas as they happened in time.
2. Cause and effect—certain conditions lead to particular consequences.
3. Comparison and contrast—looks at the similarities and differences of two items.
4. Problem and solution—Defines a dilemma, indicates a cause, and poses a variety of resolutions for the predicament.
5. Argument—presents the positive and negative aspects of a situation.
6. Category and example—presents a major category with minor members; sometimes linked with description.
7. Simple listing—gives a list in which order is not relevant. Can be descriptive.

Looking at the topic, information, and organization is essential to making a clear summary of the author's message and is a prerequisite for the critical thinking necessary to evaluate that message. As we will see later in this chapter, it is also essential for developing good diagnostic questions or retelling formats.

• Personal Response—Connections

Children respond to literature in different ways, and the nature of their response can shape and color what they comprehend (Bluestein, 2000; Martinez, Roser, & Strecker, 1998/1999; Sipe, 2000). Students who are encouraged to respond personally have exhibited an enhanced level of critical thinking about what has been read (Bluestein, 2000; Galda, 1990; McGee, 1992; Sipe, 2000). Asking for students' responses to what has been read prior to undertaking any formal retelling or questioning can often reveal preconceptions and insights that affect their comprehension.

case 5.5

Sandra—A Teacher Stimulates Personal Response

After her fourth-grade class read "The Restless Kangaroo" (see pages 201–202, Figure 5.9), she asked them to do a Point-of-View response. The students could choose any character in the story: Pete, the zookeeper, the mother kangaroo, or the joey. Sandra asked them to tell about the story from the point-of-view of one of the characters. She asked the students to hide the identity of the character and when the paragraphs were read aloud, the class attempted to identify who was speaking.

Leticia did a particularly fine job. She wrote,

> I wish we could live somewhere else. I don't know what to do about my joey. He is so naughty. He won't stay in my pouch. He keeps bringing sticks and rocks from the floor into my pouch. My pouch is sore. I wish we could move to another zoo.

Writing from the mother kangaroo's point of view was a risk for Leticia. When everyone in the class took a risk, Leticia was willing to take one herself. Sandra was pleased to see that Leticia understood the details in the story and was able to make inferences about the story that weren't specifically in the text. ■

Questions and the Development of Comprehension

The focus of direct teacher questioning affects the thinking strategies that students develop. When instructional activities use good questioning and model the process of self-questioning, students develop effective independent comprehension skills (Connor, Morrison, & Petrella, 2004; Klauda & Guthrie, 2008; Palincsar & Brown, 1983; Van den Broek, Tzeng, Risden, Trabasso, & Basche, 2001). Strategies directed toward the metalinguistic aspects of asking and responding to the questions, "What are they really asking here?" "How should I go about finding and integrating information in the text with what I know?" are critical to independent content learning (Harmon, 2000; Raphael, 1986).

It is clear that assessment involves asking good questions, interpreting responses to them, and using probing questions to follow response and recall.

• Beyond Levels of Thinking

Of the many questions that may be asked about any given text or selection of text, which one will assess fairly the comprehension of the reader?

This question has engaged the attention of experts in reading and in education generally, for a very long time. Much has been written about the kinds of questions teachers should ask. In general, teachers are urged to ask a variety of questions to give their students the opportunity to respond in a variety of ways to the materials they read. Teachers are advised to avoid overemphasizing questions that require only memory for directly stated information. They are encouraged to focus on questions that require high-level thinking to develop high-level cognitive processes. In short, questions have traditionally been approached from the standpoint of the mental processes required to answer them.

A major problem with this approach is that it is difficult to implement. A number of question-classification schemes based on this approach have been developed over the years, but even the simpler ones require distinctions between levels or types of thought that are both difficult to make and "not warranted by the current state of our knowledge about language and cognition" (Anderson, 1972, p. 149). Moreover, questions that appear to elicit high-level thinking because they cannot be answered from directly stated information may actually be quite trivial. Sanders (1966) points out that "thinking" questions cannot really be derived from insignificant subject matter, and he gives the following examples to illustrate:

text: This little pig went to market.

questions: Why? Did he go to buy or to be bought? . . . If to buy, what and for whom? Is he an informed buyer, the sort who would study the Buyers' Index and Consumers' Guide? ... If he is to be sold, what price will he bring? What will be the effect on the market price? . . .

text: This little pig had roast beef.

questions: Would you consider roast beef proper food for a pig? Which is better, nutritionally speaking, rare or well-done meat? (p. 171)

Sanders's caution is particularly relevant for the field of reading, where the "instructional diet" of simple story materials may provide little "food for thought." That is, the stories designed for developing basic reading skills do not always lend themselves to thoughtful discussion, and attempts to use them for this purpose may be unproductive.

Another problem with the mental-process or levels-of-thinking approach to questions is that it does not recognize a distinction between literal questions that pertain to important information and those that pertain to incidental detail, a point raised by Beck and McKeown (1981). Guszak (1967) alluded to this problem in his now-classic study of the kinds of questions teachers actually ask. He found that approximately 70 percent of the questions were of a literal nature, requiring only recognition (locating information in the passage) or recall (answering from memory) of factual information. Although this result is frequently cited as evidence that teachers ask too many literal questions, Guszak himself was more critical of the quality of the questions. That is, he did not feel that a seven-out-of-ten proportion of literal questions was necessarily objectionable; his objection was that many of the questions involved "retrieval of the trivial factual makeup of stories." It appeared to him that students were likely to miss "literal understanding" of story plots, events, and sequences "in their effort to satisfy the trivial fact questions of the teacher" (p. 233). But Guszak recognized, at the same time, that teachers could not employ more appropriate questioning patterns without clearer guidelines.

In sum, the traditional focus on levels of thinking in the design of questions does not effectively guard against trivialization of either nonliteral or literal questions. We believe, therefore, that questions should be approached from the standpoint of their relationship to the text as a whole rather than from the standpoint of the mental processes they elicit. We consider questions as either related to the text or beyond the text, according to whether they pertain to the information and ideas set down by the author. We also recommend that text-related questions be designed to follow the author's train of thought—that text-related questions reflect the story as a coherent whole. Beyond-text questions, on the other hand, will be those that take off where the author left off. They will go "beyond the lines" and generalize about the author's ideas, extending them to other contexts or relating them to other ideas and issues. In a sense, these questions will correlate to the ultimate purposes of reading—the enjoyment and appreciation of literature and the acquisition of knowledge and insight into human affairs. They will consist largely of the types of questions generally categorized and valued as thought provoking.

• Text-Related and Beyond-Text Questions

The rationale for our approach to questions is not just that mental process taxonomies are difficult to work with or that good thinking questions are difficult to derive from simple story materials. It lies also in recent insights into comprehension as a discourse process. These insights (described more fully in a later section) suggest that understanding "what it says" is not a trivial matter. To understand the communicative intent of a passage, readers must engage in levels of thought that are as simple or complex as the ideas communicated. They must select, combine, and integrate passage information, including information that is not explicitly stated. This means that text-related questions will generally require both literal and nonliteral (inferential) comprehension and that they must reflect the author's general intent as expressed in the passage as a whole.

In addition, our approach preserves the basic distinction between the ideas of the author (text-related) and those of the reader (beyond-text), thereby emphasizing that what is written must be understood in its own right before it can be explored in greater depth. The beyond-text questions will stimulate the reader to use the text as a springboard for reflection and conjecture. These questions will also draw on information and ideas that, although peripheral to the text, may be important to the reader.

A good set of questions, then, will consist of at least two basic parts or distinct types (see Figure 5.8). One part will be text related, in the sense that it will adhere closely to the significant content of the text, including the inferences directly motivated by text coherence. The other will go beyond the text as a communicative entity and explore its general implications and incidental detail

f i g u r e 5 . 8 • Types of Questions

Text-Related Questions	**Beyond-Text Questions**
Require literal and non-literal comprehension Must reflect Author's intent, establish the facts, and follow the sequence of the story	Use text to go beyond the lines. Cannot be answered by reading the story. Could reflect "literary analysis."
Who did what? Why did they do it? What happened as a result?	Contrast this story to another story. How did the character feel? What did the character mean when he said, "_____"? If you were in the story, what would you do?

(Gregory & Cahill, 2010; Kinniburgh & Shaw, 2009; Lee, 2010; McCollister & Sayler, 2010; Meyer, 2010; Mills, 2009/2010; Phelps, 2010; Sadow, 1982). The first part will assess the student's comprehension of the passage as a whole—of the story told therein or the aspect of human knowledge conveyed—and will be a major factor in determining the suitability of like materials for instruction. The second part will assess the student's ability to use textual detail to broaden his or her knowledge and understanding of physical and social phenomena. The difference between these two parts is illustrated by the following example.

In the opening of *Charlotte's Web* (White, 1952), Fern learns that her father is on his way to the barn, carrying an ax, with the intent of "doing away" with the runt pig that was born the night before. Fern's mother explains that the pig would probably die anyway. Outraged at the "unfairness" of killing the pig "just because it is weak and little," Fern runs after her father and pleads for the pig's life. He gives in to her plea, saying, "I'll let you start it on a bottle, like a baby. Then you'll see what trouble a pig can be" (p. 3). The text-related questions on this passage would establish the facts of the story qua story—who did what, why they did it, and what happened as a result:

1. What is a runt pig? Who is Fern? Where does she live?

2. What was Fern's father going to do?

3. Why was Fern's father going to "do away" with the pig?

4. How did Fern feel when she learned that her father was going to kill the pig?

5. What did Fern do about it?

6. How did her father respond to her?

Notice that the questions follow the sequence of the story and that they are relatively independent of each other. That is, inability to answer (2), for example, does not preclude the possibility of answering (3) and (4). In fact, (3) and (4) give the answer to (2).

The beyond-text questions, on the other hand, might explore the conflict between Fern's point of view and her father's in terms of the more universal conflict between a child's point of view and an adult's. They might also (or alternatively) address the conflict between the father's point of view as a farmer and as a father. For example:

1. Why did Fern's father "give in" to her plea? (Was he convinced that it would be unjust to kill a runt pig or was he merely being kind to his daughter?)

2. Why would Fern's father believe that it was all right to kill the pig?

It is clear that these questions cannot be answered from a reading of the passage, and it is in this sense that they are beyond the text, or reader based. It is also clear that they represent what might be called "literary analysis." If the students have read another story in which there is a similar conflict between young and old or between the dual roles and responsibilities of an individual, the teacher may ask that it be recalled and contrasted with this one. Other beyond-text questions that might be asked include these:

3. What was Fern's mother's reaction to the father's intention to kill the pig?

4. Fern's mother said, "It will probably die anyway." Why would that be likely to happen?

5. Fern's father said, "A weakling makes trouble." What is a weakling? In what way would it make trouble?

6. If you were Fern, would you be willing to take care of the pig?

• Questions and Prior Knowledge—Building Connections

The insights discussed here are important for several reasons. They highlight the reading process as a global one in which the reader is actively engaged in constructing a unified representation of text information, and they heighten our sensitivity to the "connectedness" of written prose. They strongly imply that there can be no substitute for "real" reading experiences, that is, for experiences with a variety of types of discourse text. Another important implication is that materials may be difficult to understand if they require inferences that are beyond the reader's experiential or knowledge base. Finally, these insights provide a rational basis for the design of text-related questions. They help us recognize that although such questions do not pertain to the deepest levels of meaning or the ultimate purposes of reading in the way that beyond-text questions do, they are an important intermediary step.

Recent insights emphasize, further, that text-related questions should pertain to the ideas and information that contribute in some way to the text as a whole. It is a mistake to confuse comprehension with memory for incidental details or even for incidental inferences. These insights suggest that such details are frequently forgotten because they bear so little connection to other textual information and are only superficially processed. For example, it may make no difference, in terms of other events in a story, whether a certain incident took place in the morning or afternoon, last week or this week, or whether it was first noticed by one story character or by another. In an adventure tale about a series of incidents, it makes little difference whether the incidents occurred in one order or another.

The process of following the main story line does not tend to "activate" nonessential facts, and memory for them is likely to be spotty. Good comprehension means grasping the vital information in the text and the train of thought (the low-level and high-level inferences) that binds this information together.

If text-related questions involve both "reading the lines" and "reading between the lines," then beyond-text questions may be thought of as "reading beyond the lines." These questions also involve inferential processes, but the inferences are more in the nature of "grand conclusion[s] from a number of explicit and implicit propositions combined" (Crothers, 1978, p. 55; Kinniburgh & Shaw, 2009, p. 21; Lee, 2010, p. 425; Mills, 2009/2010, p. 326). That is, they are not cued by specific linguistic devices nor by any specific inferences that are motivated by text coherence—they do not "connect" specific statements in the text. It is in this sense that beyond-text questions may be said to involve the "deeper" levels of meaning. And as with text-related inferences, the reader must draw on general knowledge to arrive at these deeper meanings.

In the case of story materials, beyond-text questions generally call on the reader to apply his or her knowledge of human events, actions, and feelings to a given situation. For example, in a story about a young boy whose father and brothers are all fishermen, we learn that what the boy wanted most was to go fishing with his father. We can understand this desire in terms of boys in general—most boys would think going fishing is fun. But we can also understand it, with reference to this boy in particular, in terms of boys' desires to do what their fathers and older brothers do, to be like them, and to feel grown up. We understand the story character's feelings and appreciate the story more fully because we recognize those feelings as consistent with what we know about little boys. Beyond-text questions should assess this application of knowledge.

Another example is provided by Miriam Schlein's (1966) story, *The Big Cheese*. In this story, a farmer decides to give his finest cheese to the king. Here we recognize the farmer's pride in his work, and it is through knowledge of this type of pride that we understand why the farmer would elect to give his cheese to the king instead of selling it in the open market and allowing "just anyone" to eat it. Also involved is the special feeling that citizens may have toward their leaders. Parallel to the farmer's pride is the pride shown by a goat herd, who insists that goats' milk makes better cheese than cows' milk. For this story, beyond-text questions require an examination of the actions and reactions of story characters from the point of view of their consistency with certain general ideas about human events. As we ask such questions, we help students develop these ideas, and we help them see the relevance of these stories to the "human condition."

A particular question may be either text related or beyond the text, depending on the answer that is expected (Kinniburgh & Shaw, 2009, p. 22; Mills, 2009/2010, p. 327; Pearson & Johnson, 1984). A text-related answer can be justified with specific reference to the text. A beyond-text answer is one that is based on insights or logical reasoning that is not clearly implied in the text. Consider the following question and some possible answers concerning *The Big Cheese* (Schlein, 1966).

> ***question:*** Why did the goat herd suggest that he and the farmer taste the cheese?

> ***answer a:*** Because it was lunchtime, and he was hungry.

> ***answer b:*** Because he didn't believe it was the best cheese (because it was not made from goats' milk).

> ***answer c:*** Because he thought the farmer should be sure it was the best cheese before he gave it to the king.

Answers B and C pertain directly to the goat herd's own statements: "Then how can it be the best cheese ever made? The finest . . . cheeses are always made from goats' milk" (p. 80), and "How can you present the king with a cheese you do not know tastes the best?" (p. 81). So answers B and C are text related and show good comprehension of the story line. Answer A goes beyond the text because there is no implication in the text that the goat herd's motives are unclear. This answer could represent good insight into the fact that people sometimes have ulterior motives. On the other hand, it could be that the student simply failed to understand the persuasive arguments of the goat herd and that the answer is really a "stab in the dark."

Beyond-text questions need not be confined to issues involving human goals, desires, and feelings. There is information of a factual nature to be gained from stories. Teachers' questions should help students "pull" this information out and make it part of their general fund of knowledge—part of the background knowledge they will be able to bring to subsequent stories. For purposes of assessment, these questions may help the teacher evaluate the adequacy of the student's background knowledge in relation to story content. This is important because it is often a lack of some specific information that leads to misunderstanding of story events. In *The Big Cheese* (Schlein, 1966), for example, students must understand that farmers sell their products at a "market" (many city children may think of "markets" only as places where families buy food). They must also grasp the fact that cheese may be made of milk from goats as well as from cows and that in "olden" days a farmer might transport his products by wheelbarrow.

• Constructing Comprehension Questions

Text-related questions recapitulate the main story line or central ideas in a text. Unfortunately, there are no objective method for determining that one idea is more important than another. Teachers must rely on their own clear understanding of the text to be used, based on a careful reading, rereading, and analysis. One way to proceed is as follows:

- First, read the text for an overview of its content and organization. You will gain insight into what the passage is like, and which parts stand out in memory.
- Try to construct a set of questions whose answers will represent a broad outline of the story's significant content (Step 1).
- A second reading of the text will enable you to "fill in" the outline (Step 2).
- A third and final reading will suggest some beyond-text questions. These are described more fully.

Because of their differences in form, content, and purpose, story materials and nonfiction are treated separately.

Story Materials. On the first reading, simply follow the story line (i.e., find out who did what, why they did it, and how it all came out). This reading will help you form the intuitive base for the group of questions that will reflect the causal essence of the story and assess story comprehension. Highly relevant to this step are the results of some recent investigations into story structure and story recall.

The derivation of text-related questions based on story structure constitutes the first step in the process of writing questions. For the second step, a second reading of the story will usually be necessary. In this step, the story outline constructed in Step 1 will be rounded out with important details. With very short stories, all or most of the details may be important for the story line. In fact, the shorter the story, the less likely it is to include incidental detail. With longer stories, however, readers are likely to forget many details, particularly if the details do not carry the story forward.

This process of question construction is illustrated for the third-grade story, "The Restless Kangaroo," shown in Figure 5.9.

figure 5.9 • Narrative Passage

The Restless Kangaroo

The zoo had a problem. The problem was Tanga who was the mother kangaroo.

She had begun to take her joey, as kangaroo babies are called, out of her pouch in the night. For two mornings Pete, who is the head keeper at the zoo, had found the cold little joey on the dirt floor of the kangaroo pen.

Each time Pete rubbed the joey with a towel until he was warm. Then he tucked him back into Tanga's pouch. And Tanga stood still because she was a gentle kangaroo.

But on the third morning the joey was found on the floor again.

"This is a problem," the zoo director said. "The joey is too young to be out of Tanga's pouch."

"It is a new problem," said Pete. "Tanga has been a good mother. She always kept her other joeys safe until they were older."

"We must find out why she does this now," said the director. "If this goes on the joey might catch a chill. He may even die."

"Tonight I will stand watch at Tanga's pen," said Pete. "Perhaps I can learn why she puts her joey on the floor."

"That is a good idea," said the director.

When night came to the zoo, Pete went to the animal barn where Tanga lived. He sat down on a chair in front of her low gate.

In the next pen the great elk, with its wide antlers, snorted. On the other side of Tanga's pen a zebra stamped its feet and then a deer sneezed.

The llamas and camels and the buffalo gazed over their gates at Pete for a long time. It was plain that they were surprised to see him there at that time of night.

But at last they all became used to him and, one by one, they went to sleep.

And Tanga lay down on her side in her own pen on her clean straw bed and went to sleep also.

The big barn was quiet and dark but for the soft glow of one light up near the roof.

Pete yawned and leaned back in his chair. He had worked hard all day. He was sleepy and it was hard to keep awake. But he did keep awake.

After a while he heard a "scritch-scratch" in the stillness. He stood up and looked into the shadows of Tanga's pen.

Tanga was sound asleep. But something was moving. It was the joey's tiny paw.

It waved back and forth, back and forth, out of the opening of Tanga's pouch. Then it dug down into the straw and Pete could hear the same "scritch-scratch" that he had heard before.

When the joey pulled a pawful of straw into her pouch, Tanga kicked her long back feet. But she did not wake up.

Soon the joey pulled another pawful of straw into the pouch. This time Tanga gave a loud sigh.

Without opening her eyes she turned on her back. She lifted the joey with her front paws and dropped him into the straw. Then she turned over on her side and was still again. And she hadn't waked up at all.

The joey scratched around a bit and then he too was still.

"I have found the answer to our problem." Pete whispered to himself. "Tanga's joey is a naughty baby."

He tip-toed into the pen and picked up the shivering joey and tucked him in his jacket. Then he felt inside Tanga's pouch with gentle hands. Besides the straw, he found sharp pebbles from the dirt floor of the pen.

"Poor Tanga!" Pete said. "No wonder you put your joey out in the cold! No kangaroo likes to be scratched by straw and pebbles!"

He cleaned her pouch and Tanga opened her eyes and blinked her long lashes as if she were saying "Thank you."

"There, Tanga," said Pete when he was through. "Go back to sleep. Things will be better from now on."

He took the joey to the zoo office. There he rolled him in a towel and put him in a box to keep warm.

When morning came Pete told the zoo director what happened.

"You see," he said, "when Tanga's joey wakes up he likes to play with the straw and pebbles. Then he takes them into his own pouch-bed. He is a naughty little kangaroo."

The director smiled. "I don't think he is naughty," he said. "He is just a restless little kangaroo. But we will fix it so this will not happen again."

As soon as all the other zookeepers heard the story about Tanga and her restless kangaroo, they went right to work.

They moved Tanga and her joey away from the animal barn and into a big cage in the zoo's main building. The cage had a smooth floor with no pebbles. And instead of straw for a bed Pete gave Tanga a blanket.

From then on there was no more trouble. When the restless joey awoke at night he pulled and tugged on the blanket until he was tired. Then he went back to sleep.

The zoo's problem was solved. The joey was not found out of Tanga's pouch again until he was old enough to climb in and out by himself—which he did, over and over again, until he finally grew so big that he could no longer fit.

Source: From *With Skies and Wings, Level 9*, pp. 207–213. In Reading 360, published by Ginn and Company, 1969. Story by Edythe R. Warner.

pause and reflect

Compose a set of questions for "The Restless Kangaroo." Then compare them with the ones in Figure 5.10. Where did you tap the same knowledge and processes? Where were your choices different?

A typical set of questions that might result from the first and second steps of question writing is shown in Figure 5.10. Although the questions derived during Step 1 are quite predictable, those written during Step 2 result from a less systematic process. There are no hard and fast rules regarding questions of detail; you must be guided by your own sense of story cohesiveness.

figure 5.10 • Questions Based on Narrative Passage[a]

Story Structure Category	Story Structure Questions (Step 1)	Detail Questions (Step 2)
Setting	S1. Where did this story take place? S2. Who is Pete? S3. Who is Tanga?	Dl. What is a joey? [What is a baby kangaroo called?]
Initiating event/problem	S4. What was the problem that the zoo was having with the kangaroos?	D2. What did Pete do with the joey each time he found him on the floor of the pen?
Internal reaction	S5. Why was that a problem? [Why were the zookeepers worried about the baby kangaroo being out of the mother's pouch during the night?]	
Action	S6. What did Pete, the zookeeper, do to find out about the problem? [Why did Pete stay up all night watching the kangaroo pen?]	
Consequence	S7. What did Pete find out when he watched the kangaroos all night? [What did the joey do in the middle of the night?] S8. Why did Tanga take the joey out of her pouch at night? S9. Why did the joey put the straw in the mother's pouch? S10. What did Pete do to solve the problem for the kangaroos?	D3. What did Pete find when he felt inside the mother kangaroo's pouch? D4. How did the new pen solve the problem? [How was the new pen different from the old one?] D5. What did the joey do in the new pen when he woke up in the middle of the night?

[a]The questions shown in brackets suggest some alternatives in terms of wording and/or emphasis that seem to be equally appropriate.

In examining the questions generated for "The Restless Kangaroo," note the relationship between Step 1 and Step 2 questions. There is usually only one correct answer to a Step 2 question, whereas Step 1 questions give the student more latitude in framing an answer. Step 2 questions are often implicit in a Step 1 question, so that Step 2 questions will often be answered in response to a Step 1 question. Step 2 questions often serve as clarifying "probes" when the answer to a Step 1 question is vague or suggests a slight misunderstanding of the question. For example, in response to question S10 (Figure 5.10), one child said, "They put him in a box," suggesting that he did not understand the zoo's final solution to the problem. In answering question D4, this child said, "There was no straw to put in the pouch," showing clear understanding of the solution.

The third and final step in the question-writing process is the creation of beyond-text items. As already explained, these deal with the story as an exemplar of something interesting and important about the way people live, work, play, and otherwise conduct their affairs, or with some thematic issue or communicative intent of the author. In searching out ideas for these questions, it is useful to look to each of the five story elements for suggestions. The zookeeper's internal reaction (worry) on finding the joey on the floor of the cage suggests that he is knowledgeable regarding the care of animals. A good question would be, "From this story, can you tell what a good zookeeper must know or be able to do?" The zookeeper's knowledge and devotion to duty, evident in the action he took to find out about the problem, suggests the following question: "If you were in charge of a zoo, would you hire Pete as a zookeeper? Why (or why not)?"

Expository Materials. Questions concerning expository texts are constructed on the same principle as narrative questions, but here it is the traditional outline form that guides the procedure. An outline shows the relative importance of text ideas, and it also specifies how ideas are related to one another. It depicts, in graphic form (the indentation and letter-number system), the superordinate-subordinate structure of passages and expresses the particular kind of superordinate-subordinate relationship that inheres between each topic and its subtopics.

For example, Figure 5.11 gives three possible outlines of an expository passage on trees. Outline 1 shows only the superordinate-subordinate relationships. There are, however, two different *kinds* of relationships between the sub-topics (A, B, C, and D) and the major topic, trees. Clearly, subtopics A and B are kinds of *trees*, whereas C and D are *uses* of trees. A third type of relationship exists between each set of minor subtopics; that is, each (1) and (2), and their superordinates, A, B, C, D. Subtopics (1) and (2) are *examples* of their superordinate topics. Thus, the subtopics of an outline are always elaborations of a topic, but there are many different kinds of elaborations. A good outline makes these explicit in some way or other. Two possible ways are shown in outlines 2 and 3 in Figure 5.11.

f i g u r e   5 . 1 1 • Possible Outlines of an Expository Passage on Trees

OUTLINE 1
Main Topic: Trees

A. Deciduous
   1. Maple
   2. Birch
B. Evergreen
   1. Spruce
   2. Fir
C. Shade
   1. Maple
   2. Oak
D. Ornamental
   1. Dogwood
   2. Hawthorn

OUTLINE 2
Main Topic: Trees

A. Kinds
   1. Deciduous
     a. Maple } Examples
     b. Birch
   2. Evergreen
     a. Spruce } Examples
     b. Fir
B. Uses
   1. Shade
     a. Maple } Examples
     b. Oak
   2. Ornamental
     a. Dogwood } Examples
     b. Hawthorn

OUTLINE 3
Main Topic: Trees

Kinds [A. Deciduous
      1. Maple } Examples
      2. Birch
     B. Evergreen
      1. Spruce } Examples
      2. Fir
Uses [C. Shade
      1. Maple } Examples
      2. Oak
     D. Ornamental
      1. Dogwood } Examples
      2. Hawthorn

In addition to the relationships exemplified here—kinds, uses, and examples—subtopics may be related to their topics as causes, effects, functions, parts, characteristics, procedural steps, or chronological sequence.

The first step in formulating expository questions is the preparation of a complete outline. This is an easy step with well-organized, clearly written passages, such as the one on forest fires in Figure 5.12.

pause and reflect

Construct an outline for "Forest Fires" (Figure 5.12). Then compare it with the outline in Figure 5.13. After evaluating your choices, compose questions for the passage and compare your questions with those in Figure 5.14. Where did you tap the same knowledge and processes? Where were your choices different?

The next step is to derive questions from the outline (Figure 5.13) using procedures similar to those described for the questions based on narrative selections. One question may be written to focus on the main topic, and one or two questions may be developed to explore each of the subtopics in the outline. We encourage you to develop questions based on the passage outline and compare them with those shown in Figure 5.14.

• **Free and Aided Recall**

Consider an aided recall procedure as an alternative to direct questioning (Morrow, 1988; Panteleo, 2007). The student is instructed to recount everything

figure 5.12 • Expository Passage about Forest Fires

Forest Fires

An important problem for forest rangers is how to protect forests from being ruined by fire. Each year thousands of trees are destroyed by fire. Careless campers do not put their fires completely out. Cigarettes are left to burn on the dry ground. These small fires in dry forests can burn thousands of trees. Fires that are spotted right away can be put out before they get too big to handle. Then fires will cause less damage to the forest. A second solution to the problem is to have experts and bulldozers ready to move in quickly to fight the fire. Bulldozers can throw huge amounts of dirt on a fire in a short time. The dirt helps put the fire out quicker. A third solution is to build fire lanes in the forests. Fire lanes are long breaks in the forest where there are no trees. These breaks prevent the fire from spreading and getting too large.

Source: The Influence of Megacognitive Knowledge of Expository Text Structure on Discourse Recall by L. M. McGee in J. A. Niles and L. A. Harris (Eds.). *New Inquiries in Reading Research and Instruction* [Thirty-first Yearbook of the National Reading Conference. Rochester, NY: National Reading Conference, 1982].

figure 5.13 • Outline Based on Expository Passage about Forest Fires

---

MAIN TOPIC: How forest rangers protect forests from fire damage

    A. Causes of fire
       1. Campfires
       2. Cigarettes
    B. Solutions to Problem
       1. Early detection
          a. Lookout stations
          b. Helicopters
       2. Quick extinction
          a. Bulldozers—throw dirt on fire
          b. Experts
       3. Preventing spread of fires
          a. Fire lanes

---

he or she can remember about the passage. The unprompted retelling reflects the student's assessment of the important story elements, and the order in which they are told gives you a clue to the organization the reader has imposed on the passage. It is also possible for you to evaluate the reader's oral language and vocabulary use based on the language he or she uses to retell the selection.

    Help the student fill in missing information by asking specific questions about important ideas or events that were not mentioned directly. This means you must be prepared with a list or outline of the main passage content against which

f i g u r e 5 . 1 4 • Questions Based on Outline of Expositore Passage about Forest Fires

---

1. What is the important problem that forest rangers must deal with? (protect trees from fire damage; forest fires)
2. How do many forest fires get started? (cigarettes and campfires)
3. How are lookout stations and helicopters used in solving the problem of forest fires? (spot fires in early stages)
4. How are bulldozers used in fighting fires? (throw dirt on fire)
5. What are fire lanes? (areas that are bare of trees)
6. How do fire lanes prevent fire damage to forest? (prevent spread of fire)
*7. The passage mentioned that "experts" are needed in fighting fires. What sorts of things might experts know that would be helpful in fighting fires? (wind conditions; how and where to approach fires; methods of fighting fires)
*8. What might be done to prevent fires from getting started in the first place? (punish wrongdoers; supervise campgrounds; educate people)

*Beyond-text question

---

you can check and evaluate the student's retelling. It would be much the same kind of outline as was recommended for the preliminary step in constructing questions. Open-ended questions (e.g., "Tell me more about____"; "Explain what you meant by ___") can be used to elicit more information following free recall. It is important to include this step because several investigations have found that students, particularly poor readers, normally store much more information than they produce in a free recall task (e.g., Bridge & Tierney, 1981; Kletzien, 2009).

summary

This chapter has presented a theoretical overview of current conceptualizations of comprehension, emphasizing that it is an active, constructive process. It has examined some reader and textual variables that affect this process. Knowledge has been applied to the issue of what makes good questions, stressing both their connection to the text (the story map and the central story issue of the author) and the need for questions to go beyond the text to foster inference and develop literary appreciation.

try it out

1. Find passages from standardized tests used in your school. Are inferencing and integration required? What background knowledge is needed for the inferences? Do your students have this knowledge?

2. Select a student in your class who has comprehension difficulties. During a reading lesson, observe the student. Can you relate any behaviors to issues raised in this chapter?

3. Choose a passage from a favorite novel. Indicate where the author expects you to make inferences (where all the information is not given—you must supply some). Bring your passage in and share it with the group.

4. Student Portfolio Ideas: (1) Have your students analyze a chapter or selection from their assigned reading. Invite them to generate questions. Compare their questions with others in their group and come up with a master list. (2) Ask students to monitor their own reading on the next assigned reading and indicate where they have trouble understanding. Share as a group and discuss why the selections are difficult. Is it knowledge, language, organization, or some combination of all three that makes selections difficult?

5. For Your Teaching Portfolio: Choose a selection from a textbook and analyze it using a map, web, or outline. Construct questions based on your analysis. Then compare your questions with those suggested in a teacher's manual. Contrast strengths and weaknesses.

for further reading

Blachowicz, C. L. Z., & Ogle, D. (2008). *Reading comprehension: Strategies for independent learners* (2nd ed.). New York: Guilford. An excellent overview of comprehension with ideas for instruction.

Pressley, M. (2000). What should comprehension instruction be the instruction of? In M. L. Kamil, P. B. Mosenthal, P. D. Pearson, & R. Barr (Eds.), *Handbook of reading research* (Vol. 3, pp. 545–561). Mahwah, NJ: Erlbaum. A timely review of research on comprehension instruction.

Taylor, B. M., Graves, M. F., & Van Den Boek, P. (2000). *Reading for meaning: Fostering comprehension in the middle grades*. Newark, DE: International Reading Association. Excellent ideas for strategic instruction.

Smith, M. W., & Wilhelm, J. D. (2002). "Reading don't fix no Chevys": Literacy in the lives of young men. Portsmouth, NH: Heinemann. The authors directly address these sometimes unsettling questions and call into question the type of literature taught in high school English programs.

Reading Comprehension: Assessment and Instructional Support

chapter goals for the reader

- To recognize the variety of ways readers can experience difficulty in understanding
- To learn how to gather data about a reader's comprehension
- To work through three cases using questioning, retelling, and think-alouds for data gathering
- To develop some alternatives for instruction related to assessment

classroom vignette

Solving Classroom Puzzles

Jim, a middle school language arts teacher, is puzzled by the performance of three of his students. Bob is a methodical student and excellent oral reader who answers factual questions with great accuracy. Yet he is silent and unresponsive whenever class discussion or written assignments move on to bigger issues. Though Andrea finishes her class reading assignments quickly, her performance in class discussions and on written work is uniformly poor. Her typical strategy is to pick some words out of the teacher's questions on a reading guide and rephrase them into an answer. Yet her oral reading is accurate if somewhat expressionless. Jake, another capable oral reader, is energetic but inconsistent in discussion and is frequently the first to want to answer questions or offer opinions. Sometimes he is right on target, but at other times his responses are way off base.

In this chapter, we will see how Jim went about gathering data on each of these students to develop a more detailed profile of their comprehension strengths and weaknesses. First he had to establish a baseline by answering the question, "What is adequate comprehension?" Next, he gathered data on these students using the selection they were reading in their literature anthology. Finally, he analyzed their performances and decided on specific instructional strategies to use with each student. By working through the cases of Bob, Andrea, and Jake, you can begin to develop an understanding of the multifaceted nature of comprehension and build a framework for assessment and instruction. ■

chapter overview

This chapter has three parts. The first section discusses the variety of comprehension difficulties that can be observed and the concept of "instructional level." The second segment focuses on data gathering and presents cases using questioning, retelling, and think-alouds to gather data on and analyze student reading performance. The third section presents instructional recommendations for developing interactive strategies, for developing the ability to reorganize information in large segments of text, and for developing sentence-level comprehension, relating these to the student cases presented earlier.

210

chapter outline

Comprehension in the Classroom

An assessment of reading comprehension serves a twofold purpose. It enables you to make an informed decision regarding the level of materials that would be appropriate for instruction, and it alerts you to a student's specific instructional needs. You would generally undertake such an assessment when you have some question concerning a student's current placement in instructional materials or the type of instructional emphasis that would enable the student to make better progress. For the most part, these questions arise when a student is not performing well during daily lessons. However, they can also arise when a student is performing extremely well, for instructional materials should be neither so difficult that the student can have little success with them nor so easy as to require little thought or attentional effort. Thus, the student who is always able to answer your questions may need more challenging materials, whereas the student who can seldom answer questions correctly may need less demanding ones. You must make every effort to see that instructional materials are optimal from this point of view.

In addition, you must be aware of the area(s) of reading in which a student is relatively weak and consequently requires special attention. A student is considered to need special attention in the area of comprehension when his or her performance on a comprehension test is inadequate (below a certain level) *and* the assessment procedures described in preceding chapters indicate that the student's print skills and vocabulary knowledge—the areas of reading underlying comprehension—are not prime sources of difficulty.

We first discuss criteria for establishing whether materials are at an appropriate level of difficulty for a student's use in reading instruction. Then we describe the general types of comprehension problems that students may encounter

figure 6.1 • Material to Be Covered

Determining Instructional Level	Identifying Common Problems	Finding Instructional Techniques
Are materials at an appropriate level of difficulty for use in reading instruction?	Is there a procedure for describing types of comprehension problems that will also provide alternative diagnostic possibilities?	Can instructional techniques help students gain proficiency in comprehension and carry out further diagnostic teaching?

and a procedure for assessing an individual student's major problem along with alternative diagnostic possibilities. Finally, we suggest some instructional techniques for helping students gain proficiency in comprehension and for carrying out further diagnostic teaching. (See Figure 6.1.)

• Determining Instructional Level

When selecting materials for use in the classroom, teachers use many types of criteria. Content, format, and language are all important elements for establishing whether materials are at an appropriate level of difficulty for a student in reading instruction. Standardized reading formulas using sentence length and word frequency are commonly used to scale commercial materials and trade books as to readability (Fang & Schleppegrell, 2010; Gunning, 2003; Ivey, 2010; Purcell-Gates, Duke, & Martineau, 2007; Weaver & Kintsch, 1991; Williamson, 2008; Winokur-Kotula, 2003). Yet teachers make these determinations without a particular child or group of children in mind, and their estimations do not take into account what the readers already know or don't know about the subject being discussed and their prior experiences with reading materials of the type and organization under examination.

A more classroom-sensitive concept is that of instructional level, a level at which a student can comprehend adequately in a challenging but teacher-supported situation.

In general, materials are considered suitable for instruction when the student, after reading them, can answer correctly a certain proportion of the questions asked. Unfortunately, there is no firm agreement among reading authorities regarding what this proportion should be. Recommendations range from 60 percent to 75 percent. Harris and Sipay (1990) suggested that 60 percent is "marginal." They also noted that a 50 to 60 percent criterion may be used with students of limited experiential background if "more time than usual will be spent [by the teacher] developing the concepts and vocabulary necessary for understanding the stories" (p. 185). Betts (1954), on the other hand, recommends 75 percent comprehension for oral reading and a substantially higher percentage for "silent reading to locate specific information." In the procedures recommended by Betts, however, the oral reading of a passage is *not* the student's first encounter with the text; it is a rereading after silent reading. (Betts is a strong advocate of the principle that silent reading should precede oral reading, although he acknowledges that oral reading at sight provides valuable information regarding word recognition skills.) Nevertheless, we believe that, with well-designed questions, a criterion of 75 percent is not unreasonable even for a first reading. We also believe, with Harris and Sipay, that this criterion should be applied flexibly. Under certain conditions, a student who scores below 75 percent on a diagnostic passage may benefit from instruction in materials at the same level of difficulty. In general, such conditions exist when a student is relatively strong in vocabulary knowledge and, if given an opportunity to review the passage, is able to answer several questions that had been missed initially. This student would be proficient in basic language skills but lacking in the ability to interrelate and organize passage information. A teacher must be ready to provide instruction that would take into account the student's struggle with this aspect of comprehension.

A teacher usually undertakes assessment to explore difficulties observed in a student's reading during classroom activities. If the teacher uses commercially prepared materials, it is often puzzling when a student selected for diagnosis performs well on the diagnostic passage that is identified as being at the same level of difficulty as the classroom materials. In such cases, you may want to consider whether the reading selection used in the diagnosis is typical of materials. It could be considerably easier in style, structure, and content, even if it came from the same reading level. If the passage appears to be typical, then the student's classroom difficulties could be due to inattention, disinterest, difficulty in working in a group setting, differences in topic and type of reading material, and the like. You must also recognize that the student has probably put forth a higher level of effort during the diagnosis than can reasonably be expected during daily classroom routines. Still, the diagnostic performance gives evidence of available strength. You should therefore discuss the results of the diagnosis with the student and elicit his or her views on the matter. Your expression of interest and concern will undoubtedly be important to the student and may help the student become more deeply involved in reading activities. Alternatively, the student may have some insights into his or her own difficulty that will be useful to you in planning and implementing classroom activities.

If a student selected for diagnosis scores extremely well in comprehension—90 percent or better—the passage should be considered at a level appropriate for independent reading. You may then administer a more difficult passage to determine the student's instructional level, or the student may simply be assigned to more difficult materials on a trial basis.

A 75 percent level of comprehension, then, indicates that the reader is gathering enough of the important information in a text for reading to be a satisfying and productive experience: The reader is successful and has a sense of accomplishment. At a much higher level of comprehension, say 90 percent or above, particularly if the answers to questions are full and unhesitating, the reader is processing information so efficiently that there is little to be gained from the instructional efforts of the teacher, as materials that present so little difficulty can be read independently.

On the other hand, when comprehension is below 75 percent, the student is normally gaining too little of the information in the text for reading to be a comfortable experience under ordinary instructional conditions. It is often possible to adjust instruction to accommodate a student who scores at least 50 percent in comprehension. A student who scores below 50 percent is following the text so poorly that even with strong instructional support in the form of extensive prereading discussion and activities, he or she will find reading a frustrating experience. Thus, comprehension scores between 50 and 75 percent represent borderline situations in which the teacher must consider the nature of the student's problem and decide whether instructional support would increase comprehension to a level that would be acceptable (75 percent or greater). For example, instructional scaffolding focused on the identification and meaning of words contained in reading selections may solve enough problems for the student to support reading with adequate comprehension.

Word recognition proficiency must also be taken into account in determining instructional level. A student who performs well in comprehension and poorly in word recognition may need to work with easier materials for a time while developing greater print skill. Easier materials may facilitate progress in this aspect of reading. On the other hand, a student may derive psychological or social advantages from working with the higher-level materials that would outweigh any difficulty with word recognition. An important consideration in this regard is the type of word recognition difficulty involved. If sight word fluency and accuracy is a major problem for the student in addition to content word difficulties, the easier materials are likely to be the better solution. If, however, identification of unfamiliar content words constitutes the student's prime difficulty, then the higher-level materials can probably be used. In the latter case, of course, you must plan to provide the student (along with other members of the reading group) prereading assistance by identifying difficult words. In addition, you must make some provision for the student to receive help with specific word identification skills.

In regard to making instructional decisions about print skills, the way to use diagnostic information is described more fully in Chapter 7. In this section we examine the implications of a specific difficulty in the area of comprehension.

• Identifying Common Problem Areas

We noted in Chapter 1 that poor comprehension is often related to inadequate print skills and/or vocabulary knowledge. Sometimes, however, comprehension is poor (below 75 percent) even though the reader can identify the important words in a passage, and their meanings are reasonably familiar. In such cases, the reading difficulty is considered to be specific to comprehension. In general, this means that the reader fails to see how ideas fit together—how one idea builds on another. Often it is causal chains that go unrecognized, but other types of relationships give rise to difficulty as well. For instance, the reader might not recognize that one statement is an amplification of another, or that it is a summary of a series of preceding statements or an example in support of a general statement.

Research tends to corroborate the view that students' specific difficulties in comprehension cannot be identified through a simple analysis of question types. In a study of sixth graders, the poorer readers answered fewer questions correctly than the good readers, but they were similar to the good readers in that they answered more main idea questions than detail questions (Meyer, 1975). A similar result was observed with good and poor readers at the college level (Marshall & Glock, 1978–1979). With regard to inferences, Bridge and Tierney (1981) found that the proportion of total information recalled that was inferential in nature was the same (approximately 40 percent) for poor readers as for good readers at the third-grade level. And, among a group of poor comprehenders at the seventh-grade level, Palincsar and Brown (1983) found no tendency for questions about implicit information to be more difficult than questions about explicit information. Although question-answering behavior may be suggestive of deeper issues, multifaceted analysis is called for in these cases.

At the same time, a growing body of evidence, consistent with the view of comprehension presented in the preceding chapter, shows that poor comprehension arises from difficulty with the integrative processes necessary for understanding discourse. For instance, Marshall and Glock (1978–1979) found that intersentence relationships were a major stumbling block for poor readers at the college level. These relationships may be made explicit through various signaling devices (*however, because, in contrast, instead, in other words, for example, first, second,* and so on) or they may be implicit. Whereas the better readers did equally well under both circumstances, the poor readers suffered a significant reduction in recall of passage information when these relationships were implied rather than directly stated. The poorer readers tended to include fewer interpropositional relations in their written recalls. Further evidence that the absence of signaling devices can be detrimental to poor readers was obtained in a study of ninth graders (Meyer, Brandt, & Bluth, 1980).

In addition, research indicates that poor readers are generally insensitive to the high-level organization of passage information. In recalling information after reading, poor readers are much less likely than good readers to follow the overall argument or pattern of discourse used by the author. Whereas awareness of textual organization at the discourse level is rarely directly relevant to classroom comprehension tasks, it facilitates the processing of lower-level information. There is a high correlation between a student's ability to use the top-level structure of text in organizing his or her recall and the total amount of information recalled (Meyer et al., 1980). A focus on text frames (Buehl, 2001), the organizational structure of texts (e.g., main idea–supporting details; problem–solution; comparison–contrast), leads to marked increases in the amount of information students recall (Bartlett, 1978; McDonald, 1978; both cited in Meyer et al., 1980; Jones, Pierce, & Hunter, 1988/1989).

Finally, there is considerable evidence that poor readers have difficulty monitoring their mental processes while reading and that they do not make appropriate adjustments when they encounter obstacles to comprehension (Kimmell & MacGinitie, 1985). For example, poor readers often fail to recognize that something does not make sense or that they do not know the answer to a question. Nor do they regularly reread portions of text in an attempt to gain clarification. In an investigation of the question-answering strategies of good and poor readers in grades four through ten, a passage was used that required the student to look back to the text for the answers to certain questions. Researchers found that the good readers in grades six and seven (although not in the lower grades) showed some awareness of comprehension difficulty on at least 50 percent of the questions that required lookbacks. That is, they indicated uncertainty or dissatisfaction with a response by shrugs, grunts, and hesitations, and by such verbal expressions as ". . . I think"; ". . . or something"; and "that's a hard one." By contrast, the poor readers in these grades showed such behaviors on less than 7 percent of the questions. However, contrary to expectation, the sixth- and seventh-grade good readers did *not* look back to the text with great frequency for the answers to the targeted questions. It was only among the good readers in eighth grade and beyond that this strategy was observed with considerable frequency (79 percent of the questions that required lookbacks). Thus, although poor readers at all grade levels tend to be unaware when they do not understand or know the answer to a question, even good readers do not employ lookbacks to resolve difficulties until they reach the upper grades (Garner & Reis, 1981).

Given this evidence, it is useful to view poor comprehension as arising in relation to difficulty with the integration of text information, both at the intersentence level and at higher levels of text structure. Underlying this difficulty are poorly developed strategies for utilizing background knowledge and recognizing and responding to failures of comprehension as they occur.

For some students, poorly developed strategies for interacting with text and organizing information represent only part of the problem. Instruction in such strategies can be effective only if students already possess the basic capacity for understanding the ideas and information with which they must interact. To provide appropriate instruction once you have determined that a student's difficulty is in comprehension, you must decide whether the student has this basic capacity. You would assess his or her comprehension for this purpose. You would provide the student with an opportunity to reread relevant portions of the diagnostic passage and answer the questions that were incorrectly answered on the initial administration of the comprehension test. If the student corrects several answers on this second trial, you can conclude that he or she has the ability to acquire basic text information and can profit from instruction in interactive and organizational strategies. On the other hand, if the student is essentially unable to correct his or her answers, then the difficulty is either at a conceptual level or at the level of acquiring basic text information, necessitating instruction in intersentence and intrasentence relationships. This latter type of instruction focuses on the anaphoric relations, the use of a pronoun as a stand-in for a previous word (Harris & Hodges, 1995, p. 9), and linguistic devices that connect sentence information. It also involves the modeling of certain thought processes or interactive strategies believed to be second nature to proficient readers.

Although the print skills required across a variety of reading situations are fairly stable and determinable by a thorough initial diagnosis, comprehension skills are not. Differences in content, organization, style, and length can make dramatically different demands on the reader, making initial diagnosis of comprehension problems more tentative and qualified (Wixson, Peters, Weber, & Roeber, 1987). It is therefore less possible to make what is called a differential diagnosis with respect to comprehension from one or two diagnostic encounters. Rather, ongoing diagnostic instruction manipulating the type and complexity of material used and degree and mode of teacher support can both pinpoint a student's abilities and disabilities and guide the appropriate sequence of instruction. We discuss these variables later in the section on instruction.

Gathering Authentic Data

If assessment of comprehension is to provide authentic data, it must involve observing students in the act of comprehending. You can gather information by interacting with readers in post-reading discussion, by having them recall what they have read (a retelling), or by involving them in oral or written introspection and retrospection as they read. Whatever the initial data-gathering choice, all comprehension assessment techniques call on the examiner to respond to the reader through direct, indirect, or probing questions at some point in the diagnostic cycle. Questioning is essential to all diagnosis, either as an initial stimulus or for later probes of what is spontaneously presented in a retelling, in introspection, or in a guided reading lesson. Further, the guidelines for designing a set of questions to accurately represent the content of a selection, presented in Chapter 5, also provide the standard for analyzing a student's free recall, introspection, or instructional contribution.

In this section we show how Jim used a classroom selection, "Two Were Left" to gather data on his students' comprehension. To carry out the assessments within the context of normal classroom routine, Jim needed to analyze the selection the students would be reading, prepare questions or a retelling format, decide on some administrative and evaluative guidelines, and decide how to work with each student. For Bob, post-reading questioning was used for assessment—perhaps the most common approach to gathering data. With Andrea, a retelling was used. For Jake, an introspective think-aloud provided a promising option for assessment. Jim frequently gave one student attention while the larger group worked independently, so he took Jake aside and worked through the selection with him. For Bob and Andrea, Jim scheduled some individual time after reading while the larger group worked on extension activities.

• Preparation

Jim read "Two Were Left" (Cave, 1969) using the process we illustrated for "The Restless Kangaroo" in Chapter 5 (see Figure 5.9, pages 201–202). He then constructed a set of questions that represented the important information in the selection.

p a u s e and r e f l e c t

Read "Two Were Left" (see Figure 6.2) and design a set of questions that you think reflect the important information and issues of the selection. Also choose some important vocabulary terms to analyze. Compare your questions and terms with those in Figure 6.3 (page 221) and to the list of important information in the retelling protocol in Figure 6.4 (page 222).

In constructing questions or a retelling protocol, Jim quite naturally has specific responses in mind. These are recorded in parentheses next to each question on the prepared question list or as entries on the retelling protocol (see Figures 6.3 and 6.4) for easy reference during testing. Then Jim can make a quick judgment regarding the quality of the student's response and assess further when doing so seems appropriate. Often an answer is correct under a slightly different interpretation of the question. For example, in connection with the story of "The Restless Kangaroo" (pages 201–202, Chapter 5) one of the questions is, "What did the zookeeper do to find out about the problem [that the zoo was having with the kangaroos]?" The expected answer is that the zookeeper stood watch over the kangaroos' pen one night while the animals slept. If a child answered, "He gave them a different pen," one must allow for the possibility that the child did not

figure 6.2 • Diagnostic Reading Selection

Two Were Left

On the third night of hunger, Noni thought of the dog. Nothing of flesh and blood lived upon the floating ice island with its towering berg except those two.

In the breakup Noni had lost his sled, his food, his fur, even his knife. He had saved only Nimuk, his devoted husky. And now the two marooned on the ice eyed each other warily—each keeping his distance.

Noni's love for Nimuk was real, very real—as real as the hunger and cold nights and the gnawing pain of his injured leg. But the men of his village killed their dogs when food was scarce, didn't they? And without thinking twice about it.

And Nimuk, he told himself, when hungry enough would seek food. One of us will soon be eating the other, Noni thought. So . . .

He could not kill the dog with his bare hands. Nimuk was powerful and much fresher than he. A weapon, then, was essential.

Removing his mittens, he unstrapped the brace from his leg. When he had hurt his leg a few weeks before, he had made the brace from bits of harness and two thin strips of iron.

Kneeling now, he stuck one of the iron strips into a crack in the ice and began to rub the other against it with firm, slow strokes.

Nimuk watched him intently, and it seemed to Noni that the dog's eyes glowed more brightly as night came.

He worked on, trying not to remember why. The slab of iron had an edge now. It had begun to take shape. Daylight found his task completed.

Noni pulled the finished knife from the ice and thumbed its edge. The sun's glare, reflected from it, stabbed at his eyes and for a moment blinded him.

Noni steeled himself.

'Here, Nimuk!' he called softly.

The dog watched him suspiciously.

'Come here,' Noni called.

Nimuk came closer. Noni read fear in the animal's gaze. He read hunger and suffering in the dog's labored breathing and awkward, dragging crouch. His heart wept. He hated himself and fought against it.

Closer Nimuk came, wary of his intentions. Now Noni felt a thickening in his throat. He saw the dog's eyes and they were wells of suffering.

Now! Now was the time to strike!

A great sob shook Noni's kneeling body. He cursed the knife. He swayed blindly; flung the weapon far from him. With empty hands outstretched he stumbled toward the dog, and fell.

The dog growled. He warily circled the boy's body. Noni was sick with fear.

In flinging away his knife he had left himself defenseless. He was too weak to crawl after it now. He was at Nimuk's mercy, and Nimuk was hungry.

The dog circled him and was creeping up from behind. Noni heard the rattle of saliva in the savage throat.

He shut his eyes, praying that the attack might be swift. He felt the dog's feet against his leg, the hot rush of Nimuk's breath against his neck. A scream gathered in the boy's throat.

Then he felt the dog's hot tongue licking his face.

Noni's eyes opened, staring, not believing. Crying softly, he put out his arm and drew the dog's head down against his own. . . .

The plane came out of the south an hour later. Its pilot, a young man of the coastal patrol, looked down and saw the large, floating ice island with the berg rising from its center. And he saw something flashing.

It was the sun gleaming on something shiny which moved. His curiosity aroused, the pilot banked his ship and descended, circling the ice. Now he saw, in the shadow of the peak of ice, a dark, still shape that appeared to be human. Or were there two shapes?

He set his ship down in a water lane and investigated. There were two shapes, boy and dog. The boy was unconscious but alive. The dog whined feebly but was too weak to move.

The gleaming object which had trapped the pilot's attention was a hand-made knife stuck point first into the ice a little distance away and quivering in the wind.

Source: From *New Worlds Ahead* by I. Willis and R. E. Willis, pp. 409–411, published by Harcourt, Brace, and World, 1969. Copyright © 1942 by the Crowell-Collier Publishing Co. Reprinted by permission of the author, Hugh B. Cave.

quite catch the words *to find out* and for this reason answered as if the question pertained to what was done *about* the problem. In such a case, it seems reasonable to clarify the question, for example, by saying, "Yes, he did that in the end. But how did he find out what the problem was?"

In other cases, the answer given might relate to an aspect of the story problem that is different from the one the teacher had in mind. In response to the question, "What was the problem the zoo was having with the kangaroos?" a student might answer, "The baby kangaroo kept putting straw into the pouch." This is, of course, the "ultimate" or underlying problem in the story, but the initial problem, in terms of the story structure, is that the baby kangaroo was found on the floor of the pen on several occasions. Again, the question should be clarified: "Yes. But they noticed a problem before they found out about that. What was the problem they noticed?" Then, if necessary, further clarification might be given: "What kept happening to the baby kangaroo because it kept putting straw into the pouch?" In general, answers that give information that is correct in terms of the story but slightly oblique in relation to the question should be probed further, either at the time of the initial response or after all the questions have been asked.

Another type of problematic response is one that is too broad or narrow. In Chapter 4 we saw that Raymond gave too narrow an answer (namely, specific examples in response to the question of what determines the kinds of housing people build), apparently because he did not fully grasp the idea that external conditions can determine what people do. He was given partial credit, however, for recognizing the examples as relevant to the question. An answer that is too broad should also be given partial credit if it represents a reasonable generalization from the evidence.

Comprehension

✓ **1.** Where were Noni and Nimuk marooned? (on an ice island)
RESPONSE: Ice island.

✓ **2.** How did Noni feel about Nimuk? (loved him very much)
RESPONSE: Liked him.

✗ **3.** Why did Noni think a weapon was essential? (Nimuk was too powerful to kill with his bare hands)
RESPONSE: To kill wild animals for food.

✗ **4.** From what did Noni make a weapon? (strips of iron from his brace)
RESPONSE: Knife.

✓ **5.** Why were they wary of each other? (they were both starving—might kill the other for food)
RESPONSE: 'Cause one might eat the other.

6. Why was Noni unable to attack the dog? (loved him too much)
✓ RESPONSE: Noni liked the dog; did not want to kill him.

7. What did Noni do with the knife? (threw it away—"far from him")
✗ RESPONSE: Tried to kill Nimuk and left it there.

8. When did Noni know that the dog would not attack him? (when he felt the dog licking
✗ his face)
RESPONSE: The dog came closer and closer.

9. Who rescued them? (a pilot in a plane)
✓ RESPONSE: A plane.

10. What was quivering in the wind which caught the pilot's attention? (the knife)
✓ RESPONSE: Knife.

Vocabulary Knowledge

1 What is a *husky*?
✓ RESPONSE: An Eskimo sled dog.

2. What does *marooned* mean?
✓ RESPONSE: Deserted on an island.

3. What does *gnawing* mean?
✓ RESPONSE: A dull pain that doesn't stop.

4. What does *essential* mean?
✓ RESPONSE: Necessary.

5. In the story, it says that Noni "steeled" himself. What does *steeled* mean?
✓ RESPONSE: Got his nerve up.

6. What does *wary* mean?
✓ RESPONSE: Careful—cautious.

7. What does *descended* mean?
✓ RESPONSE: Go down.

8. What does *feebly* mean?
✓ RESPONSE: Weakly.

9. What does *quivering* mean?
✓ RESPONSE: Shaking.

10. What does *intention* mean?
✓ RESPONSE: Going to do something.

figure 6.4 • Retelling Response Checklist for "Two Were Left": Andrea

Information	Spontaneous	Prompted
1. Noni and Nimuk	√ (no names)	½
2. marooned on ice island		
3. Both were becoming hungry	√	
4. Noni considers killing Nimuk	√	
5. Nimuk too strong to kill with bare hands		—
6. Noni began to make a knife from knee brace		—
7. Both were wary because each might harm other		—
8. Noni unable to kill Nimuk because he loved him		—
9. Noni threw knife far from him		√
10. Nimuk approached Noni	} (whole sequence missing)	—
11. Noni feared Nimuk would attack him		—
12. Nimuk licked Noni, didn't harm		—
13. Pilot found boy and dog	√	
14. because of blade's reflection		—
Percentage of comprehension:	$\frac{5.5}{14} = 39\%$	

In addition, it is good practice to give students an opportunity to sharpen their answers. For answers that are too narrow, Jim may ask for a general statement about the specific facts or examples given (e.g., "What does the use of logs from a nearby forest show about the housing people build?"). For answers that are too broad, he should ask for more precise information. For example he might use a passage about the problem of oil spills in the ocean, which discusses the fact that the oil kills animals, birds, and microscopic plant life. If a student responds to the question of why oil spills must be prevented, by suggesting they "cause pollution," the student should be asked for some specification of the harmful effects of this pollution.

• Administration

A basic principle of instruction in reading is that the reader should be given some general purpose or guiding statement before reading. This principle should be followed in assessment as well. Jim prepared the entire group for reading "Two Were Left" by setting the stage for the excerpted selection they were to read. The group hypothesized about life for the Inuit and the dangers of being stranded in the wild. He then took Jake aside for the think-aloud process, coming back to work with Bob and Andrea immediately after silent reading. For each of them, he had a "right after reading" session to tap their immediate comprehension and worked with each of them a second time to further assess their understanding.

As the procedure is teacher designed, the teacher can repeat, reword, or clarify questions. He or she must acknowledge that some questions may be ambiguous, permitting more than one interpretation, or they may elicit unanticipated, though correct, responses. For this reason, taping of the sessions is advisable so that the teacher can devote his or her attention to listening to the reader and asking thoughtful questions.

• Evaluation

After working with each student, Jim prepared an analysis. For Bob and Andrea, he used the following procedure:

1. Initial analysis: Calculate a comprehension score by determining the percentage of text-related questions that the student answered correctly. If a retelling has been used, calculate the percentage of important elements he or she recalled. If the comprehension score is less than 75 percent, analyze print skill and vocabulary knowledge to see whether these areas have interfered with comprehension. If poor comprehension is *not* attributable to either of these underlying areas, look further at comprehension.

2. Further assessment of comprehension: For each question that was answered incorrectly, have the student reread the portion(s) of the passage that are relevant and give him or her a second opportunity to answer the question or provide retelling information. The purpose is to gain insight into the student's thinking and text-processing strategies. When the student can correct his or her initial response, assume that the first difficulty was relatively superficial—the student is able to grasp basic information but has difficulty identifying or extracting the relevant information. In some cases, the student may have misunderstood the question or failed to include it in his or her retelling.

When the student is unable to respond correctly after reexamining the text, the difficulty is considered to be more severe. In such cases, a more detailed assessment should focus on the cohesive elements of the selection and the reasoning and prior knowledge necessary to make inferences. Let's look at Bob's case in more detail to see how Jim conducted his diagnostic process.

case 6.1

Bob—Using Questions

Bob, a seventh grader, read "Two Were Left" (see Figure 6.1.). This story was about an Inuit boy, Noni, who was marooned with his dog on an ice island. Because there was no wildlife or vegetation on the island, within a few days the two were near starvation. With much anguish, the boy concluded that he must kill the dog for food.

Bob showed excellent print skill when he read the story aloud. Further, the vocabulary knowledge assessment, shown in Figure 6.2, indicated that he was familiar with the key words in the story (e.g., *marooned, essential, wary, descended, intention*). The questions that Bob's teacher, Jim, developed to measure his understanding of the story are also shown in the figure, along with his responses. As you can see, Bob's comprehension score was only 60 percent. Because his print skill and vocabulary knowledge were both highly satisfactory, his main difficulty was considered to be in the area of comprehension. You should examine the questions that Bob answered incorrectly to identify possible reasons for his comprehension difficulties.

Further Assessment for Comprehension

The first question that Bob missed in the comprehension test was drawn from the following paragraph:

> He could not kill the dog with his bare hands. Nimuk was powerful and much fresher than he. A weapon, then, was essential.

The question was "Why did Noni think a weapon was essential?" Bob had initially answered, "To kill wild animals for food." (The correct answer would refer to the fact that the dog was too powerful to be killed barehanded; partial credit could be given for referring to the need to kill the dog for food.) Further assessment with regard to this question was as follows:

Jim: I'd like you to read this paragraph again and see if you can tell why Noni thought a weapon was essential.

Bob: [after reading]: To kill the dog, for food.

Jim: Yes, but why did he need a weapon?

Bob: Can't kill a dog without a weapon, with bare hands.

Jim: And why not?

Bob: It could kill you, too big.

One interpretation of this result is that Bob had initially answered as he did—"to kill wild animals for food"—because he conceived of the question as a generic one—pertaining to weapons in general, rather than to the story in particular. Another possibility is that he had forgotten—or was never really certain—that there were no wild animals on the ice island. (That information appears in the second sentence of the story, several paragraphs before the one under discussion.) Nevertheless, he was able to answer the question correctly on rereading, showing that he could, at least, understand the intersentence relationships in the paragraph.

Jim continued with another question that Bob had initially missed. This related to the part of the story that described how the Inuit boy made a knife with two strips of metal taken from a brace he was wearing on his wounded knee. The relevant paragraphs read as follows:

> Removing his mittens, he unstrapped the brace from his leg. When he had hurt his leg a few weeks before, he had made the brace from bits of harness and two thin strips of iron.
>
> Kneeling now, he stuck one of the iron strips into a crack in the ice and began to rub the other against it with firm, slow strokes.
>
> Nimuk watched him intently, and it seemed to Noni that the dog's eyes glowed more brightly as night came.
>
> He worked on, trying not to remember why. The slab of iron had an edge now. It had begun to take shape. Daylight found his task completed.

In answer to the question "From what did Noni make a weapon?" Bob had responded, "a knife." After rereading, he responded as follows:

Bob: Oh. A slab of iron.

Jim: And where did he get the iron?

Bob: His brace for his knee.

Jim: Can you explain how he made a knife out of the iron?

Bob: He rubbed it until it had an edge.

Jim: What did he rub it with?

Bob: Not sure . . . on the ice?

This was a rather difficult sequence of text. It required the reader to visualize a step-by-step procedure, and Bob was evidently unable to do this. Still, on a second reading he had gleaned the essential idea that the knife was made from a part of the brace.

The third question that Bob missed involved a crucial element of the story. Just as the boy was about to strike the dog, he was overcome with grief and "flung the weapon far from him." Bob evidently understood the boy's reluctance to kill the dog; in answer to the question, "Why was Noni unable to attack the dog?" he had replied, "Noni liked the dog; did not want to kill him." Yet, in answering the next question, "What did Noni do with the knife?" Bob had stated that Noni "tried to kill Nimuk and left it there." Thus,

Bob seemed to have two conflicting ideas about a dramatic story event. Jim explored further by having Bob reread the following segment.

> Now! Now was the time to strike!
>   A great sob shook Noni's kneeling body. He cursed the knife. He swayed blindly; flung the weapon far from him. With empty hands outstretched he stumbled toward the dog, and fell.

Then Jim asked the question again, "What did Noni do with the knife?"

Bob: Tried to kill Nimuk. Threw it far.

Jim: Did he throw it at the dog?

Bob: Yeah. But he missed him.

Because the student did not answer correctly on this second trial, the assessment then took the form of a detailed analysis of the text.

Jim: Show me the part that tells what Noni did; read it aloud.

Bob: [from passage]: "Flung the weapon far from him."

Jim: Yes, I suppose that could mean that he threw it at the dog and missed. But I think it means something else. Do you know how I know?

Bob: No.

Jim: Well, let's look at what happened before that, right after Noni finished making the knife. [The teacher points to the preceding paragraph and the student reads it aloud: "Closer Nimuk came, wary of his intentions. Now Noni felt a thickening in his throat. He saw the dog's eyes and they were wells of suffering."] Okay, so where was Nimuk when Noni threw the knife?

Bob: [No response.]

Jim: [clarifying]: Where was Nimuk in relation to Noni? How close was he?

Bob: Well, he came closer. . . . Oh, he saw the dog's eyes.

Jim: Yes, so the dog had to be pretty close to Noni. Do you see now what it means that Noni "flung the weapon far from him"?

Bob: He wasn't trying to kill the dog?

Jim: Right. We have to assume that he wasn't trying to kill the dog—that he changed his mind at the last minute and threw the knife "far from him"—far from himself and the dog.

There was, then, some plausibility to Bob's interpretation of the story character's action, at least when that action is taken by itself, out of context. It only becomes implausible that the boy meant to kill the dog when he "flung the weapon far from him" when one takes into account the dog's proximity. Bob had failed to keep one fact in mind while considering another. And, as with the first question, he did seem able to understand the language of the text at both the sentence and intersentence levels.

The fourth and final question that Bob missed involved the next event in the story. After the Inuit boy threw the knife "far from him" he lay on the ground in fear that the dog would now attack him:

> He shut his eyes, praying that the attack might be swift. He felt the dog's feet against his leg, the hot rush of Nimuk's breath against his neck. A scream gathered in the boy's throat.
> Then he felt the dog's hot tongue licking his face.

In response to the question, "When did the boy know the dog would not attack him?" Bob had answered, "The dog came closer and closer." After rereading, he was able to answer correctly, "When he felt him licking his face."

Taken together, Bob's responses on further assessment suggest that his main comprehension difficulty is in integrating story events. He seemed to consider each event an isolated phenomenon. As a result, his grasp of the story line was initially vague and impressionistic. Nevertheless, he was able to correct three out of four of his responses, indicating that he had the capability to grasp the basic information in the text. Therefore, Jim diagnosed Bob's comprehension problem as poorly developed strategies for interacting with information and for recognizing its overall structure. We comment on instruction for Bob later in this chapter. ■

● Retelling

Jim used some of the same assessment strategies with Andrea that he had used with Bob. However, because he wanted to assess Andrea's comprehension without the clues that questions sometimes provide, he used a retelling. Retelling is a process in which the student is asked to retell the story or reproduce information in his or her own words. Following a prereading orientation, the examiner does not ask specific questions but rather asks the reader to retell the selection. Working with a prepared checklist (see Figure 6.4 for an example for the selection "Two Were Left," introduced earlier), the examiner records the information supplied by the reader in the order in which it is presented. Following the student's unprompted recall, the examiner uses questions to assess further for any information the student did not supply. During or after the retelling, the assessor can also make anecdotal notes on the student's oral language.

You can score aided recall easily if the checklist of information you prepare in advance is precise and well ordered. Give the student points for each idea or fact recalled, as you would with questions. One advantage of this procedure is that it gives you some idea of the student's verbal clarity and fluency. It is more time-consuming than direct questioning, however, at least at the point of administration, and the added information may be superfluous if you have many other opportunities to observe students' verbal proficiency.

Retellings have been used extensively as a research tool and less frequently for assessment and instruction (Gambrell, Pfeiffer, & Wilson, 1985; Irwin & Mitchell, 1983; Morrow et al., 1986). They have the advantage of showing the examiner what the student sees as important without the prompt of teacher questions. Further, the sequence in which the student retells the information and the language he or she uses to express it also provide more diagnostic information.

Diagnostic use of the retelling procedure can bring certain problems, however. Morrow et al. (1986) found that students often have trouble with the process if it is unfamiliar but that repeated attempts produce more elaborated retellings. Further, children respond differently to different directions. For example, if both the reader and the examiner have read the story, students will often omit important information, assuming the examiner already knows it (Golden & Pappas, 1987). Moreover, the quality of the retelling or reproduction may reflect the student's verbal and expository skills as much as his or her comprehension. Students vary widely in their ability to organize and verbalize information. Like other integrative and language skills, this one depends a great deal on practice. Because questions serve as "cues" or "prompts," readers can usually remember much more about a passage in response to questioning than they can reproduce in a free recall. For example, Stein and Glenn (1979) report that in retelling a story, young children tended to omit information about the goals and motives of story characters and yet they were able to answer questions about these story elements.

More significant for our purposes, the tendency to provide additional information in response to questioning is much more pronounced among poor readers than among good readers. Bridge and Tierney (1981) found that of the total number of items of information that were ultimately remembered by a group of low-achieving third graders, over 40 percent were given during the further assessment task that followed free recall. Therefore, although it may be well to give students an opportunity to retell the story in order to assess their ability to do so, a good set of questions will be needed to obtain a valid estimate of their comprehension skill.

case 6.2

Andrea—Using a Retelling

Andrea, a seventh grader with good print and fluency skills, read the same story introduced earlier, "Two Were Left," about the dilemma of an Inuit boy marooned with his dog. Jim began the retelling process.

Jim: Can you tell me the story as if you were telling it to someone who hadn't read it?

Andrea: There was a kid and his dog and because nobody could live in the cold they had to keep going. So he was going to kill his dog because the dog was creeping around him. But a plane saved them in time.

Jim: Anything else you'd like to tell someone who hadn't read it?

Andrea: [pausing a long time]: Well, the kid wanted to use his knife to kill the dog.

Jim: Why was that?

Andrea: Well, it's a good weapon for killing.

Jim: Where did he get the knife?

Andrea: He carried it in his leg pocket.

Jim: Do you have any idea where this is happening?

Andrea: In the winter someplace.

Jim: How did Noni and Nimuk feel on the ice?

Andrea: Cold and hungry.

Jim: Was this a problem?

Andrea: Sure, they'd starve or freeze.

Jim: Any other problems?

Andrea: Well, that would be enough.

Jim: Why do you think he didn't kill Nimuk?

Andrea: He'd need his dog for pulling his sled later.

Jim: What happened to the knife?

Andrea: He threw it away.

Jim: Why?

Andrea: He wasn't going to use it.

Jim: How did the pilot find them?

Andrea: He must have looked around for a long time and then saw two little black dots on the ice.

pause and reflect

Cover up the right-hand side of the retelling checklist in Figure 6.4 and score Andrea's responses. Then compare with Jim's scoring. Discuss differences. How would you assess her comprehension?

Further Assessment for Comprehension

Following the first retelling and questioning, Jim did further assessment by asking Andrea to reexamine the selection. Simple reexamination did not help Andrea do a better job of answering some of the questions. For example, the issue of the knife is an important one for the selection. Jim then led Andrea through this series of questions:

1. Did Noni have his knife at the beginning of the story? What does the author tell us? (the knife was lost in the breakup of the ice)
2. Why did he need a knife? (Nimuk too big to kill with bare hands)
3. How did he get the knife? (made it from knee brace)
4. What happened to the knife? (he threw it far away)

Then Jim related the knife's reflection in the sun to the pilot's discovery of the two survivors. In doing this, he needed to go paragraph by paragraph, and sometimes sentence by sentence, through this short selection helping Andrea identify important information, sequence it, and make connections.

Unlike Bob, Andrea seemed to grasp only the most obvious information provided by the author and was unable to improve her performance without Jim's considerable support and segmenting of the selection. Andrea's problem is much more severe and requires attention to her ability to gain basic information from the text as well as her skill at integrating information across the text. ■

• Think-Alouds

In the think-aloud procedure (Lytle, 1982), the student is asked to introspect and verbalize before, during, and after reading a selection. The teacher asks the student to reflect and comment on what he or she is reading as the text is exposed line by line. In the introspection process, Lytle has noted that students comment on what they understand (signaling understanding), indicate what is causing them problems (monitoring of doubts), analyze parts of the text (analyzing) or verbally try to figure things out (reasoning), relate the author's ideas to their own knowledge (elaborating), and evaluate aspects of the author's message and style (judging).

Readers exhibit strategies when they combine the "moves" noted in parentheses earlier for a particular purpose, such as to remove a doubt. Characteristic strategies in certain situations may define a student's style, which may be consistent across various texts. Though this process is still an exploratory one, having a student "talk through" a selection may provide diagnostic insights and instructional leads.

case 6.3

Jake—Using a Think-Aloud

Here we consider an excerpt from a think-aloud protocol of Jake, a seventh-grade student, reading "Two Were Left." Jim noted that Jake is very inconsistent in his reading group. Sometimes he seems to have a good grasp of what is being read; at other times he is very confused or seems to have very different interpretations from those of the rest of the group. Jim decided to try to think-aloud with his next lesson.

When Jake arrived for his lesson, Jim told him about his plan, "Jake, I'm going to try something called a think-aloud. It will help me understand more about how reading works for you. I'm going to show you this story sentence by sentence and I want you to think out loud as you read it."

"What do you mean?" Jake asked.

"You can tell me about what you think the author is saying, what it makes you think of, where you think the author is going, what puzzles you, how you figure things out, or anything that comes into your head."

"Okay," Jake agreed.

Jim presented the text to Jake. First he displayed the title: "Two Were Left."

Jake thought for a minute, and then he observed, "It must tell about two people left off somewhere. I don't know where."

Jim didn't speak to Jake as he uncovered the first sentence of the text:

On the third night of hunger, Noni thought of the dog.

After reading, Jake spoke, "One person is Noni and he's probably worried that no one will take care of his dog while he is stuck somewhere."

Nothing of flesh and blood lived upon the floating ice island with its towering berg except those two.

"They're somewhere near an island but nobody lives there. They have been left there, alone."

In the breakup, Noni had lost his sled, his food, his fur, even his knife.

Jake read the next sentence and supposed, "He's really stuck but I still don't know who the other guy is. Maybe the other guy wants to kill Noni? That's the first guy's name, isn't it? And does the other guy have a knife?"

He had saved only Nimuk, his devoted husky.

"Well, his dog is okay. That's lucky. I'll bet the dog will find the other guy first and get him and save Noni."

And now the two marooned on the ice eyed each other warily—each keeping his distance.

Jake sat puzzled for a moment, "Well, the other guy is near enough to see him. I'm sure the dog will save him. When will they tell the other guy's name?"

It was clear to Jim from the think-aloud protocol that Jake has made an erroneous inference from the title concerning who the "two" were and that this misreading has colored Jake's understanding of the story. In retaining this schema, Jake is causing himself confusion as he continues to read the selection. He is sure another person will attack Noni and he keeps waiting for the attack. Jake interprets each of the sentences in the light of this flawed schema. Jim could tell that Jake had not attended to some essential signal words in the selection: "*except,* indicating that two are on an island, and *even,* signifying Noni's knife was gone.

After the think-aloud protocol was finished, Jake complained, "This is a really crazy story and I don't understand it at all."

"Let's go back to the beginning and work through the first paragraph," Jim patiently suggested. "If we repeat what we've just done, I'll bet the story will make more sense." Jim was thinking that Jake would not have difficulty with the narrative if he began by clearly establishing the characters and their problems and goals.

With Jim's support, Jake reread the title and the first two sentences. "Hey, I get this now," he said excitedly. "The kid is stuck on a chunk of ice with only his dog. This is a really good story. I think I understand it now."

Diagnostically, working through a selection in this manner gives Jim insight into strategy use, misuse, and overuse that can help students better approach a reading assignment. We will comment on his instruction later.

Besides its obvious diagnostic implications, Jim can use think-aloud protocols for intervention. If a student's style is nonfunctional, he can provide the types of responses *he* would make as modeling and feedback (Duffy, Roehler, & Hermann, 1988; Palincsar & Brown, 1983), can interrupt the reader and focus him on his own processes (Brown, 1986), or can have the students write his responses in a reading journal (Mayers, 1993) for later reflection, comparison, and discussion. Students can do a rereading of a selection along with an earlier audiotape to reflect on an earlier reading. Further, Jim can structure group think-alouds by using an overhead projector on which a selection is revealed chunk by chunk for group analysis and discussion. ■

Comprehension Instruction

We turn now to instruction in comprehension. How can we improve instruction for students with comprehension difficulties? Some years ago the answer would have been that we must identify areas of specific weakness and strengthen those areas through direct instruction. Educators believed that comprehension was made up of a number of subskills and that remedial efforts should be directed toward improving one or another of them. Thus, some students might need help in noting and recalling details, while others might need help in following sequences of events or grasping main ideas. This approach is now generally perceived as unduly limited and not entirely consistent with what we know about the nature of comprehension and the research on its development (National Reading Panel, 2000). Therefore, we recommend a somewhat different approach.

We noted earlier the difficulty in making a differential diagnosis for comprehension. What frequently can be determined for each reader is the degree of teacher support, the explicitness of instruction, and the length and complexity of material used in the instruction for productive comprehension. If comprehension problems are severe, adjustment may be needed in all these conditions; if problems are minimal, fewer changes may be needed. For example, some students, like Bob, require a small degree of teaching intervention and guidance to discover ways to interact better with whole texts. Others, like Jake, need heavy intervention at the start of a new selection to help them develop a schema for completing the selection unaided. Still others, like Andrea, need to be focused on very small units of text with explicit instructional demands to develop their strategies. Therefore, what differentiates comprehension instruction at the beginning of diagnosis are these three dimensions: length of the unit of text used for instruction, degree of teacher intervention, and explicitness of teacher direction. We recommend four categories of instructional procedures for helping students with poor reading comprehension. They are described in Figure 6.5.

• Developing Interactive Strategies

The directed reading lesson format common to basal reading materials has a familiar and predictable structure. You prepare concepts and vocabularies, set a prereading purpose, have the student read part or all of the selection, and ask the student discussion questions after reading. Skills are introduced and practiced at one or more places in the lesson, and reteaching, extension, and enrichment activities complete the cycle. Although this is a sensible and legitimate structure, there are many reasons to modify it for comprehension enhancement.

At the core of interactive reading is the active use of what the reader already knows. Analyses of classroom instruction (Beck, McKeown, McCaslin, & Burkes, 1979; Durkin, 1978–1979) have suggested that too little time before reading is

figure 6.5 • Instructional Procedures

Strategies that foster an interactive approach	DR-TA [Directed Reading-Thinking Activity] (Stauffer, 1990; Richek, 1987) KWL [What do you **K**now? What do you **W**ant to know? What have you **L**earned?] (Ogle, 1986)	These approaches combine implicit modeling and low-to-moderate teacher directedness; can be used with larger chunks of text.
	GIST [Generating Interaction between Schemata and Text] (Cunningham, 1982)	A technique for helping students develop short summaries.
	Reciprocal Teaching (Palincsar & Brown, 1983)	A strategy that combines small text chunks with high directedness and explicit modeling.
	Questioning the Author (McKeown, Beck, & Worthy, 1993)	Asks the reader to engage in an imaginary dialogue with the author to try to understand and query the thinking of the author as the text was constructed.
Strategies that focus on text patterns and organization	Text Structure Strategy (Alvermann, 1981; Readence, Bean, & Baldwin, 1995)	Helps students identify and utilize expository text organization in order to select an appropriate graphic organizer to better comprehend and remember informational text.
Connections within and across texts	Think-Aloud (Davey, 1983)	A method that helps readers scrutinize their own reading actions.
Relationship between questions and the text	QAR [Question/Answer Relationship] (Raphael, 1982)	Students identify the response demands of various questions ("right there," "think and search," "me and the book," "on my own") then use the knowledge to produce an answer.

devoted to developing and activating the prereading schemata necessary for effective comprehension. A second concern about the directed reading lesson is that the major part of the "work" is done by the teacher, relegating the students to the role of passive responders, not building those strategies needed to approach text independently (Stauffer, 1990). We offer several instructional alternatives to the directed reading lesson, all of which view your role as that of expert guide in leading students through a strategic approach to text. Both tacitly and explicitly these procedures call on the reader to control and monitor the reading situation.

The Directed Reading-Thinking Activity (DR-TA). The Directed Reading-Thinking Activity models the comprehension process by walking participants through a selection bit by bit rather than saving all discussion until reading has been completed. In this way you help the student experience the thinking processes that an expert reader uses in comprehending a text (Davidson & Wilkerson, 1988). The basic processes to be modeled are as follows:

1. Before I read a section of text, I use clues to make predictions about what the author will tell me.
2. I stop as I read to refine or reformulate my predictions.
3. I repeat steps 1 and 2 throughout the selection.

To plan a DR-TA, select an appropriate reading text. Choose a text that lends itself to predications and is at the student's instructional reading level. After analyzing the selection, you choose several points at which the reader might be stopped and asked for a prediction about subsequent content. The title, picture, caption, first paragraph, or some combination of these often serves as the basis for the first prediction.

After each chunk is read, you and your students discuss their prediction in the light of the clues the author has given them. Probing questions are the norm for the teacher in the DR-TA, using questions such as:

- What makes you think so?
- What did the author say that confirms that?
- What will _____ do about _____?
- Why do you think the author said that?

Students go back to the selection to find more information, to clarify a point, and to resolve conflicts, and oral reading is used to substantiate their opinions.

In the process of reasoning through the text with the author, the reader comes to a full construction of the message so that the final discussion can focus on evaluating the author's implication and craft. Writing also fits naturally into the DR-TA in that students can write predictions and evidence at various points, and they frequently want to rewrite sections of narratives that they find unsatisfactory.

The Know-Want-Learn (K-W-L) Approach. The K-W-L (Ogle, 1986) is a predictive approach to expository material. Like the DR-TA, it asks students to become active readers by specifying a purpose for reading. It has three basic strategies:

1. Brainstorm: Before reading, ask, "What do I Know?"
2. Set purpose: Ask, "What do I Want to know after I read?"
3. After reading: Ask, "What did I Learn?"

You would lead the students through brainstorming on the topic before reading and then have them list what they would like to find out. At this point you can also participate as a contributor of relevant questions. After reading, students go back to see which questions were answered by the selection, refine their knowledge, and frequently set reference goals for themselves to search out information that interests them that is not provided by the author.

Generating Interaction between Schemata and Text (GIST). Cunningham (1982) developed this collaborative learning strategy to increase understanding of expository texts by demonstrating how students can generate a summary. Although research demonstrates that summary writing can improve test scores (Radmacher & Latosi-Sawin, 1995), this genre is not easily utilized by less-skilled writers (Hare & Borchardt, 1984). However, directing students in the creation of a summary is a worthy effort that warrants the instructional time required to accomplish it satisfactorily. At least three sessions should be set aside for GIST. The teacher should model GIST as students look on, then students should be guided through a text with the teacher offering support. Finally, students should be asked to create a summary on their own. This last summation can be used as an assessment of the students' ability to generate a summary as well as a record of what the students have learned from the text.

The GIST process is as follows: The text is presented to the students with stopping points predetermined by the teacher. Students follow this two-step procedure as they read and discuss the text:

1. The meaning of the text is discussed, and vocabulary is explained.

2. A single summary sentence is negotiated.

The list of sentences generated by the students serves as a précis for the text. After the entire text has been reduced to a series of numbered sentences, students discuss how a page of text is condensed into a limited number of sentences (Frey, Fisher, & Hernandez, 2003).

Reciprocal Teaching/Modeling. Palincsar and Brown (1983) developed the Reciprocal Teaching/Modeling procedure in which students and teacher take turns leading a dialogue. The "leader" asks an important question about a small segment of text—no more than a paragraph—and is also responsible for

1. summarizing what has been read,

2. predicting what might be discussed next, and

3. clarifying anything that seems confusing.

The teacher guides students in these activities by a variety of prompting and modeling techniques:

- "Remember that a summary doesn't include a lot of detail."
- "What question would a teacher ask?"
- "That was interesting information. It was information that I would call 'detail in the passage.' Can you find the *most* important information?"
- "I would summarize by saying . . . ."
- "Being able to say in your own words what one has just read and being able to guess what questions might appear on the test are sure ways of testing oneself to see if one has understood."

The role of self-questioning, predicting, summarizing, and clarifying in enhancing comprehension, and the need for using these strategies during independent reading, must also be made explicit. Palincsar and Brown report that although seventh-grade students had considerable difficulty with the role of dialogue leader during the first few instructional sessions, by the end of ten sessions they were able to produce questions and summaries of "some sophistication." Therefore, a teacher who wishes to use this procedure should plan to use it regularly for several weeks.

An attractive feature of the reciprocal teaching format is that it emphasizes certain processes of reading while focusing on the *meaning* of segments of text. Instruction is provided within the context of "real reading" and by repeated modeling. This is in sharp contrast to the more traditional "skills" method of helping students with comprehension difficulty. Typically, in the more traditional method, specific aspects of text processing (e.g., sequencing events, recognizing causal relations) are isolated, directly taught through explanation and illustration, and then practiced by students on specially prepared materials and exercises. Students' performance on these materials is then evaluated as correct or incorrect. A major weakness of this method, aside from the isolation of particular aspects of meaning from the holistic process of reading, is that students are not *shown how* to arrive at correct solutions to the problem of meaning. Reciprocal teaching, as we have seen, directs students' attention to specific elements of text with a general focus on meaning. Therefore, we believe the method may be adapted to instruction in other features of text, particularly connective terms, as noted later.

Questioning the Author. Rather than having to memorize text content, with the Questioning the Author teaching strategy (McKeown, Beck, & Worthy, 1993), students learn to think more about *who* has written a text and how successful the writer was for them as audience or readers. They develop a dialog with the author just as they would with a person talking with them face-to-face. Students are encouraged to "query" the author, asking questions that get at a writer and content expert's decisions. Basic questions are focused on thinking about:

- Why the author included the particular information
- What the author could have said instead
- What the intent of the author was; what is the point of view
- How something could be stated more clearly

Students are *led* by their teacher in discussion of short segments of text, just as they are in Reciprocal Teaching. Only this time they focus on the author, thinking about how the author has written for them as readers/learners. After reading a paragraph in a sixth-grade history text, students may begin by asking, "Why do you think the author spent a paragraph explaining the cuneiform writing system?" Other questions may follow, such as, "What do you think it represents to the author? What else about the society might have been more important? Was it clearly written? Could something have been added to make it clearer? How would you have written this?" By questioning or querying the author, students take a different stance in relation to the text and begin to feel more active as participants in the process of communication about content topics. In classrooms where teachers use this approach, they have reported the students seem to engage more deeply with the material they are asked to read and are more willing to read "content" textbooks.

Developing the Ability to Reorganize Information

Recognizing that text information is interrelated is fundamental to comprehension. We have already discussed the role of post-reading questions in this connection, arguing that they should recapitulate the orderly progression of events and ideas that make up the story line. Similarly, students can be focused on overall selection organization, the connection across sentences, and the relationships between questions and the text that generates them. Again the length of textual units to which the strategies are applied, amount of teacher directedness, and explicitness of instruction are significant variables.

In this section we do not try to present a comprehensive range of these techniques but rather offer a selection reflecting the dimensions of teacher support and intervention discussed earlier. For example, the strategy fostered in the Question-Answer Relationship procedure (Raphael, 1986) requires explicit instruction, as do the GIST procedure (Cunningham, 1982) and the instruction on connective terms. In contrast, graphic organizers can be used as the basis for implicit instruction utilizing discovery techniques, but direct instruction of text structures is also possible. The ultimate goal of all these methods, however, is to pass the control of the process from teacher to learner.

Question-Answer Relationships (QAR). Students need to respond to questions throughout their school careers, yet Durkin (1978-1979) noted that little if any instruction focuses on the strategic processes needed to answer questions. Raphael's QAR method (1986) focuses students on the different strategies they can employ in answering a question. Her work is based on the idea that questions have several definable relationships with the selections from which they are drawn (Pearson & Johnson, 1984) and that each of these relationships suggests a different strategy for responding.

Some questions ask you merely to locate information that an author has given you explicitly and all in one place. Raphael (1986) terms these "Right There" questions; the author has answered them right there in the text for you. Other questions can be answered by looking for clues, both implicit and explicit, scattered across a text; for these you must "Think and Search." A third type of question necessitates that you add your own knowledge to what the author tells you; these are "Author and You" questions, calling for analysis, synthesis, and evaluation. A fourth type of question can be answered by you alone; these are "On My Own" questions.

For example, for the selection, "Two Were Left," some possible QARs would be these:

> *Question:*   Where were Noni and Nimuk when the selection began?
>
> *Answer 1:*   Marooned on an ice flow. (*Right There:* The student just searched for an answer given directly by the author.)
>
> *Answer 2:*   Maybe in Alaska (*Author and You:* The student used the clues of climate, terrain, sled, and husky to connect with what he knew about various locales.)

The preceding is a good example of two possible correct answers for the same question, each with a different procedure for answering.

> *Question:*   Would you say Noni loved Nimuk? Support your answer.
>
> *Answer:*   Yes, because he worried about him but he couldn't kill him. (*Think and Search:* The reader had to collect clues across the text.)
>
> *Question:*   Have you ever had to make a hard decision that scared you?
>
> *Answer:*   (Varies) (*On Your Own:* The student doesn't need to refer back to the story to answer this one.)

Raphael suggests making these categories and strategies explicit to students and having them classify and answer questions as a group. You can structure this activity as a game in which students gather evidence for a set of questions and discuss how they answered them (Sentell & Blachowicz, 1989).

Guided Reading Procedure. As originally developed by Manzo (1975), the Guided Reading Procedure is designed to enhance students' recall of expository materials. It also increases the level of student participation in class and provides challenge as well as variety. It consists of the following steps:

1. A passage of appropriate length is selected. The length is best judged in terms of the reading speed and attention span of the average reader in the group. As a rule of thumb, primary grade students might be expected to read for 3 minutes and to read a 90-word passage in that time (30 words per minute); intermediate grade students might read for 5 minutes at approximately 100 words per minute—a 500-word passage; junior high students might read for 7 minutes at 125 words per minute—an approximately 900-word passage; and high school students could probably read for 10 minutes at 200 words per minute—a 2,000 word passage.

2. The teacher prepares students for the selection by introducing the general topic—relating it to previous classroom instruction as well as to students' personal experiences—and by introducing vocabulary and new concepts. A general purpose for reading is established, and students are directed to remember as much of the passage as they can.

3. After reading, students tell whatever they remember, and all information is recorded on the chalkboard by the teacher in the order in which it is recalled. (It may be in abbreviated form to save time.) One teacher found that having students write the information in their notebooks while the teacher recorded it on the chalkboard helped sustain students' attention and interest.

4. After students have contributed all the information they can remember, the teacher directs their attention to any inconsistencies, inaccuracies, or inadequacies that may be present. Students are encouraged to consult the text for necessary corrections and additions.

5. The group is then asked to organize the information they have compiled. This may take any form that is familiar to the students—a diagram, an outline, a chronological sequence, or even a semantic web. The teacher guides this process by raising questions and making suggestions.

6. The teacher then raises some final questions to help students gain full understanding of the passage.

7. For the final step, a conventional, teacher-made comprehension test is administered. The test items can be of any kind, but they should reflect the ideas and information that were brought out during class discussion. Manzo cautions against omitting this step: "It is important to the overall design because it provides an opportunity for evaluation, feedback, and

reinforcement." He also notes that "students . . . come to look forward to these tests as opportunities to show what they have learned—a just reward for effort."[1]

Although Manzo's procedure was originally designed to be used following silent reading of an entire passage, you may also use it as a prereading activity. In this case, students first survey the passage by reading the title, headings, pictures, charts, introductory and summary paragraphs, and so on. Then they recall as much as they can, organize their recall, and check it for accuracy and completeness (as in Steps 3, 4, and 5). They then read the entire passage and take the final comprehension test (Step 7). When used as a prereading activity, the procedure demonstrates the value of surveying materials before reading and thus serves to combine the teaching of surveying skills with the teaching of specific content. After reading, the students contribute ideas while you record them on a chalkboard. Each idea is enclosed in a circle, and lines are drawn to connect the circles as appropriate. Students are permitted to refer to the text to refresh their memories or resolve conflicts.

For example, for a story about triplets, the teacher wrote the name of each triplet in a separate circle and the names of all three in a fourth circle. The four circles radiated from a central circle, the core of the web, which was left blank. The students were directed to "remember important things about each sister." After the story was read (by the teacher in this case, as a listening activity), the children recalled information on how each sister differed from the others as well as on the characteristics they all shared. The core of the web, representing the central idea, was filled in after the four strands had been completed; an appropriate statement of the central idea was arrived at through brainstorming "sisters who do the same and different things." The completed web then served as a springboard for a group discussion of individuality and family relationships.

Direct Instruction in Text Structure. Instructional techniques that focus student attention on the structure of what they read have been shown to increase comprehension, learning, and remembering if the task matches the way comprehension will later be measured (Anderson & Armbruster, 1984; Buehl, 2009; Weaver & Kintsch, 1991). That is, if students will be asked to summarize a text, instructional tasks that ask them to build a schematic representation will be useful. Such tasks would be less useful if students needed to prepare for a multiple-choice test.

Sentence-Level Comprehension. Although most instructional intervention is carried out with whole selections or large segments of text, some instruction

---

[1]From "Guided Reading Procedure" by A. V. Manzo, 1975, in *Journal of Reading, 18,* 291. Reprinted by permission of the author.

may need to focus on sentence-level comprehension and instruction. Though children come to school with fairly sophisticated knowledge of the syntactic system of their language, this competence continues to develop over the elementary school years with exposure through reading, writing, speaking, and listening as the prime avenues of this development. Therefore, we do not suggest that extensive instruction with isolated sentences be included in the instructional program. Rather, the following techniques may be tried with sentences that proved difficult within the context of a larger selection.

Highlighting Anaphoric Relations. Anaphoric relations refer to the way in which certain words can be used as substitutes for words or groups of words that occurred previously in the text. In addition to personal pronouns, anaphoric devices include pronouns that substitute for places *(here, there)* and for things and ideas *(it, this, that)*. One of the more difficult types of anaphora involves the substitution of pro-verbs *(does, can, will)* for previously mentioned verbs or verb phrases. *Mary* skates well. *John* does too. *Mary* does figure eights. *So* can *John*.

An experienced clinician (Daskal, 1983) reported that students with poor comprehension are generally responsive to instruction in anaphora. Not only do they become proficient in identifying the antecedents of anaphoric words but they also learn to attend more closely to the succession or "flow" of ideas in written materials. The procedure she follows begins with oral discussion. The student is simply asked questions that require the identification of pronoun or pro-verb antecedents. For example, given the following text,

> Harry and Josh went to the store to buy hot dogs, potato chips, and soft drinks for the picnic. But *they* were so expensive that the boys didn't have enough money to pay for *them*.

The student would be asked, "What was expensive?" or "What couldn't they pay for?" Next, the student learns to draw lines between pronouns and their antecedents. (With nonconsumable materials, a sheet of acetate is clipped to the page of print, and the student uses a china marker.) This activity enables the teacher to monitor the student's accuracy in identifying antecedents, and it helps the student develop awareness of these cohesive text elements. After several weeks of this type of instruction, students automatically relate anaphoric terms to their antecedents.

Focusing on Connective Terms. Daskal's procedure can also be applied to connective terms. These specify how ideas are related to one another. Geva (1983) provides a useful four-way classification of these terms. She points out that some of them simply *add* ideas to other ideas (e.g., *and, also, as well,* and *in addition*), whereas others express contrasting associations (e.g., *but, however,* and *on the other* *hand*). A third type signals causal interactions (*because, so, therefore, as a result, consequently*), and the final type pertains to temporal sequence (*before, after, first, next, then*). The relationships signaled by these terms can, of course, apply to information in any unit of text—to information contained in individual clauses or sentences, or in a series of sentences within a paragraph, or in several paragraphs.

Instruction in these relationships must be conducted in the context of the kinds of condition to which they refer. For example, to show students what specific temporal words mean, you need to look at situations that can be temporally sequenced. For this reason, reciprocal teaching appears to be a promising format for highlighting connectives and the relationships they signal. A series of sessions could incorporate specific emphasis on these relationships into the procedure; each time a signal word occurred in a passage segment, the dialogue leader would be expected to discuss its informational value. The particular signal words that students should look for would be introduced beforehand and displayed in a prominent place for quick reference.

Signal words can also be systematically highlighted during regular reading lessons. You simply examine the lesson materials to locate these terms and then plan interesting and appropriate ways to call attention to them during post-reading discussion. The purpose is to help students become aware of the terms and attend to them without external guidance.

Sentence Combining. Another type of exercise, one that can be presented as a game, is sentence combining. This process can be used to engage students in the construction of complex sentences from two or more simple sentences (Froese & Kurushima, 1979; Straw & Schreiner, 1982). An alternative is a sentence anagram task (Weaver, 1979) in which students learn to organize words into groups within a sentence and then into complete sentences.

Partner Reading and Content, Too (PRC2). As students move on in the grades, Ogle and Correa-Kovtun (2010) noticed that more and more reading materials were informational. At 12th grade, 70 percent of passage content on tests is informational (National Assessment Governing Board, 2008). They devised a routine that can be used effectively with English-language learners and struggling readers. It reflects these key researched-based priorities: Students need to read frequently at their instructional or independent reading level (Allington, 2007; Blachowiccz & Ogle, 2008), students need frequent opportunities to use conversation to acquire an academic vocabulary and develop new ways of expressing ideas (Shanahan & Beck, 2006), knowledge is enhanced when students use an inquiry approach to gain ownership of their learning (Almasi, 2008; Ogle, 1986), students need time for reflection and sharing their thoughts (Nichols, 2006), and students need to be made aware of the features and organization of their texts (Blachowicz & Ogle, 2008; Ogle, Kemp, & McBride, 2007).

With this research in mind, the following routine was developed: First, determine a comfortable reading level for students and highly motivating informational text that is appropriate for your students. Then place your students in matched pairs with similar reading levels and interests. The partners follow this process:

- They review the book during their first encounter with the text.
- A two-page spread is read silently by both partners.
- Each partner takes one page and prepares to read it aloud. As they read silently, they develop one question to ask their partner when their oral reading is finished. The question can be a version of the following stems:

  What was most important?

  What was most interesting?

  What connections can you make?

  What could the author make clearer?

- One partner reads orally and then asks a question of the listening partner. A discussion ensues.
- The partners switch roles. This procedure is continued until the text is finished.
- As they proceed, new academic vocabulary is added to a notebook. (Ogle & Correa-Kovtun, 2010, pp. 532–538).

• Reflecting on the Cases: Instructional Recommendations

Surveying the range of instructional possibilities, Jim decided on these courses of action for his students:

pause and reflect

Review the cases of Bob, Andrea, and Jake. What instructional suggestions from this chapter would you make for each of them? What other ideas do you have about appropriate instruction? Discuss and then compare with Jim's choices, described here.

Bob was able to improve his comprehension with some general rereading directions from Jim. The DR-TA would be a good choice, helping Bob to break a selection into slightly more manageable chunks and focusing him on monitoring his own reading more closely.

Jake formed an early, unproductive schema about reading that colored the rest of his comprehension. The GIST technique might provide a good starting point for Jake. He needs to be held closely to the text at the beginning of a reading selection to help him get on the right track. Within this process Jim helps Jake attend to small signal words to help build an appropriate initial schema to guide the rest of his reading.

Andrea had greater difficulty with her comprehension. Reciprocal Teaching could be a good starting point for her, focusing on sentences or short paragraphs. Because she also has great difficulty with vocabulary and using contextual information, much of the questioning and clarification could focus on these needs. Having Andrea work with graphic organizers would help her organize her concepts more effectively.

In addition, Jim might pair Bob and Jake to try the PRC2 strategy. This would create a more independent way for the boys to proceed through the text and give them ownership of a wide variety of strategies.

Like all instructional recommendations, these are tentative and can be modified as you observe more lessons and learn more about each student's abilities and problems. This is the nature of diagnostic instruction.

summary

You can generally make a diagnosis of difficulty in the area of comprehension once you have determined that print skill and vocabulary knowledge are not underlying sources of poor understanding. Having made this decision, you should explore further to identify the nature of the comprehension problem. In order to provide appropriate instruction, you must determine whether a student's difficulty stems from poorly developed strategies for interacting with text and organizing text information or from the inability to understand the information the text contains.

Case studies utilizing post-reading questioning, retelling, and the think-aloud procedure were presented along with a framework for specifying instruction. Variables such as level of teacher support, explicitness of instruction, and the length of the instructional text unit were identified and used to construct a framework for describing instructional strategies and for selecting the type of intervention that would be appropriate for the comprehension problems of the three cases. Examples are given of interactive instructional strategies such as The Directed Reading-Thinking Activity, GIST, Reciprocal Teaching, Question-Answer Relationships, Guided Reading Procedure, PRC2, and Direct Instruction of Text Structure.

try it out

1. Choose a passage from an upcoming lesson. Prepare questions and a retelling protocol for it. Try it with one student, using the retelling protocol first and then asking any questions not dealt with. What do you learn from each? What type of information did the questions tap that the student didn't offer independently? Compare and discuss.

2. Write a diagnostic report on one of the students analyzed in this chapter. How would you communicate, in writing, what you found out to Jim, the student's regular teacher? What examples from the student's performance would be helpful? What instructional ideas would you suggest for Jim, going beyond those in the chapter? Compare and discuss with others. What categories of information should be in such a report? What kinds of styles are appropriate?

3. **Student Portfolio Ideas:** (a) Ask students to retell a selection to one another and analyze their own retellings. Have them reflect on how they chose important ideas and how these were communicated. What insights did they gain into their own retellings as well as those of their classmates? (b) Ask students to construct a graphic or other form of retelling. Have students compare, contrast, and display their examples.

4. **For Your Teaching Portfolio:** (a) Add retelling protocols for the selections chosen for "Try It Out" in Chapter 5. Build a portfolio of sample selections of various grade levels. (b) Add a case analysis to your portfolio. Compile one for your own students or do a simulation with one of the students from this chapter.

for further reading

Baldwin, D. (2004). A guide to standardized writing assessment. *Educational Leadership, 62,* 72–76.

Bialystok, E., Shenfield, T., & Codd, J. (2000). Languages, scripts, and the environment: Factors in developing concepts of print. *Developmental Psychology, 36,* 1–20.

Blachowicz, C. L. Z., & Ogle, D. M. (2005 2nd edition). *Reading comprehension: Strategies for independent learners.* New York: Guilford.

Fang, Z. (1999). Expanding the vista of emergent writing research: Implications for early childhood educators. *Early Childhood Education Journal, 26,* 179–182.

Gambrell, L., & Almasi, J. F. (1996). *Lively discussions! Fostering engaged reading.* Newark, DE: International Reading Association.

Ogle, D., & Correa-Kovtun, A. (2010, April). Supporting English-language learners and struggling readers in content literacy with the "Partner Reading and Content, Too" routine. *Reading Teacher, 63*(7), 532–542.

Pullen, P., & Justice, L. M. (2003). Enhancing phonological awareness, print awareness, and oral language skills in preschool children. *Intervention in School and Clinic, 39,* 87–98.

Routman, R. (2005). *Writing essentials.* Portsmouth, NH: Heinemann.

Shanahan, T. (1997). Reading and writing relationships: Thematic units, inquiry learning . . . in pursuit of effective integrated literacy instruction. *The Reading Teacher, 51,* 1–12.

Taylor, B. M., Graves, M. F., & Van den Broek, P. (2000). *Reading for meaning: Fostering comprehension in the middle grades.* Newark, DE: International Reading Association.

7 Writing: A Window on Reading

- To become knowledgeable about current perspectives on writing and its development
- To develop strategies for assessing writing
- To develop strategies for integrating writing and reading assessment
- To develop a framework for assessing the reading–writing classroom

Using Writing for Authentic Assessment

"Ask Keisha. She's been doing some innovative things in her multiage class-room. First and second grade can't be all that different than fourth or fifth."

Mr. Johnson, her principal, took Keisha by surprise when he made these remarks to a primary teacher in her building. How did he know she'd intended to experiment with formative assessments in her classroom? He must have seen signs of her work when he visited her classroom in May. During the previous academic year, Keisha had developed a reading and writing workshop with her students. This fall, she planned to utilize assess-ments that would be consistent with a student-center philosophy. Over the summer, she had done some reading, and she was willing to try a variety of documentation. She had already found some well-organized assessment tools that would speak clearly to parents as well as link to instruction.

Keisha had six major problems to address:

- How could writing analysis play an important part in the assessment process?
- What are some of the structures, strategies, and models of assessment that she could develop to understand her students' writing?
- Could she use writing to find out more about her students?
- Last year Ken had a difficult time with reading, and Jennifer's writing indicated she needed word-study instruction. Could this information help her make appropriate educational plans for them?
- She also wanted to look at Cal's written summaries again. Perhaps they could provide a focus for his comprehension work this year.
- Tianna seemed unable to get started writing or, when she did, take a piece of writing through the writing process. Keisha wondered what activities would invite Tianna into the writing community in her classroom.

Keisha's work is the type of teacher reflective inquiry that underpins the goals of this chapter. ■

chapter overview

This chapter has three parts. The first section discusses contemporary perspectives on writing, including developmental and process-focused views. The second seg-ment focuses on assessing writing—from data gathering, to holistic scoring, to collecting integrated data—ending with a framework for analyzing what goes on in the reading–writing classroom. The third section suggests types of instructional support that help a teacher integrate reading and writing instruction.

chapter outline

Understanding Writing Development

• Perspectives on Writing

Knowledge of the writing process and of writing instruction has changed dramatically over the last decade. Luckily for the readers of this chapter, numerous volumes are now devoted to enriching our understanding of writing (see For Further Reading at the end of this chapter for some starting points). Our focus in this chapter is to sketch a general outline of what we know about writing and to suggest how this knowledge relates to classroom assessment. Research suggests that reading and writing are two aspects of language use that emerge at about the same time. For some children involved in early experimentation with writing, writing development may precede reading development. Children with literacy exposure generally display print awareness beyond what was recognized previously (Bialystok, Shenfield, & Codd, 2000; Clay, 1975; Pullen & Justice, 2003; Teale & Sulzby, 1986). Reading and writing are interrelated and depend on similar or overlapping knowledge, skills, and strategies (Kucer, 1985; Shanahan, 1984, 1997; Tierney & Pearson, 1983).

Clear-cut relationships between writing and reading competence are not always easy to draw (Stotsky, 1984). Examples of students' writing can provide insights into students' concepts of print and written texts, their strategies for constructing meaning, and their general language development. Students' writing can reflect their awareness of structure, organization, genre, intention, purpose, point of view, vocabulary concepts, and related comprehension capabilities.

This chapter presents an overview of current aspects of writing. We will look at ways to assess writing and examine the ways in which writing can provide insights about a student's knowledge of print, comprehension, self-monitoring, and interest. Finally, we discuss classrooms in which writing flourishes and is connected effortlessly to reading. Historically, educators focused on the products of writing, what was written, and the grammar and mechanics of writing. Evaluation of writing focused on products, with assessment typically focused on composition, grammar, usage, and mechanics. Current views give more emphasis to writing as a process that has strategic components, much as current views of reading value the development of reading strategies. Good instruction and assessment must deal not only with the products of writing but also its strategic processes. It is important to remember that writing, like all aspects of literacy, is a developmental system.

Stages and Processes

Any teacher planning to carry out good assessment must understand the developmental stages of the process being studied. Work by many researchers who watched the growth of literacy in young children (Baghban, 1984; Bissex, 1980; Fang, 1999; Hannan, 1984) suggests that learning to write in an environment that supports early learning proceeds through three typical stages (see Figure 7.1). The *emergent writer* experiments with print and shares these experimentations with others. The child who "scribble writes" a grocery list, gives love letters to her parents, and points to letters on a sign is in the emergent stage. The *beginning writer,* usually in the primary grades, gives a picture elaborated with labels, writes stories with developmental spelling, and shows an increasing knowledge of sound–symbol relationships. In later grades, the *developing writer* writes longer pieces in a variety of genres, experiments with vocabulary, and begins to expand his or her own voice. These stages are not discrete; they ebb and flow into one another as writers move toward greater control, fluency, and competence.

Beyond the developmental stages of writing, teachers are concerned with the stages in the writing process itself and observe students in this process to assess whether they need support in approaching writing strategically. Teachers

pause and reflect

Before reading this section, jot down on paper the types of writing you have seen done by preschoolers, by children in the primary grades, and by developing writers. Compare this with what is described in Figure 7.1.

figure 7.1 • Checklist for Determining Stages of Writing Development

Student Name _____

Stage	Observable Behavior	Date Observed/Notes
1. The Emergent Writer	Draws or "writes" communications and shares with others	
	Shows intention and planning with drawings and writing	
	Produces scribble writing	
	Shows interest in words and letters	
	Uses letters in writing and drawing	
	Writes names and may use some invented spelling	
2. The Beginner	Begins to label drawings and writes longer sentences and captions for them	
	Writes pattern stories and lists of sentences (e.g., James is my friend. Jake is my friend. Jesse is my friend.)	
	Uses invented spelling that shows awareness of initial spelling patterns	
	Writes longer pieces with personal content and dialogue; becomes conscious of beginning, middle, end Shows awareness of audience	
	Shows concern with spelling (asks for correct spelling) and handwriting (erases, crosses out, rewrites)	
3. The Developing Writer	Begins to use different forms of writing (e.g., inform, persuade, describe)	
	Begins to use concepts, ideas, and vocabulary from other reading and content areas	
	Becomes aware of author's style from reading and from other students	
	Shows greater awareness of need to revise and edit for audience	

of writing typically describe various stages in the writing process as prewriting or getting started, drafting an initial piece, reflecting on and revising, and "publishing" or bringing a piece to conclusion (see Figure 7.2).

The instructional environment of the classroom can also make a big difference in how students develop as writers. A print-rich environment promotes early writing development. Muzevich (1999) describes such a setting as

figure 7.2 • Stages in the Writing Process

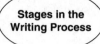

1. Prewriting

Conceptualizes a theme or topic

"Brainstorms" ideas

Makes a personal record

Envisions an audience

Uses resources as needed (e.g., other people for trying out ideas; other treatments; self-reflection)

4. "Publishing"

Produces a product of sustained effort

Presents in final form

Shows development of voice/style

Shares with others

Stages in the Writing Process

2. Drafting

Rehearses by composing, drawing, and talking

Takes risks in composing and spelling

Considers audience

Self-reflects

Uses resources (e.g., others)

3. Revising and Editing

Self-evaluates

Takes perspective of audience

Engages in Peer Conferences

Seeks other information/opinions as needed

Is willing to change/rewrite

Edits for grammar, usage, mechanics, spelling, legibility

containing alphabet charts, labeled objects (environmental print), students' names written on chairs, and a writing center. A word wall is prominently displayed. All the guided reading centers contain writing papers and a variety of pens and pencils to encourage written response. Students compose notes, poems, lists, journal entries, letters, and recipes, and they share what they produce every day. Occasionally students engage in dictation activities to promote oral phonemic awareness. Mini-lessons on conventions such as handwriting, punctuation, and capitalization encourage correct usage. In a reading–writing classroom, students are helped to see the connection between the author and the reader at all times. When they read, they ask questions about the writer's purpose and point of view. Students are invited to note how style develops. When working in content areas, they ask questions about the qualifications of the authors, the popularity of ideas, and the possible bias of texts. All these issues contribute to classrooms where writing and reading are seen as both a developmental and a strategic process. We now turn to issues of how to assess writing in a way that both reveals its richness and assists in planning instruction. To be successful, we must go beyond standardized measures of grammar and mechanics toward measures that are indicators of method and growth.

Assessing Writing

Analysis of writing samples along with observational checklists and anecdotal record keeping can give one view of a child's performance. To assess students' writing thoroughly, teachers should also collect information on both the development of students' control of the writing process and samples of their writing products. Because teachers are interested in change and development, they need to collect information over time.

Portfolios are one method being used for evaluation in many K–12 classrooms (Calkins & Martinelli, 2006; Valencia, 1990). Different types of portfolios can be compiled depending on the purpose. Simmons (1992) has researched the use of portfolios in wide-scale assessment and has proposed a schematic for different types and levels of portfolio information, including process, product, and programs (see Figure 7.3). His research compared the perceptions teachers formed about students by using standardized test results and by using portfolio information. Simmons found that portfolio assessment gave teachers much more detailed information about student writing performance. In contrast, timed essay writing failed to reveal the real strength of some students and overestimated the competence of others. This type of research, along with a groundswell of teacher support for classroom assessment, has encouraged many teachers, schools, and districts to investigate the use of portfolios.

Portfolios usually contain process data that show how a student's writing has developed over time. Other writing products such as drafts, responses, lists of personal questions, practice activities, final drafts, and completed projects may appear in a portfolio. Portfolios can contain self-evaluation information such as students' reflections on their writing products and their personal development. Teachers can compile their own class portfolios of data relevant to larger views of assessment. For these, teachers may interview their students about their writing and reading or have students interview one another (Hansen, 1987). We discuss both student and class portfolios at greater length in Chapter 9. For this chapter, we want to consider how a teacher would collect portfolio data about the writing process, how writing samples from students can be generated and collected, and how a teacher might analyze both the process of writing and the products. We also give examples of how some teachers have collected specific types of reading-related writing samples.

f i g u r e 7 . 3 • Levels of Portfolio Information

Level of Information	Purpose	Traits	Contents
Product	Assessment of written products	Ideas Organization Wording Mechanics Flavor	Best pieces: • Student choice • Teacher choice • Joint selection Required pieces
Process	Assessment of writing abilities	What I do, know, think How I do it, know it, think it What I feel How I see myself How I approach work How I use/give feedback How I challenge myself	Ordered pieces: • Student ranking • Drafts Notes, journals, logs Labels Conversations Experiences Readings Teacher, self- and peer 　evaluations Conference logs
Program	Assessment of development of writing abilities	Chances to • Discover topic • Use many forms • Confer • Keep task open • Vary length How do students and teachers • Agree on standards • Understand the other Change over time Impact on ability, 　socioeconomic status	Assignment lists Conference logs Interview data: • Length • Duration • Range • Evaluations • Expectations • Socioeconomic 　status scores

Source: "Levels of Portfolio Information" chart by Jay Simmons is reprinted from *Portfolio Portraits,* edited by Donald Graves and Bonnie Sunstein. Copyright © 1992 by Heinemann, a division of Reed Elsevier, Inc., Portsmouth, NH.

• Observing Writing

There are many ways to collect information about the writing process. A common method is to observe students during process writing instruction and practice and record your observations in a log or on a checklist. Try to observe students in various stages of the composing process to see where their strengths and needs lie. For example, Keisha observed Jessie working at the revising and editing stage of the

pause and **reflect**

How many ways can you observe and record students' writing? List the possibilities and, as you read the next section, compare your recommendations to those presented in the following segment.

writing process. In a brief conversation, Jessie indicated that she was evaluating her work to determine where she might add details. She had previously engaged in a peer conference for that purpose. Keisha made notes during and following her conference with Jessie. She noted that Jessie was taking full advantage of the opportunity to revise her work following a peer conference. During her class writing workshop, Keisha had the opportunity to observe other young writers involved in the writing process at different stages. She made notes about the various strategies they were employing. Keisha kept these notes in the students' anecdotal records.

By keeping dated records of observations focused on the writing process, you will have a better measure of the way individual students develop writing strategies. Observational checklists are good tools for collecting and organizing classroom data. To be useful, checklists must be short and simple, relate to both long-term and short-term goals, and have room for qualitative as well as quantitative data (Atwell, 2002; Heller, 1995). Figure 7.4 displays an example of a teacher-designed checklist for observing writing. Keisha found it is very powerful to meet with students to go over the checklist and set goals for future writing projects.

By setting up a systematic approach for observing students over the school term, a teacher can compare growth and set instructional goals as the term progresses. It is essential to understand that process observation and the setting of process goals are important to the development of literacy.

Along with observing students in the process of writing and as they develop strategies, a teacher needs to look at the writing students produce for other clues to their strengths and deficiencies. Collecting and analyzing writing samples is the most common approach to this challenge. Samples of student writing collected over time can provide powerful data on both process and product growth. Both finished and draft materials can provide insights into the student's writing. A teacher can also keep anecdotal records on writing and may choose to do some sort of holistic scoring to help get a global view of a student's progress. Samples might include a benchmark piece done at the beginning of the year, a piece of writing at midyear (January or February), and a piece from May or June. Throughout the year and at the end of the year, students should be invited to reflect on these pieces (Calkins & Martinelli, 2006, p. 178).

• Holistic Scoring

Holistic scoring is being increasingly used to evaluate students' writing samples. Holistic scoring aims toward an overall evaluation of the writer's ability to

f i g u r e   7 . 4 • Observing the Writing Process

Student _____

Key: I=does independently   S=does with support   N=needs development

	Date	Date	Date	Date	Date	Date	Date	Date
1. Can choose topic								
Can focus a topic								
Has diversity in topics								
2. Can write in different genres								
Shows diversity in genre choices								
3. Can brainstorm before writing								
Alone								
With group								
Keeps a record								
4. Can select relevant details to include								
5. Is willing to revise								
Can be selective about adding or deleting text								
Can use input of others								
Can self-reflect								
Can consider audience								
6. Is willing to edit								
7. Mechanical aspects to work on:								
Has knowledge of conventions of that genre								
Is concerned with accuracy in spelling and punctuation								
8. Can bring a piece to publication								
Has persistence								
Has production values								
Comments/instructional goals:								

communicate ideas to a particular audience. The rater takes a piece of writing and either matches it to another piece in a set of samples or scores it for certain features determined to be important for that type of writing. The rater does not make corrections or revisions in the paper but ranks, scores, or grades it based

pause and reflect

Before reading this section, jot down the things you think are important to evaluate in your students' writing. Then compare your list to those in the examples that follow.

on a scoring evaluation guide. Many varieties of scoring protocols and guides have been developed, with more or less direction for the evaluator, who is assumed to have practiced scoring and to have developed reliability with other raters. Typically these guides describe various aspects of a type of written work and rank the author's performance based on an evaluative scale. They can be simple (Baldwin, 2004; Deiderich, 1974; see Figure 7.5) to more complex (see Figure 7.6).

Some evaluators believe that a rubric can also involve a clear and uniform way to collect similar samples from students in various grades. In this type of rubric use, local samples are collected at designated grade levels. These local samples are selected as typical of levels of writing development at that grade. In subsequent years, students in the designated grades are asked to produce particular types of writing at predetermined times. This writing is compared to

figure 7.5 • Holistic Scoring Scale

1—Poor 2—Weak 3—Average 4—Good 5—Excellent		
		Reader _____
Quality and development of ideas	1 2 3 4 5	
Organization, relevance, movement	1 2 3 4 5	
		_____ × 5 = _____
		Subtotal
Style, flavor, individuality	1 2 3 4 5	
Wording and phrasing	1 2 3 4 5	
		_____ × 3 = _____
		Subtotal
Grammar, sentence structure	1 2 3 4 5	
Punctuation	1 2 3 4 5	
Spelling	1 2 3 4 5	
Manuscript form, legibility	1 2 3 4 5	
		_____ × 1 = _____
		Subtotal
		Total grade: _____ %

Source: Adapted from Diederich, P. (1974). *Measuring growth in English.* Urbana, IL: National Council of Teachers of English.

figure 7.6 • Kerner School Rubric for Reading Response

A-4	B-3	C-2	D-1	U-0
Accuracy of Understanding Reader demonstrates an accurate understanding of important information in the text by focusing on the key ideas presented explicitly or implicitly.	Reader demonstrates an accurate understanding of important information in the text by focusing on some key ideas presented explicitly or implicitly.	Reader demonstrates an accurate but limited understanding of the text.	Reader demonstrates little or no understanding of the text; may be inaccurate.	Reader's response is absent or does not address the task. Reader's response is insufficient to show that criteria are met.
Use of Information for Interpretation Reader uses information from the text to interpret significant concepts to make connections to other situations or contexts logically through analysis, evaluation, inference, and/or comparison/contrast.	Reader uses information from the text to interpret significant concepts to make connections to other situations or contexts logically (with some gaps) through analysis, evaluation, inference, and/or comparison/contrast.	Reader uses information from the text to interpret simplistic interpretations of the text without using significant concepts or by making only limited connections to other situations or contexts.	Reader makes little or no interpretation of the text.	Reader's response is absent or does not address the task. Reader's response is insufficient to show that criteria are met.
Textual References Reader uses relevant and accurate references; most are specific and fully supported.	Reader uses relevant and accurate references; some are specific; some may be general and not fully supported.	Reader uses irrelevant and/or limited references.	Reader uses no references or references are inaccurate.	Reader's response is absent or does not address the task. Reader's response is insufficient to show that criteria are met.
Integration Reader integrates interpretation of the text with text-based (balanced) support.	Reader partially integrates interpretation of the text with text-based support.	Reader generalizes without illustrating key ideas; may have gaps.	Reader's response does not address the task.	Reader's response is insufficient to show that criteria are met.

the local samples to give consistent and comparative measures across the school year (see Figure 7.6). Whereas standardized measures have typically focused on evaluating grammar and mechanics, holistic assessment allows a broader look at writing (Jett-Simpson & Leslie, 1994; Ray, 2006).

• Integrated Assessment

Teachers interested in integrated instruction are also interested in integrated assessment. This involves collecting assessment data as students are performing authentic language tasks and using writing as a "window to reading." In this section, we show how Keisha collected information on her students during their regular classroom activities and how she looked at writing to help her answer three important questions about some of her students:

What can students' spelling tell about their print knowledge?

What can students' writing tell about their vocabulary, concept knowledge, and comprehension?

What can their writing tell about students' self-evaluation and metacognition?

case 7.1

Keisha's Classroom

Keisha had helped her students prepare a process portfolio after they finished their first piece in writing workshop. Students spread artifacts from each step in the writing process across their desks. They chose an artifact that represented each of the following questions (adapted from Porter & Cleland, 1994):

What was the part of the process that helped you the most?
What was the part that helped you least?
Where was the place when you realized you were learning something new?
What would you change to make this process better?
What would you keep the same?
What are your goals for your next writing piece?

Students mounted their artifacts and their explanations on large sheets of art paper and shared the results with classmates, Keisha, and their parents. The parents were particularly delighted. One wrote a special note to Keisha that read, "I am thrilled. This is the first time I have seen what James is actually doing in class. Thank you." Keisha shared the portfolio and the note with other teachers at her school. Soon many of them were creating process portfolios in their classes.

For her own classroom, Keisha found an observational checklist devised by Hill and Ruptic (1994) particularly useful as a model for recording oral and written responses in a class lesson (see Figure 7.7). She adapted it for her purposes and used it in class. Companion checklists kept by students gave a second perspective on reading and writing in the classroom (see Figure 7.8). Keisha also decided to keep an anecdotal journal on each of her reading and writing classes. She would try to reflect on each entry to help her plan instruction. One of her entries looked like this:

> February 17
> The class is really having trouble with the concept of compare and contrast. Only Lashana, Joey, and Marty were able to make good comparisons between Yeh-Shen, the Chinese Cinderella, and Perrault's Cinderella. I need to construct some graphics to help. I had Patrice, Tyrone, and Stella make a list of the important aspects of Yeh-Shen: setting, characters, problem, and so on. Then Louie, Jason, and Marianne made a list of similar elements in Cinderella. I had a hard time getting Reno to work on task—I wonder if he is struggling at this level? I need to have him read a bit to see. I'll make him partners with Bette to see if that provides enough support. They work well together. Tomorrow we are going to work on putting the list together for "same"—then "different." I need to get the librarian to help me find some more Cinderella-type books (*Mufaro's Beautiful Daughter*) and to make up some Venn-diagram charts. I need to do a mini-lesson on compare and contrast and relate those terms to same–different.

Keisha's observation focused on what occurred in her class, on some specific students, and on planning for instruction. Her focus on analysis allowed her to see how students' knowledge and strategies developed from lesson to lesson.

Keisha also decided to use student journals to help assess reading. Although the writing in these journals can be very revealing about strategies and processes, research on students' responses to literature indicates that what they say about books can give real insights into their comprehension and development (Kiefer, 1988). Keisha found that she could analyze journal writing to get information on her students' comprehension as well as their knowledge of print. ■

• Analyzing the Spelling in Children's Writing

As we discussed in Chapter 2, experimentation with writing is an important component of beginning literacy. Children's spelling can be a powerful clue to their internalization of the regularities of the sound–symbol system. In this

figure 7.7 • Teacher Checklist for Discussion

Name	Finished	Spoke	Listened	Title of Piece	Other Notes
Emily	Yes	Very talkative	Not too much	"My Birthday"	Needs to work on listening
Jennifer	Yes	Responses don't always make sense	Yes	"My Dolly"	Immature subjects Doesn't always understand the topic
Ken	Yes	Had trouble reading his own spelling	Seemed distracted	"My Big Dog"	Needs work on conventional spelling
Tianna	Not sure	Summertime best days	A bit distracted	"Camping Out"	Visited Yellowstone Park. Needs to work on title
Reno	No	Sad today. Doesn't know why	No participation	"My Dog"	Resisted revision Excellent drawing
Cal	Yes	Good ideas	Looking out the window	"Twin Baby Brothers"	Says more than he writes
Cynthia	Yes	Good responses	Listened and made eye contact	"Saturdays"	Drew a picture of a child "sleeping in"
Lashana	Yes	Lots to say. Just lost a tooth	Looked away from speaker	"The Lost Tooth"	No illustration. Wanted to glue "lost" tooth on paper
Joe	Yes	Christmas was the best day	Very attentive	"Trains"	Drew trains and track Only completed one draft
Marty	Yes	Great contributions	On the ball!	"My Best Cards"	Drew a picture of a Pokemon Card
Pat	Yes	Great ideas	Helped discussion	"The Shopping Trip"	Detailed illustration
Tyrone	No	Fooled around with Lou	Was not paying attention	"The Silly Cat"	Did not finish. Should speak to Mom
Sella	Yes	What a sweet girl!	Listened well	"My Cinderella Doll"	Helps Tyrone. Organizes the group
Lou	No	Silent, sullen	Inattentive today	"The Special Day"	Refused to draw a picture. Counselor???
Jason	Yes	Helpful insights	Silent support	"Pokemon Wins the Day"	Patiently helped Lou. Offered to do a conference with him
Marianne	Yes	A little more hyper than usual	Tried hard to find focus	"My Barbie"	Call Mom about medication
Bette	Yes	Outstanding!	Always listens!	"My Bad Baby Brother"	Will help Reno with revision

Source: Adapted from B. C. Hill & C. Ruptic (1994). *Practical Aspects of Authentic Assessment: Putting the Pieces Together.* Norwood, MA: Christopher-Gordon Publishers, Inc.

figure 7.8 • Student Self-Evaluation

Date:	Title:	What I Think About My Reading & Writing:

L
R
Ⓦ   12-1-89

My Trip To space.

Beucase it is my novel.

L   11-17-89
Ⓡ
W   The Astronauts

Because I ingoy it.

Ⓛ   11-10-89
R
W   The big orange spot.

because it is funny.

L
R
W

_____

L
R
W

Legend: L = Listened to   R = Read   W = Wrote

Source: From *Reading-Writing Connections: From Theory to Practice.* By Mary E. Heller. Copyright© 1991 by Longman Publishing Group.

section, we review the developmental stages revealed through an analysis of young writers' spelling. Then we examine the spelling of Ken whom you met in Chapter 3. You will remember that his parents were concerned about his progress during first grade and had asked Eileen, his teacher, whether he should be tutored during the summer months before he was to enter Keisha's multiage, second–third classroom.

The developmental framework is also useful in examining spelling in the extended texts that children write. We consider the writing of one of Keisha's students, Jason. We also introduce an analysis sheet that a teacher can use.

Developmental Stages of Spelling. In Chapter 2, we described how the spelling strategies of children change over time. As they read and write, their knowledge of orthography (or spelling) increases. They develop greater knowledge of the elements of words, and they do so in a fairly predictable manner. Refer to Figure 2.2 on page 50 and you will see that Marni, who is in Stage 2, writes only the beginning consonants and sometimes the ending consonants of words. David, who is in Stage 3, represents the beginning and ending consonants and sometimes the medial vowel sounds, yet his spellings differ in predictable ways from Standard or Formal English spellings. In contrast, it is easy to "read" Hans's writing because he represents most of the sounds in words and writes many in standard form.

It is challenging to read the writings of Marni and David, but teachers at the kindergarten and first-grade level acquire the necessary skill to do so. To help you learn how to read these developmental spellings, it is useful to have students read their writing aloud.

You can collect writing samples in one of two ways. You may wish to have children write a set of words or you may wish to examine the writing that children produce daily in your classroom. The advantage of the spelling task is that you have the opportunity to observe how children write words that include a representative set of consonants, consonant blends, short vowels, and long vowels. The advantage of the more natural writing task is that it shows how children select and spell words to represent the meanings they wish to communicate.

A Developmental Spelling Test. The Developmental Spelling Test described here (see Figure 7.9; Ferroli & Shanahan, 1987; Morris & Perney, 1984) is particularly useful because it includes words of various complexity, and it is sensitive to changes that occur in the beginning stages of spelling. The spelling test has been used with kindergartners (Ferroli & Shanahan, 1987) and first graders (Morris & Perney, 1984) and found to be a good predictor of later first-grade achievement.

The list is composed of twelve words, as shown in Figure 7.9. Before administering the list, children must be prepared through a demonstration of spelling. First, they should be asked to listen for the letter names they hear in a few sample words not found on the list such as *mat* and *dip;* the teacher then writes these letters on the blackboard, supplying unknown letters if the children offer only a partial spelling. For example, if the children hear only the *m* and *t* in *mat,* the teacher might say, "Good," write "M_T" on the board, and say, "There's an

figure 7.9 • Developmental Spelling Test Items and Illustrative Spelling at Each Stage

Correct	Preliterate	Initial Consonant	Consonant Frame	Phonetic	Transitional
BACK	RE	BET	BC	BAK	a
SINK	E	C	SE	SEK	SINCK
MAIL	A	MM	MOL	MAL	MAEL
DRESS	S	DN	JS	GAS	DRES
LAKE	AH	L	LAE	LAK	LACE
PEEKED	TTT	PF	PT	PECT	PEKED
LIGHT	IEIX	LSIE	LAT	LIT	LIET
DRAGON	ATJA	JK	GAN	DAGN	DRAGIN
STICK	F	S	STC	SEK	STIK
SIDE	TC	ST	CI	SID	CIDE
FEET	Vv	F	FT	FET	a
TEST	ABT	TS	TST	TAST	TEEST

aNo transitional spellings were produced by the subjects for these words.

Source: L. Ferroli and T. Shanahan, 1987. Kindergarten spelling: Explaining its relation to first-rate reading. In J. E. Readance & R. S. Baldwin (Eds.), *Research in Literacy: Merging Perspectives. Thirty Sixth Yearbook of the National Reading Conference.*

A in the middle." Following this modeling, children should be encouraged to spell the list words as well as they can by writing the letter names they hear. It is important to praise them for whatever spellings they produce. Give the list as you would a spelling test.

Figure 7.9 also includes typical spellings generated for these words by children at different stages of development. On the basis of these spelling responses, you can determine whether the majority of a child's responses are preliterate, initial consonant, consonant frame, phonetic, transitional, or correct. Instruction in word elements should be geared to the child's stage of development. For example, for a child in the preliterate stage, you should check his or her knowledge of letter names to determine which, if any, need to be taught; similarly, for a child in the consonant frame stage, you should test consonants and consonant blends in final positions and short vowels to determine what word elements need to be taught.

To demonstrate this procedure, look at the cases of Ken and Jennifer, two of Keisha's students. Ken's parents have been concerned about his progress in reading. Keisha decided to look more closely at the developmental spelling test she had administered to him to assemble more information on his knowledge of word elements. Jennifer often gets discouraged when editing her own work. Keisha examined Jennifer's writing portfolio to determine her level of spelling development.

case 7.2

Ken's Spelling

At his parents' insistence, Keisha had administered the Developmental Spelling Test to Ken. In this way she hoped to describe Ken's spelling knowledge more precisely. She began the test by demonstrating how to spell two basal words: *mat* and *dip.* She had Ken listen to *mat* to see what sounds he could hear. He heard the phonate corresponding to *m* at the beginning and *t* at the end. Keisha encouraged him to write the letters associated with these sounds. She had him first say *dip* slowly to himself and write the letters he heard. When she presented the test words, she encouraged him "to write them as well as he could." The results are shown in Figure 7.10.

Keisha studied Ken's spelling and concluded that he has good command of consonants at the beginnings and endings of words, but he is not able to

figure 7.10 • Ken's Spelling

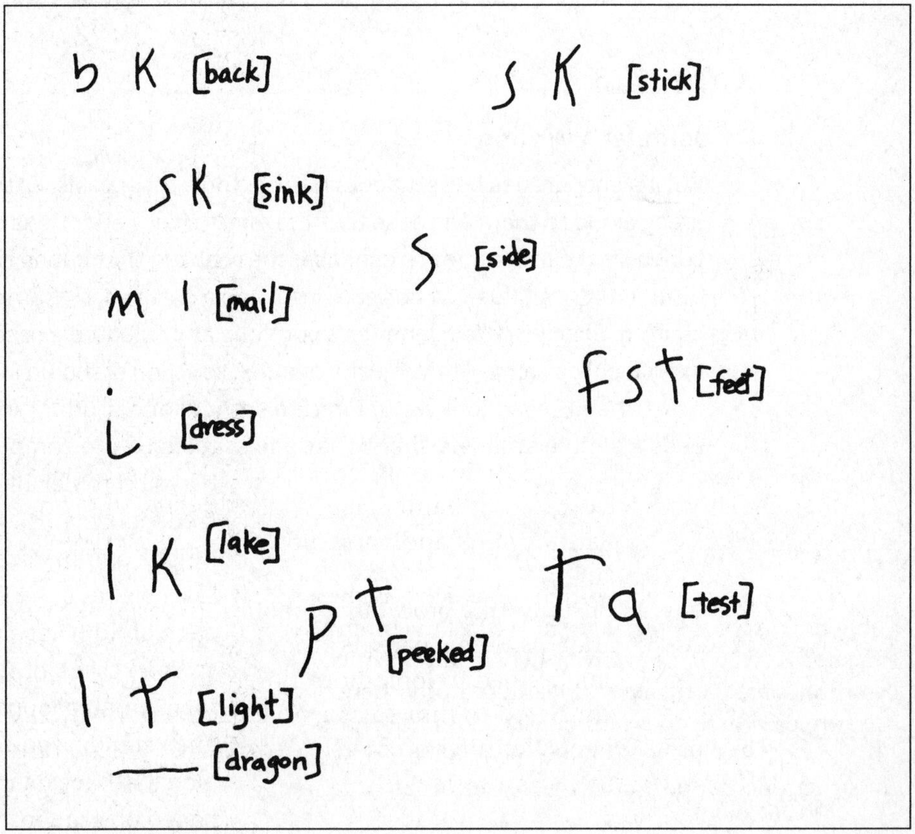

pause and **reflect**

Study Ken's spelling. How do you assess his developing knowledge of English orthography? Compare his spelling to the chart in Figure 7.9. At what stage of development is he? What ideas does this give you for Ken's instruction?

represent consonant blends and vowels. In terms of his underlying knowledge, Ken is in command of the Consonant Frame of words. From this Keisha concluded that he was ready to be introduced to the medial sounds in words. She decided to include activities

 involving sound boxes during the remaining months of Ken's small-group instruction. That is, when the children are composing an experience story and have agreed on what they want to write, she will have them participate in the spelling. If, for example, they wish to write the word *run,* she will create a sound box with three empty squares (☐☐☐), and the children will be encouraged to tell the sound they hear first, the sound they hear second, and the sound they hear last. As children identify the sound, Keisha will ask for the letter that goes with the sound and write it in the box. Other children in Ken's group are also ready for this activity. ■

case 7.3

Jennifer's Writing

Keisha encourages her students to write on a daily basis. Often she reads a story aloud to them and asks them to write their reflections on the story. When she read Jennifer's response, she realized that it was time to undertake a systematic analysis of her spelling using a naturalistic sample of Jennifer's writing. She inspected Jennifer's portfolio and selected a recent piece to examine. The sample that Keisha decided to study is shown in Figure 7.11.

When Keisha looks at a writing sample of a student in her class, she uses a simple analysis sheet that she staples to the sample and places in her own folder of student work (see Figure 7.12). On this sheet, Keisha summarizes what she learns about the knowledge of each child. These notes allow her to keep track of what she sees, form small groups of students with similar spelling needs, and plan instruction in word study based on student mastery of

pause and **reflect**

Read what Jennifer has written. In general, is she able to convey the message she wishes to communicate? Now look carefully at her spelling. Which examples are particularly revealing? Study these examples; where does Jennifer stand on the chart in Figure 7.9? Given this tentative conclusion, what instructional support might you want to provide?

figure 7.11 • A Sample of Jennifer's Writing

JeNNiFeR

THiR was a bird Namd
Joyiss. He livd IN tHe bqc
YIRD of a Hiws. a 7 YeR owld
GiRl livd IN tHe Hiws and
SHe loved Ioyiss.

spelling patterns in writing. On the basis of her study of Jennifer's writing, Keisha wrote the notes on the summary sheet shown in Figure 7.12.

Keisha concluded that although Jennifer shows many signs of spelling strength, she needs to be encouraged to notice the standard spellings of words. Several other children in the class are at the same stage. Keisha will

figure 7.12 • Keisha's Notes on Jennifer's Writing

Developmental Spelling Analysis Sheet

Student Jennifer   Date 10/15

Sample: From writing time following the reading of stories on pets.

Relevant examples: thir yird hiws yer bac
                    namd livd (note also: loved)

Analysis: Represents most sounds appropriately, but not all
          in standard form —— Is in the transitional stage.

Comments/instruction: A nice beginning to her story. Has learned
    a lot about spelling words. Needs to learn standard
    spellings.

7.3 form these children into a study group to focus on words from their writing that are close approximations of standard spelling. Simply helping children to become aware of how words are spelled in Standard English is usually sufficient to encourage them to move from the transitional stage to standard spelling. ■

case 7.4

Cal's Summary Writing

Many assessments use summary writing and question generation to help examine students' comprehension. Look at Keisha's analysis sheet of Cal's summary of *Perfect the Pig* (see Figure 7.13).

figure 7.13 • Summary, Question, Reaction Sheet

Name: Cal

Book summary—*Perfect the Pig.*

The lady found the little pig and loved it a lot. She saved her and took care of perfect. She was an artist and painted lots of pictures too. She lost perfect and another guy found it and took care of it. He got money by charging people to look at perfect. She wanted her pig back and went to the court guy and he let her have it back. They lived happily ever after.

Questions I have:

1. Why was she so mad at the guy? He found her pig and took care of it.
2. Could you go to court about a pet?

Reaction: This seemed kind of dumb. I like animal books but not this one.

Keisha's Analysis of Cal's Summary

Is It:

Accurate: In general

Complete: Skimpy about action, setting

Characters: Doesn't have any names

Plots (Actions/Motivation) Resolution: Does he understand that man mistreated the pig for own gain?

Concepts/Vocabulary: "Court guy"—probe about court concepts memory or knowledge?

Comments/Instructions: I need to ask Cal about the man's motivation to see if he understood what man was doing. His question indicates he didn't get the fact that man was exploiting Perfect. Cal really doesn't like these fantasy animal type books very much. Need to help him choose more realistic ones. Make sure he can skim to use pictures, etc., to separate fantasy from more realistic books when choosing. Needs to work on capitalization.

Based on Cal's summary, Keisha decided to probe Cal's understanding of the motivation of one of the main characters in the story. She also wanted to learn whether Cal was familiar with the concepts related to courtrooms and trials. Last, because he usually had more detailed comprehension of nonfictional selections, she wanted to verify that he realized the fantastic aspects of *Perfect the Pig* and give him some strategies to use for skimming. She would also alert Cal to the differences between fact and fiction. ■

• Analyzing Writing for Vocabulary, Concepts, and Comprehension

Writing from Models. In addition to inviting students to write summaries, teachers can use students' own written responses and their interpretation for analysis. Keisha had students read several fables, discuss them, and produce their own fables modeled after the fables they have read. She uses these writing samples to analyze what students have internalized about the fable genre. The analysis system she uses (shown in Figure 7.14) was drawn from Pappas, Kiefer, and Levstik (1990). In the future, Keisha can analyze other genres of writing that her students produce to learn which elements of each genre are clear to them and which are yet to be internalized.

Using Writing to Look at Self-Evaluation and Metacognition. Teacher observations of students in the process of reading and writing and student self-evaluations can provide insights into reading. Keisha uses an interview profile for students at the start of the year to get a picture of what strategies they employ when reading and writing. These, along with her observations of class performance, help her understand her students' metacognitive strategies (see Figure 5.2 in Chapter 5). She also asks students to self-evaluate their comprehension-monitoring strategies (see Figure 5.3 in Chapter 5) and uses these surveys not only to help her plan instruction but also to get her students to think about their own learning.

These are only a few of the types of integrated assessment strategies that Keisha and other teachers use to turn students' writing into information for reading instruction. Many other options exist, such as student critiques of assignments, best work/least satisfying work choices in portfolios, and others detailed in the many resources now available to teachers interested in reading and writing connections (see For Further Reading at the end of this chapter).

Instructional Support for Writing

Many of the strategies we have presented earlier in this book naturally connect reading and writing instruction. For example, predictive reading instruction, described in Chapter 6, involves writing down predictions, collecting ideas as

figure 7.14 • Observing Genre and Structure

Child: _____ Date: _____	
Context	
How well does the child control the genre being attempted? Are there certain beginnings, endings, sequences present to indicate a certain genre?	
Is the text complete? Are details or elaborations included?	
Interesting vocabulary used? Use of cohesive ties? Ambiguous terms?	
Any missing information? Is information ordered to make sense?	
Interesting repairs used?	
Attention to transcription of medium aspects of text?	
Fluency in composing?	
INSTRUCTIONAL IDEAS:	

Source: Keifer/Levstik/Pappas, *An Integrated Language Perspective in the Elementary School: Theory Interaction,* p. 218. Copyright ©1990 by Longman Publishers. Reproduced by permission of Pearson Education, Inc.

we read, and writing responses or refinements of our predictions after reading. Use of developmental spelling, discussed in Chapter 3, is based on writing. Because there are so many excellent resources for connecting reading and writing instruction (see For Further Reading at the end of this chapter for ideas),

pause and **reflect**

Based on what you already know about writing, what things would you expect to see in a classroom that offers appropriate instructional support for writing? Jot down a list and compare with the list in Figure 7.15.

we have framed our discussion in this section within the notion of teacher self-assessment. How can you look at your own classroom to evaluate whether you are providing instructional support for writing?

• Effective Integration in Classrooms

Research and good practice suggest that classrooms that effectively integrate reading and writing instruction have some shared characteristics. These are presented in a summarized form in Figure 7.15.

Classroom Environment. In classrooms, the environment not only supports the development of literacy skills, but also encourages and stimulates literacy as well. Students receive plenty of time to read and write. Classrooms are full of print with many types of reading materials available. Student writing is shared and "published." A supportive environment encourages students to take chances in their reading and writing.

Reader's and Writer's Workshop. Classrooms that stimulate literacy have a predictable approach to reading and writing. Teachers offer mini-lessons on skills and strategies and meet with small groups for teacher-involved guided reading. Teachers confer individually, in pairs, and in small groups about students' reading and writing. Blocks of time are provided for independent reading and writing workshops. Rich discussions take place about reading, and writers share and respond to each other's writing. Sharing of reading and writing takes place in many forms.

Comprehension. Comprehension and communication are central to many types of reading and writing lessons. Teachers scaffold good strategies for both reading comprehension and process writing. Students are encouraged to integrate what they are learning, to synthesize, and to respond both personally and critically.

Teachers Are Models. In a reading–writing classroom teachers are also learners. They read for pleasure and for professional growth and keep up with children's books. They write along with their students. Teachers communicate their love of reading and writing by reading aloud to students and by sharing their own writing.

Assessment. Teachers in reading and writing classrooms make instructional decisions based on real reading and writing. They collect portfolios of work along with anecdotal records.

figure 7.15 • Reading/Writing/Learning Self-Evaluation Form

	Implemented	Goal for next year
Classroom environment		
I increased print in the environment.	————	————
I increased shared decision making.	————	————
I provided a risk-free environment.	————	————
I increased the variety of genre and levels of difficulty of the books in the library corner.	————	————
Schedule		
I refined the schedule to provide adequate time daily for children to read and write.	————	————
Teachers as learners		
I read professionally.	————	————
I read for pleasure.	————	————
I read new children's books.	————	————
I wrote with students for authentic purposes.	————	————
Readers' workshop		
I provided a predictable structure.	————	————
I conducted mini-lessons.	————	————
I provided a block of time daily for self-selected and self-paced reading.	————	————
I held literature discussion groups.	————	————
I conferred with individual students.	————	————
I provided opportunities for children to respond to reading.	————	————
Reading aloud		
I read aloud to students.	————	————
Sharing		
I conducted shared reading (big books, charts, multiple copies).	————	————
Guided reading		
I met with small groups for guided reading sessions.	————	————
Comprehension		
I activated children's prior knowledge.	————	————
I modeled strategies good readers use.	————	————
I provided opportunities to integrate new knowledge (summarize, evaluate, synthesize).		

	Implemented	Goal for next year
Writers' workshop		
I provided a predictable structure.	_____	_____
I conducted mini lessons.	_____	_____
I provided a block of time for independent writing (student-selected topics).	_____	_____
I conferred with individual students.	_____	_____
I provided opportunities for students to share their writing.	_____	_____
Assessment		
I gathered data for students' portfolio.	_____	_____
I analyzed writing samples.	_____	_____
I took anecdotal records.	_____	_____
I used running records to evaluate miscues and strategies.	_____	_____
I made instructional decisions based on the data collected.	_____	_____
Communication with parents		
I reported student progress through use of portfolios.	_____	_____
I established a method for sharing information.	_____	_____

Source: Figure from Johnston, J. S., & Wilder, S. L. (1992, April). Changing reading and writing programs through staff development. *The Reading Teacher, 45*(8), 626–631. Reprinted with permission of the International Reading Association.

Communication with Students and Parents. In a reading–writing classroom, teachers encourage students to take control of their own learning by inviting students to construct reflective portfolios. These portfolios can be shared with parents.

One of the most significant changes in literacy education in the last twenty years has been the change in the instruction of writing. The characteristics noted earlier are hallmarks of classrooms where teachers are not only merging instructional goals but are interested in more realistic and integrated assessment as well.

s u m m a r y

In this chapter, we have presented a perspective on writing that emphasizes writing as a process with developmental and procedural stages. Knowledge of developmental stages—what characterizes an emergent, beginning, and developing writer—can help a teacher observe students significantly during the process of writing and use information gained from this observation to shape more sensitive instruction in both reading and writing. The chapter presented cases centered around spelling and summarizing to provide examples of classroom decision making based on writing. Further, teacher self-assessment of instruction and the instructional climate can help the teacher shape a classroom in which writing flourishes in close connection with reading and the other language arts.

try it out

1. **For Your Teaching Portfolio:** Observe two or three young writers in your classroom using the Checklist for Determining Stages of Writing Development (Figure 7.1) and decide at what phase these writers are working. In your journal, reflect on the range of ability you observe. You can also use this information in your anecdotal records for the children.

2. Using your observations of your students, brainstorm with other teachers to create a schoolwide holistic scoring rubric to use when you are evaluating student work. Use the examples suggested in this chapter as your starting points.

3. Assist your students in developing a personal portfolio. Ask them to choose a writing piece that represents their best work, one in which they made changes, and one that could use improvement. Invite students to describe why they chose each piece and what they learned while they were selecting these artifacts. As a final task, invite students to set three goals for future writing. Share these portfolios with parents and in class. Store the portfolios in the classroom, so students can refer to them and revise them.

for further reading

Atwell, N. (2002). *Lessons that change writers.* Portsmouth, NH: FirstHand Heinemann.

Calkins, L., & Martinelli, M. (2006). *Launching the writing workshop: Grades 3-5.* Portsmouth, NH: FirstHand Heinemann.

Fletcher, R., & Portalupi, J. (1998). *Craft lessons: Teaching writing K–8.* York, MA: Stenhouse. Seventy-eight easy-to-use mini-lessons support teachers as they assist students in making critical decisions about their writing.

Graves, D. H. (1994). *A fresh look at writing.* Portsmouth, NH: Heinemann. A valuable resource for teachers wishing to integrate portfolios, conventions, spelling, and a range of genre into their writing program.

Hill, B. C., & Ruptic, C. (1994). *Practical aspects of authentic assessment: Putting the pieces together.* Norwood, MA: Christopher-Gordon.

Ray, K. W. (2006). *Study driven: A framework for planning units of study in the writing workshop.* Portsmouth, NH: Heinemann.

Routman, R. (2005). *Writing essentials.* Portsmouth, NH: Heinemann. Based on the framework of Routman's Optimal Learning Model, this text provides teachers with practical suggestions for integrating reading into their classroom environment.

8 Using Informal Reading Inventories and Extended Passages

chapter goals for the reader

- To understand the nature and classroom uses of informal reading inventories
- To develop a framework for evaluating an informal reading inventory (IRI)
- To develop guidelines for administration and interpretation of IRIs
- To work through three cases of assessment using IRIs
- To apply IRI techniques to extended passages
- To work through two case studies using extended passages

Adding to Your Assessment Toolkit

Laura is a reading teacher in a small, two-school district. Her work takes her into elementary and high school classrooms where she works with both students and teachers. Because she sees such a wide variety of students, she needs materials on many levels to make initial assessment decisions. She also works with teachers in small workshop sessions to help them develop their observational and analytic skills. As Laura emphasizes observing students in actual reading and listening situations, she is investigating the use of informal reading inventories as materials for her assessment library. She wants to know:

What is an informal reading inventory (IRI)?

What guidelines can be used to evaluate IRIs?

How is an IRI administered and interpreted?

This chapter addresses Laura's needs and her questions. You will also be able to work through three cases of students she assessed with IRIs. ■

chapter overview

Informal reading inventories are useful tools for classroom teachers, reading specialists, and literacy coaches who need to meet with a wide range of students and who are responsible for evaluating students' reading achievement. Because IRIs are composed of reading selections and word lists that cover a large developmental span, they can be especially helpful to *classroom teachers and literacy professionals who need to assess diverse groups of students*. In this chapter we look at the ways IRIs can be used for assessment. First, we describe IRIs and comment on their history and development. Second, we share guidelines for evaluating IRIs. Third, we present procedures for administering and interpreting IRIs, describing three divergent cases of assessment using these tools. Last, we demonstrate how similar techniques and procedures used for IRIs can be used with any extended passage reading in classroom materials. Two cases using extended passages for informal assessment conclude the chapter.

chapter outline

Levels of Reading
The Informal Reading Inventory (IRI):
Description, History, and Development

Guidelines for Evaluating IRIs
Administering IRIs
  • Administering the Word Recognition Task

Levels of Reading

One of the more important instructional issues you will confront as a classroom teacher, reading specialist, or literacy coach is whether the materials being used for instruction are of appropriate difficulty for your students. Betts (1954) found it useful to characterize the appropriateness of the match between students and materials in terms of levels. The **independent** reading level is the highest level at which students can read fluently with good comprehension without instructional assistance. The **instructional** level is the highest one at which students are able to read with adequate comprehension once they are provided with appropriate instructional support. Finally, at the **frustration** level the text is so difficult that even with appropriate support, students may be unable to comprehend. In this last case, students may comprehend inadequately because of problems with print processing, vocabulary knowledge, or comprehension strategies. Figure 8.1 is a graphic representation of the difficulty levels of reading and reading materials.

Although these levels have proven historically useful to teachers looking for appropriate materials for instruction, remember that it is rarely possible to determine an exact reading level for a child, particularly for one reading beyond the primary levels (Powell, 1984). Familiarity or unfamiliarity with content, genre, and structure can cause great variability in a student's ability to read a selection with understanding. Further, for instructional purposes, different situations will require different levels of reading difficulty. For example, reading that is assigned as homework or as independent work should pose almost no print or

figure 8.1 • Levels of Reading

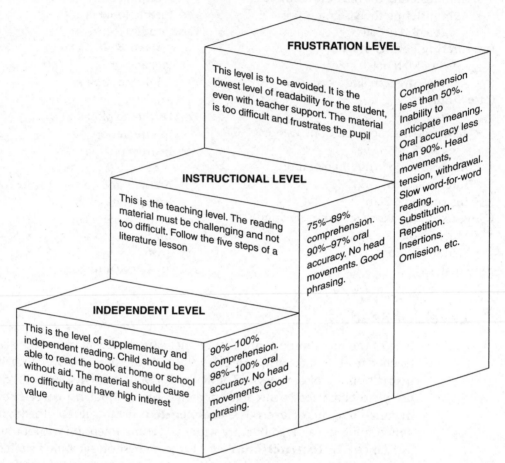

Source: Adapted from E. A. Betts, *Foundations of Reading Instruction* (p. 448), New York: American Book Company, 1954.

comprehension problems for students. They should be able to read the material orally with good intonation and phrasing or silently with ease; they should readily comprehend the main ideas and important facts. When students have difficulty correctly identifying 2 or more words in every 100, they may have problems focusing on the meaning, and these problems may hinder them from developing mature reading strategies. Failure to answer more than one question in every ten is another indication that the material is probably too difficult for independent reading. The questions you use in making this assessment should be appropriate and nontrivial. There are some struggling readers for whom no reading material is easy and who therefore should not be given an independent reading assignment unless the teacher has prepared them for the passage or provides direct support.

Given the range in reading proficiency in most classes, you should assign materials for homework and independent reading that represent a comparable range in difficulty. Students can best develop their reading strategies through contextual materials that they can read fluently with good comprehension. Unfortunately, some students never experience the pleasure of problem-free reading and are thereby deprived of appropriate reading practice.

When your students read under your direct supervision, during guided reading, for example, more problems in print skill and comprehension can be tolerated. As a rule of thumb, if a student is reading aloud, he or she should have difficulty with no more than 1 word in every 20, or 95 percent accuracy. Comprehension should be good, with at least three out of every four questions, or 75 percent, answered correctly.

You need to keep in mind not only the average performance of the group with which you are working but also the performance of individuals in your group. When individual students are missing more than half the questions posed, 50 percent, or having difficulty with more than one word in every ten, or 90 percent accuracy, the materials are inappropriate, representing frustration-level work. Instructional support cannot help a student who is reading frustration-level material advance to the point that he or she can perform at acceptable levels of print processing and/or comprehension.

By contrast, students who perform in the borderline region between frustration level and acceptable instructional level may be helped by instruction that has been developed with their particular needs in mind. Support reading, partner reading, use of taped materials prior to reading, reading guides, or group guided reading can help them accurately read and comprehend materials that might be too difficult without such support. This borderline region is characterized by an accuracy of 90 to 94 percent on oral reading and of 50 to 74 percent on comprehension. Table 8.1 presents a summary of criteria for determining

table 8.1 • Criteria for Interpreting Word Recognition, Oral Reading, and Comprehension Performance

	Functional Levels			
Task	*Frustration*	*Borderline*	*Instructional*	*Independent*
Word Recognition (Flash)	below 50%	50%–59%	60%–89%	90%–100%
Oral Reading Accuracy	below 90%	90%–94%	95%–97%	98%–100%
Comprehension (Oral or Silent)	below 60%	60%–74%	75%–89%	90%–100%

Source: Adapted from Darrell Morris (1999).

the reading difficulty levels of materials. The frequency of borderline determinations is a strong indicator that informed judgments are required as part of a thoughtful diagnosis. The guidelines for working within the borderline region are particularly applicable to the early reader.

(See For Further Reading at the end of the chapter for more on this topic.)

Consider the case of Eva, discussed in Chapter 3. Martha had her read the next story in her basal reader with little instructional support. Eva's oral reading accuracy score of 91 percent indicates performance in the borderline range. However, her comprehension was quite good at the instructional level, as she answered correctly eight out of ten questions. Eva was in the reading group needing the most teacher support, and Martha wanted her to remain there. However, the analysis of print skill difficulties indicated that her problems were severe. Martha's alternatives were either to give Eva reading instruction on an individual basis with easier materials or to try to eliminate some of the print-processing problems posed by her current basal reader through increased instructional support.

Martha decided to try the second alternative, spending more time on word identification and discussion of key story terms prior to reading. After providing such preparation, Martha listened to the quality of Eva's oral reading and found that it was more fluent than it had been, with less than 5 percent of the words causing problems. Martha then proceeded to offer this increased support to Eva's reading group as part of their regular instruction. Other students in the group seemed to profit as well. At the same time, Martha helped Eva select easy reading material for independent reading. If Eva's comprehension of the story had not been so complete, Martha might not have found it possible to keep her with the reading group.

For most teachers, the students who cause most concern are those for whom the regular, grade-level classroom reading materials are too difficult. When frustration-level reading is indicated, in terms of either oral reading accuracy or level of comprehension, the teacher must find more appropriate materials for those students experiencing difficulty. If the student's performance is in the borderline region, it may be possible to make the materials accessible through appropriate instruction. Usually, the teacher must further diagnose the student's reading strengths and difficulties to pinpoint the nature of the problem and to experiment with instructional support.

In the next section of this chapter, we describe specific procedures for determining a student's instructional reading level and for diagnosing reading strengths and difficulties, first using an informal reading inventory, then applying the diagnostic strategies used with IRIs to extended passages. Again, we illustrate with individual case studies in order to consolidate the diagnostic strategies introduced in prior chapters.

The Informal Reading Inventory (IRI): Description, History, and Development

Informal reading inventories are among the most widely used forms of instructionally based reading assessment. Typically, an IRI consists of sets of graded word lists and passages (see Appendix C for examples). Teachers use these in a systematic way to determine an individual's independent, instructional, and frustration reading levels and analyze them to provide a profile of a student's strengths and needs. Though there has been much rich dialogue surrounding these inventories, their popularity in both classroom and clinic (Harris & Lalik, 1987; Masztal & Smith, 1984) attests to their power as assessment tools.

The development of IRIs is commonly attributed to Betts (1946), although similar diagnostic processes were used in earlier clinical assessment. The original procedure was designed to help teachers construct their own inventories from their classroom instructional materials with the idea of evaluating student performance in activities that were as much like classroom activities as possible. In many ways, the original IRIs reflected the model for assessment with instructional passages that we have proposed in this book. For that reason, IRIs are often useful for drawing conclusions about reading that could easily be connected to instruction.

Besides being closely tied to classroom reading, the informal nature of the inventories encouraged teachers to take control of decision making about their use and interpretation. Criteria for evaluation in an IRI are not norm-referenced criteria, but rather criteria for mastery of such aspects of reading as word recognition and comprehension. As the popularity of IRIs grew, standards for mastery and placement were proposed. Though there has been a rich and spirited dialogue about the boundaries of these criteria and issues of the reliability of IRIs (Johns, 1993; Lipson, Cox, Iwanowski, & Simon, 1984), shared ranges of interpretation have emerged such as those presented in Table 8.1.

Guidelines for Evaluating IRIs

As IRIs grew in popularity, commercial inventories began appearing (see Table 8.2), with developers paying some attention to selecting passages that reflected mastery by representative samples of students. Further, attention was given to aiding users in making decisions about passage reading that reflected broader, more qualitative and strategic views of reading (Goodman, Watson, & Burke, 1987; Leslie & Caldwell, 2005). Whether purchasing a commercial inventory or designing one of your own, you might consider several issues:

1. In commercial IRIs, graded word lists should reflect the types of words your students will encounter in regular classroom reading. These should include high-frequency, or "sight," words, as well as content words appropriate for the grade level.

table 8.2 • Selected List of Published Informal Reading Inventories

Title/Publisher/Date	Word List Grade Ranges	Passage Grade Ranges	Forms
Analytical Reading Inventory and Readers' Passages Package, 8th Edition (Woods, M. L., & Moe, A.) Pearson, 2007	P–9	PP–9	3 Narrative 2 Expository
Bader Reading and Language Inventory and Readers' Passages and Graded Word Lists, 5th Edition (Bader, L. A.) Pearson, 2005	PP–12	PP–12	3
Basic Reading Inventory, 10th Edition (Johns, J. J.) Kendall-Hunt, 2008	PP–12	PP–12	4 PP–8 3 3–12
Classroom Reading Inventory with Teacher Resource CD-ROM and Inventory Administration Kit, 10th edition (Silvaroli, N. J., & Wheelock, W. H.) McGraw-Hill, 2004	PP–6	PP–8	3
Reading Inventory for the Classroom, 5th Edition (Flynt, E. S., & Cooter R. B., Jr.) Prentice Hall, 2003	PP–12	PP–12	5 English 4 Spanish
Qualitative Reading Inventory, 4th Edition (Leslie, L. I., & Caldwell, J.) Allyn & Bacon, 2005	PP–12	PP–12	4

2. The passages ought to represent the type of reading you do in your classroom. They should be of good literary quality with language that sounds natural. Topics should be of interest to the student to be assessed, and the selection should be of sufficient length and integrity to stand alone.

3. Questions should be clearly worded, they should be both divergent and convergent, and they should be organized to tap the important aspects of the selection. They should be "passage dependent," that is, the reader should need to read the selection to answer the questions. Good questions should call on readers to provide elaborated answers, not simple "yes" and "no" responses. (Review Chapter 5 for more ideas on questions.)

4. In commercial IRIs, the formats and directions for use should be clear and convenient, and the information the author provides about philosophy, use, and field testing should be relevant to your own school situation.

Throughout the discussion of administration and interpretation that follows, we assume that you have chosen a commercial inventory and choose to use its scoring standards, or you have constructed your own and will use the scoring standards we described earlier. In either of these cases, the judgment of the administrator is an important decision factor in how administration and interpretation will take place. The guidelines we offer should be interpreted as generic ones for dealing with using IRIs.

Administering IRIs

The general method for administering a standardized IRI is as follows. First, the word recognition test is administered and scored according to the instructions in the test manual. This provides you the basis for determining the level of the first passage to be read orally by the student. The student then reads progressively more difficult passages aloud until his or her performance falls below the oral reading accuracy and comprehension criterion levels. Next, he or she begins reading a passage silently at the instructional level established through oral reading. The student then reads progressively more difficult passages until comprehension falls below the criterion level. For silent reading, it is also important to establish the student's independent reading level; thus, he or she must also read progressively easier passages until a 90-percent comprehension or higher is achieved. On some tests, this standard may be unrealistic; if there are nine questions or fewer, it means that no questions can be missed.

Finally, beginning one level above the student's instructional level established during oral or silent reading, you read progressively more difficult passages aloud to the student until his or her comprehension falls below the specified criterion. This establishes the student's listening comprehension level. Figure 8.2 summarizes these steps in administering an IRI and the general considerations for starting and discontinuing each task.

The administration of the IRI allows you to identify the grade level of material that can be read easily by the student at an independent level, the levels that may be appropriate for alternative instructional purposes, and the levels that are too difficult. Testing usually continues until each of these levels has been established. There may be times, however, when you may wish to use the IRI to answer a more limited question (e.g., to determine a student's independent level of silent reading or instructional level for print processing). Obviously, in such cases, the procedures described here for the systematic use of the IRI would not be followed; only the relevant portion of the IRI would be used. This is an important point because diagnostic work should never blindly follow an established set of procedures. Although it is necessary for you to be familiar with the procedures involved in a comprehensive approach, it is equally necessary to know when to follow only a portion of these procedures.

figure 8.2 • Procedures for Administering Informal Reading Inventory Tasks

Word Lists
> *Begin* with the easiest list.
> *Discontinue* when the student scores below 70 percent correct on the flash (sight) presentation.

Oral Reading Task
> *Begin* with a passage at the highest level on which the student achieved 90 percent correct on the flash presentation of the word lists.
> *Discontinue* when the student's instructional and frustration levels are established.

Silent Reading Task
> *Begin* with a passage at the highest level on which the student met the criteria for instructional level in oral reading accuracy and comprehension on the oral reading task.
> *Discontinue* when the student's independent, instructional, and frustration levels are established.

Listening Task
> *Begin* with a passage one level above the highest level on which the student met the criterion for instructional level in comprehension on the oral reading or the silent reading task.
> *Discontinue* when the student's frustration level is established.

• Administering the Word Recognition Task

The word lists measure the student's instantaneous sight vocabulary (flash presentation) and word identification skills (untimed presentation). In Chapter 3, we described procedures for assessing the "basic" sight vocabulary of students through oral reading analysis. Although the primary and first-grade word lists provide a similar measure of basic sight vocabulary, the subsequent lists show how well students are incorporating other words into their store of words that are quickly recognized. Proficient readers are in command of a large store of sight words, and students during the elementary grades expand their set of sight words beyond the basic set to include most other words that they encounter frequently during contextual reading. Flash performance on the more advanced word lists shows whether the students' development of this larger sight vocabulary is grade appropriate.

The procedures for flash administration consist of using two rectangular cards, one placed just above the word to be flashed and the other covering the word. When the student is ready, quickly move the bottom card down, exposing the word. After a half-second exposure, move the top card down to cover the word. An alternative method that eliminates the need for cards is to simply have the student read the words on the list, allowing one second for "sight" recognition. Mark correct responses on the student record form with a checkmark; record incorrect responses phonetically. When the student fails to respond, record this as "NR" (no response), "DK" (don't know), or "x." No corrections are given.

When the student fails to recognize a word during the flash presentation, allow reexamination to see whether he or she can identify the word when given more time for analysis. Commercial IRIs usually direct the examiner to do this following the flash presentation of each list. Use the further exploration procedures described in Chapter 3 for determining the knowledge a student possesses about phonics. Use structural analysis with words the student reads incorrectly on an IRI as well as on a diagnostic passage.

• Administering the Oral Reading Task

The first passage the student reads is determined by the performance on the word lists. If the student's performance on this first passage is at or above the prescribed criteria, progressively more difficult passages are read until his or her performance falls below the criteria. If, on the other hand, the performance falls below the criterion for either accuracy or comprehension, this level represents the borderline or frustration level. In this case, increasingly easier passages are read until his or her instructional level is established (acceptable comprehension and oral reading accuracy).

As the student reads each passage aloud, record any errors made, using the procedures described in Chapter 3. Count the number of errors. We suggest two error counts and, thus, two accuracy scores: one for total errors that includes all mispronunciations, substitutions, omissions, and insertions; and one for significant miscues, those uncorrected errors that disrupt meaning. Although the significant miscue score, which is the more lenient score, allows for the student's attempts to make sense of the text, the total score probably better reflects the actual difficulty of the passage for that student.

When the student finishes reading a passage, ask the comprehension questions, record the answers, and determine a comprehension score. On occasion you may wish to assess comprehension by having the student retell the passage prior to asking the comprehension questions, as described in Chapter 6.

• Administering the Silent Reading Task

Following the oral reading task, ask the student to read certain passages silently. The point of this task is to determine whether the student is at least as proficient in silent reading as in oral reading. It is important to note that although many proficient readers achieve greater comprehension when they read silently than when they read aloud, this is often not the case with less proficient readers. Therefore, the first silent reading passage administered is at the *same* level of difficulty as the one the student was able to read orally with good comprehension (the instructional level). After he or she reads the passage silently, ask the comprehension questions, and record and score the answers. If the student's comprehension is below the criterion, administer successively easier passages until adequate comprehension is achieved when reading silently. On the other hand, if the comprehension score on the first silent reading passage is at or above the criterion, administer progressively more difficult passages until the frustration level is established.

Administering the Listening Task

The listening task measures a student's comprehension and underlying verbal knowledge when print skill difficulties (if any) are eliminated. As a rule, a listening task is administered only with passages that are more difficult than those the student is able to comprehend through reading alone. It is not necessary to administer as a listening task those passages that represent a level of difficulty the student can read and understand through reading alone.

The listening task usually begins with a passage one step higher in difficulty than the most difficult passage the student was able to read orally or silently with adequate comprehension. Read the passage aloud to the student, ask the comprehension questions, and record and score the student's answers. If the comprehension score is below the criterion, discontinue the listening task. The reason for discontinuing at this point is that under normal circumstances the next lower-level passages will have been read by the student with adequate comprehension during oral or silent reading. If his or her listening comprehension score on the first passage is adequate, read aloud the next higher-level passage, ask the questions, and record and score the answers. Read progressively more difficult passages until you are satisfied that the student can comprehend language on the appropriate developmental level or until his or her comprehension falls below the criterion if you are attempting to estimate capacity. Then discontinue the listening task.

If the particular IRI materials being used provide only two passages at each level of difficulty, both passages at the level that would be appropriate for the listening task may have already been administered—one for oral reading and the other for silent reading. In this case, the listening task should proceed to the next higher level.

Laura presented the case study of Carlos, a fourth grader, to a group of teachers with whom she was working on assessment procedures. First, we work through Carlos's case to see how an IRI is administered. Then we examine two more cases—Sara, a second grader, and James, a high school student—to get an idea of the range of information an IRI can provide.

pause and **reflect**

Look at Case 8.1: Carlos, which follows. Compare it with the procedures you just read. Does it make sense? Bring questions to group discussion.

case 8.1

Carlos

To illustrate the comprehensive procedures, we use the case of Carlos, a fourth grader, tested with the Ekwall Reading Inventory (Ekwall & Shankar, 1999). Laura first administered the preprimer-level word recognition list to Carlos. She exposed the words for a half-second interval (flash). If Carlos did not recognize a word, it was presented for an untimed interval. As shown in Figure 8.3, he quickly recognized all words on the preprimer list, but he failed to recognize one word out of ten on the primer list. He was able to identify that word when it was presented with time for analysis. Laura continued administering the lists, up through and including the fifth-grade list, on which Carlos's untimed score fell below 75 percent.

Second, Laura asked Carlos to read a passage aloud and answer comprehension questions. The passage selected was at the highest level at which Carlos recognized 90 percent of the flashed words, the first-grade level. Carlos's oral reading and comprehension on the first-grade passage were good, and Laura then asked him to read the second-, the third-, and finally the fourth-grade passages. Oral reading was discontinued after the

figure 8.3 • Summary of Performance on IRI: Carlos

INFORMAL READING INVENTORY SUMMARY

Test Ekwall R. I.   Child Carlos   Age 9   Grade 4   Date Jan.

| Level | Recognition Test | | Informal Reading Inventory | | | | | |
| | | | Oral Reading Task | | | Silent Reading | | |
	Flash (%)	Untimed (%)	Accuracy (%)	Comprehension (%)	Rate (wpm)	Comprehension (%)	Rate (wpm)	Listening Comprehension (%)
Preprimer	100	100						
Primer	90	100						
First	90	100	97	100	95	100	105	
Second	80	90	95	100	81	85	84	
Third	80	90	95	75	73	50	87	
Fourth	40	80	89	50	62			75
Fifth	—	60						50
Sixth								
Seventh								
Eighth								
Ninth								

fourth-grade passage because both his oral reading accuracy and comprehension dropped below the test criteria.

Third, Laura assessed Carlos's silent reading comprehension by having
him read a passage at the third-grade level, his instructional level on the
oral reading task. His comprehension of this passage fell below the criterion. Laura then administered easier passages. Testing proceeded down to
the first-grade passage in order to establish Carlos's independent level for
silent reading comprehension.

Finally, Laura administered the passages as a listening comprehension
test. That is, she read the passage aloud to Carlos and then asked him to
answer comprehension questions. Testing began at the fourth-grade level,
the level where Carlos's oral reading comprehension fell below the instructional level. Because he demonstrated adequate listening comprehension
(75 percent) on the fourth-grade passage, she administered the fifth-grade
passage. Because his comprehension was not acceptable at this level
(50 percent), the listening task was discontinued.

These procedures work well for younger poor readers and older less
proficient readers suspected of having print skill problems. However, for
some older readers for whom silent reading proficiency is of particular concern, it is useful to test silent reading comprehension first and to sample
oral reading second in order to obtain a more valid measure of their silent
comprehension. For most readers, the complete IRI can be administered at
one time, but for younger readers, the silent reading tests, when administered last, may not be valid because of fatigue. Therefore, it is advisable to
break the testing into two sessions if fatigue is noted in the students. ■

Interpreting Results of IRIs

For the teacher-constructed series of graded passages, consisting usually of a
single passage per level, the interpretation was similar to that for diagnoses
made with individual reading passages. In contrast, the standardized inventories
allow for a variety of comparisons, which provide a comprehensive basis for
understanding a student's reading strength and difficulty. For example, in addition to comparing a student's performance from level to level, as was possible
with the teacher-constructed inventory, it is now possible to compare oral and
silent comprehension and reading rates. The student's identification of isolated
words on the graded lists can be compared with his or her print processing during oral reading. Further, a student's level of vocabulary knowledge as estimated
from the vocabulary questions following each passage can be compared with his
or her listening comprehension. This variety of comparisons is complicated, but

it does increase the precision of the diagnosis. Such a comprehensive diagnosis should be unnecessary for most students in a class. Occasionally, however, a particularly perplexing problem requires a comprehensive reading inventory.

Like teacher-constructed inventories, comprehensive IRIs are interpreted in two stages. First, the teacher makes a judgment about the level of materials appropriate for reading instruction and independent reading. Then print skill, vocabulary knowledge, and comprehension are examined in order to determine relative strengths and weaknesses. The teacher's recommendations concerning the level of materials to be used for instruction are based on the first analysis; the establishment of instructional priorities is based on the second.

• Level of Materials

Instructional Reading Level. The level of instructional materials you select depends on the nature of instruction. For example, the level of material that is sufficiently challenging to foster the further development of word identification skills may be higher than the level of materials appropriate for the development of silent comprehension strategies. The instructional level for word identification is based on the student's oral reading accuracy, whereas selecting instructional material for group-based comprehension instruction is based on the student's oral reading comprehension. For instruction that emphasizes the monitoring of silent reading comprehension, material selection is based on silent reading comprehension.

Independent Reading Level. The silent reading task determines the highest level of materials the student can read silently with good comprehension. This will normally be his or her independent reading level. It represents the level at which words are recognized and identified without pronouncing them aloud and at which he or she can concentrate on meaning without instructional support.

• Areas of Strength and Need

Print Skill. Evidence from the word lists (flash and untimed), the oral reading, and the reading rate scores (silent versus oral) should all be considered in drawing conclusions about a student's print-processing skill. In addition, the listening task measures the strength of the student's comprehension skills unconfounded by his or her ability to process print. In general, if a student can, through listening, understand materials that are too difficult when read independently, you may infer that print skill difficulty interfered with reading comprehension. A detailed analysis of oral reading of one or two passages at the instructional or borderline level (as outlined in Chapter 3) should confirm this inference and reveal the specific nature of the difficulty and appropriate instructional emphasis. Evidence from the word lists (flash and untimed), the oral reading, and the reading rate scores (silent versus oral) should all be considered in drawing conclusions about a student's print-processing skill.

Vocabulary Knowledge. Information about a student's vocabulary knowledge comes from two sources. First, asking specific questions about vocabulary and phrases provides you with information on whether the student understands the key terms of a passage. Vocabulary knowledge performance on any of the three tasks (oral reading, silent reading, listening) that you administer at any one level should be combined to determine the percentage of terms the student defines or describes correctly at that level. Second, the listening comprehension score reflects a student's underlying vocabulary knowledge. A high score indicates good verbal development, whereas a low score is ambiguous because it may reflect limited vocabulary knowledge, poor comprehension strategies, or both.

Comprehension. Valuation of reading comprehension begins with a comparison of oral versus silent reading comprehension. If the student's silent reading comprehension is a grade or more lower than his or her actual grade, this indicates that strategies to monitor comprehension during silent reading have not yet been internalized. He or she is able to comprehend but because of limited practice or lack of instruction in silent reading strategies, the student has not learned to attend to meaning without the added support of pronouncing words aloud. Once a reader becomes proficient, it is not unusual for silent comprehension to exceed oral comprehension; a discrepancy in this direction is not viewed as a problem.

Next, compare the highest level of reading comprehension (oral or silent) with listening comprehension. A discrepancy here indicates that the student has print-processing problems. At the same time, the higher listening comprehension score suggests that once the print problems are solved, reading comprehension will be similar to listening.

Finally, analyze the student's responses to the reading comprehension questions. When you determine that the major problem is in comprehension, further explore his or her strategies, using the procedures described in Chapter 6.

Case Studies

The cases described show how diagnosis using an informal reading inventory was undertaken by Laura. The case of Sara provides an overview of the diagnostic thinking involved in the interpretation of the inventory. The case of James goes into much greater detail, presenting passage-by-passage evidence from an IRI.

case 8.2

Sara

Sara is in an "on-level" guided reading group in a second-grade class. The basal program being used in her class is the Houghton-Mifflin series, and

pause and reflect
What level of task should be administered first as an oral reading task?

her group currently reads from the second-grade reader. Laura, the teacher we introduced at the beginning of the chapter, decided to take a closer look at Sara's reading because of her poor comprehension of stories during guided reading in contrast to her relatively good performance on independent assignments. Laura decided to administer the Basic Reading Inventory by Johns (Kendall/Hunt Publishing Co., 2001) to gain a better understanding of Sara's reading strategies. She administered the word lists and the oral reading passages on the first day and the silent reading and listening passages on the second day. Sara worked hard and was involved in these reading activities. The results from the administration of the word lists are shown in Figure 8.4.

pause and reflect
What would you do next? Should testing be discontinued, or would you proceed to the first-grade passage?

Administration of the oral reading passage should begin at the highest level at which the student obtained at least 90 percent correct on the flash administration of the word lists. Thus, for Sara, oral reading should begin on the primer-level passage. When given this passage, she made only one oral reading error and got answered all the comprehension questions correctly. Laura then gave Sara the first-grade passage. On this she made four oral reading errors on the 100-word passage, and she missed two out of ten passage questions.

According to the scoring guide of the test, up to five oral reading errors and up to two comprehension errors represent the instructional level. Thus, oral reading should continue at the next higher level. On the second-grade passage, Sara made eight oral reading errors (8 percent of the words) and missed six of the ten questions. Because the comprehension score shows that the second-grade passage is in the

figure 8.4 • Summary of Performance on the Word Recognition Tests: Sara

Level	Word Recognition Test	
	Flash (%)	Untimed (%)
Preprimer	95	100
Primer	95	95
First	80	90
Second	70	95
Third	55	70
Fourth		
Fifth		
Sixth		
Seventh		
Eighth		
Ninth		

8.2

p a u s e and r e f l e c t

Given Sara's oral reading performance, on what level should Laura begin the silent reading task?

frustration range for Sara, oral reading was discontinued.

The next day Laura had Sara read silently at the highest level on which she last demonstrated instruction-level oral reading and comprehension. This was the first-grade level. Sara read this passage and answered all the passage questions correctly.

Laura had her read the next more difficult passage, which was at the second-grade level. On this passage, Sara read with good comprehension, missing only one of ten questions. Consequently, Laura asked her to read the third-grade-level passage. On this passage she knew the answers to only three of ten questions. Because this performance indicated the material was at Sara's frustration level, Laura discontinued the silent reading and instead had her listen to a passage that Laura read aloud.

The administration of the listening task should begin at the level above the highest level successfully comprehended when the child read either orally or silently. For Sara, this means the third-grade level. (Since Sara could comprehend at the second-grade level when reading silently, there was no need to test her listening comprehension at that level or below.) When Laura read the third-grade passage aloud, Sara missed only one

p a u s e and r e f l e c t

Given these results, what tentative conclusions can you draw about the nature of Sara's reading difficulty? What level of material should Sara be reading?

question. Thus, Laura proceeded to the next more difficult passage. On the fourth-grade passage, Sara missed only three of ten questions. Therefore, Laura read the fifth-grade passage to her. On this passage Sara was able to answer only four of the ten comprehension questions. The results from the inventory are summarized in Figure 8.5.

Scores in the vocabulary column are based on answers to passage questions. Because for each passage there were two questions about word meaning, it was possible to tabulate the total number of correct answers on these questions at each level. For example, on the second-grade level, the vocabulary knowledge percentage was based on the results from the passage read orally and that read silently. On the third-grade level, it was based on the passage read silently and the one read to Sara by her teacher. ■

figure 8.5 • Summary of Performance on IRI: Sara

INFORMAL READING INVENTORY SUMMARY

Test J. John's BRI   Child Sara   Age 8   Grade 2   Date Dec.

| | Recognition Test | | Informal Reading Inventory | | | | | | | |
| | | | Oral Reading Task | | | Silent Reading | | | | |
Level	Flash (%)	Untimed (%)	Accuracy (Total Error Score) (%)	Compre-hension (%)	Rate (wpm)	Compre-hension (%)	Rate (wpm)	Listening Compre-hension (%)	Vocabulary N	%
Preprimer	95	100								
Primer	95	95	99	100	111				2/2	100
First	80	90	96	75	91	100	100		4/4	100
Second	70	95	92	40	67	90	77		3/4	75
Third	55	65				30	71	90	4/4	100
Fourth								70	1/2	50
Fifth								40	0/2	0
Sixth										

• Tentative Instructional Conclusions

Areas of Reading Difficulty. Sara's reading diagnosis is complicated in several ways. Because her reading profile does not conform to typical patterns, it is important for Laura to understand the nature of Sara's reading strengths and difficulties before specifying the levels of materials that she should read.

With respect to reading comprehension, Sara's silent reading comprehension is better than her oral comprehension by one grade level. It is not unusual for silent reading to be better than oral reading comprehension when a reader is proficient. But other evidence from the word lists and the oral reading accuracy indicates that Sara is not a proficient reader. For example, on second-grade-level materials, where her silent reading comprehension was good, she is in the borderline region for oral reading accuracy, and the flash presentation of second-grade words indicates some problems with sight recognition. The discrepancy between oral and silent comprehension would seem to indicate that Sara can compensate for poorly developed print skills when she reads silently, but when faced with the additional demands of oral reading, she is not able to process print accurately and also comprehend at the same time.

Sara's listening comprehension shows that she possesses the necessary background knowledge to understand third- and even fourth-grade-level material. The vocabulary knowledge evidence confirms her strength in this area, at least through the third-grade level. Laura concludes that Sara's difficulty in oral reading comprehension is not a reflection of poorly developed word knowledge or vocabulary.

It is in the area of print skill that Sara's difficulties appear to lie. The results for the word lists, for example, indicate that she had difficulty with immediate recognition of some first-grade-level words. While a single error (95 percent) may occur by chance, the four errors (80 percent) on the first-grade-level list suggest that some first-grade words are not familiar to her. Even when given more time, Sara was able to correct only two of the four errors. She had even more difficulty with the flash administration of the second-grade list, although here she was able to correct all but one of her errors with time. Laura concluded that Sara's performance on the third-grade list is at the frustration level.

In addition to her problems reading isolated words, Sara made four errors on the first-grade passage and eight on the second-grade passage (each 100 words in length), and her reading rate diminished from a relatively fast rate on the first-grade passage to a slow-average rate on the second-grade passage.

These results point to print processing as the area in need of further study. Laura should analyze the errors that Sara made on the second-grade passage and explore some of her responses to the passage and word lists. Given the discrepancy between her flash and untimed scores on both the first- and second-grade lists, Laura can conclude that Sara possesses knowledge about word identification but has not done enough easy reading to consolidate this knowledge and expand her sight vocabulary. Because of this lack of experience, she is able to read orally with a high degree of accuracy only when she focuses mainly on print and somewhat superficially on meaning. And as materials become more difficult (second grade), she is no longer able to avoid errors. When reading silently, primary focus on meaning and probably less stringent monitoring of print allow her to comprehend second-grade material. However, this strategy is no longer functional at the third-grade level, where she encounters many more print problems. Thus, on the basis of the evidence, Laura concludes that Sara's major problem is in the area of print skill. Further, she speculates that the problem pertains to the consolidation and application of Sara's existing knowledge about print as well as to the development of new knowledge about word identification.

Levels of Materials. If taken alone, Sara's silent reading comprehension might suggest that her independent reading should be at the second-grade level. However, her difficulty processing print at this level suggests that it might not be the appropriate place to begin if Sara is to develop good reading strategies. Indeed, even first-grade-level material may pose print problems that require her undivided attention. The level of material that appears to pose no print skill or comprehension problems is the primer level. Although Sara may soon progress to first-grade-level materials, at the present time primer is her independent reading level and the level that will be effective in helping her consolidate good reading strategies.

To determine Sara's instructional level, Laura focuses on the area of her greatest need and then asks what level material would best serve to develop this

area. She has tentatively concluded that Sara's main reading problem involves print skill. Not only does she need to consolidate and expand her sight vocabulary through extensive reading at her independent reading level (primer and then first grade), but she also needs further to develop her word identification strategies. Whereas first-grade materials may be appropriate for instructional purposes, second-grade materials may be too difficult. Following further study of her print-processing strategies (oral reading analysis for the second-grade passage and exploring responses), Laura should examine Sara's response to second-grade-level materials when instruction is specially designed to prepare her for the reading. If Sara shows better print strategies with instructional preparation, it is appropriate to keep her with her present reading group, which is working with second-grade material, and to offer appropriate instructional support that will further develop Sara's word identification skills and permit her to focus on comprehension.

Sara's performance on the third-grade-level passage indicates that this is her frustration level. Even though she is able to understand materials at this level when they are read to her, her print-processing problems are so great that she cannot comprehend them when she is reading.

case 8.3

James

James is a freshman in high school and is in an intensive reading program. He is ranked 31st among 50 disabled readers. He was referred by Laura to the class on the basis of teacher recommendations and diagnostic reading test results. On the most recent standardized reading test, he scored a grade equivalent of 5.3 in comprehension and 6.8 in vocabulary. These scores reflect an average gain of 2.5 grade equivalents over the prior year's test. This achievement is a result of his desire to improve his reading so that he might go to college. Because of his extremely high motivation, Laura asked him if he would like to have an inventory made of his reading skills so that she could better advise him as to how he might improve his reading even further. He agreed that this would be of interest to him.

During the testing with the *Analytical Reading Inventory* by Woods and Moe (2003, 7th ed.), James was pleasant and responsive. Between passages he talked about the books he likes to read, the movies he has seen, and one of his favorite authors, Edgar Allan Poe.

Administration

First James read all the word recognition lists. He achieved 90 percent accuracy on flash administration at the fifth-grade level but 95 percent at the sixth-grade level (the highest level list). He then read the sixth-grade passage orally, followed by the passages for grades 7 through 8. Next he read the seventh-grade passage silently. Laura selected this level because it corresponded to the highest oral reading passage for which his comprehension score was at the instructional level. Because of his low comprehension on this passage, he next read the sixth- and then the fifth-grade passages silently. Finally, he was administered the eighth-grade listening passage, on which he correctly answered seven out of eight questions. Although James scored 81 percent on the next higher passage (grade 9), Laura discontinued the testing because there are no higher-level passages on this particular IRI. (The IRI records from James's performance are shown in Appendix C.) ∎

• Analysis and Further Exploration

The first step in the analysis is for Laura to examine the test records and score them (see Appendix C). On the word lists, it is necessary to determine the percentage of words correctly recognized for the flash and the untimed administrations.

The next step is to score the passages. It is useful for Laura to keep the passages in the order in which they were administered and to identify them as "oral," "silent," or "listening." For orally read passages, the number of errors is recorded line by line, and then the total is determined. The total number of errors in relation to the total number of words read and the percentage of errors are then recorded following the passage. On the sixth-grade passage (see Appendix C) James made 3 percent errors and thus read with 97 percent accuracy. In this example, it would also be important to note that the problems were concentrated in the first three sentences, with few occurring thereafter.

Next, Laura scored the comprehension questions using the expected answers as a guide. When ambiguous responses occur, it is important to ask the student to "explain further" during the administration of the test so that credit may be given if the information has been comprehended. The total number of questions answered correctly out of the total asked and the corresponding percentage figure were recorded on the passage next to the number of oral reading errors. For example, as shown for the Level 6 passage, James correctly answered eight out of eight questions, for 100 percent comprehension.

Finally, Laura determined James's rate of reading. For example, James read the Level 6 passage in 1 minute and 36 seconds, which is equivalent to 96 seconds or 1.6 minutes (96 divided by 60). Because the passage is 192 words in length, 192 is divided by 1.6 to yield a reading rate of 120 words per minute. This information was recorded next to the comprehension percentage score.

After all the orally read passages had been scored, Laura determined comprehension and rate scores for the silently read passages. These scores were also recorded following the passage. The comprehension of the passages administered as listening tasks were then scored and recorded. The final step was to transfer all

figure 8.6 • Summary of Performance on IRI: James

INFORMAL READING INVENTORY SUMMARY

Test _Woods-Moe_   Child _James_   Age _14_   Grade _9_   Date _March_

| | Recognition Test | | Informal Reading Inventory | | | | | | |
| | | | Oral Reading Task | | | Silent Reading | | | |
Level	Flash (%)	Untimed (%)	Accuracy (Total Error Score) (%)	Compre-hension (%)	Rate (wpm)	Compre-hension (%)	Rate (wpm)	Listening Compre-hension (%)	Vocabulary (%)
Primer	100	100							
First	100	100							
Second	100	100							
Third	95	100							
Fourth	95	100							
Fifth	90	100				100	109		100
Sixth	95	100	97	100	120	81	97		100
Seventh			95	88	105	56	111		25
Eighth			92	63	91			88	50
Ninth			93	25	87			81	25

accuracy percentages, comprehension percentages, and reading rates to the summary sheet, as shown in Figure 8.6.

Once the results had been summarized, the next step was to consider each area of James's reading to determine whether any of his responses should be explored further. The results pertaining to oral reading accuracy, reading rate, and isolated word recognition accuracy suggest that James is experiencing some difficulty with word identification. The Level 7 passage was selected for further analysis, and further exploration was undertaken to explore his recognition of sight words and content words presented in isolation.

Laura's comparison of James's oral reading comprehension with silent reading comprehension suggests a problem in silent reading. Because James is able to comprehend, but not without the support of oral reinforcement, the interactive and monitorial strategies described in Chapter 6 represent appropriate instructional approaches.

The results from the listening task suggest that James's vocabulary knowledge is sufficiently well developed for the comprehension of ninth-grade material. However, the vocabulary-related comprehension questions suggest otherwise. These results, summarized in Figure 8.6, show that many terms from the seventh-grade level and up are unknown to him. Thus, exploration of the Level 7 content words needs to focus on word meaning as well as recognition.

The analysis of miscues made on the seventh-grade-level passage and exploration based on this analysis are shown in Figure 8.7. The results show that James's

figure 8.7 • Analysis of Oral Reading Responses, Level 7: James

ORAL READING ANALYSIS

Name **James** Grade **9** Date **March**

Book/Page **IRI Woods Moe** Level **7**

A. Difficulty

13 / **262** **95** % Correct

Level: Independent (Instructional)
Borderline   Frustration

B. Word Learning: High-Frequency Word Errors

Printed Word	Oral Response	Further Exploration
run	return	✓
did	had ©	✓
had	[omitted]	✓
from	[omitted]	✓
a	[omitted]©	✓
the	[insertion]	✓

Evaluation

High-frequency words are known when presented in isolation. Given the number of such errors, James should be encouraged to do more easy reading to consolidate his sight recognition.

C. Word Identification: Content Word Errors

Printed Word	Oral Response	Further Exploration
turn	to ©	✓
friend	friends	✓
terrifying	terrific©	✓
miserable	miserably©	✓
wretched	wretcher©	✓
picnic	band ©	✓
vaguely	vă|vā goly©	✓

Evaluation

Ability to correct miscues indicates strong knowledge of phonics and structural analysis. Systematic syllable-by-syllable word attack, but slowness of process indicates little reading practice.

D. Integration–Fluency

Integration: Good use of content — both graphic cues and context serve as a basis for correction.

Fluency: Rate **262 / 2.5 = 105** Evaluation Below norms for 7th gr.

Phrasing Many repetitions and pauses for word identification and perhaps comprehension.

knowledge of high-frequency words and word identification is strong but that his application of this knowledge is inconsistent. Further exploration of his knowledge of word meaning reveals inconsistent understanding of vocabulary items (for example, he knew the meanings of such words as *terrifying, miserable, wretched,* and *vaguely,* but he did not know the meaning of *independent* and *belligerent*).

• Interpretation

Print Skill. Laura's analysis and exploration based on the seventh-grade passage reveal that James possesses considerable knowledge about phonic and structural analysis and that his basic sight vocabulary is well developed. Whether the larger stock of sight words that he recognizes instantaneously is grade appropriate cannot be determined from the evidence because lists beyond the sixth-grade level are not included in the test. But the fact that he experienced some difficulty with the flash presentation beginning at the third-grade level suggests that his broader sight recognition vocabulary is not as large as it should be. Indeed, some of the difficulty he experienced during passage reading may have been based on the unfamiliarity of many words that are typically recognized by students his age.

Though James is able to apply his knowledge about print effectively when he is not under the time pressure of contextual oral reading or flash presentation, he does not do so easily when he *is* under pressure. If he were more proficient reading silently than orally, these difficulties might be attributed to nervousness and be overlooked. However, because his comprehension is less adequate during silent than oral reading, Laura infers that his silent print-processing strategies are no more efficient, and probably less efficient, than his oral reading strategies.

Further exploration indicates that James does not need special instruction to learn about print but, rather, needs considerable practice with easy materials in order to consolidate and apply what he already knows. His slow reading rate reflects his current difficulty in application and should improve once he does more reading; if his reading rate does not improve spontaneously, then it may need to be the focus of special instructional intervention.

However, James's print skill difficulties may not simply be a function of too little practice. Recently, James has seen several eye doctors because of blurred vision. The conclusion from the examination is that the blurred vision stems from eyestrain and that James must learn to relax while reading. Glasses were not recommended. The eyestrain may actually be the result of his difficulty in reading print fluently rather than the cause, but in any case, James's visual difficulties should be kept in mind.

Vocabulary Knowledge. James's listening comprehension is good at the ninth-grade level (81 percent comprehension). The passage, about Pygmies (see full text in Appendix C, page 365), develops a topic with which James is unfamiliar and contains many difficult words (e.g., *equatorial, Itiru Forest, Zaire, contagious,* *blasphemy*). It would seem that when James is not faced with the task of print skill, he may be better able to compensate for not knowing the meaning of some key terms. His listening comprehension is better than might be expected on the basis of his knowledge of specific terms.

Comprehension. James's retelling of selected passages is comprehensive: He reported the sequence of events accurately and related many details. Although his comprehension following oral reading is adequate through the seventh-grade level and borderline at the eighth-grade level, his silent reading comprehension is near frustration at the seventh-grade level. These results indicate that he will have considerable difficulty reading grade-appropriate (i.e., ninth-grade) materials, particularly when he is reading silently. Within the area of comprehension, Laura decided that silent reading should be the focus of instruction for James.

Summary. On the basis of the listening test results, Laura determined that James should be able to read ninth-grade-level materials with comprehension. Currently, however, he experiences problems with eighth-grade materials and even seventh-grade material that he reads silently. Two separate problems contribute to his reading comprehension difficulties. First, his print-processing strategies are not adequately developed, and thus he reads slowly with many repetitions and corrections of miscues. Second, his knowledge of key terms is limited. While he is able to compensate for this limited knowledge when materials are read to him, when he is faced with print-processing problems as well, his comprehension fails. The fact that his comprehension failure is more severe under silent reading conditions suggests that in addition to developing his vocabulary and refining his print-processing strategies, he must learn to monitor his comprehension during silent reading.

• Instructional Plan

Materials. Laura found that materials above the seventh-grade level yielded borderline or poor comprehension results on the IRI. With instructional preparation (discussion of the meaning and pronunciation of key vocabulary), James should be able to comprehend course materials that he reads at the seventh-grade level and perhaps at the eighth-grade level when topics are familiar.

Special reading instruction should focus on three areas: consolidation of print-processing skill, development of vocabulary, and development of silent reading comprehension. For the first, the material should be easy for James when he reads silently. Thus, fifth- (and somewhat later, sixth-) grade materials should be used. The selections should be about topics of high interest to James. Vocabulary development may be undertaken along with content area instruction and should reinforce the concepts being presented in his course materials. He should begin silent reading of short passages of sixth-grade-level material followed by comprehension questions and, as rapidly as comprehension warrants, proceed to seventh- and then eighth-grade-level passages.

Instructional Priorities. Laura advised James's content area teachers that James will have difficulty reading materials independently above the sixth-grade level but that if they provide appropriate instructional support, including the discussion of the meaning and pronunciation of key terms, James can cope with seventh- and perhaps even eighth-grade-level materials.

James also needs help in improving his vocabulary. He should be taught how to prepare vocabulary cards for words from his courses that are unfamiliar and how to review and use these words orally. If possible, he should be paired with another student who could profit from vocabulary instruction so that they can discuss words together.

For James, the development of print-processing skills will be a major priority. James needs to learn to apply his good knowledge efficiently and to enlarge the set of words that he recognizes instantaneously. His fluency can best be developed by extensive reading of easy and highly interesting materials. These materials should initially be at the fifth-grade level, although James may soon progress to more difficult material. In conjunction with this reading, James should be taught a system for recording and evaluating his reading rate. A reading log should be kept of the number of pages read to provide a tangible record of his accomplishments.

Finally, Laura recommended that James be taught study strategies, such as those described in Chapter 6, for monitoring his comprehension during silent reading. It is important that the passages for this purpose be limited to several pages at most and be followed by comprehension questions so that James can have immediate feedback on the effectiveness of his comprehension strategies.

Using Extended Passages for Assessment

The same diagnostic principles that guide the use of the IRI can be used with a student reading an extended passage taken from classroom materials, trade books, or other types of textual material. Extended passage reading can be used to test the appropriateness of a particular material or level of material for a student or to "field test" an assessment made with the shorter passages of an IRI. Students sometimes perform differently on longer passages or different types of materials. The reading selection can also be taken from something that the student is using in class to provide the most realistic view of a reader's capability to handle classroom reading tasks.

• Preparation

Select from the student's instructional materials a passage that seems likely to pose some difficulty and that is similar in length to those you typically use for instruction. Prepare a photocopy or double-spaced typewritten copy of the passage.

Next, study the passage and create a set of vocabulary knowledge and comprehension questions according to the procedures described in Chapters 4 and 5. Order the comprehension questions in the sequence of the story and type or write them, leaving enough space between them to record the student's responses. The vocabulary knowledge questions should follow the comprehension questions.

Use a system like the one described in Chapter 3 to record the student's oral reading responses. You should also audio-record the session so you can check the time the student required to read the passage and the accuracy of your handwritten oral reading record.

• Administration

Make sure the student is comfortable and relaxed. Discuss briefly your reasons for the diagnosis with him or her (e.g., "to learn more about how to work with you on reading") and describe the procedures you will use. Tell the student that he or she will be asked to read a passage and answer some questions about it and that next time reading strategies will be explored more informally. When asking the student to read the selection aloud, give some version of the following directions:

> This is a selection in which . . . [theme-related preparatory statement]. Please read this story aloud for me. If you come to a word you don't know, try to figure it out, or skip it. I will not be able to help you, so do the best you can. After you finish, I will ask you some questions.

Before the student begins reading, test the audio-recording equipment. You might let the student record his or her voice and then listen to the replay. Record the student's oral reading on the photocopy or typed version of the story as well. Keep the tape recorder running while you ask the comprehension questions so the responses won't be lost if the student answers more rapidly than you can write. Use the recording to check the amount of time needed for the student to read the passage.

• Analysis

Study the student's performance on the first part of the diagnosis to determine the area(s) of reading you should explore further. If print skill accuracy is below 95 percent, select high-frequency and/or content words and develop procedures for examining the underlying resources for identifying words. If comprehension is below 75 percent, examine the questions that were answered incorrectly and plan questions that may facilitate further exploration. At the same time, consider the influence of vocabulary knowledge on comprehension and print skill; when appropriate, select additional words or phrases for presentation during this stage.

• **Further Exploration**

During a second session with the student, administer items for further exploration according to the procedures summarized in Figure 8.8. If you suspect the student is having difficulty with print skill, regardless of the adequacy of comprehension performance, you should focus first on content word identification

figure 8.8 • Summary of Procedures for Further Exploration

These procedures may be used after the student has read a passage and responded to comprehension questions.

If Student Demonstrates Difficulty Identifying Content Words
1. Select content words that the student missed during the oral reading. Write them on a blank page in list form. For each word, first see if the student can pronounce it without help. If not, use the procedures described in Chapter 3: See if the student can divide the word into syllables and pronounce them. If not, see if the student can pronounce just the first syllable (cover the remainder of the word with a finger). If not, see if the student knows the sound corresponding to the first consonant or consonant cluster, then the vowel and final consonant(s). For syllables that lend themselves to visual analogy, test to see if the student can think of a word that ends the same and on that basis identify the syllable; if not, provide such a word and see if the student can use it to identify the syllable. Test a sample of consonants, consonant clusters, vowels, word endings, and word families. Continue with successive words on the list as long as the procedure yields new information and the student is responsive.

2. Ask the student to define the words missed, using the procedures described in Chapter 4.

If Student Demonstrates Difficulty with High-Frequency Words:
1. Select high-frequency words that the student misread during oral reading. Write them on a blank page in list form. See if the student can pronounce each word. Note whether the response is immediate or delayed. Continue further exploration only as long as it yields new information and the student is able to respond attentively.

If Student Demonstrates Inadequate Comprehension:
1. Explore the student's knowledge of word meanings and/or concepts that may be interfering with comprehension, as described in Chapter 4. If vocabulary knowledge is adequate, explore comprehension further as described in the next two steps.

2. Note those questions that were answered incorrectly. Have the student reread the portion of the passage on which the question is based and reask the question. Continue this procedure for the remaining incorrectly answered questions.

3. If the student fails to answer a question correctly after rereading, explore further using the informal interview technique illustrated in Chapter 6. Note intersentence and sentence-level problems of the text that may interfere with the student's comprehension, and use informal procedures to explore these areas.

and then on content word meaning. The reason for this order is that presenting the vocabulary knowledge items first would invalidate the exploration of word identification. If high-frequency words are also a problem, explore these after identifying the content words. Record the student's responses to the print skill exploration in writing as well as on tape. It is important to make complete notes because it is often difficult on the basis of a tape recording to reconstruct the questions or word parts to which the student was responding.

Next, present the vocabulary knowledge items you selected for obtaining further evidence, if you have not already presented them in exploring print skill. Conduct further exploration of comprehension last. You may omit this stage if, by then, you are convinced that print skill and vocabulary knowledge are interfering with the student's comprehension.

Interpretation

In analyzing a student's performance on a diagnostic passage, it is useful to focus first on print skill, then on vocabulary knowledge, and finally on comprehension. Then, when you have achieved an understanding of the student's strategies in each of these areas, examine his or her relative strength using the model presented in Chapter 1.

Print Skill. The evidence concerning a student's print strategies comes from two sources: oral reading of contextual materials and identification of isolated words and word parts. The first source tells you about the student's integrated approach to print; the second yields evidence about his or her underlying knowledge of print. Though the two sources of evidence complement each other, the analyses are done separately.

The analysis of contextual reading involves four steps. First, examine the student's response to the entire passage in order to characterize general proficiency. Then, focus your analysis on responses to high-frequency sight words and, subsequently, on responses to content words so that you can determine how the student identified words that were unfamiliar. Finally, assess reading integration and fluency. Record the results of this four-step analysis on the oral reading analysis form. Your analysis of the student's performance on isolated words (further exploration) may focus on high-frequency words, content words, or both. Exploring high-frequency words should reveal whether the student recognizes them on sight when other problems involved in contextual reading are removed. Exploring content words provides answers to the following questions: Can the student divide multisyllabic words into syllables? Can simple syllables and more complex syllables (those containing blends or digraphs) be identified? Can he or she identify word endings (-*ing*, -*es*, -*ed*)? Does the student know vowel pronunciation and markers? Can he or she blend letter sounds?

Next, consolidate on the oral reading analysis form the results obtained from the oral reading analysis and further exploration in order to answer the following questions:

1. Is the passage of appropriate difficulty in terms of the student's print skill and instructional needs?

2. What is the student's strength in rapid high-frequency word recognition?

3. What resources does the student possess for identifying unknown words?

4. Are the student's print-processing skills integrated and fluent?

5. What, if any, aspect of print skills should be the focus of instruction?

In answering these and subsequent questions, you should note any supporting evidence.

Vocabulary Knowledge. You can use informal questioning and discussion to ascertain whether the student has the background experiences needed to understand the passage. However, word knowledge questions and further exploration will be needed to assess the student's knowledge of the specific words that pertain to these experiences. This step also provides evidence of whether the student is able to select the particular meaning of a word that is appropriate to the sense of the passage. This evidence concerning vocabulary knowledge should answer three questions:

1. Does the student have command of the concepts used in the passage?

2. Is this knowledge explicit and clear (definitions) or implicit and somewhat vague (sentence use)?

3. Can the student use context to select the appropriate word meaning?

Comprehension. Interpretation should begin with the evidence concerning the student's ability to respond correctly to text-related comprehension questions. In completing the comprehension–vocabulary knowledge summary form, look for answers to the following questions:

1. Did the student understand the essential information contained in the passage and the import of the message? Is the passage at an appropriate level for the student for instructional purposes?

2. If not, what are the student's strengths and weaknesses in comprehension?

3. Is the student's problem mainly in the area of comprehension, or do difficulties with print skill or vocabulary knowledge contribute to comprehension difficulties?

4. Based on your exploration of the student's comprehension, what, if any, instruction in comprehension is needed?

Summary. First, summarize your conclusions about the student's print skill, vocabulary knowledge, and comprehension. Then, determine whether his or her vocabulary knowledge or print skill difficulties interfere with comprehension. Finally, discuss with the student his or her major strengths and difficulties in reading.

• Instructional Plan

On the basis of the summary and final integration of diagnostic information, you should be able to answer the following questions:

1. Is the instructional material of appropriate difficulty for this student under ordinary conditions? Would certain forms of instructional intervention help the student cope with the material?

2. What forms of instruction will help this student further refine his or her reading strategies?

Your recommendations for instruction should follow directly from the final summary of results and should be listed in order of priority.

It is important to discuss your diagnosis and recommendations with the student in an age-appropriate manner. It is also important to ascertain how the student feels about the recommendations. The instruction can be successful only when the student becomes a part of the planning and implementation.

Case Studies

The two case studies described in the remaining sections of this chapter demonstrate how these procedures can be applied. A teacher using this form of diagnosis may wish to prepare the student for reading the passage in the manner he or she normally follows in the classroom, rather than, as we have suggested, to have the student read with only a brief introduction.

case 8.4

Sharon

Sharon is 12 years old and in seventh grade. She has difficulty in reading and is in a remedial reading class. She works hard and is very cooperative in school. She is a shy student with very little experience outside of her neighborhood. Her mother is dead, and she lives with an older sister, who is her guardian, and other sisters and brothers. She does not have many interests—"just likes to stay home and watch TV or play outside with her younger sister." Her teacher, Monica, noticed that she often had difficulty comprehending assigned materials and decided to learn more about Sharon's reading strategies. ■

• Preparation

Monica selected a passage that she thought might be of interest to Sharon. It was entitled "Bringing Light to the Blind" and was taken from a high fourth-grade reading workbook called *Adventure Trail* (Charles E. Merrill, 1969). Monica's first step was to study the passage in order to derive comprehension and word knowledge questions.

> **pause and reflect**
>
> Analyze "Bringing Light to the Blind" shown in Figure 8.9. What questions would you ask? What vocabulary knowledge would you tap? Compare these with Monica's choices in Figure 8.10.

figure 8.9 • Diagnostic Reading Passage: Sharon

Bringing Light to the Blind

Only about one-fourth of the blind people in our country can read. They read Braille (brāl). As you know, Braille is a way of printing by raised dots. The blind run their fingers over the raised dots.

Did you ever shut your eyes and run your fingers over a page of Braille printing? All the little raised dots seemed to run together. Even if you knew the Braille alphabet, your fingers could not pickout each separate dot. But the boys and girls who cannot see read stories in Braille. Their fingers are trained to be their eyes.

A Frenchman, Louis Braille, made it possible for those who cannot see, to read. When he was a small boy, he used to play around his father's harness shop. One day, he was trying to punch holes in a piece of leather with a big awl. The tool slipped and hurt Louis' eye. Before long, he became blind.

When Louis was ten years old, he was sent to a school for the blind in Paris. There he began to study music and learned to play the organ. He became a very fine musician.

Louis did not just want to become famous. He wanted to help all those who could not see. So he set to work to find an alphabet which could be read with the fingers. Today that system of writing is known as Braille.

Some books and magazines are printed in Braille for boys and girls. "My Weekly Reader Number Four" is one of them. Every week, the American Printing House for the Blind prints Braille copies of this newspaper.

There are even books that "talk." The books are like phonograph records that talk to the blind. When a blind person wants to read, he turns a key and then listens. It is as if someone were reading a book aloud to him. Our government sends the talking books free to blind people in all parts of our country.

Source: Adventure Trail, Diagnostic Reading Workbook, Grade 4, by E. M. Johnson, p. 46. In *New Diagnostic Reading Series.* Columbus, Ohio: Charles E. Merrill Publishing Co., 1969. Reprinted by permission.

figure 8.10 • Comprehension and Vocabulary Knowledge Questions: Sharon

Comprehension

1. How do blind people read? (They run their fingers over raised dots, or by Braille.)

2. What do blind people train to be their eyes? (fingers)

3. How did Louis Braille become blind? (He was hit in the eye with a tool [awl] while punching holes in leather in his father's harness shop.)

4. When Louis Braille was at school, what did he study? (music; playing the organ)

5. What did Louis Braille do for the blind? (made it possible for blind people to read by inventing an alphabet that could be read with the fingers, etc.)

6. What are books that "talk"? (like records that talk to the blind)

*7. Do you think that Louis Braille was a brave person? Why?

   *Beyond-text question

Vocabulary Knowledge

1. What is *Braille*? (printing by small raised dots that can be read by touch)

2. What is an *awl*? (a tool for punching holes)

3. What does *raised* mean? (higher; above)

4. What is a *system*? (a method)

Figure 8.10 shows Monica's comprehension and vocabulary knowledge questions and the responses that she expected. The first six comprehension questions involve text-related comprehension, whereas question 7 encourages the student to generalize beyond the text.

• Administration

Sharon was quite relaxed when she read the passage orally and responded to the prepared questions. The record of her oral reading is shown in Figure 8.11. Note the two error count tallys in the right margin: total errors and significant miscues.

Following the oral reading, Sharon was asked to retell as much of the selection as she could remember. Here is what she said: "It's (pause) . . . about blind people (pause) . . . reading and stuff. About this boy (pause) . . . he was doing something and something hurt his eye. That's all I remember." Because Sharon's retelling was so incomplete, it was necessary for Monica to administer the questions she had prepared. Sharon's responses are shown in Figure 8.12.

pause and reflect

Before reading Monica's first analysis, analyze Sharon's reading as recorded in Figures 8.11 and 8.12. Is there a problem with print? What are Sharon's strengths and difficulties? What would you explore further?

figure 8.11 • Record of Oral Reading: Sharon

Bringing Light to the Blind

③ Brālly   21
① Bra   1

Only about one-fourth of the blind people in our country can read. They read ~~Braille~~

Brālly

(brāl). As you know, ~~Braille~~ is a way of printing by raised dots. The blind run their fingers   b1*

over the raised dots.   X0

paget Bră-alky

Did you ever shut your eyes and run your fingers over a ~~page~~ of ~~Braille~~ printing? All the   b1

Brāley

little raised dots seemed to run together. Even if you knew the ~~Braille~~ alphabet, your   b1

sek-per-s

fingers could not pick out each ~~separate~~ dot. But the boys and girls who cannot see read   b2

Brāley

stories in ~~Braille~~. Their fingers are trained to be their eyes.   X0

Brāley

A Frenchman, Louis ~~Braille~~, made it possible for those who cannot see, to read. When   X0

he was a small boy, he used to play around his fathers harness shop. One day, he was   X0

a

trying to punch holes in a piece of leather with a big awl. The tool slipped and hurt Louis'   b1

eye. Before long, he became blind.

© sean

When Louis was ten years old, he was ~~sent~~ to a school for the blind in Paris. There he   1

begin   ing   could become

~~began~~ to study music and learned to play the organ. He ~~became~~ a very fine musician.   4

a

Louis did not just want to become famous. He wanted to help all those who could not   1

see. So he set to work to find an alphabet which could be read with the fingers. Today that   1

simple   it   s Brāley   skipped entire line in passage

~~system~~ of writing is known as ~~Braille~~.   #3

Brāley

Some books and magazines are printed in ~~Braille~~ for boys and girls. "My Weekly Reader   X0

Number Four" is one of them. Every week, the American Printing House for the Blind   1

Brāley

prints ~~Braille~~ copies of this newspaper.   X0

s

There are even books that "talk." The books are like phonograph records that talk to the   #1

blind. When a blind person wants to read, he turns a key and then listens. It is as if   1

someone were reading a book aloud to him. Our government sends the talking books free   X0

a

to blind people in all parts of ~~our~~ country.   1

*Dialect-based miscues occurring more than twice were not counted.

Source: Adventure Trail, Diagnostic Reading Workbook, Grade 4, by E. M. Johnson, p. 46. In *New Diagnostic Reading Series.* Columbus, Ohio: Charles E. Merrill Publishing Co., 1969. Reprinted by permission.

f i g u r e 8.12 • Responses to Comprehension and Vocabulary Knowledge
Questions: Sharon

Retelling

> …about blind people…reading and stuff. About this boy—he was doing
> something and something hurt his eye. That's all I remember.

Comprehension

✓ **1.** How do blind people read? (They run their fingers over raised dots, or by
   Braille.)
   Response: They read from Brā-ley.

✓ **2.** What do blind people train to be their eyes? (fingers)
   Response: They use their hands, don't they?

½ **3.** How did Louis Braille become blind? (He was hit in the eye with a tool
   [awl] while punching holes in his father's harness shop.)
   Response: He was doing something and he knocked something over and it
               made him blind. [Q.: What hit him in the eye?] That harness
               stuff.

✓ **4.** When Louis Braille was at school, what did he study? (music; playing the
   organ)
   Response: Music.

✗ **5.** What did Louis Braille do for the blind? (made is possible for blind people
   to read by inventing an alphabet that could be read with the fingers, etc.)
   Response: He helped them learn and put up this thing about blind.

✗ **6.** What are books that "talk"? (like records that talk to the blind)
   Response: Don't know.

✗ ***7.** Do you think that Louis Braille was a brave person? Why?
   Response: Yes, he was brave. He helped people that were blind to read
               and write.

   *Beyond-text question

Vocabulary Knowledge

✗ **1.** What is *Braille*? (printing by small raised dots that can be read by touch)
   Response: Like a thing that goes through a line or something. [Q.: can you
               explain that?] Well…not sure.

✗ **2.** What is an *awl*? (a tool for punching holes)
   Response: Don't know.

✓ **3.** What does *raised* mean? (higher; above)
   Response: You raise it…raise it up.

✗ **4.** What is a *system*? (a method)
   Response: Don't know.

• Analysis

On the basis of Sharon's oral reading of the passage and her responses to the
comprehension questions, Monica decided to explore two areas: Sharon's content word errors, to better assess her word identification skill, and her vocabulary knowledge in areas pertinent to the passage.

Further Exploration

The results from Sharon's oral reading analysis and further exploration are summarized on the oral reading analysis form in Figure 8.13. Sharon's answers indicate that she has good knowledge of basic phonics concepts but has difficulty applying this knowledge during contextual reading: She was able to identify words she had missed in the passage when these same words were presented in isolation.

pause and **reflect**

What do you see as areas of difficulty for Sharon? What are the implications of this diagnosis for Sharon's instruction?

The summary of Sharon's comprehension performance and the results from the vocabulary knowledge exploration are presented on the comprehension–vocabulary knowledge summary in Figure 8.14. Because Sharon's word knowledge was so limited, Monica felt there was no point in exploring her comprehension skills further.

Interpretation

Print Skill. High-frequency words do not seem to be a problem for Sharon, and she possesses good phonics and structural analysis skills. It is difficult to know whether her failure to apply these skills during contextual reading occurred because of the large number of unfamiliar words in the passage or because the general meaning of the passage was difficult for her to grasp. Most of the substitutions that did not make sense occurred in sentences that were too technical for her. Although it is clear that Sharon's reading of this passage was neither integrated nor fluent, the number of problems posed may simply have overwhelmed her. It will be important for Monica to have Sharon read an easier passage with fewer unfamiliar words in order to have a more valid test of her integration and fluency.

Some affixed words and verb forms posed problems for Sharon. Dialect substitutions where the final s was either omitted or inserted were eliminated from consideration. But Sharon's problem seems to extend beyond that of pluralization and possession to other affixes. Her oral language differs in certain respects from standard English; further, at times she appears to be overcorrecting for dialect. It is important to determine the extent to which Sharon's problems with affixes arise from dialect influence as opposed to lack of knowledge. Exploration results suggest that she understands affixes but during difficult oral reading becomes confused about their pronunciation.

Vocabulary Knowledge. Sharon's vocabulary and understanding of words seems to be quite limited for a seventh grader. She does not know some words typically known by students her age (*harness, system, volume*) and has vague or limited concepts of others (*separate, raised*). The possibility that she is in command of more

figure 8.13 • Analysis of Oral Reading Responses: Sharon

ORAL READING ANALYSIS

Name *Sharon*   Grade *7*   Date *Feb.*

Book/Page *Adventure Trail*   Level *4th Grade*

A. Difficulty

22 / *329*   *93* % Correct

Level: Independent   Instructional
(Borderline)   Frustration

B. Word Learning: High-Frequency Word Errors

Printed Word	Oral Response	Further Exploration	Evaluation
is	it	✓	Immediate and correct recognition of high-frequency words. High-frequency words are probably not a problem with the easier materials.
our	a	✓	
② the	[omitted]	✓	
③ a	[inserted]	✓	
could	[inserted]	✓	
[a line]	[omitted]		

C. Word Identification: Content Word Errors

Printed Word	Oral Response	Further Exploration	Evaluation
② Braille	Brǎ/Brǐly/Brāley Brǐley		Good knowledge of phonics. Application may be more of a problem. Has some knowledge of affixes and syllabication. Well-developed word identification skill; need to check application during easier contextual reading.
page	paget	✓	
known	knows	✓	
sent	sean ④	✓	
seemed	seems	✓	
learned	learning	✓	
separate	sēper ③	✓	
began	begin	✓	
became	become	✓	
system	simple	✓	
American	America	✓	

D. Integration–Fluency

Integration: *Errors are generally not contextually appropriate; infrequent correction of errors; highly dependent on graphic cues.*

Fluency: Rate *329* / *6.1* = *54*   Evaluation *Slow, even for a fourth grader.*

Phrasing *Choppy – does not read with appropriate phrasing.*

figure 8.14 • Summary of Responses to Comprehension and Vocabulary Knowledge Questions: Sharon

---

COMPREHENSION–VOCABULARY KNOWLEDGE SUMMARY

Name Sharon Grade 7 Date Feb

Book/Page Adventure Trail Level High 4th

COMPREHENSION

3½ / 6   58 % Correct

Level: Independent Instructional
(Borderline) Frustration

A. Retelling: Complete. Main Idea Partial (Inadequate)

Comments: She had a difficult time. expressing herself – limited vocabulary, problems with sentence structure.

B. Text-Related Comprehension

Item #	Response	Further Exploration	Item #	Response	Further Exploration
1	✓		6	NR *	
2	✓	(mentioned hands not fingers)			
3	½				
4	✓				
5	X				

* NR = no response

C. Beyond-Text Generalization

Item #	Response	Further Exploration	Item #	Response	Further Exploration
7	X				

VOCABULARY KNOWLEDGE

1½ / 6   25 % Correct

Item Tested	Response	Comments	Item Tested	Response	Comments
Braille	X				
awl	X				
raised	✗	knows verb form			
system	X				
separate dot (P)*	½				
harness (P)	X				

* P indicates a probe item

EVALUATION

A. Comprehension: Vague understanding of ideas in passage. Her comprehension is inadequate. – the materials are inappropriate.

B. Vocabulary Knowledge Very limited word knowledge – even unable to use words in a sentence.

knowledge than she is able to express was not supported by exploration, but Monica should undertake further observation of her vocabulary knowledge.

Comprehension. The results from Sharon's retelling and the text-related questions are consistent, and they reveal that she had difficulty understanding this selection. Even when her responses were correct or partially correct, they indicated serious limitations. She seemed to have particular difficulty describing major concepts explained in the passage. The main underlying problem seemed to be her failure to understand the technical concepts (raised dots, awl) necessary for understanding the central concepts (Braille) and events (the eye injury). However, print-processing problems may have also interfered with her understanding of *books that "talk."*

Summary. The analysis shows that Sharon's sight recognition and her phonics and structural skills are strong, even though she sometimes fails to apply this knowledge during contextual reading. Given the difficulty of the passage for her, it was not possible for Monica to evaluate Sharon's reading integration or her fluency. On this fourth-grade selection, she showed poorly integrated strategies and extremely slow reading.

Sharon's main problem is her extremely limited vocabulary knowledge. Monica assumes that her poor reading comprehension is a direct reflection of her vocabulary deficiency.

• Instructional Plan

Materials. High fourth-grade-level material is too difficult for Sharon unless the reading is preceded by extensive instructional support focused on the development of word meanings. Sharon should be reading from easier material (level to be determined) to enable her to attend to meaning, use context, and increase her reading rate.

Instructional Priorities. The major focus of Monica's instructional support should be on developing Sharon's vocabulary and her reading integration and fluency. This instruction can be provided in a group that includes other students with similar problems.

Before Sharon reads a selection, Monica should identify concepts that may be unfamiliar and encourage Sharon to speculate about their meaning and relationship to the theme of the selection. Monica should explain unfamiliar or partially known concepts. Because the goal of vocabulary development is the improvement of comprehension, thorough discussion should follow the reading of each selection in order to develop comprehension and establish its importance.

Monica can use other procedures to expand Sharon's vocabulary knowledge. For example, she can read stories to her (along with other students) and discuss new concepts, with suggestions for their use in alternative contexts. Sharon may also profit from working with another student on synonym, antonym, and root word–affix activities. To improve Sharon's reading rate, integration, and fluency, Monica can give her short selections that are easy for her. Sharon should be encouraged to concentrate on gaining meaning from everything she reads.

case 8.5

Patricia

Patricia is in ninth grade. Like 80 percent of her freshman class, she is in a double-period basic English class for students reading on a second- to fifth-grade level. On this year's California Achievement Test, she scored a grade equivalent of 5.2 on vocabulary and 3.2 on comprehension. In contrast to many other students in her class, Patricia attends regularly and does all the assigned work. She understands and enjoys the mysteries that she reads on her own but has difficulty with most of her school reading. Because Monica is able to spend some extra time with Patricia, she decided to undertake a more systematic diagnosis of Patricia's reading strategies in order to determine what should be the areas of instructional focus.

In the testing situation, Patricia was relaxed, friendly, and eager to proceed. She was asked to read a fifth-grade-level passage entitled "Rescue in a Burning Building." The record of Patricia's oral reading is shown in Figure 8.15.

pause and reflect
Look at Figures 8.15 and 8.16. What would you explore further?

She was then asked to retell the selection and to respond to the questions that Monica had prepared. Patricia's responses to the comprehension and vocabulary knowledge questions are shown in Figure 8.16. ■

Analysis and Further Exploration

On the basis of Patricia's responses to the passage and the comprehension and vocabulary knowledge questions, Monica decided that further exploration should examine her comprehension responses and her word knowledge. In addition, Monica decided to have Patricia respond to several of the content words that she had had difficulty pronouncing in order to confirm that print skill was not an area of difficulty. When questioned, Patricia responded quickly

figure 8.15 • Record of Oral Reading: Patricia

___

Rescue in a Burning Building   _5_

NEW YORK, June 17—A fireman rescued a 76-year-old woman from a burning apartment

building yesterday by tossing her off a fire escape. The woman, Mrs. Mary Rogers, landed   /

safely in the arms of another fireman waiting on the roof of an adjoining building.   /

Fireman Edward Lane had risked his life to reach the woman, who was trapped in her

        fired
smoke-~~filled~~ top floor apartment in the five-story building. The fire was blazing out of   /

control as Lane carried the almost unconscious woman onto a fire escape.

As flames threatened them, Lane tried without success to first climb to the roof and then

                  such
to go below the height of the flames. He could not do ~~so~~ while carrying the dead weight of   /

the helpless 115-pound woman.

                    motion
Then he saw another fireman, Mike Mays, ~~motioning~~ to him with his arms held out.   /

Mays was on the roof of the next building, which was level with the fire escape. A space

of only four feet separated the two buildings, but there was a fifty-foot drop to the ground.   _+ 0_

Lane tried to pass Mrs. Rogers over to Mays, but the gap was too wide.

Then the two men decided that the only chance to save the woman was to try something

very dangerous. Lane reached back and threw Mrs. Rogers across the space between the

buildings. For a moment the woman was not supported above the ground. Then Mays

caught her by the neck and shoulders, and pulled her safely onto the roof. Mrs. Rogers was

uninjured.

Lane then climbed to the roof of the burning building, went down another fire escape

         ©
and back to fighting the fire.

___

Source: From *Real Stories*, Book 1, pp. 200–202, Milton Katz, Michael Chakeres, & Murray Bromberg (Eds.), New York: Globe Book, 1969. (Originally published in *Newsday;* reprinted by permission of the publisher, Newsday, Inc., Melville, NY.)

figure 8.16 • Responses to Comprehension and Vocabulary Knowledge Questions: Patricia

---

Retelling

Response: It was a fire. He had to get this lady out of the building. They had to use the fire escape to get the lady out of the building.

Comprehension

✓ **1.** Where did Fireman Lane find the woman? (in her smoke-filled apartment, on the top floor of the building)
  Response: In the building, in the house (*house* means *apartment*)
✓ **2.** How serious was the fire? (It was blazing, out of control)
  Response: Real serious.
✗ **3.** Why couldn't Fireman Lane carry the woman up or down the fire escape? (She was too heavy in her unconscious state—"dead weight.")
  Response: Because it was too hard. [Q.: Explain how.] Just too hard.
✗ **4.** Where was the other fireman, Mike Mays? (on the roof of the next building, level with the fire escape)
  Response: Trying to get the fire out.
✗ **5.** Why couldn't Fireman Lane pass the woman to the other fireman? (The gap between the buildings was too wide—four feet.)
  Response: (Could not answer.)
✗ **6.** What did Fireman Lane finally do with the woman? (threw her across the space between the two buildings; Mays caught her)
  Response: (Could not answer.)
✓ ***7.** Why do you think the woman was "almost unconscious"?
  Response: Because of the smoke.

  *Beyond-text question

Vocabulary Knowledge

✓ **1.** What does *risked* mean, as in "He risked his life"?
  Response: Took a chance.
✓ **2.** What does *unconscious* mean?
  Response: Knocked out.
✓ **3.** What does *tossing* mean?
  Response: You throw it.
✗ **4.** What does *adjoining* mean?
  Response: Like you join a club.

and accurately to words such as *adjoining, escape,* and *motioning*. Thus, Monica made no further analysis of her oral reading responses.

Comprehension and vocabulary knowledge responses and the results of further exploration are given in the comprehension–vocabulary knowledge summary form in Figure 8.17.

pause and reflect

What do you see as areas of strength and difficulty for Patricia? What are the implications of this diagnosis for Patricia's instruction?

f i g u r e 8.17 • Summary of Responses to Comprehension and Vocabulary
Knowledge Questions: Patricia

COMPREHENSION–VOCABULARY
KNOWLEDGE SUMMARY

Name _Patricia_ Grade _9_ Date _Nov._

Book/Page _Real Stories_ Level _5ᵗʰ gr._
_200–202_

COMPREHENSION

_2_ / _6_   _33_ % Correct

Level: Independent   Instructional
Borderline   (Frustration)

A. Retelling: Complete   Main Idea   Partial   (Inadequate)

Comments: _Incomplete and inaccurate retelling; she had only the barest understanding of story._

B. Text-Related Comprehension

Item #	Response	Further Exploration	Item #	Response	Further Exploration
1	✓		6	✗	
2	✓				
3	✗				
4	✗				
5	✗				

C. Beyond-Text Generalization

Item #	Response	Further Exploration	Item #	Response	Further Exploration
7	✓	_possesses some background knowledge of fires_			

VOCABULARY KNOWLEDGE

_6_ / _8_   _75_ % Correct

Item Tested	Response	Comments	Item Tested	Response	Comments
risked	✓		motioning (P)	✓	
unconscious	✓		gap (P)	✗	
tossing	✓				
adjoining	✗				
blazing (P)*	✓				
dead weight (P)	✓				

* P indicates a probe item

EVALUATION

A. Comprehension: _Does not seem to understand the situation — e.g., where the second fireman was and what the problem was. May need to work on visualizing situations. Dense prose and expository materials may be particularly difficult for her._

B. Vocabulary Knowledge _Some concepts are unknown, but generally she shows good strength in word knowledge._

- **Interpretation**

Print Skill. Patricia seems to have almost no problems with high-frequency word recognition and word identification. Most of her errors on content words involved word endings (*-ed, -ing, -s*). Examination of the passage shows that typically she does pronounce these endings. In fact, she often pronounces endings that she drops during oral conversation. When words were presented in isolation during further exploration, she pronounced the affixes according to standard English. Thus, it is clear that Patricia possesses knowledge about word endings. Print processing does not appear to be a problem area that interferes with her comprehension. Nevertheless, her reading rate is slower than the average range for fifth graders, so some improvement in integration and fluency may be needed. It is difficult for Monica to evaluate her use of context because her word attack skills are strong but her comprehension is low.

Vocabulary Knowledge. Patricia knew three-quarters of the vocabulary items tested. The two she missed, although not key words, would definitely have aided her comprehension. They also indicate that Patricia probably does not know many words typically known by ninth graders. Verbal knowledge is a possible area of weakness that may contribute to Patricia's comprehension difficulties. Nevertheless, as is also suggested by the results from the standardized reading test, her comprehension is lower than might be expected on the basis of her vocabulary knowledge.

Comprehension. Patricia's retelling (incomplete and inaccurate) showed that she had only the barest understanding of the situation in the story. Her answers to the factual questions (two correct out of six) support this. Even her two correct answers were not specific. In further exploration, where she had an opportunity to reread most of the text orally and silently, she still did not grasp the point of the story. She reread the key paragraph many times before she comprehended it.

Summary. Patricia's main area of reading difficulty lies in comprehension. Because she could not answer the questions after rereading, her problem appears to be at the sentence and intersentence level. Her vocabulary knowledge is relatively strong and does not seem to account for the comprehension difficulty. Print processing represents an area of strength, although work may be needed to improve integration and fluency.

- **Instructional Plan**

Materials. Although the currently used fifth-grade-level material is appropriate for Patricia for instructional purposes with respect to print-processing demands, it represents frustration level (below 50 percent) with respect to her comprehension.

Given the test results, her instruction should begin with material with very familiar concepts or with a lower-level selection.

Instructional Priorities. Instruction should focus directly on the development of basic text-processing strategies, particularly those that are useful for expository materials. Key terms should be discussed as needed.

1. Patricia's comprehension may be improved through individual work. She needs instructional materials (on a third- or fourth-grade level) that ask specific questions about information presented and provide corrective feedback. At least once a week Monica should review Patricia's work with her. At this time, Monica may wish to engage in reciprocal teaching of comprehension strategies. Patricia should then be encouraged to concentrate on comprehending what she reads, paraphrasing sentences to herself, and interacting with the text as described in Chapter 6. Work on anaphora and connectives is also appropriate.

2. Students with comprehension problems similar to Patricia's should be brought together into a group. The group should learn to speculate—on the basis of titles, headings, and initial paragraphs—what a selection may be about. Discussion should follow each main segment of the article to check the accuracy of group predictions. For both expository and narrative selections, the group should be given help in organizing information as described in Chapter 6.

3. Patricia should be encouraged to read on her own and to expand her reading interests. She could be given mysteries or exciting biographies that are slightly harder than the ones she presently reads. Her integration and fluency should be checked on these high-interest materials.

summary

One purpose of diagnosis is to establish the level of materials that students can read easily (independent level) and the level students can read with teaching support (instructional level). It is also important to identify those materials that are extremely difficult and should be avoided (frustration level). We have described criteria for oral reading accuracy and comprehension accuracy that will be helpful in making judgments about the reading levels appropriate for your students.

Both informal reading inventories and extended passage reading give you observational information on readers. By combining and interpreting information that you obtain concerning student skill with print, vocabulary knowledge, and reading comprehension, you can draw conclusions about the levels of materials that are appropriate for students and the type of teaching support they need. A formal analysis of reading involves six steps: (1) selection of an informal reading inventory or preparation of the reading selection and questions, (2) administration of the task, (3) analysis of the results, (4) further exploration of reading strengths and difficulties, (5) interpretation of results, and (6) instructional planning. In the classroom setting, your procedures will be more informal as you gather and interpret relevant information over a period of time.

We have shown, through detailed presentation of case studies, how the procedures introduced in preceding chapters may be used to diagnose students' reading problems and modify your instruction in accordance with students' needs. Although the process of acquiring expertise in using these procedures may be time consuming, it leads to deeper understanding of the various facets of reading and provides you with a framework for making sense of students' successes and failures and for refining your instructional approaches.

try it out

1. Collect as many commercial informal reading inventories as possible. Working in a group or with a partner, use the evaluation criteria presented in this chapter to select those that you think might be useful to you. Add them to Table 8.2 and update with a column of personal comments.
2. **For Your Teaching Portfolio:** Use a commercial IRI to assess a child in your class. Tape-record the assessment and share with a classmate. Compare and contrast your procedures and conclusions about instruction. List shared questions or problems and how you resolved them.
3. **Student Portfolio Ideas:** Share your assessment with the student and discuss findings. Have students reflect, in writing, on your assessment and plans or steps *they* might take to improve performance. This is more appropriate for the older reader than for the younger or beginning reader.

for further reading

Afflerbach, P. (2005). National reading conference policy brief: High stakes testing and reading assessment. *Journal of Literacy Research, 37,* 151–162.

Hurley, S. R., & Tinajero, J. V. (2001). *Literacy assessment of second language learners.* Boston: Allyn & Bacon. Authentic literacy assessment for second language learners is described.

International Reading Association. (1999). *Reading assessment: Principles and practices for elementary teachers.* Shelby J. Barrentine (Ed.). Newark, DE: Author. This is a collection of articles from *The Reading Teacher.*

Johns, J. L., & Berglund, R. L. (2005). *Fluency: Strategies and assessments* (2nd ed.). Dubuque, IA: Kendall Hunt. Ideas are presented for assessing and improving reading fluency.

Nilsson, N. L. (2008). A critical analysis of eight informal reading inventories. *The Reading Teacher, 61*(7), 526–536.

Paris, S. G., & Carpenter, R. D. (2003). FAQs about IRIs. *The Reading Teacher, 56,* 578–580. Essential information for teachers about informal reading inventories for early reading assessment is presented.

Decision Making: Organizing, Using, and Communicating Assessment Information

chapter goals for the reader

- To understand the nature and classroom uses of standardized tests
- To understand the nature and uses of class and student portfolios
- To develop a framework for using assessment information in forming flexible, need-based groups; selecting materials; and developing appropriate instructional strategies
- To develop an understanding of how to share information with parents, students, and specialists
- To understand the relationship of curriculum-based assessment to the school data collection and interpretation process

classroom vignette

Assessment in Tessa's Classroom

In Chapter 1, you were introduced to Tessa, an experienced teacher recently reassigned to fourth grade in an inner-city school. Her classroom contains fourth-grade and third-grade basal readers and a small library of trade books on many levels. Many of her students are new to the school, and the records on some of them are sketchy, although there is a standardized test score as well as information on third-grade reading group placement for each of the children. Tessa also has a student teacher and wants to help him frame some basic questions for starting the school year. Together they list their questions:

> What kinds of information can help us get started?
>
> How can we best interpret and use standardized test data?
>
> How should we develop our portfolio records?
>
> On what basis should we organize students for instruction, select appropriate materials, and provide appropriate instruction?
>
> About what should we be communicating with students, parents, and specialists?

These are questions related to basic classroom decisions that must be made to get instruction underway at the start of a new school year. ■

chapter overview

In this final chapter we consider how the model for curriculum-based assessment informs and is informed by the testing program of the school; instructional decisions made throughout the school year; and communication with parents, students, and specialists. Because standardized reading tests are particularly useful to the classroom teacher for making decisions at the beginning of the school year, and because they are routinely administered in most schools, we believe teachers should be knowledgeable about them. In addition, various portfolio systems provide a way to organize information that will inform instructional decision making and communication with others.

The first section of this chapter considers the types of standardized tests available, characterizes their strengths and limitations, and discusses how to evaluate and interpret results from them. The second section describes two forms of portfolio assessment—class portfolios and student portfolios—that are useful in organizing information about student progress. The third section discusses strategies for (1) assessing students' individual reading needs at the beginning of the school year in order to form initial pairs, teams, or groups for instruction, (2) selecting appropriate materials, and (3) developing appropriate instruction. The fourth section describes procedures for communicating with students, parents, and professionals about student needs and progress.

chapter outline

Understanding Assessment Information

We strongly believe that for you to obtain information that is directly relevant to planning instruction for your students, you must learn to undertake curriculum-based assessment. That is, you must learn to observe and interpret oral reading responses and to construct vocabulary and comprehension questions and interpret students' responses to them, ideally with existing materials and instructional tasks. Such evidence provides a valid basis for shaping instruction to better meet the needs of your students.

We believe it is important for you to be familiar with the characteristics of standardized tests and to understand both the advantages and limitations of this form of assessment information. In Chapter 1, we gave an example of the use of standardized and other measures at the beginning of the school year. In this section, we first consider the nature of standardized tests: the kinds of tests there are, their problems, and how to use information from them at the beginning of the school year. As the year progresses and as you have the opportunity to observe the reading and writing of your students, standardized test information becomes much less important. But as you gather information on your students, you need to develop systems for organizing this information. We recommend two procedures: a class portfolio in which you gather the information on your students, and student portfolios, kept by each student in your class, containing samples of their reading and writing. In this section, we describe these class and student portfolios, illustrating them by showing you the ones that Tessa and her students developed.

Understanding Criterion-Based and Standardized Tests

In this book we have proposed a framework for curriculum-based assessment in which teachers use instructional materials and curriculum tasks to structure classroom diagnosis. The term *testing,* however, refers to a much larger realm of school assessment. In this section we describe the types of formal measures with which you must be familiar, explain some concepts basic to these measures, and give examples of how you might adapt more formalized assessment instruments to provide instructional information.

Formal measures are basically of two types: criterion referenced and norm referenced, the latter frequently referred to as "standardized" tests. A recent variation of the criterion-referenced test is the standards-based assessment, also discussed in this section. It is important to understand the ways in which these types of tests differ.

• Criterion-Referenced Tests

The goal of criterion-referenced tests (CRTs) is to compare a particular student's performance with mastery goals set by a curriculum program, or predetermined body of knowledge. These instruments provide qualitative information on the skills and knowledge considered basic for progressing in a particular curriculum. For example, a curriculum goal might be that students should be able to divide compound words into their constituents. Figure 9.1 shows a criterion-referenced test item designed to assess achievement of this goal.

Along with the curricular goal, CRTs frequently indicate a performance standard to be met. Although 70 to 80 percent is a common mastery standard, criteria vary by age of student and by item being tested. For example, an appropriate mastery level for naming the letters of the alphabet for first graders might

figure 9.1 • Criterion-Referenced Test Item: Division of Compound Words

> **Goal:** Students will divide compound words into their constituent words.
>
> **Direction:** Give each student a duplicated sheet with the following words.
>
> **Say:** These words are all made up of two or more words. Draw a line between the words that make up the compound.
>
> **Example:** mail/man
>
> **Items:**
>
> | | |
> |---|---|
> | truckload | railroad |
> | dishpan | baseball |
> | fireman | joystick |

be 100 percent. Though this type of testing is very much like teacher-created informal testing, many CRTs are part of larger, purchasable instruction and management systems (Idol, Nevin, & Paolucci-Whitcomb, 1986), or those provided by commercial reading programs.

You must address several issues when you use criterion-referenced measures for either assessment or placement. Questions to ask include the following:

1. Are the objectives related to essential skills, strategies, and knowledge? Frequently the items most essential to the reading task are the most difficult to conceptualize as discrete objectives, and the items most easily tested may not be essential for effective reading.

2. Is the performance required a real measure of the goal? Does circling a digraph on a worksheet, for example, measure how well a student can use graphophonic knowledge of that cluster for reading, or is it just an isolated measure? How genuine is the reading in the testing situation?

3. Is the criterion level appropriate for the age and ability of the student?

All these relate to the larger issues of reliability and validity, which we discuss later in this section. In sum, CRTs can provide specific information about the particular skills of a particular student. However, in their use you must be sure that you are not just assessing one-time mastery of peripheral behaviors, but rather focusing on knowledge, skills, and strategies important to the reading act.

• Standards-Based/Performance-Based Assessments

The goal of standards-based or performance-based assessments is to compare a particular student's performance with a standard that has been set for students of the same learning level, typically an age or grade level. Often these assessments stress broader goals than those of the more atomistic criterion-based measurement. For example, a standards-based assessment might call for a third-grade student to construct a two-paragraph response after reading a short nonfiction piece. The response would be scored by a rubric that looked at inclusion of important points, coherence, and use of specific vocabulary. Use of any performance-based measure assumes three things: appropriate standards, benchmark samples displaying acceptable and unacceptable types of performance, and a rubric for evaluation. The assessments are directly linked to the standards of local, state, and national construction. Many states have designed and are using their own standards-based assessments to match their state standards. Currently, there is a movement toward Common Core Standards, which can inform state processes (see http://www.corestandards.org/). Also, "Looking at Student Work" (www.lasw.org) can be useful for formulating standards that relate to student performance.

Both of these sites provide samples of student performance at various levels. The "Looking at Student Work" site also encourages teacher dialogues about evaluation of samples.

It is important to remember that *standards based* and *standardized* are not the same thing. Standards-based testing, like CRTs, grade students on predetermined standards of what students should know at a certain grade/age level. Standardized tests, discussed next, measure a student against the knowledge of other students taking the same test.

• Norm-Referenced Tests

The purpose of **norm-referenced tests (NRTs),** or standardized tests, is to allow the evaluator to compare the performance of a student or group of students to a larger group for the purpose of identifying potential problems or for assessing group achievement. Most norm-referenced tests are group tests, but a small number are individually administered both for achievement estimates (e.g., the Peabody Individual Achievement Test) or for diagnostic purposes (e.g., Woodcock Reading Mastery Test, Gilmore Oral Reading Test). Criterion–referenced and -standardized-based assessments can also be normed (for explanation, see following section page) to suggest typical performance at a particular age or grade point, though that is not their primary goal. Most group reading tests are called "survey" tests and give an overview of global reading performance. Diagnostic tests are designed to give a profile of student strengths and weaknesses.

A standardized test is an *objective, normed* measure of a *sample* of behavior. Let's look at each of these key words to try to understand some basic concepts about this type of test.

Objective. When we say a friend is objective in deciding arguments, we mean that that person treats everyone the same way and does not show favoritism. The same sense of the term applies to *objective* in standardized tests. In order to treat each test taker alike, these tests are designed with a set of answers from which test takers select so that the answers can be scored impartially. Time limits, specific directions for explaining and administering the test, and answer sheets all help ensure that the test-taking, answering, and scoring process is as much alike as possible for all students.

Normed. Tests that are normed are developed and tested on a large group of diverse students so that the test designers are able to calculate the average performance of many students in differing age and geographic groups. Tests can have *nationwide* norms, norms that reflect a broad spectrum of geographic and ethnic diversity, or they can provide *local* norms so that the user can compare the performance of a particular group of students with closely matched peers, such as, for example, rural midwestern students.

Normed scores are used to place a value on the *raw* score (the number of correct answers), which, without a standard for comparison, cannot by itself tell the teacher how well a group has performed. For example, a raw score of 24 out of 26 might seem good. However, it becomes very clear that such a score is not good when you know the task is naming the letters of the alphabet and the test taker is applying for graduate school.

The most common normed scores are stanines, percentile scores, and grade-equivalent scores. The word **stanine** is a contraction of standard-nine because stanines represent divisions of the normal curve divided into nine equal or standard parts. Stanines place students in a broad performance band and allow comparisons across tests, with stanines 4 to 6 considered average, 5 being the mean, stanines 1 to 3 below average, and stanines 7 to 9 above average.

Percentiles, better called percentile ranks, are often confusing for teachers and parents, who confuse them with percentages, indicators of the number of items correct. Ranging from 1 to 99, **percentile rank** indicates a student's relative position in the norming group. For example, a score of 60th percentile means a student did better than 60 percent of the other students taking the test; it does not mean that the student scored only 60 percent correct.

Grade scores indicate a level of achievement in terms of years and months in school; for example, 6.3 would indicate an average level of performance for a sixth grader in the third month of school. Such scores assume great importance because grade organization is most familiar to parents, children, and teachers. There are some very significant problems in the use of grade scores, however.

The first of these is the question of growth across the school years. Consider the observable changes in reading from the beginning of first grade to the beginning of second grade. Normally these are significant changes in what we would call reading performance. Then imagine the change from junior to senior year of high school. These changes would be harder to detect and harder to describe. A year's growth at earlier levels may not indicate the same amount of change as at later levels, and using grade scores to discuss growth can have similar problems of equivalence.

A second problem is typified by interpreting a high score gained by a young child. For example, a good second-grade reader may score 4.6 on a standardized test, but when placed on fourth-grade materials, the child is unable to function. Why? It is important to remember that the score of 4.6 was obtained on a test meant for second graders. That indicates that the able second grader did as well as a fourth grader in the sixth month of school would do *on second-grade material.* Both the reporting and interpreting of grade scores require care.

Sample. When you have your blood tested, the technicians or doctors don't require that all the blood be removed from your body and analyzed. Rather, they work with a sample that they assume represents that quantity. In the same way, reading tests take a short **sample** of what you do and extrapolate to a larger estimate of your performance. Like a medical test, there are two important requirements: that this test be reliable and that it be valid.

1. *Reliability.* **Reliability** refers to the degree of consistency a test has. If a particular blood-testing technique is correct 9 times out of 10, it is fairly reliable; tests must also be reliable in the way they rank students who take them. Tests are also checked for consistency of items across the test and for equivalency of different forms. Every test manual describes one or more ways in which reliability is estimated and expresses this reliability as a decimal, a coefficient of reliability; the closer to 1.0 a coefficient of reliability is, the more consistent a test is.

    Along with a high reliability, look for a low **standard error of measurement (SEM).** This figure indicates how accurate given scores on a test are and emphasizes that no score is absolute, that each is subject to a certain degree of error. For example, with a raw score SEM of 2 points, a child whose obtained raw score is 43 can be estimated to have an actual raw score between 41 and 45 with about 70 percent surety. If we double the value of the standard error of measurement to 4, we can be 90 percent sure that the score is between 39 and 47. The smaller the standard error of measurement, the more likely that the child's obtained test score and actual score are close together. SEM can also be useful in helping report scores as ranges, often with grade-level variations of 0.3 to 0.6 a year, rather than an absolute, to give parents and others a better picture of the student's performance.

    Reliability alone, however, is not sufficient to make a test good. Consider our initial metaphor of a blood test. A blood test can give us the same data each time and be highly reliable. Yet it is useless as a test for vision because it has no real connection with that trait.

2. *Validity.* A test is **valid** when it measures what it is intended to measure. For a reading test to be valid, it must measure those things that we think are important to reading. For example, a test that assesses only decoding might better be called a decoding test than a reading test because no comprehension is involved. Validity is assessed by evaluating the content of the test and comparing it with one's own definition of or curriculum for reading. Frequently tests are deemed valid by testimony of experts or by a comparison of their content with that of other, more established tests. Nothing substitutes, however, for examining and taking a test oneself.

> **pause and reflect**
>
> Before reading the next section, Problems with Standardized Tests, reflect on your own test-taking history. What problems have you experienced with standardized tests? What problems have you encountered in classrooms? List and compare with those that follow.

Problems with Standardized Tests

Standardized tests are useful for gathering large-scale statistics but may often be misleading when used for analyzing a particular student. In addition to the difficulties inherent in reliability, error of measurement, and reporting, teachers are normally aware of other problems, a few of which we discuss here.

• High Floor Problem

You may have received a new student into your class with records suggesting that he has a low but measurable reading level, yet he is unable to read at the primer level. How is it that a nonreader can receive a score, one that goes up each time he or she is tested? The answer lies in the way increasing grade forms of tests are designed. It is almost impossible for any student to receive a zero raw score. By chance a few of the answer marks will find the right space, giving the students the lowest possible score on the test. Although this score will remain in stanine 1 over the years, the lowest grade possible becomes *higher* on each higher level of a test. Therefore, even a student who can't read gets a score, one that goes up each year.

• Test-Question Independence

In the 1970s, Tuinman (1974) did some interesting research on test construction. He allowed students to see the comprehension questions on some standardized tests without having read the passages to which the questions referred. Then they were asked to answer the questions as well as they could. Tuinman found that many questions on tests were test independent; that is, they tested a student's knowledge and reasoning rather than the reading of the passage. For example, a question, "What did the monkey eat?" is very likely to elicit the answer "bananas," regardless of whether you have read the selection. Since the publication of Tuinman's work, test questions have undergone more stringent evaluation, but it is still possible for students with specific prior knowledge to answer from their knowledge base rather than from their reading of material.

• Task Validity

The formats of most standardized reading tests have received major criticism. The passages are generally short and unrelated, switching from narrative to exposition, from topic to topic. Further, unlike real-life comprehension tasks, test tasks look for one right answer. Developments in state-based assessment (Valencia & Pearson, 1986; Wixson, Peters, Weber, & Roeber, 1987) have recognized these as serious difficulties. As teachers are more responsible for using data to inform instruction, the issue of task validity becomes critical for all members of the school community.

• Specific Sources of Test Information

The Mental Measurement Yearbooks provide an invaluable aid to the practitioner. Begun by Oscar Buros in 1938, the yearbooks are issued and revised periodically and contain reviews on most standardized instruments. Their index volumes, *Tests in Print I and II* (Murphy, 2011), can be used to locate initial and subsequent surveys of particular tests, but this information is most easily accessed via the World Wide Web at www.unl.edu/buros/ or using the ERIC test locator. In addition, professional journals such as the *American Psychologist, Journal of Educational Measurement, Psychological Bulletin, The Reading Teacher,* and *The Journal of Reading* contain regular test reviews.

In Chapter 1, you were introduced to the ways in which Tessa and her assistant used standardized test data to make some screening decisions about her students and to decide about further assessment. (See Figure 1.2 on page 19.) The following section describes some other ways to collect information about students as the year progresses.

Portfolios

• Building a Class Portfolio

This section on building a class portfolio may be among the most important in the book, for if you do not find a way to record and organize the information and insights you develop, they will be of limited use to you. A class portfolio differs from a teacher portfolio: In the first, you organize your reflections about the students in your class; in the second, you gather samples and reflections about your own life as a professional.

How should you go about devising a system to organize the knowledge you are developing about your students? There are many different systems, and we describe some. The system you develop may turn out to be a unique hybrid.

You should use several steps as guidelines in making a class portfolio. These include (1) specifying your goals in the areas of reading and writing, (2) thinking about the activities in your class that may yield valuable information, (3) selecting the type of information you want to include in the class portfolio, (4) determining the physical form of the portfolio, and finally, (5) making sense of your portfolio records.

Specifying Your Goals. Your goals in the areas of reading and writing will directly reflect the prior learning of your students. Many schools, teachers, and curriculum designers routinely use "backward mapping" from goals and standards to plan instruction (Wiggins & McTighe, 1998). If you are teaching first grade, your goals will differ somewhat from those of a sixth-grade teacher. Further, the children in your class will differ from each other, and your goals must reflect these developmental differences. In Tessa's case, for example, the goals she sets for Walter will differ considerably from those for Grace, who you will meet later in this chapter.

Yet, there is general learning in the area of literacy that will apply to all children: knowledge of print, reading fluency, vocabulary development, comprehension strategies, love of reading, knowledge of types of writing (narrative and nonfiction), writing fluency, and ability to organize ideas. The Upper Arlington City Schools include among their assessment guidelines for teachers four main categories that capture many of these areas. Their guide is shown in Figure 9.2.

From the large set of possible goals, you must select the subset (from four to ten) that you will evaluate during the year. Some teachers prefer to define a limited number of general goals; others identify a larger number of more specific goals. But whatever the number, they will be the areas in which you gather information in an ongoing fashion.

Thinking about Class Activities. Another way to define your assessment activities is to think about the activities that your children do each day or week and to identify those that may lend themselves to evaluation. Tessa's class includes large- and small-group reading instruction, reader's workshop, independent reading and writing time, and book club activities. During the independent reading and writing time, she meets individually with students to discuss their recent work and to enter selected work into their literacy portfolios. Each of these activities offers Tessa different opportunities to increase her understanding of her students' reading and writing. During the individual conferences, for example, she can explore her students' understanding of and reflection on books they have recently read, she can study samples of their writing, and she

figure 9.2 • A Holistic Reading Assignment Observation Form

UPPER ARLINGTON CITY SCHOOLS
Holistic Reading Assessment Observation Form

Date _____   Holistic Reading Score _____

Student's Name _____   Grade _____

Teacher _____   Observer _____

BOOK SELECTION FOR HOLISTIC READING ASSESSMENT

Book Title _____

Child selected _____   Teacher selected _____

WIDE READING

■ *May I see your book list?* (comment on books read)

Book List: Limited _____   Adequate _____   Extensive _____

Comments:

■ *How do you choose a book to read?*

■ *What is one of your favorite books? Why?*

■ *What are you reading now?*

■ *What do you think you will choose to read next? Why?*

CONSTRUCTING MEANING / RESPONSE

■ Tell me about the book you have selected for this conference.

Student discusses story idea _____   major events _____

characters _____   story ending _____

(Prompting may be used to elicit additional information; i.e., Tell me more about the story idea.)

Prompted with additional questions _____

No additional prompting necessary _____

■ Why do you think the author wrote this book?

■ Would you recommend this book? Why or why not?

(continued)

figure 9.2 • Continued

SILENT / ORAL READING / USE OF STRATEGIES

- Find a passage in your book to read aloud. You can read it to yourself first if you like.

Estimated Accuracy: 95–100% _____ 90–95% _____ Less than 90% _____

Do miscues interfere with meaning? yes _____ no _____

Rate: slow _____ adequate _____

Fluency: (Intonation, phrasing, repetitions) fluent _____ some fluency _____ nonfluent _____

Observation of student strategies: (self-correction, prediction, use of cues) Comments:

- *Tell me in your own words about what you've just read.* (Comment on reading and retelling).

ATTITUDE / SELF-ASSESSMENT

- Do you like to read? Why or why not?
- What are your strengths as a reader? (What do you do well as a reader?)
- What would you like to improve about your reading?

PLANNED INTERVENTIONS:

---

can ask questions and listen carefully to assess their feelings and reflections about their literacy activities. During reader's workshop, she can note who works with whom and the reading activities they undertake.

Selecting Portfolio Information. The information gathered in a class portfolio should represent areas of literacy that coincide with instructional goals (i.e., that are important aspects of literacy) and that permit assessment of learning over time. For example, Linda Pils, a teacher in a first-grade, whole-language classroom, gathered the following:

- Writing samples (considered for their content, number of known words, sentence structure, and punctuation)
- Number of words read aloud in one minute (assessed in September, January, and May)
- Ten-minute writing samples (at three-month intervals throughout the year)

- Lists of books read and to be read (kept during buddy reading time)
- Challenge cards (lists of unknown words and their sources)
- Conference records (students' interests in reading, how themes of books are alike and different, what they are currently writing about)

These samples are either easily obtained (number of words read aloud in one-minute and ten-minute writing samples) or can be gathered during the course of instruction. All are in keeping with Pils's literacy goals for her first graders. Some samples that are gathered may be kept best in student portfolios (discussed in the following section) and some in a class portfolio. For example, from the samples listed here, students should keep in their portfolios the writing samples, the list of books already read and to be read, and the challenge cards. The other information (one-minute word reading sample, ten-minute writing sample, and conference records) may be kept best in the class portfolio.

You must decide how to record the observations you make during ongoing instruction, and two systems that have been developed by teachers may work for you. One involving anecdotal records is described by Rhodes and Nathenson-Mejia (1992). They offer three guidelines: "Describe a specific event or product. Report rather than evaluate or interpret. Relate the material to other facts that are known about the child" (adapted from Thorndike & Hagen, 1977, p. 503). A sample provided in Figure 9.3 illustrates the nature of anecdotal records.

figure 9.3 • An Anecdotal Record of Eleanor's Reading

Eleanor

STRDAIPADENBSNO
(Yesterday I played in the snow)

STRDA = yesterday
I = I
PAD = played
EN = in
B = the (said "du" and thought she was writing "D")
SNO = snow

Showed her how to stretch her words out like a rubberband—doing it almost on own by SNO. E does have a fairly good grasp of sound/letter relationships. However, has a hard time isolating words and tracking words in sentences in her mind. That may hold up progress for awhile. Asked her—at end—what she did in writing today that she hadn't done in previous writing. She said, "I listened to sounds." Told her to do it in her writing again tomorrow.

Source: Rhodes, L. K., & Nathenson-Mejia, S. (1992). Anecdotal records: A powerful tool for ongoing literacy assessment. *The Reading Teacher, 45* (7), 503.

A somewhat different system is also described by Pils (1991). Her portfolio materials include strips of blank mailing labels attached to a clipboard. Each morning she dates several of these; then as she walks around the room she records her observations of children's works. For example, her records on Stacy might include the following:

(9/24) *Stacy:*   I can read *Hop on Pop* all by myself.
(10/5) *Stacy:*   Stacy and Alan very good buddies. Stacy helps Alan with
                  words. She read all of helper chart when she selected her job. (p. 48)

Pils has a three-ring binder with a section for each child. At the end of the day, she places the recorded labels on the sheets named for each child she observed.

Although it is important to use some more formal observational procedures, such as the Upper Arlington City Schools Holistic Reading Assessment form (see Figure 9.2), it is also important to ensure that your daily observations are represented in your class portfolio.

Determining the Physical Form of the Portfolio. The portfolio may take many forms. It may be a set of manila folders, one for each child, to be kept in your file drawer. It may be a loose-leaf notebook with a section for each child. It may be an accordion file with a section for each of your children. The form should be one that will be easy for you to use. You should have the physical form of the portfolio established before the beginning of the school year.

Making Sense of Your Portfolio Records. The final step is the most important. The best-kept records in the world will do you little good if you fail to reflect on what you have observed over time and make sense of the patterns you see. Your records should be descriptive rather than interpretive. At least once a month, read over your portfolio entries for each child in your class and ask what they tell you about the child's literacy development. You will begin to see recurring patterns in some areas and marked departures in others. When we do this sort of study, we usually record our thoughts and ideas in writing as we read the record. It is possible to identify patterns and inconsistencies in our insights and emerging understandings.

On the basis of the patterns you see and the changes that have occurred, identify the current reading and writing strengths and weaknesses of the child. These tentative conclusions will form the

pause and **reflect**

Select a grade level that you either currently teach or would like to teach in the future. Describe your goals for student reading and writing. What are the activities you will undertake to help your students achieve these goals? What type of information will you want to include in your class portfolio? Describe the procedures you will follow and the physical form of your portfolio record-keeping approach.

basis for setting new short-term goals. During your next conference with the child, you will be able to discuss and confirm the patterns you believe you see and use this as the basis for discussing goals for reading and writing.

The insights and new understandings you derive from your study of the portfolio entries should be recorded in brief form in the portfolio. The study will better prepare you for your next observations of the student's reading and writing.

• Building Student Portfolios

A student portfolio is like the portfolio of an artist, which contains a representative sample of the artist's work, revealing the essence of who the artist is and what he or she is trying to accomplish. A similar collection of work can be developed by students in your class. Building a portfolio is important for two reasons. It becomes a window into the student's thinking, revealing his or her aspirations, interests, and goals. It is a powerful educational tool that can encourage students to assume control of their own learning (Lipson & Mosenthal, 1997).

Paulson, Paulson, and Meyer (1991) and colleagues developed the following definition: "A **portfolio** is a purposeful collection of student work that exhibits the student's efforts, progress, and achievement in one or more areas. The collection must include student participation in selecting content, the criteria for selection, the criteria for judging merit, and evidence of student self-reflection" (p. 60). Although portfolios can be defined in other ways, we have selected this definition because it captures what we believe are several important aspects of them.

First, the collection of student work must be purposeful; it must relate to the goals that you and the student have established in the area of literacy. Do not assess too many areas. For example, it may be sufficient to collect work in three areas: writing; a list of books read, with brief entries; and writing that relates to reading activities. More activities related to the development of print may be included for younger children (spelling samples, words known, challenge words, and the like).

Second, the work collected must show the "efforts, progress, and achievements" of the child. The samples must be judiciously selected to show work reflecting effort (e.g., multiple drafts of the same paper) and must be collected over time to show progress. Not all the child's work should be included or the task of examining the collection will become overwhelming. The work should be selected with a purpose in mind. More samples will be collected at the beginning of the year to represent the year's starting point; some of these may be eliminated as the year progresses. The portfolio is organic in nature and may profit from being pruned periodically.

In addition, the student will be involved in selecting content, establishing the criteria for selection, and judging merit. Part of the value of student portfolios lies in the student's assuming responsibility for his or her own reading and writing development. This can occur only if the student's goals and values influence what is kept in the portfolio and influence the criteria by which merit is judged. For many teachers, the interactive process of considering work, discussing its strengths and weaknesses, and judging its merits is a new one. Those who have been doing it for some time have learned to become very good listeners when they interact with their students. Teachers who wish their students to keep portfolios must set aside time for individual conferences every week or two for younger students and at least every three weeks for older ones. Conferences should be more frequent at the beginning of the year than later. Usually the focus of the conference is on the new work the student has placed in his or her portfolio. On the basis of the conference, some of this work will be kept in the portfolio and other work will be sent home, displayed, shared, or discarded.

Finally, evidence of student self-reflection will be included in the portfolio. By encouraging students' self-reflection on their work, the portfolio collection gives students opportunities to take charge of their own learning. Prior to several conferences with their teachers (for example, at midyear and a time or two thereafter), students can be encouraged to study the work they have recently collected, compare it with previous work, and draw conclusions about their progress. Paulson, Paulson, and Meyer (1991) provide some useful illustrations of student reflection. These are shown in Figure 9.4. Writing about what they have learned becomes an important part of the process for students and a valuable part of the record.

The sort of informal assessments that we have described must be recorded and organized in some way. The procedures for building class portfolios and student portfolios represent solutions to the problem of organization. They become useful educational tools for assessing student learning and progress and for planning instruction. In the following section, we consider how the information that you have gathered and organized helps you make informed instructional decisions.

• Electronic Portfolios

Electronic portfolios are another way to keep student work. Teacher Charlotte Diller at Baker Demonstration School at National-Louis University assists students in constructing electronic portfolios using Hyperstudio. Portfolio template programs are another effective way to begin collecting data electronically. Many electronic versions are now available. For an example, consult www.scholastic.com.

Using Information

Gathering information and making observations are useful only if you learn to make good decisions based on the understanding that you are developing about each of your students. As you reflect on the characteristics of each child, you must pose certain questions:

1. How will I organize my class for various instructional activities?

figure 9.4 • Samples of Students' Reflections on the Writing Samples They Included in Their Portfolios

5-11-90

At the beginning of the year.
I hevit been yoosng periods
and I am now.
At the beginning of the year,
I hayit been yoosng sentence
and I am now.
At the beginning of the year.
I hayit been yoosng elaboration
and I am now the End

Today I looked at all my
stories in my writing folder
I read some of my writing since
September. I noticed that I've
impaved some stuff. Now I edit my
stores, and revise, Now I use periods,
quotation mark. Sometimes my stories
are longer I usd to misrspell my
words and now I look in a
dictionary or ask a friend and now
I write exciting and scary stories
and now I have very good endings
Now I use capitals I usd to leave out
words and wrote short simple stories.

Source: Paulson, F. L., Paulson, P. R., & Meyer, C. A. (1991). What makes a portfolio a portfolio? *Educational Leadership, 48*(5), 62–63. Reprinted with permission from ASCD. All rights reserved.

2. What level of materials can each of my students read independently and with support?

3. What kind of support should I provide each of my students?

• Assessment Walls—Using data to monitor progress

Roberta Buhle, Director of the National Louis University Literacy Coaching Institute, describes Assessment Walls as mechanisms for data analysis (Frost, Buhle, & Blachowicz, 2009) to help teachers use assessment information. An Assessment Wall is a tool for engaging teachers in the analysis of group data with a visual representation of student performance (Dorn, French, & Jones, 1999; Frost, Buhle, & Blachowicz, 2009). A card is made for each child indicating an instructional level, overall performance on an assessment or some other feature being tracked through performance assessment. The cards are arrayed on a grid, in a pocket chart, or in some other visual representation. The goal is for teachers to use this visual representation (see Figure 9.5) to open discussions about the progress trends of their students over time.

At its best, the discussion evolves into problem-solving the ways that might accelerate the progress of those children who are moving so slowly that they are falling more and more behind. It also allows teachers to discuss the progress of children who are either on grade level or who might be reading above grade level. Although it uses cards that represent individual students, the Assessment Wall is not intended to highlight the progress of individual children. Instead, it focuses on the trends of groups or children who are or are not making appropriate literacy progress. The following steps can set up an Assessment Wall:

1. Create one card for each student.

2. Set up a sentence strip chart or bulletin board in a private area where teachers can view the Assessment Wall, with an area in front of it where they can sit and talk.

3. Place one row of cards across the top, with each signifying a different reading level, arranged from lowest to highest from left to right.

4. Initially, place each child's card under the row that identifies the book level at which that child is currently determined to be reading with proficiency. At the beginning of the year, the first level may be determined by making a running record of the child's reading. Later, it can be determined by the level of text used in the child's reading group.

5. At predetermined times (every three weeks in our institute), teachers move the cards of those children who have moved up one or more reading levels since the last time.

figure 9.5 • Assessment Wall

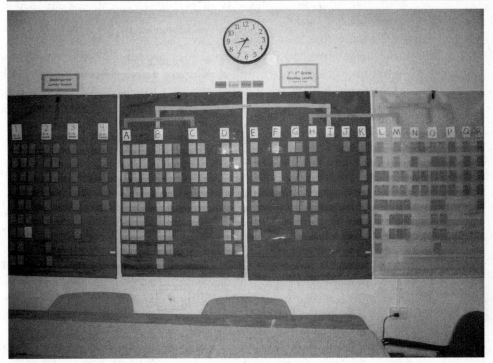

Source: By permission of Murphy School, Chicago, Illinois.

6. After making these changes, teachers problem-solve instructional interventions that might help children to make better progress. At its best, the Assessment Wall prompts teachers to *ask questions* that get at the root causes of children who are not making progress.

7. Some teachers decide to include other information than the child's name (or number) on the card, for instance, whether the child is in ELL, special education, or gifted classes.

Teachers use their discussion around the Assessment Wall to observe and problem-solve about their children's progress in their team meetings over the course of the year.

• Organizing Students for Instruction

Classroom children are grouped for reading instruction in most elementary school classrooms. Further, in most classrooms a variety of organizational structures are used for reading and writing: pairs, teams, ability groups, or total class. The grouping arrangements you select depend on your instructional goals. The problem for you as a teacher is to think about the composition of your class and your own goals and values. Then you must consider what forms of grouping may work for you.

Historically, most grouping for reading instruction was done on the basis of achievement (Barr & Dreeben, 1991). More recently, teachers have developed repertoires of flexible grouping strategies to meet students' individual needs in reading. Students work in large groups with support strategies in place for less able readers. They are grouped cooperatively for paired and shared learning. Teachers have mini-lessons for both small and large groups and continue to work with individuals when the larger class is involved in independent work. The type of group that is formed depends on the needs of the students, the goals you have for instruction, the constraints of the classroom, and the stages of reading represented in the classroom (Barr, 1995).

Most reading researchers agree that the beginning stages of reading differ in certain fundamental ways from subsequent stages. Most important, beginning readers must learn about the nature of print and how print relates to their spoken language. Chall (1983) described the initial stages of reading as learning to decode and then learning to read fluently. Typically, this focus on reading occurs in the first two or three grades of elementary school. The developmental nature of learning to read during this period becomes obvious. Children who are able to read beginning, first-grade-level materials usually have extreme difficulty reading second- or third-grade-level materials because they have not yet acquired the needed sight vocabulary nor the skill to identify unknown words.

As we described in Chapter 3, once children have learned a substantial number of words and can identify them easily, they consolidate this learning to become fluent readers. For most children, this integration occurs sometime during the second or third grade. Learning about print is no longer a major emphasis of instruction; reading instruction focuses even more on the strategies that children must acquire in order to comprehend effectively and critically. The materials that children encounter in the intermediate grades pose many new problems for them: Often the vocabulary is unfamiliar; the structure of reading in science and social studies differs from the narrative forms experienced in the basal series; and children are expected to read longer selections silently.

Most important to our discussion here, what children need to learn to become effective readers is no longer developmentally organized. Whereas in the early stages children's skill with print relates directly to the level of the material they will be able to read, in later stages their interest in and prior knowledge about the topic are more important. Accordingly, in the intermediate grades and above, it becomes more difficult to predict whether a child can comprehend a particular story or article. As we discussed in Chapter 4, prereading discussions encourage students to share their knowledge about the topic of a selection and thereby better prepare them to comprehend the selection. Several useful teaching strategies, developed to encourage students to think about what they may learn from the text and what they already know about the topic, were described in Chapters 5 and 6. Remember, however, that word identification and fluency will still have a bearing on the reading of low-achieving students; special instructional provisions may need to be made to accommodate deficiencies in these areas.

Grouping children by their reading proficiency may make it easier for you to match closely the demands of selections with students' developing knowledge. And yet, children grouped together on the basis of achievement, particularly groups composed of those developing their reading skill most slowly, may be deprived of the more stimulating discussions that characterize groups including a cross section of children.

Children who are less well prepared for a reading or writing task can participate in the activity with their peers who are more proficient readers if you help them with one of several instructional strategies. Even children in the beginning stages of reading are able to read fairly demanding books (for which they know few sight words) when the story is familiar to them. You can make the books familiar by reading them aloud previously in class or by asking parents to read them to their children at home. Reading in pairs or choral reading provides support for children who are experiencing difficulty learning print. Finally, rereading stories helps children develop and consolidate their knowledge of print.

Beyond the beginning stages of reading, all children can be supported through instruction in a way that will enable them to read selections with comprehension. In particular, some of the strategies for sharing prior knowledge discussed in Chapter 4 enable even students with limited experiences to read and comprehend.

When you are thinking about how to organize your students for different aspects of instruction, consider your goals, the characteristics of your students, and the instructional support they require to be active participants. When you choose to form groups that are diverse in reading ability, you will need to provide special support for those children who are developing their reading strategies more slowly than others in your class. Figure 9.6 shows how Tessa used her information to form groups.

• Large Scale Initiatives—RTI

Response to Intervention/Instruction (RTI) was conceived within the Individual with Disabilities Act (2004) as an option for assessment for identifying students who could benefit from special education placement and instruction. The common paradigm for assessment and selection was the IQ discrepancy model, looking at the difference between intellectual ability and academic achievement, which had been critiqued from both within the special education community (Lyon et al., 2001) and from the educational community at large (Allington, 2007).

figure 9.6 • Standardized Test Results: Third-Grade Grouping and Hypothetical Groups Based on Comprehension Scores

Student	Reading Vocabulary	Reading Comprehension	Third-Grade Group	Tessa's Hypothetical Group
Ann	3.4	3.7	L	G
Candy	4.1	3.8	M	G
Carol	3.0	4.3	L	G
Connie	4.3	4.0	M	G
Cornelia	4.1	3.9	H	G
Daniel	4.1	3.8	H	G
David	4.0	4.3	M	G
Denise	4.5	4.0	H	G
Donald	4.8	3.7	H	G
Dorothy	4.3	5.1	M	I
Dottie	3.1	3.1	L	S
Gary	3.4	3.9	M	G
Gordon	3.7	3.9	M	G
Grace	3.5	3.0	H	S
Greta	4.4	3.9	H	G
Jean	2.9	2.0	M	S
Jeff	5.7	4.9	H	I
John	3.1	2.8	L	S
Kay	4.3	4.0	H	G
Lois	3.4	3.3	M	G
Lottie	2.7	1.8	L	S
Tia	4.5	3.9	H	G
Walter	1.9	2.2	L	S
Wanda	2.2	2.7	L	S

There is no one model or approach to RTI, and many possible variations can be conceptualized (National Joint Committee on Learning Disabilities [NJCLD], 2005). In fact, the federal government purposely provided few details for the development and implementation of RTI procedures, stating specifically that states and districts should have the flexibility to establish approaches that reflect their community's unique situation. In this book we emphasize assessment used for good first instruction and for connecting assessment with instruction, both components of what are called Tiers 1 and 2 in a three-tiered model. However, a three-tiered model, though widely used, is neither mandated nor the only possible approach to RTI. Similarly, the statute and regulations do not mandate screening assessments or any particular assessment per se, although they do require data-based documentation of repeated assessments of achievement at reasonable intervals.

To bring clarify to this discussion, The International Reading Association has disseminated six principles for sound RTI programs (2009):

I. Instruction. RTI is first and foremost intended to prevent problems by optimizing initial language and literacy instruction. Good core classroom instruction is the bedrock of literacy instruction.

II. Responsive Teaching and Differentiation. The RTI process emphasizes increasingly differentiated and intensified instruction/intervention in language and literacy. There is no scientifically validated "one size fits all" approach.

III. Assessment. An RTI approach demands assessment that can inform language and literacy instruction meaningfully.

IV. Collaboration. RTI requires a dynamic, positive, and productive collaboration among professionals with relevant expertise in language and literacy. Success also depends on strong and respectful partnerships among professionals, parents, and students.

V. Systemic and Comprehensive. RTI must be part of a comprehensive, systemic approach to language and literacy assessment and instruction that supports all pre-K–12 students and teachers.

VI. Expertise. All students have the right to receive instruction from well-prepared teachers who keep up to date and supplemental instruction from professionals specifically prepared to teach language and literacy (IRA Position Statement on Children's Rights, 2000).

• Selecting Appropriate Material

Children read materials they select as well as those selected by teachers. It is your responsibility, as teacher, to make sure that the materials your students read are at the appropriate level—not frustrating and not too easy. It is also your responsibility to see that children read a variety of text: nonfictional materials (science and social studies articles, biography, history) as well as narratives. In the past, there had been a clear bias by teachers toward the selection of narrative materials. Studies have shown that even young children—particularly boys, but girls as well—prefer nonfiction (Pappas, 1993).

Reflecting this new viewpoint, in the past decade, there has been an increased effort by many teachers to balance selections of fiction and nonfiction.

We believe that one useful way to approach the selection of materials is to decide on one or several themes that you and the class will pursue during the year. In her class, Tessa has selected the theme of "Challenge." She has already examined the basals in her class and found narratives that fit this theme. Now she needs to locate articles, some of which are nonfiction, that also develop this idea. Typically, teachers over the years develop appropriate collections of trade books or nonfiction materials from which they draw. These collections must be reviewed and supplemented to remain current and interesting to specific classes of students.

The selection of materials occurs on two levels. On one level, teachers select what they believe will be interesting and conceptually challenging reading experiences for their students. On another level, teachers attempt to ensure that the assigned materials, the "normal reading task demands," can be read by all children to whom they are assigned. Selection of materials in this second sense involves knowing enough about the reading strengths of students to be able to develop an appropriate match. Reading comprehension or the ability to construct meaning from text is viewed as the central and most important goal. Thus, if children cannot read the assigned materials with comprehension, then either easier materials need to be found or greater instructional support needs to be provided. We believe that children will continue to develop their reading strategies if the normal reading task demands permit reading with comprehension. Text that is too difficult will lead them to develop maladaptive strategies.

At the beginning of the school year, teachers must work from limited information to determine whether the materials they have selected are appropriate. In the earlier section on instructional organization, the decision of how to cluster children for appropriate instruction was based mainly on a decision about materials. That is, the instructional arrangements selected are influenced to a great extent by the diversity of the class in reading skill. If class members are quite similar in reading comprehension, there is no need for special materials and instructional strategies. On the other hand, if a class is highly diverse, the teacher will need to have materials available at several different levels of difficulty so that all children can read with comprehension.

Tessa made her decision about the selection of materials on the basis of her past experience with similar children, the standardized test scores of the present class, and information from their third-grade teachers. She decided that children scoring low on the comprehension section of the standardized test would find the fourth-grade basal narrative and nonfiction selections too demanding, and that they would make better progress reading less challenging materials.

A teacher must exercise considerable caution in using standardized test scores in this way. As discussed in earlier sections of this chapter, scores may not be accurate estimates of reading ability for some children for a variety of reasons. Thus, although we believe that scores can be used as one piece of information, we are concerned when instruction is established solely on this basis.

Scores can be used as an initial estimate if, and only if, teachers faithfully examine and reexamine earlier decisions by observing the reading and writing of their students.

Similarly, the level at which children were reading during the prior school year should also be treated in a tentative fashion. The reading progress of children does not occur in a straight line, nor do all children progress through the same stages. Reading development is somewhat like growth in height; at times there can be periods of amazing growth. Further, you don't know that children during the prior year were being instructed at the appropriate level. Glynn and associates (1989) report that New Zealand children who had participated in Reading Recovery (a first-grade tutorial program) were reading in books more than four levels (about a half year) below where they were capable of reading as indicated by passage tests. Thus, when children have made spurts in their reading development, their earlier basal placement may be inaccurate. The main point is that no single observation or piece of information should underlie a major instructional decision. Rather, decisions, particularly those made at the beginning of the school year, should be viewed as tentative and subject to modification as you gather other information about children's reading and writing.

Book leveling for primary grades can be facilitated by adopting one of the many systems that has been derived from Reading Recovery leveling. One of the most used is that constructed by Fountas and Pinnell (2010). Books are leveled by teams of expert teachers who look at the following:

- Sentence structure

- Number of words on a page

- Vocabulary and conceptual familiarity

The discussion concerning leveling in Chapter 2 and the work of Fountas and Pinnell and their associates provides excellent direction for determining benchmarks for book difficulty.

Once Tessa has made her initial decisions, during subsequent months she must study the comprehension of her children in order to identify those who are ready to read with the large group. Her observations during reader's workshop, where she has the entire class read the same short stories will be particularly informative. This flexibility will help her to achieve her goal of having all children in her class reading in the large group before the end of the year. Studies of grouping show that effective teachers have a pattern of moving their students into higher-achieving groups during the course of the school year (Barr & Dreeben, 1983).

case 9.1

The Case of Grace

Tessa was particularly uncertain about the decision she had made for Grace. In third grade, Grace had been in the high reading group, yet her comprehension score suggested that she was reading only as well as students at the beginning of third grade. This conflicting information raised questions in Tessa's mind about whether Grace should be reading with the small group Tessa had selected for her. To pursue this question, Tessa decided to have Grace read aloud for her the initial portion of a story from the fourth-grade basal. After Grace had finished reading the story silently, Tessa asked her to summarize it. She did so fluently and with enthusiasm. Figure 9.7 shows a sample of Grace's oral reading and her retelling.

Tessa was pleased with Grace's reading. Her print strategies appeared to be well developed, certainly good enough to cope with most of the fourth-grade basal selections. Her retelling was brief, but suggests that she comprehended most of the story. On the basis of this evidence, Tessa decided to have Grace read with the large reading group. She asked Grace if she remembered taking the reading test at the end of third grade. Grace told Tessa that she always gets extremely nervous when she takes tests and that she had difficulty concentrating. On the basis of Grace's reading, Tessa decided that Grace's test scores were invalid. ■

p a u s e and r e f l e c t

Study the sample of Grace's oral reading shown in Figure 9.6. In terms of her strategies for dealing with print, is this passage at an appropriate level of difficulty? How did you arrive at your decision? Now examine her retelling. Does she represent the most important ideas? On the basis of this information would you have her read from easier material in the small group or the fourth-grade-level material in the large group?

• Developing Appropriate Instructional Support

Just as decisions about the appropriateness of materials and grouping of students have implications for each other, the development of appropriate instructional support is also involved. Through instruction, you can prepare students to read a story or article. Selections that might otherwise be too difficult for them can be made accessible through various prereading activities. Thus, in making selections, you can select more complex materials if you are able to prepare students to read them. On the other hand, if the possibilities for instructional support are limited, children may not be able to bridge the gap between the difficulty of the reading materials and their reading skill.

figure 9.7 • A Record of Grace's Oral Reading and Retelling of "Cheating" by Susan Shreve

Cheating
by
Susan Shreve

che-©

I cheated on a unit test in math class this

morning during second period with Mr. Burke.

Afterward, I was too sick to eat lunch just

thinking about it.

I came straight home from school, went to

my room, and lay on the floor trying to decide

whether it would be better to run away from home

now or after supper. Mostly I wished I was dead.

assident ©

It wasn't even (an) accident that I cheated.

an rocked

Yesterday Mr. Burke announced there'd be a

unit test and anyone who didn't pass would have

partic ly

to come to school on Saturday, most particularly

me, since I didn't pass the last unit test. He said

that right out in front of everyone as usual. You

im-ag-in

can imagine how much I like Mr. Burke.

Retelling: This is a story about a kid who wasn't very good in math. Anyway, he didn't study for a test and he decided to cheat. But he came home from school and felt sick . . . didn't eat his dinner. He started feeling awful about himself . . . thinking maybe he was really bad. His dad asked what was wrong, and finally, he told him the truth. His dad made him call his teacher.

Source: The World Is Round Just Like an Orange (pp. 26–36). Glenview, IL: Scott Foresman, 1993. Reprinted by permission of Pearson Education, Inc.

The size of the group is also an important consideration. If a group is small, you have greater opportunity to listen to and interact with students. You can thereby personalize the support you offer to your students.

In Tessa's class, for example, she will have all students in her large fourth-grade-level group take part in the initial background setting and final discussion for each selection. She will individualize instruction by having her more independent learners (I), who tend to finish their reading faster, meet with their cooperative book club teams while others finish their reading. At the same time, Tessa will work with those students needing more guidance in this larger group (G), typically by working through some of the guided reading techniques described in Chapter 6.

Tessa will introduce a similar set of reading techniques to her smaller group(s) who are reading less-demanding text. At the same time, she will also focus on the development of print strategies (see Chapter 3) and vocabulary concepts (see Chapter 4). Her instruction will be responsive to the specific needs of group members.

There will also be discussions of the total class focusing on the theme of challenge in which subgroups of students will describe the new insights they have gained from their reading and writing. Students will draw not only from their reading instruction but also from their independent reading and writing, their content area reading, and the selection read as a part of reader's workshop.

Communicating Information

You will gain new insights through conversations with students, their parents, and professional colleagues. Such conversations will help you check the accuracy of what you are learning about your students. In this final section, we discuss ways you can learn and share knowledge with these three important groups.

• Talking with Students

Conversations with students are particularly informative. They let you learn how students see themselves as readers and writers; what their immediate and long-term goals are; and how they feel about reading, writing, and the classroom instructional program. It is through such conversations that you will gain your best insights into the feelings of students and their ideas about how you may help them most in developing their reading and writing strategies.

Conversations are usually most informative when they focus on specific activities. An approach we recommend is to meet with each student once every two or three weeks during the independent reading and writing period or a silent sustained reading period. Meetings should be more frequent with younger students.

Use the student's daily portfolio as the focus of your conversations. During this time, students will describe the reading they are doing at home and at school and tell you what they have particularly enjoyed, and why. They will also share drafts of their most recent writing so that you will be able to see the progress they have made. You may wish to have students reflect on their progress and to identify areas in which they will focus their attention.

On the basis of this conversation, the two of you can make joint decisions about what reports on their reading and samples of their writing should be placed in their permanent portfolios. Because these portfolios will be shared with parents, they should contain the samples that most clearly illustrate the progress students are making.

Meeting with Parents

Parent–teacher conferences typically create some degree of uneasiness, but this discomfort can be alleviated in several ways. First, try to establish relationships with parents from the beginning of the year. Some schools have a tradition of holding open house during the first month of school, which gives teachers the opportunity to describe their programs and allows parents to ask questions. If this is not the tradition in your school, an alternative is to send brief letters home to parents describing the activities on which you and the students are working. Invite phone calls and e-mails when parents have questions.

A second way is to plan for conferences with parents by gathering samples of their children's work that provide insight into the children's learning. You may wish to have children identify the work of which they are most proud, the areas in which they feel that they have made most progress, and ways in which they believe their parents could support their reading and writing work at home.

It is important to frame your comments about a child's work in objective terms, beginning with positive statements about the child's strengths, continuing with areas of concern, and ending with a statement about progress that has been made. Having examples of children's work is a powerful tool. For children still developing their skill with print, oral reading tapes may be useful. Written summaries of stories children have read can be used to illustrate their skill in reading comprehension and writing. These may also indicate the children's attitudes and enjoyment of reading. Children's work communicates much better than letter grades or summary comments because parents can see for themselves their children's strengths and weaknesses in reading and writing.

It is extremely useful to have children attend at least some of the conferences with parents so they can display their own work. When problems exist, it is helpful to have the child as a participant in the conference to consider alternative solutions. Planning for the conference by the child and teacher represents an authentic evaluation activity.

Conferring with Professionals

Teachers interact with specialists in related areas (psychologists, social workers, learning disability personnel, special educational professionals) in several ways. They frequently receive reports from other specialists concerning the academic achievement and abilities of their students; they attend staff conferences in which the placement of one of their students is being considered; on occasion, specialists observe children in the teachers' classrooms; specialists also work on school student performance and/or data analysis teams. In this section, we first discuss the unique insights of teachers concerning the learning of their students and how this information contributes to the decision-making process. Then we consider how the reports from specialists may provide further insight into the learning and adjustment of a child.

Participation in Staff Conferences. As a teacher, you have a unique role to play in staff conferences because you interact with your students on a day-in, day-out basis. That is, you have had the opportunity to observe your students over a long period of time as they interact with other children and engage in schoolwork. In terms of our earlier discussion, your knowledge of children is based on a highly valid set of experiences. How can you share your knowledge at a staff conference?

Like parents, other specialists appreciate judiciously selected samples of a child's work, particularly when these permit assessment of the student's progress over time. Samples of writing, for example, collected at three points during the year may reveal little progress, erratic changes, or considerable development. Similarly, tape recordings of a child's oral reading will enable other participants to appreciate the integration of his or her strategies for dealing with print. Written summaries of stories and answers to comprehension questions will let them judge the child's ability to comprehend and reason. The complexities of these behavioral samples provide a complementary richness to normative scores.

Equally important are your entries into your class portfolio. These are observations you make periodically as significant events occur. Taken together they yield insight into a child's adjustment and progress in the classroom.

To illustrate the contribution you can make at a staff conference, let us consider the comments Tessa made at a staffing for her student, Walter, in the middle of October. She brought his portfolio, which contained samples of his writing and a running record of his oral reading. In addition, she shared the entries she had made for Walter during the first months of school. They read as follows:

8/30 *Walter:*   Eager and attentive, but rarely volunteers to answer questions

9/13 *Walter:*   Read aloud from a trade book (second grade); showed good correction strategies

9/23 *Walter:*   A wonderful artist; works with Jason who helps him write his stories in exchange for illustrating Jason's work

10/5 *Walter:* Took running record on story his small group was reading; recognized most sight words, but had difficulty decoding two three-syllable words

From this variety of evidence, it is clear that Walter is adjusting well to the class and forming good relations with peers. Further, he seems to be responding well to instruction. On the basis of the conference, the team decided not to refer him for further assessment for special education placement.

Reports from Specialists. A specialist typically sees a student for a limited period of time for the specific purpose of evaluating his or her achievement and abilities. The evaluation is typically based on interviews and/or a variety of standardized and informal tests of adjustment, aptitude, and achievement. This form of assessment views the progress of a child normatively, in terms of what children, on average, typically know or can do. Unlike teachers who consider children's relationships to other children in their class or school, specialists use national samples as their frame of reference.

c a s e   9 . 2

Walter's Reading Progress

In order to consider the value of reports to teachers, we examine here a report that Tessa received from a reading specialist concerning Walter. As you will recall from Figure 9.6, Walter's test scores are fairly low (1.9 in vocabulary and 2.2 in comprehension). Last year he met with the lowest reading group. Tessa received the report the first week of September. The report, shown in Figure 9.8, includes diagnostic information on Walter's areas of reading strength and weakness, a description of the tutorial program in which he had participated the prior summer, and recommendations for further instruction.

p a u s e and r e f l e c t

Read the report shown in Figure 9.8. What do you learn about Walter's reading skill from this report? In what areas (skill with print, prior knowledge and vocabulary, and reading comprehension) does he need to receive instruction? As Walter's teacher, would you find this a useful report?

Tessa found this report to be useful in delineating the areas on which she would continue working with Walter. The results from the diagnosis were consistent with the results from his standardized tests. But after the diagnostic testing, he had received daily tutorial instruction for about six weeks. Thus, during the independent reading time, Tessa had him read some first-grade-level books. She was amazed at his fluency. He seemed

figure 9.8 • Walter's Reading Diagnostic and Instructional Report

Midwest College of Education Reading Center

Student's name: Walter Smith   Date of testing: 6/12–13

School: Hillside School   Date of instruction: 6/14–7/7

Grade: Entering grade 4   Reading Specialist: Kathleen Brown

Age: 9

INITIAL DIAGNOSIS

Walter was given the Basic Reading Inventory (Johns), which is a series of graded word lists and passages that are read orally and silently. After reading, he responded to literal and inferential comprehension questions. Parallel forms of these passages are also used to assess listening comprehension. From an analysis of oral reading and comprehension responses, the level at which Walter can read material independently, the level at which he needs instructional support, and the level at which he becomes frustrated by the material were determined. These results are summarized below:

	Independent	Instructional	Frustration
Oral Reading	1st	2nd	3rd
Silent Reading	1st	1st–2nd	2nd
Listening		4th	

On the passages he read orally, Walter experienced considerable difficulty with word recognition at the third-grade level although he was still able to comprehend. On the passages he read silently, he experienced some comprehension difficulty at the second-grade level and considerable difficulty at the third. Walter's strengths include his use of context to self-correct decoding errors as well as to derive meaning of unfamiliar vocabulary. He also refers to the text to find factual information he has forgotten. Yet, his listening comprehension is strong. Moreover, a definite strength is his positive attitude about reading and his willingness to persevere on difficult tasks. Walter's reading weaknesses include his poor sight word vocabulary and very slow rate of reading. His print strategies, particularly his ability to decode vowel sounds, are also weak (e.g., he read *men* as *man* and *tan* as *ten*). His weak comprehension is also of concern, although this may reflect his problems with print.

Walter was also given the Developmental Spelling Test (Morris & Perney, 1984), involving a list of 10 words which he was asked to write. This test was used to assess his awareness of the sound segments in words and his knowledge of the spelling patterns of English. His spellings included correct beginning and ending sounds, as well as the correct long vowels and appropriate short vowel substitutions. The results of this test suggest that he has knowledge of letter–sound associations that he is not yet able to apply during word identification.

TUTORIAL PROGRAM

Based on the results of diagnostic testing, goals were established to help Walter improve his reading in the following areas: sight vocabulary, fluency, decoding, and comprehension

figure 9.8 • Continued

strategies. To achieve these goals, several instructional approaches were followed: reading and rereading of easy materials, sorting short words on the basis of spelling patterns, sentence writing, and the K-W-L comprehension strategy.

Reading and rereading of easy materials. During each session Walter read a new predictable book and several previously read patterned books. This intense reading practice on material with which he experienced few word identification problems helped him to increase his sight vocabulary, improve his fluency, and increase his self-confidence and independence in reading.

Sorting words and sentence writing. Through the Word Sort, children become aware of the likeness and differences among words. Walter worked on words that included the following patterns: *ap, at, an, am,* and *ack.* He is now able to say how words are similar and to read words containing these patterns with various beginning consonant sounds, blends, and digraphs. Through composing sentences and writing some of the words involved, Walter became more aware of the sounds in words and their written representation.

Comprehension strategies. In the K-W-L strategy, the student brainstorms all he knows about a particular subject prior to reading a selection. He is then asked to list questions about what he would like to learn about the subject. Walter was able to assume control over these two strategies after about 10 instructional sessions. In working on his literal comprehension, the third step of K-W-L was employed: He was asked to formulate statements about what he had learned from reading the selection. Walter is most successful when he is asked to retell what he learned after each individual page; he is becoming able to generate a retelling that captures the overall idea of a section as well as individual facts.

PROGRESS AND RECOMMENDATIONS

Despite the short length of the program, Walter made definite progress in developing his sight vocabulary and fluency, in becoming more aware of the spelling patterns of words, and in becoming a more strategic comprehender. Walter needs further individual or small group work to continue his progress in these areas.

to have a fairly good knowledge of sight words and showed some facility with word identification. Walter's reading of selections from the third-grade basal was more labored and required considerable prior support. Perhaps because of his good listening comprehension, and with highly supportive instruction, he would be able to make progress reading this level of materials.

Tessa's experiences are not exceptional. As a teacher, you will be called on to provide information and your thoughts about some of the children in your class who may be experiencing difficulties either at home or at school. Your ability to be a good observer during class instruction will increase the value of your reports. ▪

summary

In this chapter we have focused on standardized tests, which we believe are a useful supplement to other information available to you about the reading of your students, particularly at the beginning of the year. In order to make good use of standardized test information, you must understand the advantages and problems with such tests and know how to interpret scores based on them.

Class portfolios provide ways to organize your own observations about your students' reading and writing. Records made on single days, when considered together, form patterns that can lead you to further awareness and searching. Such records are useful in tracing the progress of students, and in this capacity they complement other available assessment procedures.

Student portfolios provide ways for you to help your students organize and value their work. These records are particularly useful when you meet individually with your students to discuss their progress. They are also helpful in conferring with parents and other specialists.

The information you collect and organize will help you in making key instructional decisions. This includes the varieties and levels of materials that your students will read, how they will be paired or grouped together to accomplish their work, and the degree of support you will offer.

conclusion

Learning to diagnose the reading problems of students is not a simple process. This is because the process of learning to read is itself extremely complex, and there are important differences from one stage of reading development to another. We believe that you must understand the nature of this development in order to be an effective diagnostician. This means having an overview of the reading process and a thorough understanding of its component processes. Instead of providing a simple "cookbook" solution to problems, we have in this book attempted to build, step-by-step, a conceptual framework for viewing the component process of reading development: (1) print skill, (2) vocabulary and prior knowledge, and (3) reading comprehension. But it is not enough to understand how the three components work as separate entities. You must also understand how they combine to form a balanced and smoothly operating system—and to recognize when imbalances occur that interfere with effective literacy development.

One way we attempted to show the nature of these imbalances was through detailed case studies of students with various reading problems and teacher diagnoses of their problems. We carefully selected the cases to reflect major types of problems that students encounter as they attempt to establish a balance among the component processes of reading.

Just as we believe that students are active problem solvers responding to the demands of their instructional materials, so we believe that you as teachers must become active problem solvers as you learn to diagnose reading problems. To this end, we have focused on developing the observational skills you need for gathering evidence about reading and the interpretive skills you must have for making sense of the evidence. In presenting the case studies, we encouraged you to assume an active role in assessing the observational evidence, drawing conclusions, and deriving appropriate instructional recommendations. We included specific Pause and Reflect activities to encourage your active involvement and problem solving.

But skill in diagnosis can be acquired only if you go beyond this book, carrying out projects that build on the concepts and skills presented here. To this end, we included Try It Out activities to help you apply your newly acquired concepts to your teaching practice. This book will have been used most effectively if you undertook such projects as you read each chapter of the book. And this is just the beginning. The development of diagnostic skill is in many ways similar to the development of literacy skill. Just as your students need to undertake much contextual reading and writing to become proficient, so must you continue to study the reading and writing problems of your students in order to consolidate your diagnostic strategies.

Finally, we emphasize once again that the purpose of diagnosis is to create instruction that is responsive to the needs of students. If this last step is omitted, the diagnosis is an idle exercise. There are two prerequisites to effective instructional planning. One is to understand the strengths and difficulties of a student well enough that instruction is "on the mark." In this book we have attempted to provide the basis for such an understanding. The second—and more difficult, perhaps—is to create instruction that captures the interest and energy of students and leads them to assume an active role. Accordingly, many of the instructional procedures we have described are designed to create active learners. As in the development of diagnostic skill, you will become more expert in providing high-quality instruction through experimentation with these and other procedures.

try it out

1. Collect standardized test and portfolio information from your class and analyze it. How does it match with the grouping and organizational decisions you've made during the year? If you are not in your own classroom, analyze someone else's data and then compare it with the teacher's perceptions.

2. Reflect on your own class or interview a teacher. Choose several children whose standardized test results are a poor match for their portfolio performance. Can you determine why the test results did not reveal true performance?

3. **For Your Teaching Portfolio:** Take the standardized tests administered in your school or district and record your observations. Then examine the manual that describes reliability and validity. Critique content, format, and validity. See if you can locate a review of the measure in *Mental Measurements Yearbook* (Buros, 1938–1985) or an electronic search that leads you to journals and other resources. Retain this to help you interpret standardized test performance for yourself and for parental communication.

4. **Student Portfolio Ideas:** Where appropriate, share your class portfolio results with individual students and use them for planning goals. Include goal plans in their portfolios.

for further reading

Lipson, M. Y. (2006). Intelligent action as the basis for literacy instruction in classroom and clinical settings. *Research at work* (pp. 394–402). New York: Guilford and Newark, DE: International Reading Association.

Paris, S. G., Calfee, R. C., Filby, N., Hiebert, E. H., Pearson, P. D., Valencia, S. W., & Wolf, K. P. (1992). A framework for authentic literacy assessment. *The Reading Teacher, 46*(2), 88–98.

Describes a framework for examining seven critical dimensions of literacy programs in schools and districts.

Wixson, K. K., & Carlisle, J. F. (2005). The influence of large-scale assessment of reading comprehension on classroom practice: A commentary. In S. G. Paris & S. Stahl (Eds.), *Children's reading comprehension and assessment* (pp. 395–405). Mahwah, NJ: Erlbaum.

Dolch Basic Sight Vocabulary

a _____	call _____	funny _____
about _____	came _____	gave _____
after _____	can _____	get _____
again _____	carry _____	give _____
all _____	clean _____	go _____
always _____	cold _____	goes _____
am _____	come _____	going _____
an _____	could _____	good _____
and _____	cut _____	got _____
any _____	did _____	green _____
are _____	do _____	grow _____
around _____	does _____	had _____
as _____	done _____	has _____
ask _____	don't _____	have _____
at _____	down _____	he _____
ate _____	draw _____	help _____
away _____	drink _____	her _____
be _____	eat _____	here _____
because _____	eight _____	him _____
been _____	every _____	his _____
before _____	fall _____	hold _____
best _____	far _____	hot _____
better _____	fast _____	how _____
big _____	find _____	hurt _____
black _____	first _____	I _____
blue _____	five _____	if _____
both _____	fly _____	in _____
bring _____	for _____	into _____
brown _____	found _____	is _____
but _____	four _____	it _____
buy _____	from _____	its _____
by _____	full _____	jump _____

just ____	pretty ____	those ____
keep ____	pull ____	three ____
kind ____	put ____	to ____
know ____	ran ____	today ____
laugh ____	read ____	together ____
let ____	red ____	too ____
light ____	ride ____	try ____
like ____	right ____	two ____
little ____	round ____	under ____
live ____	run ____	up ____
long ____	said ____	upon ____
look ____	saw ____	us ____
made ____	say ____	use ____
make ____	see ____	very ____
many ____	seven ____	walk ____
may ____	shall ____	want ____
me ____	she ____	warm ____
much ____	show ____	was ____
must ____	sing ____	wash ____
my ____	sit ____	we ____
myself ____	six ____	well ____
never ____	sleep ____	went ____
new ____	small ____	were ____
no ____	so ____	what ____
not ____	some ____	when ____
now ____	soon ____	where ____
of ____	start ____	which ____
off ____	stop ____	white ____
old ____	take ____	who ____
on ____	tell ____	why ____
once ____	ten ____	will ____
one ____	thank ____	wish ____
only ____	that ____	with ____
open ____	the ____	work ____
or ____	their ____	would ____
our ____	them ____	write ____
out ____	then ____	yellow ____
over ____	there ____	yes ____
own ____	these ____	you ____
pick ____	they ____	your ____
play ____	think ____	
please ____	this ____	

Blachowicz Informal Phonics Survey

This informal survey gives subtests for many sound–symbol correspondence patterns. It is rarely useful or advisable to give the *whole* test to any student. It should be used after an oral reading diagnostic test to pinpoint those areas that look like possible weaknesses.

Because the test utilizes nonsense syllables, some mispronunciations will be artifacts of the test. Often a child will try to make a nonsense syllable into a real word. All conclusions from this test should be verified in real reading situations. For example, if you think a student has done badly on *bl-*, you might want him or her to read a paragraph containing words like *blue, blend, blood,* and so forth. Never lose sight of the fact that phonics used in context is the important tool.

General Guidelines

1. The subtests get harder. For very young children, start at subtest 1. For most students, subtest 3 is a good starting point.
2. For subtests 3 and up, always write down what the student says when he or she mispronounces a stimulus item. This is essential for final analysis.
3. Stop whenever the student shows signs of distress. If you want to give other subtests, do them another day.
4. Always tell the students what you are doing and why. Be sure to tell them that THESE ARE NOT REAL WORDS and that they are not expected to know them all.
5. Give praise and encouragement whenever you can. Start a child on an easy subtest to give success. If a student flounders, you can go back to an easier subtest to end with success.
6. Try to modify the materials to make them more usable. You might want to cut and mount the subtests for the student's copy. This makes the order less obvious.
7. A most effective use of the material is to turn it into a board game. Place the stimulus items on index cards, and have the student draw cards and move spaces for each one correctly pronounced. You can put different subtests on different colored cards for easy use and sorting.

Source: Blachowicz Informal Phonics Survey. C. L. Z. Blachowicz (Unpublished assessment device). Evanston, IL: National College of Education, 2001. Reprinted by permission.

Analysis

1. Look for patterns.
2. Test your conclusions with real reading materials.
3. Try to break down the task into its parts when conclusions don't add up. For example, if the student could recognize *up,* knows the consonant sound associated with *t,* but could not pronounce *tup,* perhaps he or she cannot blend sounds.
4. Keep a record of your findings to check out in the real-life reading situation. Remember, testing is always artificial.

Test Items

1. *Naming upper- and lowercase letters.* Circle those not known when pointed to.

a	S	q	I	R	h	k
s	J	d	A	f	O	U
l	w	z	Q	v	X	B
n	H	T	b	e	G	P
V	N	j	y	K	w	f
F	r	Z	x	l	m	O
E	o	C	D	P	g	A
i	M	t	u	c	Y	d
w	p					

2. *Sound-values of isolated consonant.* Point to each letter and ask the child to tell you what sound "this letter makes" or to give you a word that starts with this letter. Circle those not known.

b	c	k	j	g	t	v	d	m	h	r
p	z	I	f	n	s	u	w	y	q	u

3. *Short-vowel phonograms blended with initial consonants.* Check to see if the student knows the following simple sight word phonograms: *up, it, am,* and *on.* (If they are not known, try to train the student to recognize them, or choose phonograms the child does know.) Point to each item, and have the child pronounce it. If an item is mispronounced, write the mispronunciation above it for later analysis.

Mup	zam	yup	sam	con	rit	gam	kno
Dup	vit	hon	quam	bup	pon	wup	jam
Nit	fup	lam	yup				

4. *Consonant blends plus short-vowel phonograms.* This and all subsequent tests follow the same procedure as test 3. Have the child pronounce each item, and write in any mispronounced words.

brup	scon	plit	skam	slup	twit	dron
gram	swis	spup	fron	blit	snam	glup
clam	trit	flon	smam	slup	cron	prit

5. *Consonant digraphs plus short-vowel phonograms.*

chup	shon	thup	whit	pham	shup	whon
chon	thon					

6. *VCe pattern plus initial consonants.*

dake	mime	fole	tule	mede	tate	fope
dute	dite	sede				

7. *Long-vowel digraphs.*

leat	mied	boad	tay	ley	moe	teef
buel	moes	lail	bie	toat	meep	tay
lue	bain	leam				

8. *R-controlled vowels.*

mer	tir	hur	dir	fer	dar	mor	tur
sar	dor	bur					

9. *Ending-blend phonograms.*

selt	mext	basp	mick	dunch	mulk	tand
goft	sunch	mimp	kent	munk	jung	dulf
baft	dilk	nolt	satch	fodge	hink	disp
folt	namp	dist	gelf	mond	bant	ting
dast	holf	fask	rept	felp	nold	hent

10. *Ending-digraph phonograms.*

that	fash	nich	baph	dith	sosh	tach	ruph

11. *Alternate sounds of c and g.*

gap	gity	cot	came	gend	cend	git	cim

12. *Three-letter blends.*

splan	chrin	thrup	schon	strat	scrup
squit	spron	chris	thrat	scris	spron
strup	splup	squis	schan	shrat	

13. *Diphthongs.*

dow   doy   dound   doint   doy   doud   oil   down

14. *Silent letters.*

talf	tamb	demn	falm	knop	wrid	gnap
knop	ghat	word	gnom	phot	pnip	psin

15. *Multisyllabic words.* Show division points in responses with slash marks.

buffle	hotrat	rewant	sunting	fendle
inserg	unpottle	rembat	rebark	bullingable
minkfall	refizwissing	wenkerfil	mendle	submarkable
raction	bunded	madsion		

Complete Records of Performance on an IRI: James

Analytical Reading Inventory, Word Lists

Level 3	Flash	Untimed	Level 4	Flash	Untimed
1. beginning	✓		1. worm	✓	
2. thankful	✓		2. afford	afforded	✓
3. written	✓		3. player	✓	
4. reason	✓		4. scientific	✓	
5. bent	✓		5. meek	✓	
6. patient	✓		6. rodeo	✓	
7. manage	✓		7. festival	✓	
8. arithmetic	✓		8. hillside	✓	
9. burst	✓		9. coward	✓	
10. bush	✓		10. boom	✓	
11. gingerbread	✓		11. booth	✓	
12. tremble	treb–	✓	12. freeze	✓	
13. planet	✓		13. protest	✓	
14. struggle	✓		14. nervous	✓	
15. museum	✓		15. sparrow	✓	
16. grin	✓		16. level	✓	
17. ill	✓		17. underground	✓	

Source: Analytical Reading Inventory, 7th ed., by M. L. Woods & A. J. Moe. 2003. Word lists and questions reprinted by permission of Pearson Education, Inc. Passages reprinted by permission of original sources.

Analytical Reading Inventory, Word Lists (*Continued*)

	Flash	Untimed		Flash	Untimed
18. alarm	✓		18. oxen	✓	
19. cool	✓		19. eighty	✓	
20. engine	ing-✓		20. shouldn't	✓	
Number correct	95	100	Number correct	95	100

Level 5	Flash	Untimed	Level 6	Flash	Untimed
1. abandon	✓		1. seventeen	✓	
2. zigzag	✓		2. annoy	✓	
3. terrific	✓		3. dwindle	dind-	✓
4. terrify	✓		4. rival	✓	
5. plantation	✓		5. hesitation	✓	
6. loaf	✓		6. navigator	✓	
7. hike	✓		7. gorge	✓	
8. relative	✓		8. burglar	✓	
9. available	✓		9. construction	✓	
10. grief	✓		10. exploration	✓	
11. physical	✓		11. technical	✓	
12. commander	Commanded	✓	12. spice	✓	
13. error	✓		13. spike	✓	
14. woodcutter	✓		14. prevail	prev	
15. submarine	✓		15. memorial	✓	
16. ignore	✓		16. initiation	✓	
17. disappointed	✓		17. undergrowth	✓	
18. wrestle	✓		18. ladle	ladle✓	
19. vehicle	vick	✓	19. walnut	✓	
20. international	in-ter	✓	20. tributary	tri-✓	
Number correct	90	100	Number correct	95	100

Analytical Reading Inventory, Form A, Level 6
(192 Words, 12 Sentences)

- ### Examiner's Introduction

Dr. Charles Drew overcame many obstacles to become a remarkable black American surgeon. Dr. Drew, who died in an auto crash at the age of forty-six, lived a life of dedication and kindness. The following information was derived from a book entitled *Black Pioneers of Science and Invention,* by Louis Haber.[1]

"Thousands of people are dying on the battlefields from loss of blood," $\underline{5}$

said Dr. Charles Drew. "I must give(my) time to solving the problems of blood   /

trans fer
~~transfusion~~."   /

© physics
~~Physicians~~ had studied blood transfusion for years. However, they had   /

met with many difficulties because the whole blood spoiled within days, and

the matching of blood types was time-consuming. Nevertheless, Dr. Drew

palsma
found there were fewer problems if ~~plasma~~, instead of whole blood, was used   /

palsma
in transfusion. ~~Plasma~~, the liquid part of the blood without the cells, could be   /

stored much longer and made the matching of blood types unnecessary.

palsma
Anybody could be given ~~plasma~~, and this was important on the battlefields of   X O *

World War II.

In 1940 the Blood Transfusion Association set up a program for war-
palsma
torn France. Dr. Drew asked them to send ~~plasma~~ rather than whole blood.   X O

But, it was started too late since France had fallen into the hands of the

enemy.

Later, when Great Britain suffered heavy losses from air raids, Dr. Drew
palsma
was asked to run a program called "~~Plasma~~ for Britain." He organized the   X O

entire project, and thousands of Americans gave blood to help the British.

* *Miscues occurring more than twice were not counted.*

___
[1]Excerpt from *Black Pioneers of Science and Invention,* copyright © 1970 by Harcourt, Inc., reprinted by permission of the publisher.

Errors : $5/192$ = 3%

Comp: $8/8$ = 100%

Rate : 96 sec = 1.6 min

192 words / 1.6 min = 120 w/m

• Comprehension Questions and Possible Answers

✓ **1.** What was the area of Dr. Drew's major work?
(blood transfusion) *blood — transfusions*

✓ **2.** What is meant by the word *difficulties*?
(problems) *problems*

✓ **3.** Why did Dr. Drew decide to devote his time to solving the problems of blood transfusion?
(Thousands were dying on the battlefields of World War II.)
because of men dying— World War II

✓ **4.** What is *plasma*?
(the liquid portion of the blood without cells)
part of blood - not cells

✓ **5.** In 1940 what program was organized to aid war-torn France?
(Blood Transfusion Association)
Blood Transfusion Program — No, Association

✓ **6.** What is meant by the phrase "fallen into the hands of the enemy"?
(France had lost battles to the enemy.)
You lose a battle to the enemy.

✓ **7.** Why did Americans give blood to help their British neighbors?
(Britain had suffered heavy losses from air raids.)
Because air raids killed lots of them

✓ **8.** What is said in this story that makes you think more people survived injuries on the battlefield because of Dr. Drew's work in blood transfusion?
(Stated: Plasma could be stored longer; with plasma, blood typing was unnecessary; anybody could be given plasma.)

*There were fewer problems with plasma —
it didn't spoil as easy as blood.*

Retelling: This doctor, Drew was his name, discovered plasma. Because it didn't spoil as easy as blood, it was better for transfusions — and blood types didn't have to match. It was used during World War II, not in France because it was too late, but in Britain for air raid victims

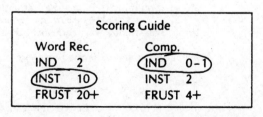

Scoring Guide	
Word Rec.	Comp.
IND 2	IND 0-1
INST 10	INST 2
FRUST 20+	FRUST 4+

Analytical Reading Inventory, Form A, Level 7 (262 Words, 14 Sentences)

• Examiner's Introduction

S. E. Hinton wrote a very sensitive book called *The Outsiders*,[2] showing the loyalties teenagers in gangs have toward one another. In this passage, Johnny is in serious trouble, and his friends, Ponyboy and Dally, prefer to stick by him until he can decide how best to solve his problem. Please read a retelling of one of the incidents from this memorable book.

13

While he had been hiding out for the past five days, Johnny had given serious thought to the whole mess. He had decided to return home, turn *2* himself in to the police, and take the consequences of his crime. Being only sixteen, he was too young to have to run away for the rest of his life. He knew */* the fight had been in self-defense, but the fact still remained that he had killed another person, and the thought of that miserable night in the city */* park sent Johnny into a terrifying panic. */*

He told Dally and Ponyboy of his decision, and now Dally reluctantly began the long drive home. Dally had gone to jail before, and this was one wretched experience he did not want his friend to have to endure. *3*

As they reached the top of Jay Mountain, Dally slammed on the brakes! */* The old church where Johnny and Ponyboy had been hiding was in flames! Ponyboy and Johnny bolted from the car to question a bystander who ex- */* plained that they were having a school picnic when the church began to burn. *2*

Suddenly, the crowd was shocked to hear desperate cries from inside! Ponyboy and Johnny ran into the burning church, and the boys lifted the children one by one through a window to safety. Chunks of the old roof were already beginning to fall as the last child was taken out. Ponyboy leaped through the window, vaguely hearing the sound of falling timber. Then, as he */* lay coughing and exhausted on the ground, he heard Johnny's terrifying scream!

---

[2]Hinton, S. E. (1967). *The Outsiders*. New York: Viking.

Errors: $^{13}/262 = 5\%$
Comp: $^7/8 = 88\%$
Rate: 150 sec = 2.5 min
262 words/2.5min = 105 w/m

• Comprehension Questions and Possible Answers

✓ **1.** What difficult conflict did Johnny have to solve?
(He had committed a crime, and he had decided to turn himself in to the police or to run away.) *whether to go home and turn himself in or stay out.*

✓ **2.** What is meant by the phrase, "take the consequences"?
(take the punishment for his crime) *he would take whatever punishment they gave him.*

✓ **3.** Where did the crime take place?
(in the city park) *in New York. (James was familiar with the book.)*

✓ **4.** Why were Dally and the boys returning home?
(Johnny had decided to return home and turn himself in.)
So Johnny could turn himself in.

✓ **5.** Why did Dally slam on the brakes?
(He saw the burning church.) *because the church was burning.*

✓ **6.** How did the boys get the children out of the burning church?
(lifted them through the window) *They ran in and the roof was caving in — the boy jumped out the window with the children.*

✗ **7.** What is meant by the word *vaguely*?
(not clearly defined, unclear) *D.K.*

✓ **8.** What is said in the story that makes you think Johnny thought he should turn himself in?
(Stated: He said that he was too young to run and hide for the rest of his life; the fact still remained that he had killed another person, and this was apparently something he felt he couldn't live with.)
He was running and hiding and things and he just didn't want to stay away from people and be afraid of everyone.

Scoring Guide	
Word Rec.	Comp.
IND 2–3	IND 0–1
INST 13	INST 2
FRUST 26+	FRUST 4+

Analytical Reading Inventory, Form A, Level 8 (286 Words, 15 Sentences)

• Examiner's Introduction

Witch-hunts took place in England back in the 1600s. The following information was derived from an article entitled "East Anglican and Essex Witches," from *Man, Myth, and Magic: An Illustrated Encyclopedia of the Supernatural.*

Witch-hunts were common in ^the^ seventeenth-century England. The mere $\frac{22}{1}$

presence of a witch-hunter in a village caused such fear among the people

that children would even denounce their parents.

© ~~Belee~~ ~~Belief~~ in magic was common in those days. Perhaps some of the victims   /

of these hunts did think themselves guilty of witchery, but history has proven

that the majority of men and women accused and tortured by witch-hunters

© put
were ~~but~~ poor, defenseless victims of the times.   /

One of the best-known methods ~~for~~ ^of^ the detection of@ witch was the   2

© orderly
"swimming test." In this ~~ordeal~~ the suspect was dragged into a pool or stream   /

suspect'
after he was already tired from torture and fear. If the ~~suspect~~ floated to the   /

top(he)was found guilty, and long pins were plunged into his body in search of   /

devil
the ~~devil's~~ marks. If he sank to the bottom, he was presumed innocent.   /

1945
In ~~1645~~ a man who titled himself, Witchfinder General Matthew Hop-   /

© of   ragging
kins, led a severe and cruel hunt. Because a civil war was ~~raging~~ in England at   2

© tense
the time, ~~tensions~~ and fears were common among the people. The time was   /

prosecution
ripe for ~~persecution~~.   /

At
~~In~~ that same year Hopkins imprisoned as many as 200 persons, all   /

and
charged with witchcraft. Among eighteen of those who died by hanging ~~was~~   /

© and
one John Lowes, a seventy-year-old clergyman who had been accused of   /

the   © inter
witchcraft by ~~his~~ congregation. After undergoing ~~intolerable~~ torture, the old   2

a leggled
man admitted ownership of an evil spirit which he ~~allegedly~~ ordered to sink a   /

ship. No one bothered to check out the existence of such a vessel or to ask

© an   © over
about ~~any~~ reported sinkings on that day, and he was hanged ~~after~~ reading his   2

own burial service.

Errors: 22/286 = 8%
Comp: 5/8 = 62.5%
Rate: 188 sec = 3.13 min
      286 words / 3.13 min = 91 w/m

• Comprehension Questions and Possible Answers

✓**1.** What commonly happened in seventeenth-century England?
(witch-hunts) *they had trials of bewitched*

✓**2.** According to this passage, what has history proven about witch-hunts?
(Most of the men and women accused and tortured for being witches
were but poor and defenseless people.) *that there really is no such
thing as witchcraft.*

✗ **3.** Why would children even denounce their parents as witches?
(The mere presence of a witch-finder caused such fear among the people
and children.) *if their parents got mad at them and accused
them and told.*

✓ **4.** What is meant by the phrase, "method of detection"?
(way of finding something out) *it's a test to see if a person's
a witch or evil*

✓ **5.** In seventeenth-century England, why was the time ripe for persecution?
(A civil war was raging, causing tension and fear.) *a civil war*

✗ **6.** What is meant by the word *allegedly*? *he said he would sink a ship*
(asserted to be true or exist but not proven) *and the people thought
he was a witch because they got no report.*

✗ **7.** What did John Lowes allegedly do?
(owned an evil spirit which sank a ship) *he was the guy who committed
people to death was in the witch hunts.*

✓ **8.** What is implied in the story that makes you think the swimming test
was unjust?
(Unstated: If the accused person sank, thus being proven innocent, he or
she was probably dead from drowning.) *If they weren't a witch, they
would die anyway. If they were innocent, they would die anyway.*

Scoring Guide			
Word Rec.		Comp.	
IND	3	IND	0–1
INST	15	INST	2
FRUST	30+	FRUST	4+

Analytical Reading Inventory, Form A, Level 9 (339 Words, 18 Sentences)

• Examiner's Introduction

This selection, based upon information from two articles appearing in a 1973 issue of *Plain Truth,* entitled "Who's That Polluting My World?" and "How One Town Solves Pollution and Saves Water," describes some interesting facts concerning pollution and its control.

"This lake is all treated sewer water," the old gentleman murmured in admiration. The old man sat on a bench as close to the bank as possible with his elbows resting on his knees while gazing at the rippling water. The breeze sweeping across the lake caused the sailboats to glide about with amazing ease.

"We are making great ecological strides," he thought to himself. He knew well the story of this remarkable lake nestled in the foothills of southern California. He swelled with pride to recall the wise choice the Santee citizens had made when they elected not to join the metropolitan sewage system where the waste would have been discharged into the Pacific with only inadequate primary treatment. Rather, the residents constructed their own sewage facility, reclaiming the sewer water, thus extending their own supply to provide basic needs and clean recreational extras.

"This is probably the only city park in the world which is built just yards downstream from a sewer plant," the gentleman thought. He leaned forward scooping up a handful of water. "This lake is more sanitary than most natural streams."

It has taken ingenious foresight to make this unprecedented plan viable. Its resourcefulness lay in the fact that clean water provided not only lucrative recreational facilities, but the sewage waste solids furnished marketable soil conditioners and plant fertilizers.

As the old gentleman arose he caught sight of paper trash carelessly
⟵
         content   © charged
tossed beside the shore. His ~~contented~~ expression ~~changed~~ to one of concern. 2
                                    discharged
He already knew that twenty million tons of paper are ~~discarded~~ each year in 1
                       © thirty
the United States representing a net loss of 340 million trees to the envi- 1
                                  © needle
ronment. The gentleman shook his head to think of this ~~needless~~ waste. He 1

knew the United States comprises only 6 percent of the world's population,
the
yet ~~its~~ citizens consume 30 percent of the world's total energy output, only to 1

waste half of it. The old gentleman shuddered at these thoughts as he picked

up the discarded paper and placed it into the trash container.

Errors: 24/339 = 7%

Comp: 2/8 = 25%

Rate: 234 sec = 3.90 min

      339 words / 3.9 min = 87 w/m

• Comprehension Questions and Possible Answers

X **1.** What is the main idea of this passage?
(We are making progress in pollution control, but still there is needless
waste.) *how many people think bad thoughts about pollution.*

X **2.** What is meant by the phrase *inadequate primary treatment*?
(insufficient water treatment) *does not give good treatment to the water*

✓ **3.** Where is this remarkable lake?
(in Santee in southern California) *in a city park — in California*

X **4.** What happened when the Santee citizens constructed their own sewage
facility?
(It provided basic needs and clean recreational extras.)
to stop pollution and sewage from going into the lake

X **5.** What is meant by the phrase *an unprecedented plan*?
(one not done before)
it wasn't given to them — it wasn't stated to them

X **6.** How much of the world's total energy does the United States use?
(30 percent) *350%*

✓ **7.** Why did the old gentleman's expression change when he got up from the bench?

(He caught sight of paper trash carelessly tossed beside the shore.)

He saw a piece of paper and it kills the beauty and the trees around the lake

✗ **8.** What is said in the story that makes you think the Santee plan to reclaim sewage water was an ingenious and well thought-out ecological one?

(Stated: The clean water provided not only lucrative recreational facilities, but the waste solids furnished marketable soil conditioners and plant fertilizers.)

He would stop pollution going into the lake.

Scoring Guide	
Word Rec.	**Comp.**
IND 3–4	IND 0–1
INST 18	INST 2
FRUST 36+	(FRUST 4+)

Analytical Reading Inventory, Form B, Level 7 (234 Words, 15 Sentences)

• Examiner's Introduction

Dave's Song, a book by Robert McKay, is a very sensitive story about a young girl who finds out that she can learn to appreciate and care for someone quite different from other young adults in her class. Please read a retelling of some of the information from this memorable book.

Kate sat in her senior biology class, but she wasn't hearing a single word the teacher was saying since her mind was thoroughly preoccupied. She could only think about Dave and her date with him last Friday night.

The entire thing was so confusing and distracting that she kept glancing sideways to where he was sitting near the windows. He was by far the most handsome boy at Tylerton High. He was tall, strong, with shaggy hair, and brilliant blue eyes, but there was something very different about Dave Burdick which she found difficult to accept. She knew that he was independent, and at times he seemed actually defiant. She found this disturbing. He always neglected his appearance as if he didn't care what others thought. He was an excellent football player, probably the best in the entire school, but he quit the team. He was stubborn and belligerent, and he would argue with anyone over anything. He never hung around the other kids, so it seemed to her that he was a loner. He drove an old Ford pickup, which had chicken feathers and farm tools scattered all over the floor. Kate felt that he was more interested in raising chickens than in having friends. Yet, even knowing all of these things, there was something crazy going on in her mind. To her surprise she found Dave Burdick fascinating and quite to her liking.

Comp: 4½/8 = 56%
Rate: 126 sec = 2.1 min
        234 words/2.1 min = 111 w/m

• Comprehension Questions and Possible Answers

✓ **1.** Why was Kate confused and distracted?
(Dave was very different from her other friends but she still found that she liked him.) *cause she kept thinking about the last date she had with Dave*

✓ **2.** Why didn't Kate hear anything the biology teacher was saying?
(She was preoccupied.) *cause she was too interested in dreaming about Dave*

✗ **3.** What is meant by the word *independent*?
(not dependent upon others) *he's dedicated to work*

✓ **4.** What did Kate find disturbing about Dave?
(his defiant attitude) *he didn't care for other people.*

✗ **5.** What is meant by the word *belligerent*?
(hostile, waging war) *D.K.*

✓ **6.** What did Dave's truck have in it?
(chicken feathers and old farm tools) *chicken feathers and farm equipment*

✗ **7.** Why did Kate think Dave was a loner?
(because he never hung around other kids) *because he wouldn't talk at all—just sit around and think to himself.*

½ **8.** What is said in the story that makes you think Dave had a negative attitude?
(Stated: He seemed defiant, stubborn, belligerent.) *The one date he had with the girl — she said he was too much to himself. If anyone said something about him, he didn't care what they said about him.*

Retelling : *It's about this one girl saying about she was in class— she was sitting there dreaming about that one last dream that she had with Dave and she felt that he was the cutest boy in school — she saw how strong he was and she said he has furry hair and he was skinny and had shaggy hair and all — he was on the football team — he was the best one on the football team and he quit the team and he drove a pick-up truck that had feathers in the back of it. She knew that he was more interested in farming than he was in school.*

Scoring Guide			
Word Rec.		**Comp.**	
IND	2–3	IND	0–1
INST	13	INST	2
FRUST	26+	FRUST	4+

Analytical Reading Inventory, Form B, Level 6 (186 Words, 12 Sentences)

• Examiner's Introduction

Garret A. Morgan, a black American inventor, was born in 1877. He not only invented the first electric traffic signal but also other important inventions. The following information was derived from a book entitled *Black Pioneers of Science and Invention,* by Louis Haber.[3]

The explosion was horrible that tragic day in Cleveland, Ohio, in 1916. Thirty-two men were trapped in a tunnel 250 feet below Lake Erie. No one could enter the smoke-filled tunnel to rescue the survivors.

"Someone get Garrett Morgan to help those men down there," shouted a man from the crowd. "Morgan and his breathing device are the only chance those men have!"

Garrett Morgan and his brother quickly came to the aid of the men trapped in the tunnel. Morgan had invented what he called a "Breathing Device," later to be known as the *gas mask.* Two years before, Morgan's invention had been tested by filling an enclosed tent with the foulest, thickest smoke possible. Placing the device over his head, a man entered this suffocating atmosphere, stayed twenty minutes, and emerged unharmed! Later, using a poisonous gas in a closed room, another test also provided the same successful results.

Although not all lived, every man was brought to the surface by the brothers. It was Morgan's concern for safer working conditions that saved lives that day and in the years to come.

Comp: 6½/8 = 81%
Rate: 115 sec = 1.92 min
186 words/1.92 min = 97 w/m

---

[3]Excerpt from *Black Pioneers of Science and Invention,* copyright © 1970 by Harcourt, Inc., reprinted by permission of the publisher.

• Comprehension Questions and Possible Answers

✓ **1.** What did Garrett Morgan invent?
(gas mask — breathing device) *a gas mask*

✓ **2.** Where was the tunnel located in which the men were trapped?
(250 feet below Lake Erie) *Cleveland, Ohio - 250 feet down*

½ **3.** What happened as a result of the terrible explosion in Cleveland?
(thirty-two men were trapped) *gas filled the tunnel*

✓ **4.** What is meant by the phrase, "this suffocating atmosphere"?
(the air in the tent was without oxygen)
run out of air - can't breathe - you'll die

✓ **5.** What is meant by the word *device*?
(something intricate in design; a machine)
Something used to help someone — like a camera is a device.

✓ **6.** What happened to the man who stayed in the tent for twenty minutes?
(He emerged unharmed.) *he survived — he got out of it*
— he could breathe

✗ **7.** What was used to test the gas mask the second time?
(a poisonous gas) *smoke — I don't know*

✓ **8.** What is said in the story that makes you think Morgan cared for the safety of others?
(Stated: It was Morgan's concern for safer working conditions which saved lives that day.)

He came as fast as he could with the breathing thing —
and he invented it to save lives.

Scoring Guide	
Word Rec.	Comp.
IND 2	IND 0-1
INST 10	(INST 2)
FRUST 20+	FRUST 4+

Analytical Reading Inventory, Form B, Level 5 (197 Words, 12 Sentences)

• Examiner's Introduction

This is a story about Robyn Smith, who left a career as a movie star to become one of the first female jockeys. The following information was derived from an article appearing in *The Lincoln Library of Sports Champions*.

"I know that I was last in the race," announced Robyn Smith, "but I am determined to be the best woman jockey! I want to ride race horses!"

It was a rainy morning in 1969, and as Robyn stood outside talking to the trainer, Frank Wright, she was so dripping wet that water came running out of the top of her boots. Many people had doubts about Robyn's riding ability, but Wright was sure she could be a successful rider. He decided to give her a first big chance.

By December of that same year she had proven herself by placing fourth in a race. Robyn not only had skill as a jockey, but she also had a way with horses which made them run fast for her.

Soon, she became accepted by others as an excellent rider. She went on to highlight her career with a surprising victory riding a horse named North Star. This horse was known for being wild on the track, but Robyn was able to handle him. Together they outran a horse named Onion. This was a special victory for Robyn because later, in another race, Onion defeated the famous horse, Secretariat!

Comp: 8/8 = 100%
Rate: 108 sec = 1.8 min
197 words / 1.8 min = 109 w/m

• Comprehension Questions and Possible Answers

/ 1. What was Robyn Smith determined to be?
      (the best woman jockey) *the best woman jockey*

✓ 2. Why did water run out of the top of Robyn's boots?
      (because she was standing outside in the rain)
      She was in the rain

✓ 3. What did Frank Wright do for Robyn?
      (gave her a first big chance) *Gave her a chance to ride*

✓ 4. What is meant by the phrase, "proven herself"?
      (She showed that she could ride well.) *to show she could do it*

✓ 5. What did others think of Robyn when she proved her riding skill?
      (She was accepted as a good jockey.)
      thought she was a good jockey

✓ 6. What was North Star known for?
      (being wild on the track) *being wild and hard to handle*

✓ 7. Why was this a special victory for Robyn?
      (North Star defeated Onion; Onion defeated the famous horse Secretariat.) *because she beat the horse who later beat Secretariat*

✓ 8. What is said in the story that makes you think Robyn's trainer had confidence in her riding?
      (Stated: Wright was sure she could be a successful rider; she had a way with horses which made them run fast for her; she had skill as a rider.)
      Because he gave her a chance

Scoring Guide	
Word Rec.	Comp.
IND 2	IND 0–1
INST 9	INST 2
FRUST 18+	FRUST 4+

Analytical Reading Inventory, Form C, Level 8 (257 Words, 15 Sentences)

- ### Examiner's Introduction

The next selection you are to read is about vampires. At one time in our history vampires and other supernatural beings were believed to exist. The following information was derived from an article entitled "Vampires," from *Man, Myth, and Magic: An Illustrated Encyclopedia of the Supernatural.*

"I am . . . Dracula," murmured a black-caped, fanged-toothed, pointed-eared monster. "I never drink . . . wine," he declared as movie-goers sat petrified in their seats.

In 1931, a novel by Irish author Bram Stoker became vividly alive on the movie screen as thousands flocked to see this re-creation of the vampire superstition which dates back to the sixteenth century.

According to the novel, a vampire looks pale, lean, and has a death-like icy touch. His eyes gleam or flash red, his ears are pointed like those of a werewolf, and his fingernails are curled and sharp. Some tales describe him as skeletal and often dressed in a black costume. His limited diet of blood gives him a foul-smelling breath. Old legends depict him with only one nostril and a barbed tongue. These creatures have the power to change their form into a cloud of mist or a bizarre nocturnal animal.

Despite modern disbelief in vampires, during the seventeenth century many thought they existed. It was believed that once a person died he could possibly return as a vampire. A corpse was often fastened in its grave with pegs or iron skewers to prevent a potential vampire from escaping.

Since the vampire was dormant during the day, graves were examined for small holes through which the monster could escape. If a grave was discovered with such holes, vampire hunters would remove the body and destroy it. This procedure took place during the daytime hours and all the

hunters returned to their homes before sunset.

Comp: $\frac{7}{8}$ = 88%

• Comprehension Questions and Possible Answers

✓ 1. What is the main idea of this article?
(Belief in vampires existed in the 16th and 17th centuries.)
they used to believe in vampires

✓ 2. What are a vampire's eyes supposed to look like?
(gleaming or flashing red) *flash red*

✓ 3. What is meant by the phrase, "bizarre animal"?
(unique or strange) *strange*

✓ 4. How did old legends describe a vampire?
(one nostril and a barbed tongue) *one nostril [Anything else?]*
a funny tongue - a barb tongue

✗ 5. What is meant by the phrase, "barbed tongue"?
(a forked or pointed tongue) *D.K.*

✓ 6. Why were iron skewers used to fasten a corpse to its grave?
(to prevent it from escaping) *to stop it from getting away*

✓ 7. Why were the graves examined during the day?
(There was less danger as vampires slept during the day.)
the vampires slept then

✓ 8. What is said in this story that makes you think people in the 16th and
17th centuries believed in and feared vampires?
(Stated: They fastened corpses in their graves with iron skewers; they
searched graves for perforations and if holes were found they destroyed
the corpse.) *they went hunting for them*

Scoring Guide	
Word Rec.	Comp.
IND 3	IND 0-1
INST 15	INST 2
FRUST 30+	FRUST 4+

Analytical Reading Inventory, Form C, Level 9 (315 Words, 17 Sentences)

• Examiner's Introduction

Jean-Pierre Haller, a Belgian explorer and author, was born and raised in the Belgian Congo. Because his childhood playmates had been members of the Efé Pygmy society, he returned in 1957 to become an adopted member and assist them in their dramatic struggle for survival. The following information was derived from an article entitled "To Save a People," appearing in a 1975 issue of *The Plain Truth*.

A young Pygmy stood in the parching equatorial African sun. He stood but five feet tall and his stature was bent from hard labor. His skin was golden brown and his hair was short and curled tightly to his head. His feet were bare and his clothes tattered. His eyes had the dull stare of a man once proud and free, but now deprived of the will to maintain his own gentle life-style.

The Pygmies are central Africa's oldest known surviving people and in the 1930's about 35,000 proudly lived in the Itiru Forest of the eastern Congo, now called Zaire. By 1957 their population had fallen to 25,000.

During the fifties, the Pygmies' ancestral forest was wastefully chopped down by lumber industrialists, robbing them of the vegetation and game they depended upon for survival. Consequently, the people were forced into the blistering sun to which they were unaccustomed. Large plantations closed in on their environment. National parks and game reserves were established, but no land was set aside to aid the Pygmy societies in their struggle for survival. Tourists brought contagious diseases to which the Pygmies had no immunity, and as a result their population continued to decline.

In 1960 the Belgian Congo received political independence, becoming the nation of Zaire. This political change brought civil war for which the nonaggressive Pygmies were the first to suffer and their number rapidly dwindled to 15,000. They became victims of new burdens such as paying income taxes, being drafted into the Zaire army, further loss of cultural identity, and by 1975 their size numbered some 3,800.

The Pygmies have a warm and gentle life-style with a dignified moral code which forbids killing, lying, theft, devil worship, sorcery, disrespect for elders, and blasphemy. They do not engage in cannibalism, mutilation, ritual murder, intertribal war, initiation ordeals, or other cruel customs sometimes associated with equatorial Africa.

Comp: $6\frac{1}{2}/8 = 81\%$

• Comprehension Questions and Possible Answers

✓ 1. What is the main idea of this passage?
(This Pygmy tribe is facing near extinction.) *about how Pygmies were forced to become like our society*

✓ 2. Where is the Itiru Forest?
(eastern Congo, now called Zaire) *in Africa*

½ 3. What happened to the Pygmy society when their forests were chopped down?
(They were robbed of the vegetation and game they depended upon for survival.) *they weren't used to the sun beating down on them*

✓ 4. What is meant by the word *immunity*?
(condition of being able to resist a particular disease) *if a person isn't immune to a sickness, they'll probably get it*

✓ 5. What did tourists bring to the Pygmies?
(contagious diseases) *diseases*

✗ 6. What is meant by the phrase, "nonaggressive Pygmies"?
(nonhostile, nonwarlike) *you're not selfish, like someone who is crazy and always wanting something, they're nonaggressive*

✓ 7. In 1960, what happened when the Belgian Congo received political independence?
(civil war and new suffering for the Pygmies) *they had to pay taxes and were drafted into the army.*

✓ 8. What is said in this story that makes you think no one cared enough to protect the Pygmies' rights?
(Stated: Lumber industrialists wastefully chopped down the Pygmies' forests; parks and game reserves were set aside but no land was saved for the Pygmies.)

they had to move to the cities and countryside with people

Scoring Guide		
Word Rec.		Comp.
IND	3-4	IND 0-1
INST	18	INST 2
FRUST	36+	FRUST 4+

Assessment Instruments

Norm-Referenced Reading Tests

Name	Grades	Individual or Group	Time	What Is Assessed	Publisher
Stanford Diagnostic Reading Test, 4th ed.	K–13	Group	85–120 min.	Phonetic analysis, vocabulary, fluency, phonemic awareness, comprehension, reading strategies, retelling, attitudes	Pearson (800) 328-5999 www.pearsonassessments.com
Gates-MacGinitie Reading Tests, 4th ed.	K–12, adult	Group	55–100 min.	Reading survey test, emphasis on comprehension	Riverside Publishing (800) 323-9540 www.riverpub.com
Nelson-Denny Reading Test	9–16, adult	Group	35–56 min.	Progress in vocabulary comprehension & reading rate	Riverside Publishing (800) 323-9540 www.riverpub.com
CDRT (California Diagnostic Reading Test)	1–12	Group	2–2½ hours	Word analysis, vocabulary, comprehension, applications	CTB McGraw-Hill (800) 538-9547 www.ctb.com
DATA-2 (Diagnostic Achievement Test for Adolescents)	7–12	Individual	Varies	Spoken language ability & academic achievement including receptive vocabulary & grammar, expressive vocabulary & grammar, word ID, reading comprehension, math, spelling, writing composition	Pro-Ed (800) 897-3202 www.proedinc.com
GORT-4 (Gray Oral Reading Tests)	Age 6–18	Individual	20–30 min.	Measures growth in oral reading rate & accuracy, comprehension, provides a miscue analysis, overall ability	Pearson (800) 328-5999 www.pearsonassessments.com
Reading Progress Tests	Age 5–11	Both	50 min.	Early reading skills, comprehension	New Zealand Council for Educational Research www.acer.edu.au/products.edresources/500
Degrees of Reading Power Test	1–12	Group	Varies	Reading comprehension, holistic reading, links student reading ability to text difficulty	Questar Assessment, Inc. 1-800-800-2598 www.questarai.com
Brigance CBS-R Comprehensive Inventory of Basic Skills	PK–9	Both	Varies	Measures present level of performance or academic achievement and functional performance	Curriculum Associates, Inc. (800) 225-0248 www.curriculumassociates.com

Diagnostic Batteries

Name	Grades	Individual or Group	Time	What Is Assessed	Publisher
Brigance System II	PreK–9	Both	Varies	General knowledge, comprehension, speech & language, gross & fine motor skills, math, reading readiness, basic reading skills, manuscript writing	Curriculum Associates, Inc. (800) 225-0248 www.curriculumassociates.com
SAM (Skill Assessment Modules)	Adults (Levels A–M)	Both	Varies	Basic literacy skills	Wright Group/McGraw Hill Contemporary (800) 621-1918 www.mhcontemporarybooks.com
New Gap Test	2–5	Both	20 min.	Expressive language using the cloze technique reading comprehension	Academic Therapy Publications (800) 422-7249 www.academictherapy.com
McLeod Assessment of Reading Comprehension	2–5, 6–8	Both	15 min.	Reading comprehension by using cloze procedure	Arena Press (800) 422-7249 www.mcleod-educational.com
Measures of Academic Progress (MAP) *	K–2, 3–8	Both	Varies	Phonological awareness, phonics, number sense, computation, reading, language	Northwest Evaluation System (NWEA) (503)624-1951
Reading Power Essentials *	3–8	Both	Varies	Vocabulary, fluency, and word decoding for struggling readers	Questar Assessment www.questarai.com

Individual Diagnostic Battery

Name	Grades	Individual or Group	Time	What Is Assessed	Publisher
Woodcock-Johnson III Tests of Achievement 2000	Ages 2–90+	Individual	Varies, 35–65 min.	Academic achievement in reading, math, written language, & knowledge	Riverside Publishing (800) 323-9540 www.riverpub.com
Woodcock Diagnostic Reading Battery (WJ III DRB)	Ages 2–90+	Individual	50–60 min. 5–10 min. per subtest	Specific reading & reading-related strengths & weaknesses	Riverside Publishing (800) 323-9540 www.riverpub.com
Diagnostic Assessments of Reading (DAR) 2005, 2nd ed.	K–adult	Individual	untimed, appx. 40 min.	Word recognition, word analysis, oral reading, silent reading comprehension, spelling, word meaning	Riverside Publishing (800) 323-9540 www.riverpub.com
Hammill Multiability Achievement Test (HAMAT)	1–12	Individual	30–60 min.	Reading comprehension & word knowledge measured via cloze procedure; writing (spelling, punctuation, capitalization); math, knowledge of fact (basic science, social studies, history, and literature	Pro-Ed (800) 897-3202 www.proedinc.com
DAB-3 (Diagnostic Achievement Battery), 3rd ed.	Age 6–14	Individual	90–120 min.	Listening, speaking, reading, writing, & math; assesses global strengths & weaknesses	Pro-Ed (800) 897-3202 www.proedinc.com
GORT-D (Gray Oral Reading Tests-Diagnostic) GDRT-2	Age 6–13.11	Individual	45–60 min.	Specific abilities & weaknesses of oral reading based on the three major cueing systems of reading	Pro-Ed (800) 897-3202 www.proedinc.com
GSRT (Gray Silent Reading Tests)	Age 7–25	Both	Varies	Measures an individual's silent reading comprehension ability	Pro-Ed (800) 897-3202 www.proedinc.com
GORT-4 Oral Reading Tests, 4th ed.	Age 6–18	Individual	20–30 min.	Fluency and accuracy scores, comprehension, diagnosis of reading difficulties	Pro-Ed (800) 897-3202 www.proedinc.com

Name	Grades	Individual or Group	Time	What Is Assessed	Publisher
CTOBS-2 (Criterion Test of Basic Skills)	Age 6–11	Individual	15–20 min.	Letter recognition, letter sounds, blending, sequencing, common spelling patterns, multi-syllabic words, sight-word recognition	Academic Therapy Publications (800) 422-7249 www.academictherapy.com
Bader Reading & Language Inventory, 6th ed.	K–adult	Individual	Varies	Effectiveness of specific reading strategies, literacy difficulties, word recognition, spelling, phonics, expressive & receptive oral language, handwriting, written language expression, math	Prentice-Hall School Division (800)350-3693 www.prenticehall.com
TORC-4 (Test of Reading Comprehension), 4th ed.	1–12	Both	45 min. or less	Silent reading comprehension, rational vocabulary, sentence completion, paragraph construction, text comprehension, contextual fluency	Pro-Ed (800)897-3202 www.proedinc.com

Standardized Achievement Tests

Name	Grades	Individual or Group	Time	What Is Assessed	Publisher
Iowa Tests of Basic Skills (ITBS)	K–8	Group	30 min. or less per test	Reading, language arts, math, social studies, science, information sources	Riverside Publishing (800) 323-9540 www.riverpub.com
SAT9 (Stanford Achievement Test)	K–13	Group	260–290 min.	Reading, math, language, spelling, study skills, listening, science, social studies, environment; multiple choice & open-end questions	Pearson (800) 328-5999 www.pearsonassessments.com
CAT/5 (California Achievement Test)	K–12	Group	1½–5½ hours	Reading, math, language, spelling, study skills, science, social studies; draws on authentic literature & reflects life-like situations	CTB/McGraw-Hill (800) 538-9547 www.ctb.com
Terra Nova CTBS	K–12	Group	45 min.– 5 hrs 20 min.	Reading, language arts, math, science, social studies, word analysis, vocabulary, language mechanics, spelling	CTB/McGraw-Hill (800) 538-9547 www.ctb.com
Terra Nova Performance Assessments	3–12	Group	1–3 hours	Language arts, math, science, social studies; to be used independently or in conjunction with CTBS or CAT; measures broad objectives or integrated outcomes that cut across content areas	CTB/McGraw-Hill (800) 538-9547 www.ctb.com
Metropolitan Achievement Tests (MAT 8)	K–12	Group	105–225 min.	Reading, math, language, science, social studies; critical thinking in a realistic context	Pearson (800) 328-5999 www.pearsonassessments.com
DIBELS (Dynamic Indicators of Basic Literacy Skills)	K–6	Individual	10–15 min.	Early literacy–phonemic awareness, alphabet, fluency	www.dibels.uoregon.edu
Brigance IED-II (Inventory of Early Development)	Birth–7 years	Both	Varies	Diagnoses delays, disabilities, giftedness, provides present level of performance, guides instruction, supports alternate assessment needs	Curriculum Associates, Inc. (800) 225-0248 www.curriculumassociates.com
Brigance Early Childhood Screens	0–35 months, 3–5 years, K and 1st grade	Individual	10–15 min.	Diagnoses learning delays, giftedness in language, motor, self-help, social-emotional, & cognitive skills	Curriculum Associates, Inc. (800) 225-0248 www.curriculumassociates.com

Phonemic Awareness

Name	Grades	Individual or Group	Time	What Is Assessed	Publisher
Comprehensive Test of Phonological Processing (CTOPP)	K–24 years	Individual	30 min.	Phonological awareness, phonological memory, rapid naming	Pro-Ed (800) 897-3202 www.proedinc.com
TOPA (Test of Phonological Awareness)	Ages 5–8	Both	15–45 min.	Awareness of the individual sounds in words: initial sound—same, different, letter/sound; ending sound—same, different	Academic Therapy Publications (800) 422-7249 www.academictherapy.com
LAC-3 (Lindamood Auditory Conceptualization Test)	K–12	Individual	20–30 min.	Ability to discriminate one speech sound from another & to segment a spoken word into its phonemic units, multisyllable level of processing	Pro-Ed (800) 897-3202 www.proedinc.com
Phonological Awareness Test 2	K–4	Individual	40 min.	Segmentation of phonemes, phoneme deletion, & substitution, rhyme	Lingual Systems (800) 776-4332 www.linguisystems.com
Yopp-Singer Phoneme Segmentation Test	K–1	Individual	8 min.	Ability to isolate & pronounce individual phonemes in words	International Reading Association The Reading Teacher March 1995, Vol. 48, No. 6

Informal Reading Inventories

Name	Grades	Individual or Group	Time	What Is Assessed	Publisher
DRA-2 (Developmental Reading Assessment)	K–8	Individual	Varies	Book & print awareness, phonemic awareness, graphophonemic knowledge, oral reading, comprehension, written response	Pearson (800) 328-5999 www.pearsonassessments.com
SRI-2 (Standardized Reading Inventory)	Age 6–14	Individual	30–90 min.	Oral reading accuracy, silent reading, comprehension, & predictive comprehension	Pro Ed (800) 897-3202 www.proedinc.com
Flynt-Cooter Reading Inventory for the Classroom	1–9	Individual	Varies	Oral reading & analysis of miscues, silent reading comprehension, interest, & attitude	Pearson/Merrill Publishing (800) 328-5999 www.pearsonassessments.com
QRI-4 (Qualitative Reading Inventory)	K–8	Individual (parts can be whole class)	30–60 min.	Reading levels, considers prior knowledge, miscue analysis, retellings, text type, predictions	Allyn & Bacon/Pearson (800) 328-5999 www.pearsonhighered.com
Classroom Reading Inventory, 11th ed.	Primary to adult	Individual	Varies	Elementary—word recognition, listening capacity, spelling, comprehension, functional reading level; secondary school to adult—word recognition, comprehension	McGraw-Hill (800) 338-3987 www.ctb.com
Ekwall/Shanker Reading Inventory, 5/E, (ESRI)	K–9	Both	Varies	Oral & silent reading, listening comprehension, sight words, letter knowledge, phonics, interest survey	Allyn & Bacon/Pearson (800) 328-5999 www.pearsonhighered.com
Spadafore Diagnostic Reading Test (SDRT)	K–adult	Individual	30–60 min.	Word recognition, oral & silent reading comprehension, listening comprehension	Academic Therapy Publications (800) 422-7249 www.academictherapy.com
Stieglitz Informal Reading Inventory: Assessing Reading Behaviors from Emergent to Advanced (SIRI 3E)	1–9	Individual	20–30 min.	Reading levels, sight words, differences between a student's reading of narrative or expository text	Allyn & Bacon/Pearson (800) 328-5999 www.pearsonhighered.com

Name	Grades	Individual or Group	Time	What Is Assessed	Publisher
Analytic Reading Inventory (Woods & Moe), 8th ed.	K–12	Both	Varies	Level of word recognition, oral & silent reading performance, comprehension, reading potential	Allyn & Bacon www.allynbaconmerrill.com
Basic Reading Inventory (Johns), 10th ed.	PP–12	Individual	Varies	Reading using word lists & passages, reading levels, word reading, comprehension, listening	Kendall Hunt Publishing (800) 228-0810
Burns/Roe Informal Reading Inventory	PP–12	Individual	Varies	Reading levels, listening, examines miscues & comprehension	Riverside Publishing (800) 323-9540 www.riverpub.com
Diagnosing Reading Skills Through Passage Reading	PP–12	Individual	Varies	Comprehension, reading speed, vocabulary, strategies	National Reading Diagnostics Institute (630) 717-4221
Informal Reading Comprehension Placement Test (Edson & Insel)*	1–12	Individual	35–50 min.	Comprehension skills (computer based)	Educational Activities (800) 645-2796 www.edact.com

Word Identification Tests

Name	Grades	Individual or Group	Time	What Is Assessed	Publisher
WRAT-4 (Wide Range Achievement Test)	Age 5–95	Both	15 min. per subtest	Letter & word ID, spelling & letter production, math, reading, spelling, reading comprehension	Pro-Ed (800) 897-3202 www.proedinc.com
TOWRE (Test of Word Reading Efficiency)	Age 6–25	Individual	5–10 min.	Accuracy & fluency of word reading (both real words & nonwords)	Pro-Ed (800) 897-3202 www.proedinc.com
Differential Ability Scales: Word Reading Test II	Age 2–18	Individual	Varies	Ability to recognize & pronounce out-of-context words of increasing difficulty	Psychological Corp. (800) 228–1752 www.psychorp.com www.pearsonassessments.com

Early Reading

Name	Grades	Individual or Group	Time	What Is Assessed	Publisher
Developmental Tasks for Kindergarten Readiness–II (DTKR-II)	Age 4.6–6.2	Individual	20–30 min.	Child's skills & abilities as related to successful performance in kindergarten	Pro-Ed (800) 897-3202 www.proedinc.com
TERA-3 (Test of Early Reading Ability), 3rd ed.	Age 3.6–8.6	Individual	15–30 min.	Reading ability; measures knowledge of contextual meaning, alphabet, conventions	Pro-Ed (800) 897-3202 www.proedinc.com
TKFGRS (Test of Kindergarten/First Grade Readiness Skills)	Age 3.6–6	Individual	20 min.	Basic skills in reading, spelling, math, abilities & readiness for kindergarten & first grade	Academic Therapy Publications (800) 422-7249 www.academictherapy.com
Concepts about Print Test: Sand and Stone, No Shoes, Follow Me Moon (M. Clay)	Non-readers	Individual	Varies	Concepts about book orientation print, directionality, relationship between written & oral language	Heinemann (800) 793-2154 www.pearson.com
DRA2 (Development Reading Assessment)— Beavers	K–3	Individual	15–25 min.	Students' fluency & comprehension; supports Reading Recovery in the classroom	Pearson (800) 328-5999 www.pearsonassessments.com
ERSI (Early Reading Screening Instrument) (Morris)	K–1	Individual	15 min.	Early reading skills: alphabet, concept of word, phonemic awareness, word recognition	See article in IL Reading Council Journal (1998, Vol. 26, No. 2, pp. 30–40, Howard Street Tutoring Manual 1999). New York: Guilford.

Name	Grades	Individual or Group	Time	What Is Assessed	Publisher
PALS (Phonological Awareness & Literacy Screening), 1998	K–1	Both	Varies	Rhyme, beginning sound, letter sounds, letter ID, concept of word, word recognition	McGuffey Reading Center, U. of Va. (804) 982-2780 E-mail: adk3x@virginia.edu
Watch Me Read & Write Assessment Package (Butler)	K–3	Individual	Varies	Emerging literacy; uses running records observation guides, literacy continuum	Pearson (800) 328-5999 www.pearsonassessments.com
Illinois Snapshots of Early Literacy (ISEL)	K–2	Individual	20–30 min.	Determines early literacy development: letter recognition, story listening, letter/sound awareness, phonemic awareness, concepts about print, word recognition, developmental spelling, passage reading	The Technology Center for Teaching and Learning http://tctl.org/
Strategic Teaching and Evaluation of Progress (STEP)	K–3	Individual	Varies	Formative assessment provides information about reading strengths in a developmental spectrum: concepts about print, letter recognition, letter/sound awareness, running records, comprehension, writing, retelling, developmental spelling	Urban Education Institute 773-834-1136

Miscellaneous

Name	Grades	Individual or Group	Time	What Is Assessed	Publisher
TEWL-2 (Test of Early Written Language)	Age 3–11	Individual	30–45 min.	Ability to construct a story, mechanics of writing; normed	Pro-Ed (800) 897-3202 www.proedinc.com
TWS-4 (Test of Written Spelling)	1–12	Both	20 min.	Spelling; normed	Pro-Ed (800) 897-3202 www.proedinc.com
TOWE (Test of Written Expression)	Age 6.6–14.11	Both	20 min.	Essay writing, writing skills, achievement writing skills	Pro-Ed (800) 897-3202 www.proedinc.com
Reading Miscue Inventory: Alternative Procedures	K–adult	Individual	45–60 min.	Causes of miscues, quality of miscues, specific & repetitive problems	Richard C. Owen Publishers (800) 336-5588
Reading Style Inventory	1–adult	Both	Varies	Preferred learning styles	National Reading Styles Institute (800) 331-3117
Retrospective Miscue Analysis	Pre-school–adult	Individual	Varies	Helps readers to analyze their own miscues; uses a tape recorder	Richard C. Owen Publishers (800) 336-5588
STAR Reading (Accelerated Reader)*	1–12	Both	10 min.	Computer-adaptive assessment program to the Accelerated Reader; reading level	Renaissance Learning (800) 338-4204
Words Their Way Qualitative Spelling Inventory	K–8	Both	10–15 min.	Types of spelling errors; classifies skills into developmental spelling stages	Prentice-Hall School Division (800) 350-3693 www.prenticehall.com
Words Their Way Qualitative Spelling Inventory with English Learners (2009)	K–8	Both	10–15 min.	Types of spelling errors; classifies skills into developmental spelling stages	Prentice-Hall School Division (800) 350-3693 www.prenticehall.com
Degrees of Power Reading (DPR)*	Age 3–adult	Group	45–60 min.	Size of students' reading vocabulary by measuring understanding of words in natural contexts	Questar Assessments, Inc. (914) 277-4900 www.questarai.com

Name	Grades	Individual or Group	Time	What Is Assessed	Publisher
Test of Written Language-4 (TOWL-4)	Age 9–17.11	Both	60–90 min.	Components of writing through contrived & spontaneous formats	Pro-Ed, Inc. (800) 897-3202 www.proedinc.com
Stanford Writing Assessment Program	3.5–12	Group	50 min.	Descriptive, narrative, expository, & persuasive writing	Pearson (800) 328-5999 www.pearsonassessments.com
Written Language Assessment (Gill & Kirwin) WLA	Age 8–18	Both	20 min.	Essay writing quantitatively & qualitatively	Academic Therapy Publications (800) 422-7249 www.academictherapy.com
Spanish Reading Inventory (Johns)	PP–12	Both	Varies	Reading levels	Kendall Hunt Publishing (800) 228-0810
AIMSWeb Reading CBM*	K–8	Individual	1 min.	Reading Achievement based on the number of words read correctly	Pearson Clinical (866) 313-6194
SSSmart Content Area Reading Program*	4–8	Both	Varies	Assesses science, social studies, math, and reading knowledge, skills and strategies for textbooks	Questar Assessment, Inc. www.questarai.com
MAC II*	K–12	Both	Varies	Measures English proficiency in speaking, listening, reading, writing, and comprehension	Questar Assessment, Inc. www.questarai.com

Phonics

Name	Grades	Individual or Group	Time	What Is Assessed	Publisher
Roswell-Chall Screening Tests (Auditory Blending Test, Diagnostic Reading Test of Word, Analysis Skills)	K–4	Both	10 min.	Phonemic awareness, word analysis, word recognition, yields qualitative & quantitative results	Educators Publishing Service, Inc. (800) 225-5750 www.epsbooks.com
Phonics Surveys (Assessing Reading: Multiple Measures for K–Eighth Grade—Consortium on Reading Excellence)	K–8	Individual	10–15 min.	Phonics & phonics-related skills	Academic Therapy Publications (800) 422-7249 www.academictherapy.com
Linksman Phonics Diagnostic Test	K–adult	Individual	Varies	Letter–sound relationships, reading multisyllabic words, word parts	National Reading Diagnostics Institute (630) 717-4221

Resources for Leveling Books

Fountas, G. S., & I. Pinnell (1999). *Matching books to readers*. Portsmouth, NH: Heinemann. Contains ideas for building, organizing, and managing a leveled book collection; descriptors for the levels in the Fountas and Pinnell text gradient; and an extensive list of leveled book titles.

www.hubbardscupboard.org

www.home.comcast.net

www.registration.beaverton.k12.or.us

references

Adams, M. J. (1990). *Beginning to read: Thinking and learning about print.* Cambridge, MA: MIT Press.

Afflerbach, P. (2005). National Reading Conference policy brief: High stakes testing and reading assessment. *Journal of Literacy Research, 37,* 151–162.

Afflerbach, P., Pearson, P. D., & Paris, S. G. (2008). Clarifying differences between reading skills and reading strategies. *Reading Teacher, 61,* 364–373.

Allington, R. L. (1983). Fluency: The neglected reading goal. *The Reading Teacher, 36,* 556–561.

Allington, R. L. (2007). Intervention all day long: New hope for struggling readers. *Voices from the Middle, 14*(4), 7–14.

Almasi, J. F. (2008). Using questioning strategies to promote students' active discussion and comprehension of content area material. In D. Lapp, J. Flood, & N. Farnan (Eds.), *Content area reading and learning* (3rd ed., pp. 487–513). New York: Erlbaum.

Alvermann, D. E. (1981). The compensatory effect of graphic organizers on descriptive text. *Journal of Educational Research, 75,* 44–48.

Anderson, R. C. (1972). How to construct achievement tests to assess comprehension. *Review of Educational Research, 42,* 145–170.

Anderson, R. C., & Freebody, P. (1981). Vocabulary knowledge. In J. Guthrie (Ed.), *Comprehension and teaching: Research reviews.* Newark, DE: International Reading Association.

Anderson, T. H., & Armbruster, B. B. (1984). Studying. In P. D. Pearson, R. Barr, M. Kamil, & P. Mosenthal (Eds.), *Handbook of reading research* (pp. 657–679). White Plains, NY: Longman.

Anglin, J. M. (1977). *Word, object, and conceptual development.* New York: Norton.

Arciuli, J., & Monaghan, P. (2009, January/February). Probabilistic cues to grammatical category in English orthography and their influence during reading. *Scientific Studies of Reading, 13*(1), 73–93.

Asch, S. E., & Nerlove, H. (1960). The development of double-function terms in children: An exploratory investigation. In B. Kaplan & S. Wapner (Eds.), *Perspectives in psychological theory: Essays in honor of Heinz Werner.* New York: International Universities Press. Cited in Gardner, H., Winner, E., Bechhofer, R., & Wolf, D. (1978). The development of figurative language. In K. E. Nelson (Ed.), *Children's language* (Vol. 1). New York: Gardner.

Atwell, N. (2002). *Lessons that change writers.* Portsmouth, NH: FirstHand Heinemann.

Bader, L. A. (2005). *Bader reading and language inventory and readers' passages and graded word lists* (5th ed.). Upper Saddle River, NJ: Pearson.

Baghban, M. (1984). *Our daughter learns to read and write: A case study from birth to three.* Newark, DE: International Reading Association.

Bakhtin, M. M. (1981). *The dialogic imagination.* Austin: University of Texas Press.

Baldwin, D. (2004). A guide to standardized writing assessment. *Educational Leadership, 62*(2), 72–75.

Baldwin, R. S., Luce, T. S., & Readence, J. E. (1982). The impact of subschemata on metaphorical processing. *Reading Research Quarterly, 17,* 528–543.

Bannon, E., Fisher, P. J. L., Pozzi, L., & Wessel, D. (1990). Effective definitions for word learning. *Journal of Reading, 34,* 301–302.

Barr, R. (1974). Influence of instruction on early reading. *Interchange, 5,* 13–22.

Barr, R. (1995). What research says about grouping in the past and present and what it suggests about the future. In M. Radencich & L. McKay (Eds.), *Flexible grouping in the elementary grades.* Needham Heights, MA: Allyn & Bacon.

Barr, R., Blachowicz, C. L. Z., Buhle, R., Chaney, J., Ivy, C., & Sourez, S. G. (2002). *Illinois snapshot of early literacy.* Springfield: Illinois State Board of Education.

Barr, R., & Dreeben, R. (1983). *How schools work.* Chicago: University of Chicago Press.

Barr, R., & Dreeben, R. (1991). Grouping students for reading instruction. In R. Barr, M. Kamil, P. Mosenthal, & P. D. Pearson (Eds.), *Handbook of reading research* (Vol. 2, pp. 885–910). White Plains, NY: Longman.

Barron, R. (1969). The use of vocabulary as an advance organizer. In H. L. Herber & P. L. Sanders (Eds.),

Research in reading in the content areas: First year report. Syracuse, NY: Syracuse University Reading and Language Arts Center.

Bartlett, B. J. (1978). Top-level structure as an organizational strategy for recall of classroom text. Unpublished doctoral dissertation, Arizona State University. Cited in Meyer, B. J. F., Brandt, D. M., & Bluth, G. J. (1980). Use of top-level structure in text: Key for reading comprehension of ninth-grade students. *Reading Research Quarterly, 16,* 72–103.

Bass, M. L., & Woo, D. G. (2008). Comprehension windows strategy: A comprehension strategy and prop for reading and writing informational text. *The Reading Teacher, 61*(7), 571–575.

Baumann, J. F., Ware, D., & Edwards, E. C. (2007). Bumping into spicy, tasty words that catch your tongue: A formative experiment on vocabulary instruction. *The Reading Teacher, 62,* 108–122.

Bean, T. W., Singer, H., & Cowan, S. (1985). Acquisition of a topic schema in high school biology through an analogical study guide. In J. A. Niles & R. V. Lalik (Eds.), *Issues in literacy: A research perspective* (Thirty-fourth yearbook of the National Reading Conference). Rochester, NY: National Reading Conference.

Bear, D. R., Invernizzi, M., Templeton, S., & Johnston, F. (2008). Words their way: Word study for phonics, vocabulary, and spelling instruction (4th ed.). Upper Saddle River, NJ: Pearson Prentice Hall.

Beck, I. L., & McKeown, M. G. (1981). Developing questions that promote comprehension: The story map. *Language Arts, 58,* 913–918.

Beck, I. L., & McKeown, M. G. (2007). Increasing young low-income children's oral vocabulary repertoires through rich and focused instruction. *Elementary School Journal, 107,* 251–271.

Beck, I. L., McKeown, M. G., Hamilton, R. L., & Kucan, L. (1997). *Questioning the author: An approach for enhancing student engagement with text.* Newark, DE: International Reading Association.

Beck, I. L., McKeown, M. G., & Kucan, L. (2002). *Bringing words to life: Robust vocabulary instruction.* New York: Guilford.

Beck, I. L.,McKeown, M. G., McCaslin, E. S., & Burkes, A. M. (1979). *Instructional dimensions that may affect reading comprehension: Examples from two commercial reading programs.* (LRDC Publication 1979/20). Pittsburgh: University of Pittsburgh, Learning Research and Development Center.

Beck, I. L., McKeown, M. G., & Kucan, L. (2007). *Bringing words to life: Robust vocabulary instruction.* New York: Guilford.

Beck, I. L., Omanson, R. C., & McKeown, M. G. (1982). An instructional redesign of reading lessons: Effects on comprehension. *Reading Research Quarterly, 17,* 462–481.

Beck, I. L., Perfetti, C. A., & McKeown, M. G. (1982). The effects of long-term vocabulary instruction on lexical access and reading comprehension. *Journal of Educational Psychology, 74,* 506–521.

Becker, W., Dixon, R. C., & Inman-Anderson, L. (1980). *Morphographic and root word analysis of 26,000 high-frequency words.* Eugene: College of Education, University of Oregon.

Beers, K. (2003). *When kids can't read: What teachers can do: A guide for teachers 6–12.* Portsmuth, NH: Heinemann.

Berne, J. I., & Clark, K. (2008). Focusing literature discussion groups on comprehension strategies. *The Reading Teacher, 62*(1), 74–79.

Betts, E. A. (1946). *Foundations of reading instruction.* New York: American Books.

Betts, E. A. (1954). *Foundations of reading instruction* (rev. ed.). New York: American Book Company.

Bialystok, E., Shenfield, T., & Codd, J. (2000). Languages, scripts, and the environment: Factors in developing concepts of print. *Developmental Psychology, 36,* 1–20.

Biemiller, A. (1970). The development of the use of graphic and contextual information as children learn to read. *Reading Research Quarterly, 6,* 75–96.

Biemiller, A. (1979). Changes in the use of graphic and contextual information as functions of passage difficulty and reading achievement level. *Journal of Reading Behavior, 11,* 307–318.

Bissex, G. L. (1980). *GNYS AT WRK: A child learns to write and read.* Cambridge, MA: Harvard University Press.

Blachowicz, C. L. Z. (1977). Cloze activities for primary readers. *The Reading Teacher, 31,* 300–302.

Blachowicz, C. L. Z. (1986). Making connections: Alternatives to the vocabulary notebook. *Journal of Reading, 20,* 643–49.

Blachowicz, C. L. Z. (1993). C2QU: A metacognitive model for context instruction. *The Reading Teacher, 47*(3), 268–269.

Blachowicz, C. L. Z., & Fisher, P. J. L. (1989). Defining is an unnatural act: A study of written definitions. In S. McCormick & J. Zutell (Eds.), *Cognitive and social perspectives for literary research and instruction* (Thirty-eighth yearbook of the National Reading Conference). Chicago: National Reading Conference.

Blachowicz, C. L. Z., & Fisher, P. J. L. (2000). Vocabulary Instruction. In M. L. Kamil, P. B. Mosenthal, P. D. Pearson, & R. Barr, (Eds.), *Handbook of Reading Research* (Vol. 3, pp. 503–523). Mahwah, NJ: Erlbaum.

Blachowicz, C. L. Z., & Fisher, P. J. L. (2010). *Teaching vocabulary in all classrooms* (4th ed.). Columbus, OH: Prentice Hall.

Blachowicz, C. L. Z., & Fisher, P. J. L. (2010). *Teaching vocabulary in all classrooms* (4th ed.). Columbus, OH: Prentice Hall. Blachowicz, C. L. Z., Fisher, P. J. L., Costa, M., & Pozzi, M. (1993). *Researching vocabulary learning in middle school cooperative reading groups: A teacher–researcher collaboration.* Paper presented at the Tenth Great Lakes Regional Reading Conference, Chicago.

Blachowicz, C. L. Z., Fisher, P. J. L., Massarelli, J., Moskal, M. K., & Obrochta, C. (2000). *Everybody reads: An effective school program for fluency development.* Report to the Illinois State Board of Education.

Blachowicz, C. L. Z., & Obrochta, C. (2005, November). Vocabulary visits: Developing content vocabulary in the primary grades. *The Reading Teacher, 59*(3), 262–268.

Blachowicz, C. L. Z., & Ogle, D. (2001). *Reading comprehension: Strategies for independent learners.* New York: Guilford Press.

Blachowicz, C. L. Z., & Ogle, D. (2008). *Reading comprehension: Strategies for independent learners* (2nd ed.). New York: Guilford.

Blachowicz, C. L. Z., Watts-Taffe, S., & Fisher, P. J. L. (2006). *Integrated vocabulary instruction: Meeting the needs of diverse learners in grades 1–5.* Naperville, IL: Learning Point Associates.

Blachowicz, C. L. Z., & Zabroske, B. (1990). Context instruction: A metacognitive approach for at-risk readers. *Journal of Reading, 33,* 504–508.

Block, C. C., & Mangieri, J. (2006a). *The effects of powerful vocabulary for reading success on students' reading vocabulary and comprehension achievement.* Research Report 2963-005 of the Institute for Literacy Enhancement. Retrieved June 15, 2008, from http://teacher.scholastic.com/products/powerfulvocabulary/pdfs/1521-PVfRS_eff_rep.pdf

Block, C. C., & Mangieri, J. (2006b). *Exemplary literacy teachers.* New York: Guilford.

Bloodgood, J. W. (1999). What's in a name? Children's name writing and literacy acquisition. *Reading Research Quarterly, 34,* 342–367.

Bloome, D., & Egan-Robertson, A. (1993). The social construction of intertextuality in classroom reading and writing lessons. *Reading Research Quarterly, 28,* 304–333.

Bluestein, N. A. (2002, February). Comprehension through characterization: Enabling readers to make personal connections with literature. *Reading Teacher, 55*(5), 431–435.

Bormuth, J. R. (1967). Comparable cloze and multiple-choice comprehension test scores. *Journal of Reading, 10,* 291–299.

Bortnick, R., & Lopardo, G. (1973). An instructional application of the cloze procedure. *Journal of Reading, 16,* 296–300.

Boulineau, T., Fore, C., III, & Hagan-Burke, S. (2004, Spring). Use of story-mapping to increase the story-grammar text comprehension of elementary students with learning disabilities. *Learning Disability Quarterly, 27*(2), 105.

Bradley, L., & Bryant, P. E. (1983). Categorizing sounds and learning to read: A causal connection. *Nature, 301,* 419–421.

Bridge, C. A., & Tierney, R. J. (1981). The inferential operations of children across the text with narrative and expository tendencies. *Journal of Reading Behavior, 13,* 201–214.

Brown, C. (1986). *A tutorial procedure for enhancing the reading comprehension of college students* (Doctoral dissertation, University of Pennsylvania). Dissertation Abstracts International, 47, 3719A.

Bruce, D. (1964). Analysis of word sounds by young children. *British Journal of Educational Psychology, 34,* 148–169.

Buehl, D. (2001). *Classroom strategies for interactive learning.* Newark, DE: International Reading Association.

Buehl, D. (2007). The author says/I say. On WEAC. Retrieved from www.weac.org/News/2006-2007/june07/readingroom.htm

Buehl, D. (2009). *Classroom strategies for interactive learning.* Newark, DE: International Reading Association.

Buehl, D., & Stumpf, S. (2007). Literacy demands in content classrooms. In *Adolescent Literacy Toolkit* (pp. 33–51). Madison: Wisconsin Department of Public Instruction.

Buikema, J. L., & Graves, M. J. (1993). Teaching students to use context clues to infer word meanings. *Journal of Reading, 36*(6), 450–457.

Buros, O. K. (Ed.). (1938–1985). *Mental measurements yearbook* (Vols. 1–8). Highland Park, NJ: Gryphon Press.

Buros, O. K. (Ed.). (1968). *Reading tests and reviews I.* Highland Park, NJ: Gryphon.

Bussis, A. M., Chittenden, E. A., Amarel, M., & Klausner, E. (1985). *Inquiry into meaning: An investigation of learning to read.* Hillsdale, NJ: Erlbaum.

Cain, K., & Oakhill, J. (2006). Profiles of children with specific reading comprehension difficulties. *British Journal of Educational Psychology, 76,* 683–696.

Caldwell, J. S., & Ford, M. P. (2002). *Where have all the bluebirds gone? How to soar with flexible grouping.* Portsmouth, NH: Heinemann.

Calkins, L., & Martinelli, M. (2006). *Launching the writing workshop: Grades 3–5.* Portsmouth, NH: FirstHand Heinemann.

Carlo, M., August, D., McLaughlin, B., Snow, C., Dressler, C., Lippman, D., Lively, T., & White, C. (2004). Closing the gap: Addressing the vocabulary needs of English language learners in bilingual and mainstream classrooms. *Reading Research Quarterly, 39,* 188–215.

Carpenter, P. A., & Just, M. A. (1977). Reading comprehension as eyes see it. In M. A. Just & P. A. Carpenter (Eds.), *Cognitive processes in comprehension.* Hillsdale, NJ: Erlbaum.

Carr, E., & Wixson, K. K. (1986). Guidelines for evaluating vocabulary instruction. *Journal of Reading, 29,* 588–595.

Carver, R. P. (1983). Is reading rate constant or flexible? *Reading Research Quarterly, 18,* 190–215.

Cave, H. B. (1969). Two were left. In I. Willis & R. E. Willis (Eds.), *New worlds ahead* (pp. 409–411). San Diego, CA: Harcourt, Brace, and World.

Chall, J. S. (1983). *Stages of reading development.* New York: McGraw-Hill.

Chall, J. S., & Squire, J. R. (1991). The publishing industry and textbooks. In R. Barr, M. Kamil, P. Mosenthal, & P. D. Pearson (Eds.), *Handbook of reading research* (Vol. 2, pp. 120–146). White Plains, NY: Longman.

Clark, E. V. (1973). What's in a word? On the child's acquisition of semantics in his first language. In T. E. Moore (Ed.), *Cognitive development and the acquisition of language.* New York: Academic Press.

Clarke, L. K. (1989). Encouraging invented spelling in first graders' writing: Effects on learning to spell and read. *Research in the Teaching of English, 22,* 281–309.

Clay, M. M. (1967). The reading behavior of five year old children: A research project. *New Zealand Journal of Educational Studies, 2,* 11–31.

Clay, M. M. (1975). *What did I write?* Portsmouth, NH: Heinemann Educational Books.

Clay, M. M. (1979). *Reading: The patterning of complex behavior.* Auckland, N Z: Heinemann.

Clay, M. M. (1985). *The early detection of reading difficulties* (3rd ed.). Portsmouth, NH: Heinemann.

Clay, M. M. (1991). Introducing a new storybook to young readers. *The Reading Teacher, 45*(4), 264–273.

Clay, M. M. (1993a). *An observation survey of early literacy achievement.* Portsmouth, NH: Heinemann.

Clay, M. M. (1993b). *Reading recovery—A guidebook for teachers in training.* Portsmouth, NH: Heinemann.

Clay, M. M. (2006). *An observation survey of early literacy achievement.* Portsmouth, NH: Heinemann.

Cohen, A. S. (1974–1975). Oral reading errors of first grade children taught by a code emphasis approach. *Reading Research Quarterly, 10,* 616–650.

Connor, C. M., Morrison, F. J., & Petrella, J. N. (2004, December). Effective reading comprehension instruction: Examining child X instruction interactions. *Journal of Educational Psychology, 96*(4), 682–698.

Cramer, R. L. (1989). *Scott, Foresman language.* Glenview, IL: Scott, Foresman.

Crothers, E. J. (1978). Inference and coherence. *Discourse Processes, 1,* 51–71.

Cunningham, A. E., & Stanovich, K. E. (1998, Spring/Summer). What reading does for the mind. *American Educator,* 8–17.

Cunningham, J. W. (1982). Generating interactions between schemata and text. In J. A. Niles & L. A. Harris (Eds.), *New inquiries in reading research and instruction.* (Thirty-first yearbook of the National Reading Conference). Washington, DC: National Reading Conference, 42–47.

Cunningham, P. M. (1975–1976). Investigating a synthesized theory of mediated word identification. *Reading Research Quarterly, 11,* 127–143.

Cunningham, P. M. (1978). Decoding polysyllabic words: An alternative strategy. *Journal of Reading, 21,* 608–614.

Cunningham, P. M. (1979). A compare/contrast theory of mediated word identification. *The Reading Teacher, 32*, 774–778.

Dahl, K. L., & P. A. Freppon, (1991). Literacy learning in whole-language classrooms: An analysis of low socioeconomic urban children learning to read and write in kindergarten. In J. Zutel & S. McCormick (Eds.), *Learner factors/teacher factors: Issues in literacy research and instruction* (pp. 149–158; Fortieth yearbook of the National Reading Conference). Chicago: National Reading Conference.

Daskal, J. (1983). *Basic strategies for improving comprehension of written materials.* Unpublished manuscript, Chicago.

Davey, B. (1983). Think-aloud—modeling the cognitive processes of reading comprehension. *Journal of Reading, 27*, 44–47.

Davidson, J. L., & Wilkerson, B. C. (1988). *Directed reading-thinking activities.* Monroe, NY: Trillium.

Davis, F. B. (1968). Research in comprehension in reading. *Reading Research Quarterly, 3*, 499–544.

Dearborn, W. F. (1906). The psychology of reading. *Archives of Philosophy, Psychology and Scientific Methods, 1*, 71–132.

Diederich, P. B. (1974). *Measuring growth in English.* Urbana, IL: National Council of Teachers of English.

Dodge, R. (1905). The illusion of clear vision during eye-movement. *Psychological Bulletin, 12*, 193–199.

Dodge, R. (1907). An experimental study of visual fixation. *Psychological Review Monograph Supplements, 8*, 1–96.

Dolch, E. W. (1936). Basic sight vocabulary. *Elementary School Journal, 36*, 456–460.

Dole, J. A., Sloan, C., & Trathen, W. (1995). Teaching vocabulary within the context of literature. *Journal of Reading, 38*, 452–460.

Dorn, L., French, C., & Jones, T. (1999). *Apprenticeship in literacy: Transitions across reading and writing.* York, ME: Stenhouse.

Dowhower, S. L. (1994). Repeated reading revisited: Research into practice. *Reading and Writing Quarterly, 10*, 343–358.

Draper, A. G., & Moeller, G. H. (1971). We think with words (therefore, to improve thinking, teach vocabulary). *Phi Delta Kappan, 52*, 482–484.

Drum, P. A. (1983). Vocabulary knowledge. In J. A. Niles & L. A. Harris (Eds.), *Searches for meaning in reading/language processing and instruction* (Thirty-second yearbook of the National Reading Conference). Rochester, NY: National Reading Conference.

Duffelmeyer, F. A. (1980). The influence of experience-based vocabulary instruction on learning word meanings. *Journal of Reading, 24*, 35–40.

Duffy, G., Roehler, L., & Hermann, B. (1988). Modeling mental processes helps poor readers become strategic readers. *The Reading Teacher, 41*(8), 762–767.

Duffy-Hester, A. M. (1999). Teaching struggling readers in elementary school classrooms: A review of classroom reading programs and principles for instruction. *The Reading Teacher, 52*, 480–495.

Duke, N. K., Bennett-Armistead, V. S., & Roberts, E. M. (2003). Bridging the gap between learning to read and reading to learn. In D. M. Barone & L. M. Morrow (Eds.), *Literacy and young children: Research-based practices* (pp. 226–242). New York: Guilford.

Durkin, D. (1978–1979). What classroom observations reveal about reading comprehension instruction. *Reading Research Quarterly, 14*, 481–533.

Ehri, L. C. (1979). Linguistic insight: Threshold of reading acquisition. In. T. G. Waller & G. E. MacKinnon (Eds.), *Reading research: Advances in theory and practice* (Vol. 1., pp. 63–114). New York: Harcourt Brace Jovanovich.

Ehri, L. C. (1980). The development of orthographic images. In U. Frith (Ed.), *Cognitive processes in spelling.* London: Academic Press.

Ehri, L. C. (1983). How orthography alters spoken language competencies in children learning to read and spell. In J. Downing & R. Valtin (Eds.), *Language awareness and learning to read.* New York: Springer Verlag.

Ehri, L. C. (1991). Development of the ability to read words. In R. Barr, M. Kamil, P. Mosenthal, & P. D. Pearson (Eds.), *Handbook of reading research,* (Vol. 2, pp. 383–417). White Plains, NY: Longman.

Ehri, L. (1998). Grapheme-phoneme knowledge is essential for learning to read words in English. In J. Metsala & L. Ehri (Eds.), *Word recognition in beginning literacy* (pp. 3–40). Mahwah, NJ: Erlbaum.

Ehri, L., Carins, H. S., & Zipke, M. (2009, July–September). Using semantic ambiguity instruction to improve third graders metalinguistic awareness and reading comprehension: An experimental study. *Reading Research Quarterly, 3*, 300–321.

Ekwall, E. E. (1976). *Diagnosis and remediation of the disabled reader.* Boston: Allyn & Bacon.

Ekwall, E. E., & J. L. Shankar (1999). *Ekwall reading inventory.* Boston: Allyn & Bacon.

Elkonin, D. B. (1963). The psychology of mastering elements of reading. In B. Simon (Ed.), *Educational psychology in the U.S. S. R.* London: Routledge & Kegan Paul.

Eller, R. G., Pappas, C. C., & Brown, E. (1988). The lexical development of kindergartners: Learning from written context. *Journal of Reading Behavior, 20,* 5–24.

Evers, A. J., Lang, L. F., & Smith, S. V. (2009). An ABC literacy journey: Anchoring in texts, bridging language, and creating stories. *The Reading Teacher, 62*(6), 461–470.

Fang, Z. (1999). Expanding the vista of emergent writing research: Implications for early childhood educators. *Early Childhood Education Journal, 26,* 179–182.

Fang, Z., & Schleppegrell, M. J. (2010). Disciplinary literacies across content areas: Supporting secondary reading through functional language analysis. *Journal of Adolescent & Adult Literacy, 53*(7), 587–597.

Farr, R., & Carey, R. F. (1986). *Reading: What can be measured?* Newark, DE: International Reading Association.

Feifel, H., & Lorge, I. (1950). Qualitative differences in the vocabulary responses of children. *Journal of Educational Psychology, 41,* 1–18.

Fernald, G. M., & Keller, H. (1926). The effect of kinesthetic factors in the development of word recognition in nonreaders. *Journal of Educational Research, 4,* 355–377.

Ferreiro, E. (1984). The underlying logic of literacy development. In H. Goelman, A. Oberg, & F. Smith (Eds.), *Awakening to literacy.* Portsmouth, NH: Heinemann Educational Books.

Ferreiro, E., & Teberosky, A. (1982). *Literacy before schooling.* Portsmouth, NH: Heinemann Educational Books.

Ferroli, L., & Shanahan, T. (1987). Kindergarten spelling: Explaining its relation to first-grade reading. In J. E. Readence & R. S. Baldwin (Eds.), *Research in literacy: Merging perspectives* (Thirty-sixth yearbook of the National Reading Conference). Rochester, NY: National Reading Conference.

Fisher, P. J. L., Blachowicz, C. L. Z., & Smith, J. C. (1991). Vocabulary learning in literature discussion groups. In J. Zutell & S. McCormick (Eds.), *Learner factors/teacher factors: Issues in literacy research and instruction* (pp. 201–209; Fortieth yearbook of the National Reading Conference). Chicago: National Reading Conference.

Fitzgerald, J. (1989). Enhancing two related thought processes: Revision in writing and critical reading. *The Reading Teacher, 43*(1), 42–48.

Fletcher, R., & Portalupi, J. (1998). *Craft lessons: Teaching writing K–8.* York, ME: Stenhouse.

Flynt, E. S., & Cooter R. B., Jr. (2003). *Reading inventory for the classroom* (5th ed.). Upper Saddle River, NJ: Prentice Hall.

Fountas, I., & Pinnell, G. S. (1999). *Matching books to readers: using leveled books in guided reading, K–3.* Portsmouth, NH: Heinemann.

Fountas, I., & Pinnell, G. S. (2010). *The Fountas & Pinnell leveled book list, K–8+: 2010–2012 edition,* Print Version (F & P Professional Books and Multimedia). Portsmouth, NH: Heinemann.

Freebody, P., & Anderson, R. C. (1983a). Effects of differing proportions and locations of difficult vocabulary on text comprehension. *Journal of Reading Behavior, 15,* 19–39.

Freebody, P., & Anderson (1983b). Effects of vocabulary difficulty, text cohesion, and schema availability on reading comprehension. *Reading Research Quarterly, 18,* 277–294.

Frey, N., Fisher, D., & Hernandez, T. (2003). "What's the gist?" Summary writing for struggling adolescent writers. *Voices from the Middle, 11,* 43–49.

Froese, V., & Kurushima, S. (1979). The effects of sentence expansion practice on the reading comprehension and writing ability of third graders. In M. L. Kamil & A. J. Moe (Eds.), *Reading research: Studies and applications* (Twenty-eighth yearbook of the National Reading Conference). Clemson, SC: National Reading Conference.

Frost, S., Buhle, R., & Blachowicz, C. L. Z. (2009). *Effective literacy coaching: Building expertise and a culture of literacy: An ASCD action tool.* Alexandria, VA: ASCD.

Galda, L. (1990). A longitudinal study of the spectator stance as a function of age and genre. *Research in the Teaching of English, 24*(3), 261–278.

Gambrell, L., & Almasi, J. F. (1996). *Lively discussions! Fostering engaged reading.* Newark, DE: IRA.

Gambrell, L., Morrow, L., & Pressley, M. (2007). *Best practices in literacy instruction* (3rd ed.). New York: Guilford.

Gambrell, L., Pfeiffer, W., & Wilson, R. (1985). The effects of retelling upon reading comprehension and recall of text information. *Journal of Educational Research, 7*, 216–220.

Gardner, H., Winner, E., Bechhofer, R., & Wolf, D. (1978). The development of figurative language. In K. E. Nelson (Ed.), *Children's language* (Vol. 1). New York: Gardner.

Garner, R. (1987). *Metacongnition and reading comprehension.* Norwood, NJ: Ablex.

Garner, R., & Reis, R. (1981). Monitoring and resolving comprehension obstacles: An investigation of spontaneous lookbacks among upper-grade and poor comprehenders. *Reading Research Quarterly, 16*, 569–582.

Geva, E. (1983). Facilitating reading comprehension through flowcharting. *Reading Research Quarterly, 18*, 384–405.

Gilbert, D. W. (1959). *Breaking the reading barrier.* Englewood Cliffs, NJ: Prentice Hall.

Gilbert, D. W., & Foret, C. I. (1990). *Breaking the reading barrier* (3rd ed.). Englewood Cliffs, NJ: Prentice Hall.

Gillet, J. W., & Temple, C. (1986). *Understanding reading problems: Assessment and instruction.* Boston: Little, Brown.

Gillet, J. W., Temple, C., Crawford, A. N., Cooney, B., & Crawford, A. (2003). *Understanding reading problems: Assessment and instruction* (6th ed.). Needham Heights, MA: Allyn & Bacon.

Glynn T., Crooks, T., Bethune, N., Ballard, K., & Smith, J. (1989). *Reading recovery in context.* Wellington, NZ: New Zealand Department of Education.

Golden, J. M., & Pappas (1987). *A critical review of retelling procedures in research on children's cognitive processing of written text.* Paper presented at the annual meeting of the National Reading Conference, St. Petersburg, FL.

Goldenberg, C. (1992/1993). Instructional conversations: Promoting comprehension through discussion. *The Reading Teacher, 46*(4), 316–326.

Goodman, K. S. (1965). A linguistic study of cues and miscues in reading. *Elementary English, 42*, 639–643.

Goodman, K. S. (1967). Reading: A psycholinguistic guessing game. *Journal of the Reading Specialist, 6*, 126–135.

Goodman, K. S. (1969). Analysis of reading miscues: Applied psycholinguistics. *Reading Research Quarterly, 5*, 9–30.

Goodman, K. S. (1976). Reading: A psycholinguistic guessing game. In H. Singer & R. Ruddell (Eds.), *Theoretical models and processes of reading.* Newark, DE: International Reading Association.

Goodman, Y. M., Watson, D. J., & Burke, C. L. (1987). *Reading miscue inventory: Alternative procedures.* New York: Richard C. Owen.

Goswami, U., & Bryant, P. E. (1990). *Phonological skills and learning to read.* Hillsdale, NJ: Erlbaum.

Goswami, U., & Mead, F. (1992). Onset and rime awareness and analogies in reading. *Reading Research Quarterly, 237*, 152–162.

Gourley, J. W. (1978). This basal is easy to read—or is it? *The Reading Teacher, 32*, 174–182.

Graves, D. H. (1994). *A fresh look at writing.* Portsmouth, NH: Heinemann.

Graves, M. F. (2000). A vocabulary program to complement and bolster a middle-grade comprehension program. In B. M. Taylor, M. F. Graves, & P. van den Broek (Eds.), *Reading for meaning: Fostering comprehension in the middle grades* (pp. 116–135). New York: Teachers College Press.

Graves, M. F. (2006). *The vocabulary book.* New York: Teachers College Press.

Graves, M. F., & Prenn, M. (1986). Costs and benefits of various methods of teaching vocabulary. *Journal of Reading, 29*, 596–602.

Gray, C. T. (1922). *Deficiencies in reading ability: Their diagnosis and remedies.* Boston: D.C. Heath.

Gray, W. S., & Holmes, E. (1938). *The development of meaning vocabularies in reading* (Publications of the Laboratory Schools, No. 6). Chicago: University of Chicago.

Gray, W. S., with D. Kibbe, L. Lucas, & L. W. Miller (1922). *Remedial cases in reading: Their diagnosis and treatment* (Supplemental Educational Monograph). Chicago: University of Chicago Press.

Gregory, A. E., & Cahill, M. A. (2010, March). Kindergarteners can do it, too! Comprehension strategies for early readers. *The Reading Teacher, 63*(6), 515–520.

Griffith, P. L., & Olson, M. W. (1992). Phonemic awareness helps beginning readers break the code. *The Reading Teacher, 45*, 516–523.

Gunning, T. G. (2003). The role of readability in today's classroom. *Topics in Language Disorders, 23*(3), 175–189.

Guszak, F. J. (1967). Teacher questioning and reading. *The Reading Teacher, 21*, 227–234.

Guthrie, J. (2007). *Engaging adolescents in reading.* Sherman Oaks, CA: Corwin.

Hafner, L. E. (1977). *Developmental reading in middle and secondary schools: Foundations, strategies, and skills for teaching.* New York: Macmillan.

Hagtvet, B. E. (2003). Listening comprehension and reading comprehension in poor decoders: Evidence for the importance of syntactic and semantic skills as well as phonological skills. *Reading and Writing: An Interdisciplinary Journal, 16*, 505–539.

Hannan, E. (1984). Writing: What to look for, what to do. *Language Arts, 61*, 364–366.

Hansen, J. (1987). *When writers read.* Portsmouth, NH: Heinemann.

Hare, V. C., & Borchardt, K. M. (1984). Direct instruction of summarization skills. *Reading Research Quarterly, 20*, 62–78.

Harmon, J. M. (2000, March). Assessing and supporting independent word learning strategies of middle school students. *Journal of Adolescent and Adult Literacy, 43*(6), 518–528.

Harris, A. J., & Jacobson, M. D. (1982). *Basic reading vocabularies.* New York: Macmillan.

Harris, A. J., & Sipay, E. R. (1980). *How to increase reading ability: A guide to developmental and remedial methods* (9th ed.). White Plains, NY: Longman.

Harris, A. J., & Sipay, E. R. (1990). *How to increase reading ability: A guide to developmental and remedial methods* (9th ed.). White Plains, NY: Longman.

Harris, L. A., & Lalik, R. M. (1987). Teacher's use of informal reading inventories: An example of school constraints. *The Reading Teacher, 40*, 624–630.

Harris, T. L., & Hodges, R. E. (1995). *A dictionary of reading and related terms.* Newark, DE: International Reading Association.

Harste, J., Woodward, V., & Burke, C. (1984). *Language stories and literacy lessons.* Portsmouth, NH: Heinemann Educational Books.

Hasbrouck, J. E., & G. Tindal (1992, Spring). Curriculum-based oral reading fluency norms for students in grades 2–5. *Teaching Exceptional Children,* 41–44.

Heller, M. F. (1995). *Reading-writing connections: From theory to practice* (2nd ed.). White Plains, NY: Longman.

Henderson, E. H. (1981). *Learning to read and spell.* DeKalb, IL: Northern Illinois University Press.

Henderson, E. H. (1985). *Teaching spelling.* Boston: Houghton Mifflin.

Henderson, E. H., & Beers, J. W. (Eds.). (1980). *Developmental and cognitive aspects of learning to spell: A reflection of word knowledge.* Newark, DE: International Reading Association.

Hiebert, E. H. (1981). Developmental patterns and interrelationships of preschool children's print awareness. *Reading Research Quarterly, 16*, 236–260.

Hiebert, E. H. (1999). Text matters in learning to read. *Reading Teacher, 52*, 552–566.

Hill, B. C., & Ruptic, C. (1994). *Practical aspects of authentic assessment: Putting the pieces together.* Norwood, MA: Christopher-Gordon.

Huckin, T., & Bloch, J. (1993). Strategies for inferring work meanings in context: A cognitive model. In T. Huckins, M. Haynes, & J. Coady (Eds.), *Second language reading and vocabulary learning* (pp. 153–178). Norwood, NJ: Ablex.

Huey, E. B. (1898). Preliminary experiments in the physiology and psychology of reading. *American Journal of Psychology, 9*, 575–586.

Huey, E. B. (1968). *The psychology and pedagogy of reading.* Cambridge, MA: MIT Press. (Originally published in 1908.)

Hughes, A., Bernier, S. A., & Gurren, L. (Eds.). (1979). The eagle and the baker. In *The Gold Book, The Headway Program.* LaSalle, IL: Open Court.

Hurley, S. R., & Tinajero, J. V. (2001). *Literacy assessment of second language learners.* Boston: Allyn & Bacon.

Idol, L., Nevin, A., & Paolucci-Whitcomb, P. (1996). *Models of curriculum-based assessment* (2nd ed.). Austin, TX: Pro-Ed.

Illinois State Board of Education. Illinois standards achievement test sample reading materials. www.isbe.net/assessment/isat.htm

International Reading Association. (1999). *Reading assessment: Principles and practices for elementary teachers.* Shelby J. Barrentine (Ed.). Newark, DE: Author.

International Reading Association. (2009). *Response to intervention: Guiding principles for intervention.* Retrieved August 29, 2011, from http://www.reading.org/General/Publications/Reading Today/RTY-0902-rti.aspx

Invernizzi, M., & Hayes, L. (2004). Developmental-spelling research: A systematic imperative. In R. M. Bean, N. Heisey, & C. M. Roller (Eds.), *Preparing reading professionals.* Newark, DE: International Reading Association.

Irwin, P. I., & Mitchell, J. N. (1983). A procedure for assessing the richness of retellings. *Journal of Reading, 2*, 391–396.

Ivey, G. (2010). Texts that matter. *Educational Leadership, 67*(6), 18–23.

Ivey, G., & Broadus, K. (2001). "Just plain reading: A survey of what makes students want to read in middle school classrooms." *Reading Research Quarterly, 36*, 350–377.

Jett-Simpson, M., & Leslie, L. (1994). *Ecological assessment: Under construction*. Schoenfield, WI: Wisconsin State Reading Association.

Johns, J. J. (2001). *Basic reading inventory* (8th ed.). Dubuque, IA: Kendall Hunt.

Johns, J. J. (2010). *Basic reading inventory* (10th ed.). Dubuque, IA: Kendall Hunt.

Johns, J. L. (1993). *Informal reading inventories: Annotated reference guide*. DeKalb, IL: Communitech International Corp.

Johns, J. L. (2005). Fluency norms for students in grades one through eight. *Illinois Reading Council Journal, 33*(4), 3–8.

Johns, J. L., & Berglund, R. L. (2005). *Fluency: Strategies and assessments* (2nd ed.). Dubuque, IA: Kendall Hunt.

Johnson, D. D. (2001). *Vocabulary in the elementary and middle school*. Boston: Allyn & Bacon.

Johnson, D. D., & Pearson, P. D. (1984). *Teaching reading vocabulary* (2nd ed.). New York: Holt, Rinehart & Winston.

Johnson, E. M. (1969). *Adventure trail,* diagnostic reading workbook, Grade 4, In *New diagnostic reading series*. Columbus, OH: Charles E. Merrill Publishing Co., p. 46.

Johnston, F. R. (1999). The timing and teaching of word families. *The Reading Teacher, 53*, 64–75.

Johnston, P. H. (1997). *Knowing literacy: Constructive literacy assessment*. New York: Stenhouse.

Jones, B. F., Palincsar, A. S., Ogle, D. S., & Carr, E. G. (1987). *Strategic teaching and learning: Cognitive instruction in the content areas*. Alexandria, VA: Association for Supervision and Curriculum Development.

Jones, B. F., Pierce, J., & Hunter, B. (1988/1989). Graphic arts teaching. *Educational Leadership, 46*, 20–26.

Joseph, L. M. (1998/1999). Word boxes help children with learning disabilities identify and spell words. *The Reading Teacher, 52*, 348–356.

Juel, C., & Minden-Cupp, C. (1999). *Learning to read words: Linguisstic units and strategies*. Ann Arbor, MI: Center for the Improvement of Early Reading Achievement.

Juel, C., & Roper-Schneider, D. (1985). The influence of basal readers on first grade reading. *Reading Research Quarterly, 20*, 134–152.

Kameenui, E. J., Carnine, D. W., & Freschi, D. (1982). Effects of text construction and instructional procedures for teaching word meanings

on comprehension and recall. *Reading Research Quarterly, 17*, 367–388.

Karpova, S. N. (1955). *Osoznanie slovesnogo sostava rechi rebenkom doshkol'nogo vozrasta* (The preschooler's realization of the lexical structure of speech). Voprosy Psikhol, No. 4, 43–55.

Katz, C. A., Polkoff, L., & Gurvitz, D. (2005). Shhh … I'm reading.: Scaffolded independent-level reading. *School Talk, 10*(2), 1–3.

Ketch, A. (2005). Conversation: The comprehension connection. *The Reading Teacher, 59*(1), 8–13.

Kibby, M. W. (1979). Passage readability affects the oral reading strategies of disabled readers. *The Reading Teacher, 32*, 390–396.

Kiefer, B. (1988). Picture books as contexts for literary, aesthetic and real world understanding. *Language Arts, 65*(3), 260–271.

Kimmel, S., & MacGinitie, W. H. (1985). Helping students revise hypothesis while reading. *The Reading Teacher, 37*, 768–771.

Kinniburgh, L. H., & Shaw, E. L. (2009, Winter). Using question-answer relationships to build reading comprehension in science. *Science Activities, 45*(4), 19–26.

Klauda, S. L., & Guthrie, J. T. (2008, May). Relationships of three components of reading fluency to reading comprehension. *Journal of Educational Psychology, 100*(2), 310–321.

Klenk, L., & Kibby, M. W. (2000). Re-mediating reading difficulties: Appraising the past, reconciling the present, constructing the future. In M. Kamil, P. Mosenthal, P. D. Pearson, & R. Barr (Eds.), *Handbook of reading research* (Vol. 3, pp. 667–690). Mahwah, NJ: Erlbaum.

Kletzien, S. (2009). Paraphrasing: An effective comprehension strategy. *The Reading Teacher, 63*(1), 73–77.

Knoblauch, C., & Johnston, P. H. (1990). Reading, writing, and the prose of school. In R. Beach & S. Hynds (Eds.), *Developing discurse practices in adolescence and adulthood* (pp. 318–333). Westport, CT: Ablex.

Kong, A., & Fitch, E. (2002/2003). Using book club to engage culturally and linguistically diverse learners in reading, writing, and talking about books. *The Reading Teacher, 56*(4), 352–362.

Kotula, A. W. (2003). Matching readers to instructional materials: The use of classic readability measures for students with language learning disabilities and dyslexia. *Topics in Language Disorders, 23*(3), 190–203.

Krashen, S. (1989). We acquire vocabulary and spelling by reading: Additional evidence for the input hypothesis. *The Modern Language Journal, 73,* 404–440.

Kucan, L., & Beck, I. S. (1997). Thinking aloud and reading comprehension research: inquiry, instruction, and social interaction. *Review of Educational Research, 67,* 271–299.

Kucer, S. (1985). The making of meaning: Reading and writing as parallel processes. *Written Communication, 2,* 317–336.

LaBerge, D., & Samuels, S. J. (1974). Toward a theory of automatic information processing in reading. *Cognitive Psychology, 6,* 293–323.

Lake, M. L. (1971). Improve the dictionary's image. *Elementary English, 48,* 363–365.

Lapp, D., Fisher, D., & Grant, M. (2008). You can read this text—I'll show you how: Interactive comprehension instruction. *Journal of Adolescent and Adult Literacy, 51,* 372–383.

Lee, A. (2010, February). A way of understanding the world of science informational books. *The Reading Teacher, 63*(5), 424–428.

Leslie, L., & Caldwell, J. (2005). *Qualitative reading inventory* (4th ed.). Boston: Allyn & Bacon.

Liberman, I., Shankweiler, D., Fischer, F., & Carter, B. (1974). Explicit syllable and phoneme segmentation in the young child. *Journal of Experimental Child Psychology, 18,* 201–212.

Lipson, M. Y., Cox, C., Iwanowski, S., & Simon, M. (1984). Explorations of the interactive nature of reading: Using commercial IRIs to gain insights. *Reading Psychology, 5,* 209–218.

Lipson, M. Y., & J. Mosenthal (1997, April). *The differential impact of Vermont's writing portfolio assessment on classroom instruction.* Paper presented at the annual meeting of the American Educational Research Association, Chicago.

Lubliner, S., & Smetana, L. (2005). The effects of comprehensive vocabulary instruction on Title I students' metacognitive word-learning skills and reading comprehension. *Journal of Literacy Research, 37,* 163–200.

Lundberg, I., Frost, J., & Petersen, O. (1988). Effects of an extensive program for stimulating phonological awareness in preschool children. *Reading Research Quarterly, 23,* 263–284.

Lyon, G. R., Fletcher, J. M., Shaywitz, S. E., Shaywitz, B. A., Torgensen, J. K., Wood, F. B., Schulte, A., & Olson, R. (2001). Rethinking learning disabilities. In C. E. Finn, Jr., R. A. Rotherman, & C. R. Hokanson, Jr. (Eds.), *Rethinking special education for a new century* (pp. 259–287). Washington, DC: Thomas B. Fordham Foundation and the Progressive Policy Institute.

Lytle, S. L. (1982). *Exploring comprehension style: A study of twelfth grade readers' transactions with text.* Unpublished dissertation, University of Pennsylvania, Philadelphia.

Manzo, A. V. (1975). Guided reading procedure. *Journal of Reading, 11,* 287–291.

Maro, N. (2001). Reading to improve fluency. *Illinois Reading Council Journal, 29*(3), 10–18.

Marshall, N., & Glock, M. (1978–1979). Comprehension of connected discourse: A study into the relationships between the structure of text and information recalled. *Reading Research Quarterly, 16,* 10–56.

Martinez, M., Roser, N. L., & Strecker, S. K. (1998/1999). "I never thought I could be a star"; A Reader's Theatre ticket to fluency. *The Reading Teacher, 52,* 326–334.

Mason, J. (1980). When do children begin to read: An exploration of four-year-old children's letter and word reading competencies. *Reading Research Quarterly, 15,* 203–227.

Masonheimer, P. E., Drum, P. A., & Ehri, L. C. (1984). Does environmental print identification lead children into word reading? *Journal of Reading Behavior, 16,* 257–271.

Masztal, N. B., & Smith, L. L. (1984). Do teachers really administer IRIs? *Reading World, 24*(1), 80–83.

Mayers, P. (1993). *Experiencing a novel: The thoughts, feelings, and motivation of adolescent readers.* Unpublished doctoral dissertation, National-Louis University, Evanston, IL.

McClanahan, B. (2009). Help! I have kids who can't read in my world history class! *Preventing School Failure, 53*(2), 105–111.

McCollister, K., & Sayler, M. F. (2010, Winter). Lift the ceiling: Increase rigor with critical thinking skills. *Gifted Child Today, 33,* 1.

McDonald, G. E. (1978). *The effects of instruction in the use of an abstract structural schema as an aid to comprehension and recall of written discourse.* Unpublished doctoral dissertation, Virginia Polytechnic Institute and State University. Cited in Meyer, B. J. F., Brandt, D. M., & Bluth, G. J. (1980), Use of top-level structure in text: Key for reading comprehension of ninth-grade students. *Reading Research Quarterly, 16,* 72–103.

McGee, L. M. (1992). Exploring the literature-based reading revolution (Focus on Research). *Language Arts, 69*(7), 529–537.

McGee, L. M., & Richgels, D. J. (1985). Teaching expository text structure to elementary students. *The Reading Teacher, 38*, 739–748.

McKeown, M. G. (1985). The acquisition of word meaning from context by children of high and low ability. *Reading Research Quarterly, 20*, 482–496.

McKeown, M. G., Beck, I. L., & Worthy, M. J. (1993). Grappling with text ideas: Questioning the author. *The Reading Teacher, 46*, 8.

Meek, M. (1986). *Learning to read.* Portsmouth, NH: Heinemann.

Memory, D. M. (1990). Teaching technical vocabulary: Before, during or after the reading assignment. *Journal of Reading Behavior, 22*, 39–53.

Mendelman, L. (2007/2008). Critical reading and thinking. *Journal of Adolescent and Adult Literacy, 51*(4), 300–302.

Meyer, B. J. F. (1975). Identification of the structure of prose and its implications for the study of reading and memory. *Journal of Reading Behaviour, 7*(1), 7–47.

Meyer, B. J. F., Brandt, D. M., & Bluth, G. J. (1980). Use of top-level structure in text: Key for reading comprehension of ninth-grade students. *Reading Research Quarterly, 16*, 72–103.

Meyer, K. (2010, February). Diving into reading: Revisiting reciprocal teaching in the middle years. *Literacy Learning: The Middle Years, 18*(1), 41–52.

Meyers, J., & Lytle, S. (1986). Assessment of the learning process. *Exceptional Children, 53*(2), 138–144.

Mezynski, K. (1983). Issues concerning the acquisition of knowledge: Effects of vocabulary training on reading comprehension. *Review of Educational Research, 53*, 253–279.

Miller, G. A. (1977). *Spontaneous apprentices.* New York: Seabury Press.

Miller, G. A., & Gildea, P. M. (1987). How children learn words. *Scientific American, 257*, 94–99.

Mills, K. A. (2009, December/2010, January). Floating on a sea of talk: Reading comprehension through speaking and listening. *The Reading Teacher, 63*(4), 325–329.

Mokhtari, K., & Thompson, H. B. (2006). How problems of reading fluency and comprehension are related to difficulties in syntactic awareness skills among fifth graders. *Reading Research and Instruction, 46*(1), 73–93.

Morgan, W. P. (1896). A case of congenital word blindness. *British Medical Journal, 2*, 1378.

Morris, D. (1980). Beginning readers' concept of word. In E. H. Henderson & J. W. Beers (Eds.), *Developmental and cognitive aspects of learning to spell: A reflection of word knowledge.* Newark, DE: International Reading Association.

Morris, D. (1982). Word sort: A categorization strategy for improving word recognition ability. *Reading Psychology, 3*, 247–259.

Morris, D. (1986). Teaching reading in kindergarten: A language-experience approach. *Occasional Paper No. 13.* Evanston, IL: The Reading Center, National College of Education.

Morris, D. (1988). The relationship between word awareness and phoneme awareness in learning to read: A longitudinal study in kindergarten. *Occassional Paper No. 17.* Evanston, IL: The Reading Center, National College of Education.

Morris, D. (1999). The role of clinical training in the teaching of reading. In D. E. Evensen & P. B. Mosenthal (Eds.), *Advances in reading/language research* (Vol. 6, pp. 69–100).

Morris, D. (2008). *Diagnosis and correction of reading problems.* New York: Guilford.

Morris, D., Bloodgood, J., Lomax, K., & Perney, J. (2003). Developmental steps in learning to read: A longitudinal study in kindergarten and first grade. *Reading Research Quarterly, 38*, 302–328.

Morris, D., & Perney, J. (1984). Developmental spelling as a predictor of first-grade reading achievement. *Elementary School Journal, 84*, 441–457.

Morrow, L. (1988). Retelling stories as a diagnostic tool. In S. M. Glazer, L. W. Searfoss, & I. M. Gentile (Eds.), *Reexamining reading diagnosis: New trends and procedures* (pp. 128–149). Newark, DE: International Reading Association.

Morrow, L. (1992). The impact of literature-based program on literacy achievement, use of literature, and attitudes of children from minority backgrounds. *Reading Research Quarterly, 27*, 250–275.

Morrow, L., Gambrell, L., Kapinus, B., Koskinen, P. S., Marshal, N., & Mitchell, J. (1986). Retelling: A strategy for reading assessment and instruction. In J. A. Niles & R. Lalik (Eds.), *Solving problems in literacy: Learners, teachers, and researchers* (Thirty-fifth yearbook of the National Reading Conference), San Diego, CA, December 3–7, 1985.

Morrow, L. M., Tracey, D. H., Woo, D. G., & Pressley, M. (1999). Characteristics of exemplary first-grade literacy instruction. *The Reading Teacher, 52*, 462–476.

Morrow, L. M., & Weinstein, C. S. (1986). Encouraging voluntary reading: The impact of a literature program on children's use of library centers. *Reading Research Quarterly, 21*(3), 330–346.

Moskal, M. K., & Blachowicz, C. L. Z. (2006). *Partnering for fluency.* New York: Guilford.

Moustafa, M., & Maldonado-Colon, E. (1999). Whole-to-part phonics instruction: Building on what children know to help them know more. *The Reading Teacher, 52,* 448–458.

Murfett, R., Powell, M. B., & Snow, P. C. (2008, March). The effect of intellectual disability on the adherence of child witnesses to a *"story grammar"* framework. *Journal of Intellectual & Developmental Disability, 33*(1), 2–11.

Murphy, L. (2011). *Tests in print VIII.* Lincoln: University of Nebraska Press.

Muzevich, K. (1999). Emergent writing in the kindergarten classroom. *Reading Today, 17,* 9.

Nagy, W. E. (1988). *Teaching vocabulary to improve reading comprehension.* Urbana, IL: National Council of Teachers of English.

Nagy, W. E., & Herman, P. A. (1987). Depth and breadth of vocabulary knowledge: Implications for acquisition and instruction. In M. G. McKeown & M. E. Curtis (Eds.), *The nature of vocabulary acquisition.* Hillsdale, NJ: Erlbaum.

National Assessment Governing Board. (2008). *Reading framework for the 2009 NAEP.* Washington, EC: U.S. Government Printing Office.

National Joint Committee on Learning Disabilities. (2005). *Responsiveness to intervention and learning disabilities.* Available from http://www.ldonline.org

National Reading Panel. (2000). *Teaching children to read: An evidence-based assessment of the scientific research literature on reading and its implications for reading instruction.* Washington, DC: National Institute of Child Health and Human Development, National Institutes of Health.

Nelson, K. (1974). Concept, word, and sentence: Interrelations in acquisition and development. *Psychological Review, 81,* 267–285.

Nelson, L. J., & Morris, D. (1988). Echo reading with taped books. *Illinois Reading Council Journal, 16,* 39–42.

Neuman, S. B., & Dickinson, D. K. (2001). *Handbook of early literacy research.* New York: Guilford.

Nichols, M. (2006). *Comprehension through conversation: The power of purposeful talk in the reading workshop.* Portsmouth, NH: Heinemann.

Nilsson, N. L. (2008). A critical analysis of eight informal reading inventories. *The Reading Teacher, 61*(7), 526–536.

Ogle, D. M. (1986). K-W-L: A teaching model that develops active reading of expository text. *The Reading Teacher, 39,* 564–570.

Ogle, D. M., & Correa-Kovtun, A. (2010, April). Supporting English-language learners and struggling readers in content literacy with the "Partner Reading and Content, Too" routine. *Reading Teacher, 63*(7), 532–542.

Ogle, D. M., Kemp, R. M., & McBride, W. (2007). *Building literacy in social studies: Strategies for improving comprehension and critical thinking.* Alexandria, VA: Association for Supervision and Curriculum Development.

Orellana, M. F., & Hernandez, A. (1999). Talking the walk: Children reading urban environmental print. *Reading Teacher, 52,* 612–619.

Otto, W. S., & Askov, E. (1972). The Wisconsin design for reading skill development. Minneapolis, MN: National Computer System.

Page, W. D., & Barr, R. C. (1975). Use of informal reading inventories. In W. D. Page (Ed.), *Help for the reading teacher: New directions in research.* Urbana, IL: National Conference on Research in English, ERIC Clearinghouse on Reading and Communication Skills, National Institute of Education.

Palincsar, A. S., & Brown, A. L. (1983). *Reciprocal teaching of comprehension-monitoring activities* (Technical Report No. 269). Champaign: University of Illinois, Center for the Study of Reading.

Pantaleo, S. (2007). Interthing: Young children using language to think collectively during Interactive Read-alouds. *Early Childhood Education Journal, 34*(6), 439–447.

Pappas, C. (1993). Is narrative "primary"? Some insights from kindergarteners' pretend readings of stories and information books. *Journal of Reading Behavior, 25,* 97–129.

Pappas, C., Kiefer, B. Z., & Levstik, L. S. (1990). *An integrated language perspective in the elementary school: Theory into action.* White Plains, NY: Longman.

Paris, S. G., & Carpenter, R. D. (2003). FAQs about IRIs. *The Reading Teacher, 56,* 578–580.

Paris, S. G., Cross, D. R., & Lipson, M. Y. (1984). Informed strategies for learning: A program to improve children's reading awareness and comprehension. *Journal of Educational Psychology, 76,* 1239–1252.

Parker, S. L. (1984). *A comparison of four types of initial vocabulary instruction.* Unpublished master's thesis, University of Minnesota, Minneapolis.

Paul, R., & Elder, L. (2004). Critical thinking ... and the art of close reading, part III. *Journal of Developmental Education, 28*(1), 36–37.

Paulson, F. L., Paulson, P. R., & Meyer, C. A. (1991). What makes a portfolio a portfolio? *Educational Leadership, 48*(5), 60–63.

Pearson, P. D., & Johnson, D. D. (1984). *Teaching reading comprehension* (2nd ed.). New York: Holt, Rinehart & Winston.

Pelosi, P. L. (1977). *The origin and development of reading diagnosis in the United States: 1896–1946.* Unpublished doctoral dissertation, State University of New York at Buffalo.

Perfetti, C. A. (1985). *Reading ability.* New York: Oxford University Press.

Phelps, M. (2010, Spring). Gateways to experience: Real-time teaching and learning. *Kappa Delta Pi Record, 46*(3), 132–134.

Pikulski, J. A. (1974). A critical review: Informal reading inventories. *The Reading Teacher, 28,* 141–153.

Pils, L. L. (1991). Soon anofe you tout me: Evaluation in a first-grade whole language classroom. *The Reading Teacher, 45,* 46–50.

Pinnell, G. S., Pikulski, J., Wixon, K. K., Campbell, J. R., Gough, P. B., & Beatty, A. S. (1995). *Listening to children read aloud. Data from the NAEP Integrated Reading Performance of Grade 4.* Washington, DC: U.S. Government Printing Office.

Porter, C., & J. Cleland (1994). *The portfolio as a learning strategy.* Portsmouth, NH: Boynton/Cook.

Powell, W. R. (1970). Reappraising the criteria for interpreting informal reading inventories. In D. L. Deboer (Ed.), *Reading diagnosis and evaluation.* Newark, DE: International Reading Association.

Powell, W. R. (1984). Mediated (emergent) reading levels: A construct. In J. Niles (Ed.), *Changing perspectives on research in reading language processing and instruction* (pp. 247–251). Rochester, NY: National Reading Conference.

Powell, W. R., & Dunkeld, C. G. (1971). Validity of the IRI reading levels. *Elementary English, 48,* 637–642.

Pressley, M. (2000). What should comprehension instruction be the instruction of? In M. L. Kamil, P. B. Mosenthal, P. D. Pearson, & R. Barr (Eds.), *Handbook of reading research* (Vol. 3, pp. 545–561). Mahwah, NJ: Erlbaum.

Pressley, M., Levin, J. R., & Miller, G. E. (1981). How does the keyword method affect vocabulary comprehension and usage? *Reading Research Quarterly, 16,* 213–226.

Pressley, M., & Wharton-McDonald, R. (1997). Skilled comprehension and its development through instruction. *School Psychology Review, 26* (3), 448–467.

Pullen, P., & Justice, L. M. (2003). Enhancing phonological awareness, print awareness, and oral language skills in preschool children. *Intervention in School and Clinic, 39,* 87–98.

Purcell-Gates, V., Duke, N., & Marineau, J. A. (2007). Learning to read and write genre-specific text: Roles of authentic experience and explicit teaching. *Reading Research Quarterly, 42*(1), 8–45.

Radmacher, S. A., & Latosi-Sawin, E. (1995). Summary writing: A tool to improve student comprehension and writing in psychology. *Teaching of Psychology, 22,* 113–115.

Raphael, T. E. (1982). Question-answering strategies for children. *The Reading Teacher, 36,* 186–190.

Raphael, T. E. (1986). Teaching question-answer relationships, revisited. *The Reading Teacher, 39,* 516–522.

Raphael, T. E., & Pearson, P. D. (1985). Increasing student's awareness of sources of information for answering questions. *American Educational Research Journal, 22*(2), 217–235.

Ray, K. W. (2006). *Study driven: A framework for planning units of study in the writing workshop.* Portsmouth, NH: Heinemann.

Read, C. (1971). Preschool children's knowledge of English phonology. *Harvard Educational Review, 41,* 1–34.

Readence, J. E., Baldwin, R. S., & Rickelman, R. J. (1983). Instructional insights into metaphors and similes. *Journal of Reading, 27,* 109–112.

Readence, J. E., Bean, T. W., & Baldwin, R. S. (1995). *Content area reading: An integrated approach* (5th ed.). Dubuque, IA: Kendall Hunt.

Rhodes, L. K., & Nathenson-Mejia, S. (1992). Anecdotal records: A powerful tool for ongoing literacy assessment. *The Reading Teacher, 45,* 502–509.

Richards, M. (2000). Be a good detective: Solve the case of oral reading fluency. *The Reading Teacher, 53,* 534–539.

Richek, M. A. (1987). DRTA: Five variations that facilitate independence in reading narratives. *Journal of Reading, 30,* 632–636.

Robinson, H. M. (1937). The study of disabilities in reading. *Elementary School Journal, 38,* 15–38.

Rogoff, B. (1990). *Apprenticeship in thinking*. New York: Oxford University Press.

Rosch, E. H. (1973). On the internal structure of perceptual and semantic categories. In T. E. Moore (Ed.), *Cognitive development and the acquisition of language*. New York: Academic Press.

Rosenblatt, L. M. (1985). Viewpoints: Transaction versus interaction—A terminological rescue operation. *Research in the Teaching of English, 19*, 96–107.

Roser, N., & Juel, C. (1982). Effects of vocabulary instruction on reading comprehension. In J. A. Niles & L. A. Harris (Eds.), *New inquiries in reading research and instruction* (Thirty-first yearbook of the National Reading Conference). Rochester, NY: National Reading Conference.

Rosner, J., & Simon, D. (1971). The auditory analysis test: An initial report. *Journal of Learning Disabilities, 4*, 384–392.

Routman, R. (2005). *Writing essentials*. Portsmouth, NH: Heinemann.

Sadow, M. W. (1982). The use of story grammar in the design of questions. *The Reading Teacher, 35*, 518–522.

Samuels, S. J. (1979). The method of repeated readings. *The Reading Teacher, 32*(4), 403–408.

Sanders, N. M. (1966). *Classroom questions: What kinds?* New York: Harper & Row.

Schlein, M. (1966). The big cheese. In B. Martin, Jr. (Ed.), *Sounds of the storyteller*. New York: Holt, Rinehart & Winston.

Schwartz, R., & Raphael, T. (1985). Concept of definition: A key to improving students' vocabulary. *The Reading Teacher, 30*, 198–205.

Scott, C. (2009). A case for the sentence in reading comprehension. *Language, Speech, and Hearing Services in Schools, 40*, 184–191.

Senechal, M., Pagan, S., Lever, R., & Ouellette, G. P. (2008). Relations among the frequency of shared reading and 4-year-old children's vocabulary, morphological and syntax comprehension, and narrative skills. *Early Education and Development, 19*(1), 27–44.

Sentell, C., & Blachowicz, C. L. Z. (1989). Comprehension court: A process approach to inference instruction. *The Reading Teacher, 42*, 347–348.

Shanahan, T. (1984). The reading-writing relation: An exploratory multivariate analysis. *Journal of Educational Psychology, 76*, 466–477.

Shanahan, T. (1997). Reading and writing relationships: Thematic units, inquiry learning … in pursuit of effective integrated literacy instruction. *The Reading Teacher, 51*, 1–12.

Shanahan, T., & Beck, I. L. (2006). Effective literacy teaching for English-language learners. In D. August & T. Shanahan (Eds.), *Developing literacy in second-language learners: Report of the National Literacy Panel on language-minority children and youth* (pp. 415–488). Mahwah, NJ: Erlbaum.

Shinn, M. R. (1989). *Curriculum-based measurement: Assessing special children*. New York: Guildford Press.

Silvaroli, N. J., & Wheelock, W. H. (2004). Classroom reading inventory with teacher resource CD-ROM and inventory administration kit (10th ed.). Boston: McGraw-Hill.

Simmons, J. (1992). Portfolios for large scale assessment. In D. Graves & B. Sunstein (Eds.), *Portfolio portrait*. Portsmouth, NH: Heinemann.

Sipe, L. R. (2000, April–June). The construction of literacy understanding by first and second graders in oral response to picture storybook read-alouds. *Reading Research Quarterly, 35*(2), 252–275.

Slobin, D. (1966). English abstract of Soviet studies of child language. In F. Smith & G. Miller (Eds.), *The genesis of language*. Cambridge, MA: MIT Press.

Slosson, R. L. (1990). *The Slosson oral reading test*. East Aurora, NY: Slosson Educational Publications.

Slosson, R. L. (2002). The Slosson oral reading test. Aurora, NY: Slosson Educational Publishers.

Smith, F. (1971). *Understanding reading*. New York: Holt, Rinehart & Winston.

Smith, M. W., & Wilhelm, J. D. (2002). *"Reading don't fix no Chevys": Literacy in the lives of young men*. Portsmouth, NH: Heinemann.

Snow, C. E., & Kim, Y. (2007). Large problem spaces: The challenge of vocabulary for English language learners. In R. K. Wager, A. E. Muse, & K. R. Tannenbaum (Eds.), *Vocabulary acquisition: Implications for reading comprehension* (pp. 123–139). New York: Guilford.

Spiro, R. (1980). Constructive processes in prose comprehension and recall. In R. Spiro, B. Bruce, & W. Brewer (Eds.), *Theoretical issues in reading comprehension*. Hillsdale, NJ: Erlbaum.

Stahl, S. A. (1983). Differential word knowledge and reading comprehension. *Journal of Reading Behavior, 15*, 33–50.

Stahl, S. A. (1992). Saying the "p" word: Nine guidelines for exemplary phonics instruction. *The Reading Teacher, 45*, 618–625.

Stahl, S. A., Duffy-Hester, A. M., & Stahl, K. A. D. (1998). Everything you wanted to know about phonics (but were afraid to ask). *Reading Research Quarterly, 33*, 338–355.

Stahl, S. A., & Fairbanks, M. (1986). The effects of vocabulary instruction: A model-based meta-analysis. *Review of Educational Research, 56*, 72–110.

Stahl, S. A., & Vancil, S. (1986). Discussion is what makes semantic maps work in vocabulary instruction. *The Reading Teacher, 40*, 62–69.

Stanovich, K. E. (1980). Toward an interactive-compensatory model of individual differences in the development of reading fluency. *Reading Research Quarterly, 16*, 32–71.

Stanovich, K. E. (1986). Matthew effects in reading: Some consequences of individual differences in the acquisition of literacy. *Reading Research Quarterly, 21*, 360–407.

Stauffer, R. G. (1981). *The language experience approach to the teaching of reading* (2nd ed.). New York: Harper & Row.

Stauffer, R. G. (1990). *Directing reading maturity as a cognitive process.* New York: Trillium Press.

Stein, N. L., & Glenn, C. G. (1979). An analysis of story comprehension in elementary school children. In R. O. Freedle (Ed.), *Advances in discourse processes: Vol. 2. New directions in discourse processing.* Norwood, NJ: Ablex.

Sternberg, R. (1987). Most vocabulary is learned from context. In M. G. McKeown & M. E. Curtis (Eds.), *The nature of vocabulary acquisition.* Hillsdale, NJ: Erlbaum.

Stotsky, S. (1984). Research on reading/writing relationships: A synthesis and suggested directions. In J. Jensen (Ed.), *Composing and comprehending* (ED 243 139, pp. 7–22). Urbana, IL: ERIC Clearinghouse on Reading and Communication Skills and the National Conference on Research in English.

Straw, S. B., & Schreiner, R. (1982). The effect of sentence manipulation on subsequent measures of reading and listening comprehension. *Reading Research Quarterly, 17*, 339–352.

Strecker, S. K., Roser, N. L., & Martinez, M. G. (1998). Toward understanding oral reading fluency. In T. Shanahan & F. V. Rodriguez-Brown (Eds.), *National Reading Conference Yearbook* 47 (pp. 295–310). Chicago: National Reading Conference.

Sulzby, E. (1985). Children's emergent reading of favorite storybooks: A developmental study. *Reading Research Quarterly, 20*, 458–481.

Taylor, B. M., Graves, M. F., & Van Den Boek, P. (2000). *Reading for meaning: Fostering comprehension in the middle grades.* Newark, DE: International Reading Association.

Taylor, D. (1983). *Family literacy: The social context of learning to read and write.* Portsmouth, NH: Heinemann Educational Books.

Taylor, S. E. (1965). Eye movements in reading: Facts and fallacies. *American Educational Research Journal, 2*, 187–202.

Teale, W. H., & Sulzby, E. (1986). *Emergent literacy: Writing and reading.* Norwood, NJ: Ablex.

Thorndike, E. L. (1917). Reading as reasoning: A study of mistakes in paragraph reading. *Journal of Educational Psychology, 8*, 323–332.

Thorndike, R. L. (1973). *Reading comprehension education in fifteen countries.* New York: Wiley.

Thorndike, R. L., & Hagen, E. P. (1977). *Measurement and evaluation in psychology and education* (4th ed.). New York: Wiley.

Tierney, R. J., & Pearson (1983). Toward a composing model of reading. *Language Arts, 60*, 568–580.

Tierney, R. J., Readence, J. E., & Dishner, E. K. (1995). *Reading strategies and practices: A compendium.* Boston: Allyn & Bacon.

Treiman, R. (1985). Onsets and rimes as units of spoken syllables: Evidence from children. *Journal of Experimental Child Psychology, 39*, 161–181.

Tuinman, J. J. (1974). Determining the passage-dependency of comprehension questions in five major tests. *Reading Research Quarterly, 9*, 207–223.

Tunmer, W. E., Herriman, M. L., & Nesdale, A. R. (1988). Metalinguistic abilities and beginning reading. *Reading Research Quarterly, 23*, 134–158.

Uhl, W. L. (1916). The use of the results of reading tests as a basis for planning remedial work. *Elementary School Journal, 17*, 266–275.

Vacca, R. T. (1981). *Content area reading.* Boston: Little, Brown.

Valencia, S. W. (1990). A portfolio approach to classroom assessment: The whys, whats, and hows. *The Reading Teacher, 43*, 338–340.

Valencia, S. W., & Pearson, P. D. (1986). Reading assessment: Time for a change. *The Reading Teacher, 40*, 726–732.

Valenzuela, J., & Hilferty, J. (2007). Music, modularity and syntax. *International Journal of English Studies, 7*(1), 101–115.

Van den Broek, P., Tzeng, Y., Risden, K., Trabasso, T., & Basche, P. (2001, September). Inferential questioning: Effects on comprehension of narrative texts as a function of grade and timing. *Journal of Educational Psychology, 93*(3), 521–529.

VanTassel-Baska, J., Bracken, B., Feng, A., & Brown, E. (2009). A longitudinal study of enhancing critical thinking and reading comprehension in title 1 classrooms. *Journal for the Education of the Gifted, 33*(1), 7–37.

Vaughan, J. L., Castle, G., Gilbert, K., & Love, M. (1982). Varied approaches to preteaching vocabulary. In J. A. Niles & L. A. Harris (Eds.), *New inquiries in reading research and instruction* (Thirty-first yearbook of the National Reading Conference). Rochester, NY: National Reading Conference.

Vellutino, F. R., Scanlon, D. M., & Jaccard, J. (2003). Toward distinguishing between cognitive and experiential deficits as primary sources of difficulty in learning to read. In B. R. Foorman (Ed). *Preventing and remediating reading difficulties* (pp. 73–120). Baltimore: York.

Venezky, R. (1970). *The structure of English orthography.* The Hague: Mouton.

Venezky, R. L. 1970. Principles for the design of practical writing systems. *Anthropological Linguistics, 12,* 256–270.

Villaume, S. K., & Brabham, E. G. (2002). Comprehension instruction: Beyond strategies. *The Reading Teacher, 55*(7), 672–675.

Vygotsky, L. S. (1978). *Mind and society.* Cambridge, MA: Harvard University Press.

Walker, B. J. (2003). *Diagnostic teaching of reading* (5th ed.).Columbus, OH: Prentice Hall.

Weaver, C. A., & Kintsch, W. (1991). Expository text. In R. Barr, M. Kamil, P. Mosenthal, & P. D. Pearson (Eds.), *Handbook of reading research* (Vol. 2, pp. 230–245). White Plains, NY: Longman.

Weaver, P. A. (1979). Improving reading comprehension: Effects of sentence organization instruction. *Reading Research Quarterly, 15,* 129–146.

Weber, R. (1968). The study of oral reading errors: A review of the literature. *Reading Research Quarterly, 4,* 96–119.

Whaley, J., & Kibby, M. W. (1981). The relative importance of reliance on intraword characteristics and interword constraints for beginning reading achievement. *Journal of Educational Research, 74,* 315–320.

White, E. B. (1952). *Charlotte's web.* New York: Harper & Brothers.

Wiggins, G., & McTighe, J. (1998). *Understanding by design.* Alexandria, VA: ASCD.

Wilkinson, G. S. (1993). *The wide range achievement test 3.* New York: McGraw-Hill.

Wilkinson, G. S. (2006). *The wide range achievement test 4.* New York: McGraw-Hill.

Williamson, G. L. (2008). A text readability continuum for postsecondary readiness. *Journal of Advanced Academics, 19*(4), 602–632.

Winokur-Kotula, A. (2003). Matching readers to instructional materials: The use of classic readability measures for students with language learning disabilities and dyslexia. *Topics in Language Disorders, 23*(3), 190–203.

Wittrock, M. C., Marks, C. B., & Doctorow, M. J. (1975). Reading as a generative process. *Journal of Educational Psychology, 67,* 484–489.

Wixson, K. K., & Lipson, M. Y. (1991). Perspectives on reading disability research. In R. Barr, M. Kamil, P. Mosenthal, & P. D. Pearson (Eds.), *Handbook of reading research* (Vol. 2, pp. 539–570). White Plains, NY: Longman.

Wixson, K. K., Peters, C. W., Weber, E. M., & Roeber, E. D. (1987). New directions in statewide reading assessment. *The Reading Teacher, 40,* 749–754.

Wolman, R. N., & Barker, E. N. (1965). A developmental study of word definitions. *Journal of Genetic Psychology, 107,* 159–166.

Wood, E., Pressley, M., & Winne, P. H. (1990). Elaborate interrogation effects on children's learning of factual content. *Journal of Educational Psychology, 82*(4), 741–748.

Woods, M. L., & Moe, A. (2003). *Analytical reading inventory: Comprehensive assessment for all students including gifted and remedial.* Colombus, OH: Prentice Hall.

Woods, M. L., & Moe, A. (2007). *Analytical reading inventory: Comprehensive assessment for all students including gifted and remedial.* Colombus, OH: Prentice Hall.

Yan P. X., Wiles, B., & Yu-Ying L. (2008, November). Teaching conceptual model-based word problem *story grammar* to enhance mathematics problem solving. *Journal of Special Education, 42*(3), 163–178.

Yopp, H. K. (1992). Developing phonemic awareness in young children. *The Reading Teacher, 45*(9), 696–703.

Zembat, R., & Zulfikar, S. T. (2006). An investigation of conversation and story telling activities used by preschool education teachers. *Educational Sciences: Theory & Practice, 6*(2), 602–608.

Zirbes, L. (1918). Diagnostic measurement as a basis for procedure. *Elementary School Journal, 18,* 507–523.

name index

subject index